QUESTIONING
CREOLE

QUESTIONING CREOLE

Creolisation Discourses in Caribbean Culture

IN HONOUR OF
KAMAU BRATHWAITE

Editors

Verene A. Shepherd
Glen L. Richards

Ian Randle Publishers
Kingston

James Currey Publishers
Oxford

First published in Jamaica, 2002 by
Ian Randle Publishers
11 Cunningham Avenue
Box 686
Kingston 6

ISBN 976-637-039-7 paperback

A catalogue record of this book is available
from the National Library of Jamaica.

First published in the United Kingdom, 2002 by
James Currey Publishers
73 Botley Road
Oxford, OX2, OBS

ISBN 0-85255-477-X paperback

A cataloguing in publication record for this book is available
from the British Libray

Cover art: Jamaica – A Coloured Lady on a Race-course from
"The West Indies", illustrated by A.S. Forrest. Courtesy of the
University of the West Indies Library, Mona.

Cover and book design by Robert Harris
E-mail: roberth@cwjamaica.com

Set in Schneidler 9.5/14 x 27

Printed and bound in the United States of America

CONTENTS

FOREWORD

This collection of essays is a tribute to the contribution made by Kamau Brathwaite to the rich dialogue on creolisation which continues apace throughout the Caribbean, comprising the archipelago of island and mainland states that are now home to "the people who [originally] came" – (Brathwaite's "arrivants") – many of them involuntarily. I welcome the significant contribution made by the editors, Verene A. Shepherd and Glen L. Richards, in assembling this anthology in the form of serious critique and straightforward tribute from academicians drawn from diverse disciplines as sociology, history, gender studies, literature, linguistics, musicology and poetry.

Such a range of contributions is fitting since Kamau Brathwaite is himself not only historian, but also lecturer, critic, essayist, music (jazz) enthusiast and always poet. He now has a chair in poetry at the New York University (NYU) and most of his substantive work since the 1980s has been in the art of his poetry. He has also held a chair as professor in Cultural History at the University of the West Indies. It was as professor of Cultural History that he influenced the two editors each of whom also makes substantial contributions to this collection.

As editor of *Caribbean Quarterly*, I was delighted that some of these essays first formed part of the special double issue (vol. 44: 1 and 2, 1998) appropriately published on the eve of a new millennium and coinciding with the occasion of the University of the West Indies' fiftieth Anniversary. That moment was an opportune time to look back from whence we have come, to mark where we are and map our future, cognisant that the map is not the journey. We thank Kamau Brathwaite for enlightening us on the journey we must traverse.

As Stewart Brown in his introduction to a collection of essays on the *Art of Kamau Brathwaite* (Poetry Wales Press, 1995) reminds us, that "journey" involves the challenges of "rebirth, rediscovery, reclamation of identity for West Indian people through an examination of their roots in the African past". The acceptance of those roots, insists Brathwaite, "will begin to heal the negative self-images established by the experience of the middle passage, plantation and colonial life".

Rex Nettleford

PREFACE

With the exception of the essays by Percy Hintzen, Paul Lovejoy and David Trotman, Pat Mohammed and Glen Richards, the articles in this collection appeared in a special double volume of *Caribbean Quarterly* (vol. 44: 1 and 2) in 1998. That special issue, like this anthology, was designed to honour Kamau Brathwaite, an internationally acclaimed historian and poet, during the fiftieth-anniversary celebrations of the University of the West Indies (UWI) in recognition of his great contribution to the intellectual life of the institution in particular and the region in general. A former professor in the Department of History at the Mona campus of the UWI, Kamau Brathwaite now holds a chair in poetry at NYU and teaches comparative literature. Well-known for his pioneering work, *The Development of Creole Society in Jamaica*, published in 1971, Brathwaite remains a leading participant in the discourse on creolisation in the African diaspora – a discourse in which – as is evidenced by the articles in this anthology, many more scholars have since become engaged. The perspectives from which these scholars have analysed "Creole", "créolité", "creolisation" and "Creole Society/Culture" have not been unified. Not surprisingly, then, the volume reflects both support for, and opposition to, the concept of "Creole" and "creolisation" in the study of Caribbean culture; but this divergence of views has only served to give rise to a lively conceptual debate which testifies to the durability and fundamental nature of Brathwaite's work.

Several people helped us along the way as we compiled this volume. First, we thank all the contributors to the initial journal version for revising their articles for publication in this present collection. The support of Joe Pereira, dean of the Faculty of Arts and Education and director of the Institute of Caribbean Studies must also be acknowledged; for a few of these essays are final versions of lectures given as part of the ICS's 1997/98 Lecture Series. Thanks go to Ahmed Reid for help with proofreading and to Professor Paul Lovejoy (director) and Professor David Trotman (associate director) of the York University/UNESCO/Nigerian

Hinterland Project for facilitating Verene's 2000–2001 Network Professorship which gave her time off to work on various projects, including this anthology.

Finally, for permission to include the articles from the special *Caribbean Quarterly* issue in this collection, we thank Professor Rex Nettleford and the quarterly's managing editor, Dr. Veronica Salter.

Verene A. Shepherd
Glen L. Richards

Verene A. Shepherd/Glen L. Richards

INTRODUCTION

Historians have for decades been pre-occupied with the often contentious issues of cultural change and the formation of new ethnic identities in situations of multiple ethnic contact. They have also attempted to label the process and end result of cultural changes in the Americas, forming theories around such concepts as creolisation, ethnogenesis, inter-ethnic fusion, hybridisation, merger, transculturation and pluralism. In his seminal work, *The Development of Creole Society in Jamaica, 1770–1820*, published in 1971, Kamau Brathwaite sought to expose the essentially "Jamaican" nature of the identity that developed in this island society at the interstices between the cultures of Europe and Africa. At the time that Brathwaite published his work, the term "Creole" as a description of specific New World cultures and societies was already in widespread and general use. In a seminar presented in 1957, which influenced the evolution of Brathwaite's ideas, Richard Adams described "Creole culture" as the "ways of life that have emerged in the New World specifically in those societies where plantations have served as a dominant element in the . . . social structure."[1] Brathwaite, however, took the concept of Creole society beyond mere description by articulating a clear and poetically engaging intellectual model of the process of cultural change that defines, and distinguishes, Creole societies – a process, which he termed "creolisation". In his subsequent study, *Contradictory Omens: Cultural Diversity and Integration in the Caribbean*, Brathwaite defined "creolisation" as "a cultural process . . . which . . . may be divided into two aspects of itself: ac/culturation, which is the yoking (by force and example, deriving from power/prestige) of one culture to another (in this case the enslaved/African to the European); and inter/culturation, which is an unplanned, unstructured but osmotic relationship proceeding from this yoke. The creolisation which results (and it is a process not product) becomes the tentative cultural norm of the society."[2]

Brathwaite's Creole-society model contrasted sharply with its predecessor, the plural-society model as advanced by M.G. Smith (1921–1993), which by the end of the 1960s was perhaps the dominant sociological interpretation of Caribbean social reality. It was an interpretation of which Brathwaite was cognisant but with which he did not engage directly, focusing his attention instead on advancing his more positive vision of the Caribbean's past and future. The late Lloyd Brathwaite (1919–1995) was a contemporary Caribbean scholar who shared Kamau Brathwaite's vision and whose role in refining and developing the Creole-society model must be acknowledged. A Trinidadian sociologist and a critical contributor to the concept of Creole society, Lloyd Brathwaite, while recognising that the fundamental differences in the cultural framework of the various ethnic groups of his homeland meant that Trinidadian society "could be accurately described as in some sense a plural society", sought, rather, to emphasise the incorporation by these ethnic groups of "universalistic values", which, he argued, made it "possible to conceive of a system of common values ... that may overcome the tendencies toward disintegration already apparent in the social system."[3]

Since the publication of *The Development of Creole Society in Jamaica*, Creole studies has emerged as a multi-disciplinary field in its own right. The temporal and spatial breadth of this field of study has impeded its incorporation into the emerging fields of Atlantic World studies as scholars, particularly in the discipline of linguistics, engage in systematic cross-comparisons of creolisation patterns in Atlantic and Pacific communities or into post-colonial studies with the recognition that creolisation began with the earliest plantations in the Western world in a period preceding the systematic European colonisation of non-European territories.[4] Although Creole studies is being increasingly shaped, almost independently, by the discipline of linguistics, the creolisation concept is now undeniably the dominant intellectual construct in the fields of Caribbean and Atlantic World history and informs all the historical presumptions of the leading historians in these fields today. As Barry Higman points out, the wide diffusion of the creolisation concept has given it "a significance comparable to the globalisation model" and even those historians who have not fully embraced the concept in the writing of Caribbean history have "taken its essence into their work". Indeed, as Higman notes, the emergence of an indigenous historical tradition in the English-speaking Caribbean and the challenge posed by indigenous historians such as Kamau Brathwaite to the British imperial historical tradition has been described as the "Creolisation of West Indian history".[5]

The concept of creolisation has evolved significantly since Brathwaite's critical publications of 1971 and 1974. The publication in 1976 of *An Anthropological Approach to the Afro-American Past* by Sidney Mintz and Richard Price (republished in 1992 as *The Birth of African-American Culture: An Anthropological Perspective*) marked a critical turning point in the evolution of the discourse on creolisation.[6] This work has largely set the parameters of the subsequent debate on the concept between those who, like Mintz and Price, see Creole cultures as almost entirely new creations which seek to adapt to new social and geographical environments and those who, like Mervyn Alleyne and many Caribbean linguists, stress cultural continuity between Africa and the Caribbean and advance Afrogenesis as an explanation of many of the cultural patterns described as Creole.[7] In response to the rise of Africentric scholarship in the field of Creole studies, especially to the emphasis on the dominance of African culture in the creolisation process, some (Eurocentric?) scholars such as William Green have gone to great lengths to stress that "resistance to a Euro-Caribbean value system" was not as strong or universal as argued by Africentric scholars and that many people of Colour, "the most Creole of West Indians" were inexorably drawn to the European sector. Green notes that "many influential people of colour . . . wanted to preserve both the plantation society and a White planter elite whose presence would continue to afford European cultural influences to the society at large."[8] Such a perspective has not diminished the zeal of Africentric scholars. Brathwaite himself has come down firmly and unapologetically on the side of Afrogenesis. In his discussion of Caribbean Creole language, he describes the "submerged language" of the Caribbean enslaved population as "moving from a purely African form to a form which was African but which was adapted to the new environment and adapted to the cultural imperative of the European language." While he recognises the "plurality" of the Caribbean experience, he sees Caribbean English Creole (or nation-language) as "much more closely allied to the African aspect of experience in the Caribbean" adding, for emphasis, that "it is English and African at the same time".[9] The strongest rejection of the Afrogenetic thesis has come from the French Caribbean in the form of the concept of créolité. In their *Eloge de la créolité*, Raphael Confiant and Patrick Chamoiseau have advanced their distinct Creole identity declaring: "Neither Europeans, nor Africans, nor Asians, we proclaim ourselves Creoles."[10] Confiant has gone even further to assert that not a "fragment of Africanness" has persisted in the Creole culture of Martinique.[11]

The entrenched divisions that have emerged within the ranks of the adherents to the creolisation concept have challenged the very validity of the concept itself and have given rise to vigorous polemics, with scholars emerging to support or oppose Brathwaite's theory. They have also led to an interesting revival of the plural-society model, its leading theoretical rival, within the very body of creolisation theory itself. In *Afro-Creole: Power, Opposition, and Play in the Caribbean,* Richard Burton recasts the model of "segmentary creolisation", a cultural process which produces a "continuum of overlapping and competing cultural forms, all of them Creole or creolised . . . 'Euro-Creole', 'Meso-Creole' . . . and 'Afro-Creole'".[12] The revival of the plural-society model, while staying within the broad parameters of the creolisation thesis, seeks to address some of the theoretical uncertainties that have become increasingly glaring, particularly in light of the revival of ethnic polarisation which today marks Caribbean societies. Despite the theoretical weaknesses and the widening academic divide among the adherents to the theory, no competing model has yet emerged with the power to explain the obvious and, despite the politically engineered ethnic polarisation, arguably deepening cultural integration of Caribbean societies.[13] Today, approximately 30 years after its public launching, Kamau Brathwaite's Creole-society model is accepted by many as the leading interpretation of Caribbean and, to a large extent, Atlantic World societies. As a description of Caribbean society during slavery, it seems more appealing to those who question the slave-society and plantation-society constructs. Although it has indeed generated widespread critique, whether through support or opposition, the creolisation discourse has been widely incorporated into the scholarship of the region and resonates in diverse fields of Caribbean and Atlantic World studies, spreading far beyond the confines of the discipline of history. The publication, over the last decade, of a host of scholarly works engaging with Caribbean and Atlantic World culture has demonstrated a marked revival of interest in the creolisation concept and a new intensity in the discourse on creolisation.[14] As the study of cultural change in the Caribbean and the Atlantic World deepens and the field of cultural studies matures, the debate over the creolisation concept authored by Brathwaite should lead to its further refinement and its broader utilisation in the field of cultural studies on a global level.

Brathwaite's intellectual influence has already been widely diffused internationally and much contemporary post-colonial discourse and literary criticism is infused with the spirit and style of his poetic concept. Mary Louise Pratt conveys Brathwaite's Creole-society concept in her use of the term "transculturation" which she argues "treats the relations among colonisers and colonised . . . not in terms of separateness or apartheid, but in terms of coprescience, interaction, interlocking understandings and practices, often within radically asymmetrical relations of power."[15] Homi Bhabha's concept of "hybridity" also seems to share in the spirit and poetic expression of Brathwaite's work when he writes that if "the effect of colonial power is seen to be the *production* of hybridisation rather than the noisy command of colonialist authority or the silent repression of native traditions, then an important change of perspective occurs."[16]

But Brathwaite's influence has been most strongly felt and is most clearly recognised in the field of Caribbean studies that has been the focus of his scholarship. The breadth and diversity of the articles in this volume embracing the fields of economic and political history, anthropology and sociology, linguistics, literary criticism and cultural studies demonstrate his wide intellectual impact. While these articles are presented as a tribute to Brathwaite, it should be stated from the outset that the contributors are also involved in a process of "re-engagement" with, and a "re-assessment" of, his ideas. Put differently, this collection represents a dialogue, a "conversation" – if you will – with a distinguished colleague and mentor outside of the context of a conference table. Among the contributors, for example, there are those like O. Nigel Bolland who feel that there is need for a more dialectical approach which will acknowledge the "centrality of relations of domination/subordination, including class relations" in shaping Caribbean society thereby providing a more realistic understanding of creolisation "not (as) a homogenising process, but rather (as) a process of contention between people who are members of social formations and carriers of cultures . . .". Scholars such as Rhoda Reddock, Pat Mohammed, Veronica Gregg and Percy Hintzen point to the problematic issue of the applicability of the Creole-society model to countries where the dominant relations are not Black/White. Nevertheless, the very act of engagement is testimony to the on-going impact of Brathwaite's work, some 30 years after the appearance of *The Development of Creole Society in Jamaica.* As Gregg rightly observes, regardless of the problematic aspects of his theorising, Brathwaite, at the very least, opened a discursive space with which and through which scholars can think differently. Thus by complicating, interrogating or even defying his position, writers and scholars underscore its impact and influence. Indeed, as Carolyn Allen points out, non-Caribbean scholars have increasingly turned to the Caribbean for theoretical tools – such as the concept of creolisation – with which to decipher global culture.

The volume has been divided into six sections organised around distinct themes for convenient reading. Section one, entitled "Barbadian Genesis" starts not with the post-1971 controversies, but rather at the beginning, with a biographical account by Mary Morgan, Brathwaite's sister, of the early life experiences and influences which have shaped his vision – the sea, ever present in his early life, linking Africa to the Caribbean; his mother's insistence on her African connections; and the countless relatives whose stories sensitised him to issues little discussed in the colonial educational system to which he was exposed. After reading this article one is left in little doubt as to why Brathwaite's exploration and interpretation of the Caribbean is one of hope, and an affirmation of the creative possibilities of Caribbean peoples who have been forged in the cauldron of slavery and colonialism.

Section two, "Creolisation and Creole: Definitions, Meanings and Models Critiqued", includes essays that engage with the significance, applicability and multiple meanings and interpretations of the concepts "Creole", "créolité", "Creole-society model" and "creolisation" (with many warnings against the generalised application and homogenised interpretation of these terms). The essays by O. Nigel Bolland and Carolyn Allen intervene in the on-going interpretive debate on the meaning and origin of the terms "Creole" and "creolisation". Bolland, sociologist and historian, in his "Creolisation and Creole Societies: A Cultural Nationalist View of Caribbean Social History", undertakes a theoretical exploration of Brathwaite's Creole-society model which he describes as "ill-defined and ambiguous". Bolland identifies the source of this ambiguity as the false dualism, fashioned by Brathwaite, between enslaver and enslaved; Black and White; metropole and colony; colonial and Creole. These elements, which Brathwaite presents as opposites, Bolland argues, are from the dialectical point of view, "the differentiated parts of a whole" which "have no independent existence from each other, but are defined in their relation with each other". According to Bolland, Brathwaite's dualistic approach "leads to the portrayal of creolisation as a 'blending' process, a mixing of cultures that occurs without reference to structural contradictions and social conflict".

In "Creole: The Problem of Definition", Allen uses as her starting point one of Brathwaite's ideas for understanding the cultural dimensions of Caribbean history: that is, as a process in which the arrivants and their progenitors forge a complex dynamic of group identity and interrelations. She reviews works that reinforce the particular significance that the terms "Creole" and "creolisation" hold for the region, especially for its interdisciplinary study, but also poses the problem of their unstable, diverse and contradictory meanings in the scholarship. Clearly writers and scholars do not all mean the same thing when they use the terms "Creole" and "creolisation"; so, is the word "Creole" an expression emerging out of the trans-Atlantic crossing and colonisation, or is its origin African (as Maureen Warner-Lewis also maintains in this volume)? What is the "history" of its use? As a preliminary step towards seeking solutions to these problematic questions surrounding the word "Creole", Allen seeks to extract from dictionary definitions in three languages (English, Spanish, French), as well as from selected scholarly pieces primarily on the Caribbean, concepts that may serve as the principles of co-identification in the variety of Creole-designated phenomena. Despite the variations and contradictions which her survey of the use of the concept "Creole" reveals, from its etymology to its many definitions, Allen still maintains that "there is an identifiable, though not stable, group of principles associated with the notion wherever it is found."

The articles in section three address "Class, Gender, Ethnicity and Identity" and explore empirically many of the theoretical problems raised in the preceding section demonstrating, in particular, the ways in which the ethnic diversities of the region complicate meanings and traditional theoretical formulations. The article "Enslaved Africans and their Expectations of Life in the Americas: Towards a Reconsideration of Models of 'Creolisation'" by Paul Lovejoy and David Trotman, directly critiques the interpretation of the creolisation process advanced by Sidney Mintz and Richard Price who regarded the African background of enslaved Africans as having only a "generalised influence on slave culture" and stressed the "newness" of their cultural creations. In exploring how the mental map which enslaved Africans brought with them was adapted in, and helped them to adapt to, their new social situation, they remind us that the attitudes and expectations of enslaved Africans in the Atlantic World were shaped by their knowledge and experience of slavery in Africa and that their actions and responses in their new social situations and geographical settings were strongly influenced by the expectations that they brought with them. Lovejoy and Trotman question the prevailing approach of studying Africans in the Americas, and their descendants, in isolation from their African homeland and without reference to their prior experience, directly or indirectly, of systems of slavery. They explore how the racialisation of slavery in the Americas and resistance to this, for the Africans, caused new forms of enslavement to be reinforced, or altered the ethnic identities of enslaved Africans, at times retreating into specific ethnic allegiances, at others, forging "pan-ethnic unions" which promoted a broader Creole identity, African or Black. They also point to the often ignored and under-researched fact of the existence of "an important network for the trans-Atlantic and circum-Atlantic flow of information", which permitted West Africans some limited knowledge about the fate of enslaved Africans on the other side of the Atlantic, a historical reality which must have helped to shape African expectations of and responses to life in the Americas.

"Race and Creole Ethnicity in the Caribbean" by Percy Hintzen examines the critical function of race and ethnicity in determining Caribbean Creole identity. He argues, along similar lines to Robert Burton's segmentary creolisation thesis, that to "be Caribbean is to occupy the hierarchical, hybridised 'Creole' space between two racial poles that serve as markers for civilisation and savagery". Hintzen, like William Green, points to the enduring dominance of European value-systems in this "hybridised, 'Creole' space" and notes that, even after the triumph of the Creole nationalist project, creolisation still involves the implicit "rejection of Africa" and the "embrace of Europe" with the cultural poles of Europe and Africa being replaced by a White-Black polarity at the opposite ends of the Creole continuum. The "possibility of whiteness", which operated as an integrative mechanism in colonial society during and after slavery, opens new doors for the members of a new Black political elite who accept the economically-dominant White Creoles as mentors, allies and emissaries in diplomatic relations with the former colonial powers. Hintzen argues that the creolisation process can also be seen in minority communities of the Portuguese, Lebanese, Syrians, Jews and post-indenture Chinese, whose intermediate position in the colonial economy "became the springboard for the structural and social insertion of their members into colonial Creole society". Even the most problematic population group in terms of Creole inclusiveness, the Asian Indians, reveal Creole tendencies in their patterns of socialisation. Miscegenation between Asian Indians and Africans has produced a Creole variant, the so-called "Douglas", and Westernised education, religious conversion and socio-economic progress have provided the basis for the Creole inclusion of an Asian Indian economic elite. Despite their historical exclusion from the Creole definition and the intellectual rejection, by a significant section of the Asian Indian population, of what they describe as a "bastardised" and corrupted Creole culture for the ideal of Hindu purity, Hintzen argues that the Asian Indian population of the region has indeed engaged in "a form of creolisation that comes with little sacrifice to Hindu identity".

Rhoda Reddock's "Contestations Over Culture: Class, Gender and Identity in Trinidad and Tobago: The 'Little Tradition'" explores the implication for the post-Columbian Caribbean of the immigration of diverse ethnicities. One implication is that next to family, the issues of race, ethnicity and social differentiation have become central to scholarship and everyday life in the region, giving rise to theoretical formulations to grapple with the evident socio-cultural diversity. She critiques the various theoretical offerings of sociologists and historians and, in particular, explains why the application of Brathwaite's Creole-society model to the southern Caribbean with mixed ethnic populations is potentially problematic. Her basic point of departure seems to be that the Creole-society model was developed in societies characterised by White/Black, dominant/subordinate relations and is more difficult to apply uncritically to countries like Trinidad and Guyana where "Creole" signifies "African/Black" to segments of the population who wish to embrace alternative cultural norms. She examines the reasons why the construction of group identity, of a national culture in places like Trinidad and Tobago would have been complicated and also, unlike traditional theorists, shows the ways in which gender makes the existing theoretical constructs more complex.

In her essay "The Creolisation of Indian Women in Trinidad", the Indo-Trinidadian Patricia Mohammed, while admitting that "Creole" and "creolisation", when applied to ethnic and cultural intermixture involving Indian women can have negative connotations, particularly among those in the Indian and Indo-Trinidadian communities, uses the terms in a more expansive framework. She focuses on those on-going and dynamic processes – acculturation, commitment to one's country of birth, reactions against external cultures and inter-culturation – which have been associated with "Creole", "Creole society" and "creolisation". She cautions that discussions of cultural changes in society must take political movements and modernisation effects on competing cultures into account. In other words, cultural change does not only occur because of simple inter-ethnic interaction. Her main intention, though, is to show how Indian women fit into this matrix of cultural change in Trinidad and Tobago. Her key questions are, firstly, how did they contribute to the process and, secondly, how were they affected by it? In order to answer these questions she explores the pre- and post-independence periods, the former characterised by indentureship, spatial separation from African-Trinidadians, lack of access to education and the cash economy, traditional expectations of Indian women as keepers of the culture, sexual disparity within indentureship, gender relations among indentured Indians and other ethnic groups, the profile of those women who were indentured, how Indian women negotiated their gender roles within their traditional cultures and the degree to which they either tried to recreate traditional culture (though with greater power), or adapt to new cultures, especially as they moved out of the plantation community and interacted more with African-Trinidadians. She outlines those aspects of Indian culture that showed evidence of change. In the post-independence period, greater access to education and the cash economy, urbanisation and modernisation all caused changes among Indian women. However such changes, she argues, did not imply creolisation in the sense of commitment to country of birth/settlement and physical engagement with the society so that the existing cultures are mixed and enriched in the process. The "creolisation" process, therefore, if complicated by other groups apart from African and European, forces different conclusions/interpretations. The conclusion seems to be, then, that we must be cautious of the tendency to see culture changes as indicative of creolisation or to interpret the reasons for such changes within the creolisation discourse.

In "'Yuh Know Bout Coo-Coo? Where Yuh Know Bout Coo-Coo?': Language and Representation, Creolisation and Confusion in 'Indian Cuisine'", Veronica

Gregg acknowledges the "slipperiness" of Brathwaite's concept of creolisation: a "surface slipperiness [which] is but the deeply entrenched struggles for and about language and representation in terms of Caribbean identities". Like Mohammed, Gregg introduces a perspective which centres women into the creolisation discourse, also showing, like Reddock, how creolisation links with race as much as with sex, sexuality and gender. She agrees with Brathwaite that it was in the intimate area of sexual relationships that the most significant (and lasting) inter-cultural creolisation took place, but at the same time holds that there is much that is problematic in this key concept "because of what it simultaneously assumes and overlooks about the constructions of sex, gender and race in terms of power". Her essential question in this essay, then, is how does the construction of sex, gender and race in terms of power shape our understanding of Caribbean identities? Associated with this concern (fuelled partly by Mohammed's essay which hints at Indian separation from the African-Caribbean "Other") is the need to call attention to the way in which "the prevailing interpretations of creolisation and Indianness are constitutively entangled, within the terms of a cruelly binary logic." She demonstrates this problematic through her critique of the short story Indian Cuisine written by an Indo-Caribbean woman, Ramabai Espinet. Gregg suggests that " 'Indian Cuisine' . . . can be read as a fictional reworking of the concept of creolisation" using Standard English to represent the rhythms and inflections of Trinidadian Creole, without departing from Standard English spelling and punctuation, and through its use of English words, such as " 'privilege', 'agriculture', 'gambler', to convey Caribbean meanings while retaining their original English". Gregg highlights the short story's depiction of the process of interculturation occurring, in this instance, between the two historically subordinate racial majority groups of Trinidad, the Indians and the Africans: a process which displays, as Gregg suggests, the "permeability of boundaries and identities within a shifting multi-racial society". This essay also testifies to the fact that Caribbean people of Indian ancestry "do not speak with one voice", and that "the social and discursive construction of Indianness in terms of the Caribbean remains a dynamic and contested site."

The articles in section four, "Creolisation in Caribbean Economy, Society and Politics during Slavery and Freedom" by Verene A. Shepherd, Hilary McD. Beckles, Glen Richards and Swithin Wilmot are located firmly within the historical context of Jamaican and wider British-colonised Caribbean societies during the slavery and post-slavery periods, highlighting issues surrounding the economic, demographic, social and political dimensions of Brathwaite's "Creole-society model". They use the term "Creole" in the sense of being born in the region and participating in "local" as opposed to "external" economics and politics.

Shepherd's "Questioning Creole: Domestic Producers in Jamaica's Plantation Economy" engages with Brathwaite's discussion of a "Creole economy" in his seminal work *The Development of Creole Society in Jamaica*. In that work, Brathwaite raised the issue of the need to diversify the island's colonial economy to combat the effects of over-reliance on external supplies, a situation which was amply exposed during and immediately after the American War of Independence. She argues that although non-sugar producers, specifically the livestock farmers ("pen-keepers"), rallied to the call for diversification and supplied a significant portion of the island's livestock needs, thus contributing to the local economic sector, they faced tremendous odds. The conservative planter elite embraced the traditional ties with external suppliers of plantation inputs and never seriously challenged the mercantilist arrangements; and the potential for sugar estates to act as a dynamic element in the development of local industries was never realised. The livestock farmers themselves never wholeheartedly embraced "Creole culture/society/economy". Their challenge to the institutional arrangement of the society in which the sugar sector was influential was not totally successful. Indeed, some, like their wealthier sugar-planting counterparts aspired to external cultural values. Her article expands Brathwaite's and Edward Long's explanations for the failure of Jamaican society to become truly creolised in all its dimensions – economic, social, cultural and political, and shows that there was not necessarily a dichotomy between "Creole" and "colonial".

Hilary McD. Beckles, in "Creolisation in Action: The Slave Labour Elite and Anti-Slavery in Barbados", focuses on the relationship between the creolisation of the enslaved population, occupational differentiation as a distinguishing feature of demographic creolisation, and the enslaved's anti-slavery politics. He hypothesises that the politics of enslaved peoples in Creole society suggests that they engaged the ruling classes with a sophisticated dialogue that targeted liberty as the central and ultimate objective. He uses Barbados, arguably then the most demographically creolised sugar plantation complex in the age of abolitionism, to explore the extent to which the hypothesis can be supported by evidence drawn from the culture of everyday life among the enslaved. Clearly, the high level of creolisation and community development in Barbados shaped the politics of enslaved peoples in fundamental ways: enslavers indicated that enslaved people who were locally born/Creole were less committed to violent anti-slavery activities than those who were African-born. Much of the enslaved community's rejection of organised armed violence must then be attributed to the rapidly diminishing numbers of enslaved peoples who were African-born. Beckles argues, therefore, that enslaved Creoles, particularly those among the slave elite, seemed more responsive to negotiable arrangements and patronage; and the enslavers no doubt capitalised on this for as long as they could. But, of course, as nineteenth century events in Barbados were to show, as soon as the "slave elite" perceived that it had maximised the privileges and rights that seemed possible, it determined to remove by violent means the remaining obstacles in the path of freedom.

Glen Richards' article, "Driber Tan Mi Side", problematises the issue of labour bargaining strategies employed by enslaved peoples in the Caribbean alongside the expected revolutionary challenges to the entire plantation system. Using the examples of St Kitts and Nevis, he argues that the development of labour bargaining strategies by the enslaved populations of the Caribbean, and their free descendants, reflects both their acceptance of their historical reality and their concerted efforts to change that reality by transforming the economic relations that bound them to enslavers and employers. Like Beckles, he admits that the drivers and headmen on individual plantations and the elite class among the enslaved, in general, had a strong personal interest in the success of these strategies – for success meant an increase in their material benefits and a strengthening of their social position, though this did not mean total acceptance of the slave system. He engages with the Creole-society model in his argument that the evolution of labour bargaining strategies signalled the increasing social investment of enslaved Africans and their descendants in plantation society and their emerging Creole sensibilities and growing commitment to the only home that they knew. Following Mintz and Price, he emphasises the "newness" of these strategies and questions the likelihood of these social patterns of collective engagement between enslaved Africans and their European enslavers being based upon memories or past experiences derived from their African background. This latter viewpoint will, no doubt, spark debate among those who believe that Africans arrived in the Caribbean with an already developed sense of labour bargaining.

Swithin Wilmot's "The Politics of Samuel Clarke: Black Creole Politician in Free Jamaica, 1851–1865", explores the intriguing case of one of the earliest, and largely forgotten, Black Creole politicians in Jamaica, Samuel Clarke, who became involved in electoral politics as early as March 1849. As Wilmot points out, the involvement of Clarke, and the Black small freeholders whom he organised, in parochial politics, their creation of embryonic political parties like the "St David's Liberal, Recording and Election Association" founded in 1849, and their full participation as electoral campaigners and voters in the 1851 general elections to the Jamaican Assembly "underscored the extent to which rural Blacks had been integrated into the political culture of the island within a decade and a half of the granting of full freedom in 1838." Clarke and his supporters upheld the "universalistic values" of peace, freedom and justice upon which Creole Jamaican society claimed to be based, and demanded that the existing rights and privileges of colonial subjects be extended to all, regardless of race. Wilmot's exploration of the violent and antagonistic political contest between Black Creole peasants and labourers, on the one hand, and White and Coloured Creole planters and merchants, on the other, rightly places the focus on colonial power relations and adopts the analytical approach which Bolland urges needs to be integrated into the Creole-society model.

Section five, "Creolisation and Caribbean Cultural Forces", focuses on the creolisation process in the cultural life of enslaved Africans and their descendants. Maureen Warner-Lewis's authoritative discourse entitled "Creolisation Processes in Linguistic, Artistic and Material Cultures" approaches the Creole/creolisation discourse from the perspective of a linguist and cultural studies specialist. For her, "Creole" (which was first recorded in a 1570s Mexican text), ". . . is a term denoting various types of hybridity in the socio-historical evolution of Latin America, the Caribbean, and francophone areas of the United States South"; but the roots of this meaning, she insists, are traceable to insular and coastal peoples of Portuguese West and West Central Africa, and in British-colonial Sierra Leone. The abstract concept "creolisation", she argues, has been derived from "the person- and culture-specific referent 'Creole' ". But since the word signified "outsiders", "the identity of the 'outsider' modulates according to the identity of the 'insider' in any given context", and is thus characterised by situational and temporal values. Her essay attempts to analyse various Caribbean cultural configurations of the creolisation process as a way of demonstrating its multiple, dynamic and often paradoxical manifestations. She examines the creolisation processes through the lens of African language texts from the island of Trinidad recovered during the 1960s and 1970s. Among her important findings are that ethnic clustering on plantations and in maroon communities encouraged native language function; and that the language changes which have traditionally been highlighted as features of creolisation were not only those resulting from the contact between European and African, but also from the contact among African people of different ethnic and linguistic backgrounds – for example, Oyo, Ekiti and Ijesha. Thus, in tracing creolisation processes in Caribbean languages, more attention clearly needs to be paid to inter-dialect contact and consolidation among Africans in the Americas. The same caution should apply, obviously, to analyses of culture contact and changes in other aspects of Caribbean/African/European material culture. Indeed, the creolisation process, Warner-Lewis points out, is dialectical, charcterised by erasure, syncretism, adaptation, innovation and wholesale importation.

Lucie Pradel and Carolyn Cooper view the issue of creolisation through the lens of religious tradition and popular music, discussing the impact of African religious and musical "sounds" in particular, on contemporary Caribbean culture. Pradel, in "African Sacredness and Caribbean Cultural Forms" examines how the "converging traditions" of religious belief and practice from four continents have shaped Caribbean spirituality as expressed as much through the dominant faiths – Hinduism, Islam, Christianity and Judaism – as through "Vaudou, Santeria and the worship of divinities such as Mariama, Mahabir or Kali". Her main focus, however, is on the impact of one of the religious "great traditions", in the form of African sacred thought, on Caribbean spirituality and secular life. Pradel demonstrates the process of creolisation by showing how the major African divinities, "Ogun Shango, Yemaya, Egungun, Fa, Oshossi, along with a plethora of secondary entities", have been secularised and incorporated into Caribbean oral traditions, literatures and other art forms, and cultural festivals, including Carnival and Jonkonnu.

Carolyn Cooper in "Hip-Hopping Across Cultures: Crossing Over From Reggae to Rap and Back", uses as her starting point Brathwaite's reverberant metaphor "bridges of sound", employed to evoke the substrate cultural ties that reconnect Africans on the continent to those who have survived the dismembering middle passage. She points out that the paradoxical construct, "bridges of sound", conjoins the ephemerality of aural sensation with the technological solidity of the built environment and confirms the capacity of Africans in the diaspora to conjure knowledge systems "out of nothing, as it were". Her article demonstrates the ways in which Africans were able to rebuild material culture from the blueprint of knowledge carried in their collective heads across the "musical bridge/the transitional passage". Reggae, rap and ragga were three of the products reconstructed in the African diaspora and they all originated in a complex and contested ideological space in which everyday issues of race, class and gender were voiced in what she calls "the noisy discourse of African diasporic popular music".

Section six, the final section, entitled "Poetic Discourses" consists, fittingly, of a poetic tribute to Brathwaite. The two poems by Lorna Goodison, "Angel of Dreamers" and "My Uncle", are, in themselves, poetic expressions and representations of the very process of creolisation. Goodison paints the cultural heterogeneity of Caribbean life through the eyes of her protagonist in "Angel of Dreamers", the visionary seer and seller of dreams, "great granddaughter of a psalmist and griot Guinea woman", whose protection from the cuss-cuss and obia of her market competitors is the "power of [supposedly Christian] prayer". In "My Uncle", Goodison depicts the quintessential Creole figure of the late nineteenth and early twentieth centuries, the multi-talented peasant farmer, born a slave or descendant of slaves (or indentured or free immigrant labourers), who had embraced the social opportunities of "Full Freedom" and had ensured that his children learnt the rudiments of Western education and the technical skills needed to ensure upward social mobility in colonial society. Proud, defiant, a respecter of the law and an upholder of established social norms, a church goer and respected community figure, this Creole personality, perhaps more than any other, is the true father of modern Caribbean Creole nations (the father of Marcus Garvey, the father of Fidel Castro, the father of Cheddi Jagan) whose heart was weighed and "was not found wanting". Jean Small's "Po'm for Kamau" was written as a poetic introduction for Brathwaite when he delivered the annual Sir Phillip Sherlock Lecture in February 1995. A biographical tribute recounting his Barbadian past, his life, career and his intellectual accomplishments, the poem praises Brathwaite's role as poet, literary critic and cultural historian – the Griot of the Caribbean – and extols him for "telling the tale . . . of the Gods of the Middle Passage".

In his exploration and interpretation of Caribbean societies, Brathwaite's vision provides an alternative to the pluralist vision of M.G. Smith. Brathwaite's Creole-society model suggests that these societies are not doomed to tear themselves apart in ethnic and class conflict unless held together by some coercive authority. Brathwaite asserts that the evolution of Creole society, and the process of creolisation itself, provides a basis for the creation of a national society and economy in the Caribbean. Perhaps, most importantly, the model refutes the nihilistic views of V.S. Naipaul who achieved notoriety with his description of his Caribbean homeland as "unimportant, uncreative, cynical" and his conclusion that the history of the Commonwealth Caribbean "can never be satisfactorily told" because, as he dismissively observed, "History is built around achievement and creation; and nothing was created in the West Indies."[17]

The Creole-society model will continue to inform debate for some time to come. David Buisserret, together with a new generation of scholars, has already started to mine the rich historical data of the seventeenth and late nineteenth centuries to test the applicability of this model for the different periods of Jamaican history; others are probing the extent to which a Creole society has persisted in the modern Caribbean. The field is now being further opened up by those seeking to compare the exact nature of the Jamaican society of the eighteenth and nineteenth centuries with those of the French and Spanish-speaking Caribbean of the same period.[18]

Brathwaite's hopeful vision, then, has contributed enormously to our understanding of the evolution and nature of Caribbean societies and of the process of cultural change and interaction in colonial social formations. This collection is a tribute to Brathwaite's creative intellect and the positive impact of his vision on those who today are seeking to change Caribbean reality. It is also an acknowledgement of his inspirational role as a teacher and mentor to a generation of students, including the editors, at the University of the West Indies, Mona Campus, who were touched by the poetic vision of his lectures and who were lifted by his conviction that, in the words of Aimé Césaire, "it is not true that the work of man is finished . . . and no race has a monopoly of beauty, intelligence, strength, and there is room for all at the rendez-vous of conquest."[19]

NOTES

1.   Richard Adams, "On the Relation between Plantation and 'Creole' Cultures", in *Plantation Systems of the New World* (Washington, D.C.: Pan American Union, 1959), p. 78. This paper was presented at a seminar held in San Juan, Puerto Rico, in November, 1957.

2.   Kamau Brathwaite, *Contradictory Omens: Cultural Diversity and Integration in the Caribbean* (Mona: Savacou Publications, 1974), p. 6.

3.   Lloyd Brathwaite, "Social Stratification and Cultural Pluralism", in Vera Rubin, ed., *Social and Cultural Pluralism in the Caribbean* (Annals of the New York Academy of Sciences, vol. 83, art. 5, 1960), p. 826.

4.   In their review of the growth of Atlantic Creole languages, William Washabaugh and Sidney Greenfield trace the beginnings of the creolisation process in the Atlantic World back to the earliest plantations established by the Portuguese in the Atlantic islands. See W. Washabaugh and S. Greenfield, "The Development of Atlantic Creole Langauges", in E. Woolford and W. Washabaugh, eds., *The Social Context of Creolization* (Ann Arbor, Michigan: Kanoma Publishers Inc., 1983), pp. 106–19.

5.   B.W. Higman, *Writing West Indian Histories* (London and Basingstoke: Macmillan Education Ltd., 1999), p. 6.

6.   See S. Mintz and R. Price, *The Birth of African-American Culture: An Anthropological Perspective* (Boston: Beacon Press, 1992).

7.   See, for example, M. Alleyne, *Roots of Jamaican Culture* (London: Pluto Press, 1988).

8.   William Green, "The Creolization of Caribbean History: The Emancipation Era and a Critique of Dialectical Analysis", in H. Beckles and V. Shepherd, eds., *Caribbean Freedom: Economy and Society from Emancipation to the Present* (Kingston and London: Ian Randle and James Currey Publishers, 1993), p. 35.

9. Kamau Brathwaite, *History of the Voice* (London and Port of Spain: New Beacon, 1984), pp. 7–13.

10. Quoted in Maryse Conde, "Créolité without Creole Language?", in Kathleen Balutansky and Marie-Agnes Sourieau, eds., *Caribbean Creolization:Reflections on the Cultural Dynamics of Language, Literature and Identity* (Gainesville and Kingston: University Press of Florida and UWI Press, 1998), p. 105.

11. See Richard Burton, *Afro-Creole: Power, Opposition, and Play in the Caribbean* (Ithaca and London: Cornell University Press, 1997), pp. 4, 2.

12. Ibid, pp. 5–6.

13. The evolution of chutney soca in Trinidad and the universalisation of dancehall music and culture from Jamaica along with its spin-off, dancehall soca, provide strong testimony to the deepening cultural integration of the region.

14. Some recent scholarly works in the field of Caribbean and Atlantic World history that utilise the concept of creolisation include Philip D. Morgan, *Slave Counterpoint: Black Culture in the Eighteenth Century Chesapeake and Low Country* (Chapel Hill and London: University of North Carolina Press, 1998); and Paul Lovejoy, ed., *Identity in the Shadow of Slavery* (London and New York: Continuum, 2000).

15. Marie Louise Pratt, *Imperial Eyes: Travel Writings and Transculturation* (London and New York: Routledge, 1992), p. 7.

16. Homi Bhabha, "Signs taken for Wonders", in Bill Ashcroft, et al., eds., *The Post-colonial Studies Reader* (London and New York: Routledge), p. 35.

17. V.S. Naipaul, *The Middle Passage* (Harmondsworth, England: Penguin Books, 1969), pp. 29, 43.

18. One example is work being done by Paul Scott of the University of California, Berkeley, on "Creolisation in the long 19th century".

19. Aimé Césaire, *Return to my Native Land* (Paris: Presence Africaine, 1971), pp. 138–40.

PART ONE

Barbadian Genesis

Chapter 1

HIGHWAY TO VISION

THIS SEA OUR NEXUS*

We were brought up by the sea. I do not mean merely that as island people we saw the sea always there, but that our home was actually by the sea; the Round House where we grew up looked out on Brown's Beach and Carlisle Bay. We came to appreciate, and to learn, the movement of the sea, which forms so much a part of Kamau's work. The sea, our highway out (migration, to study);[1] our wave-ride back – back to what he calls "the centre", after England and Ghana: "I had, at that moment of return, completed the triangular trade of my historical origins."[2]

The sound and rhythm, the movement, the restlessness and indeed the changeable nature of the sea are constantly reflected in his writing, especially in *Mother Poem*[3] and *Sun Poem*,[4] his two long works about growing up in Barbados.

I remember how the beach used to change from being a small beach to no beach at all and then later again to the wide expanse of white sand where the boys would play cricket. Sometimes during the hurricane season a storm would suddenly blow up, and we would watch from the back windows of our house as the waves rolled in from far out.

The sound of the waves would punctuate our sleep, and next morning some of the small fishing boats that were moored offshore would be wrecked on the beach, or sometimes there would be no beach and the waves would be lapping against the breakwater on which our beachgate and paling (sea fence) were built. We would then run down the stone steps from the pantry and dive right into the sea from our gate. In a few weeks the sea would recede, and we again had a beach behind our house; and there were times, our mother told us, when the sea went out as far as – indeed beyond – the place where the fishing boats now lie at anchor, so that once upon a time there was cultivated land where the sea now was. In the poem *Soweto*, of all places, Kamau transforms this into "and we are rowing out to sea/where the woman lived/with her pipe and her smoke/shack . . ./and we are rowing out to sea 'where there were farms' ".[5] It taught us, among other things, the importance of breakwaters, of protection against this sea that we loved but which could change so easily, so dangerously. It was from this that my brother developed his notion of Caribbean "tidalectics", a way of interpreting our life and history as sea change, the ebb and flow of sea movement; and with the suggestion of surf comes the contrapuntal sound of waves on the shore: "the peace of the Lord is upon her/lost: they will single her out/hurt: they will balm her/afraid: she will find their flicker underneath her door".[6]

The sea was also the means by which we all, "the people who came",[7] came to our islands, became fused, smelted in the encounter of fire blood sun lust hate tyranny servitude . . . love. And the awareness of this fusion is everywhere in Brathwaite's work, echoes of the stories that Mother and Cousin Jeanie Stuart used to tell: family stories, some of them about slavery days; dream stories[8] (the image I just quoted from *Soweto*), and others. For instance, Mother felt convinced that she was a reincarnation of an Ethiopian or Egyptian princess; so she read all she could about Egypt and Ethiopia and passed this on to us at night when she was sitting ironing.[9] This is how we knew that the pharaohs were Black while everybody else assumed they were White (as they were pictured in "the books"); and we always had this joke about the Sphinx's nose – that the English "discoverer" had broken it off so that the flatness wouldn't show!

E
gypt
in Af-
rica
Mesopo-
tamia
Mero-
ë
the
Nile
silica
glass

and brittle
Sa-
hara, Tim
buctu, Gao
the hills of
Ahafo, winds
of the Ni-
ger, Kumasi
and Kiver
down the
coiled Congo
and down
that black river
that tides us to hell

Hell
in the water
brown
boys of Bushongo drowned in the blue and the bitter salt
of the wave-gullied Ferdinand's sea
Soft winds
to San Salvador, Christopher, Christ, and no Noah
or dove to promise us, grim
though it was, the simple sal-
vation of love.[10]

There were duppy stories too. Gordon Rohlehr and Stewart Brown[11] have spoken about Kamau's concept of the circle and its spiritual significance: "they will light wicks to honour her circle/standing all night to hinder her ghosts from rising from surface of mirrors/through the long wax of stars and the blood's surfage".[12]

Also significant in Brathwaite's work is the image of the stone, with so many different nuances: the stone as creation and beginning and vision, as in "Calypso",[13] the stone as instrument of destruction, as used against Mikey Smith in the poem "Stone",[14] and often the stone as catalyst and agent of change ("out of the living stone, out of the living bone of coral").[15] Inevitably, there is a connection between the stone and the circle. When we were children running on the beach behind our house, Kamau and his friends used to skim the surface of the sea with a stone. I could never do it well, but they could, so that you could follow the flight of the stone with your eye – in a dead straight line or in a beautiful curving arc, which sometimes, like our archipelago itself, seemed about to close to a circle. But whatever the pattern, as the stone tipped the water each time, it rippled out into a circle, into circles, widening, sparkling, in the sun – which eventually becomes Kamau's alternative, as he puts it, to Wordsworth's "Daffodils": "Me stone had skidded arc'd and bloomed into islands: /Cuba and San Domingo/Jamaica and Puerto Rico/Grenada Guadeloupe Bonaire".[16]

Mother Poem and *Sun Poem* are replete with echoes of childhood; not all are truly autobiographical, but many are recognisable. "Occident", for example, captures our warm, loving, almost overpowering upbringing round our mother, with her concerns, her worries, her aggressions, her angers, her visions, her dreams, her determination concerning our education and future. Our father, on the other hand, was a very quiet person – not "marginal", as the textbooks say Caribbean fathers are supposed to be, but just quiet. Our mother, among other things, was, as far as we were concerned, a great quarreler. Our father was not. Refusing to quarrel, he just walked away. "Fish was a sign of peace inside our house."[17]

Mile and Quarter, St Peter, where our father came from, was also a significant "other shore" – not surf-sound here, but the sea-sound of cane fields and "country people". That place, a mile and a quarter from Speightstown,[18] has as much influence on Brathwaite's poetry as the sea outside Round House, Bay Street, Bridgetown.

And at the centre of it all, our grandfather, his sister-in-law, our Aunt May Agard, his brother-in-law Bobby O'Neale (Bob'ob, who becomes Ogoun in Brathwaite's poetry) and "all the aunts and uncles" we remembered in our prayers each night.

The actual, wonderful now-fading photo portrait of "Granpa" still hangs on the sitting-room wall at Mile and Quarter: "He drove the trap/himself, slap of the leather reins/along the horse's back and he'd be off/with a top-hearted homburg on his head: black English country gentleman".[19]

In addition to this open "trap", there was also a great assortment of horses, cows, lorries in various stages of repair or disrepair, including the magical ruin of a V-8 Ford: "the car had two horns: black bubble bugle: *paa paa paadoo*/and the round electric button nose inside the steering wheel: /*aa aa aaoooooga*: which we all preferred".[20] Next door to Granpa was Bob'ob – his home upstairs, where he and his two daughters, the musicians Miriam and Mabel lived; downstairs was the carpenter shop, now famous in Kamau's poetry (though the house and shop no longer exist) through the poem "Ogun".[21]

Like our mother and Grampa's sister-in-law, Aunt May Agard, Bob'ob also told us stories – of the Emperor Haile Selassie, of Mussolini and the Abyssinian War, of Marcus Garvey, the Sphinx, the pyramids and pharaohs of Africa. The closing stanzas of "Ogun" reveal how Brathwaite remembered, nourished, and transformed these things into his now well-known images of middle passage/re-connection.

And yet he had a block of wood that would have baffled
them.

With knife and gimlet care he worked away at this on
Sundays,

explored its knotted hurts, cutting his way
along its yellow whorls until his hands could feel

how it had swelled and shivered, breathing air,
its weathered green burning to rings of time,

its contoured grain still tuned to roots and water.
And as he cut, he heard the creak of forests:

green lizard faces gulped, grey memories with moth
eyes watched him from their shadows, soft

liquid tendrils leaked among the flowers
and a black rigid thunder he had never heard within his hammer

came stomping up the trunks. And as he worked within
his shattered
Sunday shop, the wood took shape: dry shuttered

eyes, slack anciently everted lips, flat
ruined face . . .

. . . the heavy black

enduring jaw; lost pain, lost iron;
emerging woodwork image of his anger.[22]

We were all writing in the late 1940s and early 1950s: in school magazines, in newspapers, in school newspapers like the one started by Kamau and friends at Harrison College. Thanks to Frank Collymore, Kamau's work, like that of Derek Walcott's in St Lucia, started appearing in *Bim*,[23] while others of us were successfully entering newspaper competitions (Kathleen McCracken, later Drayton, in the *Trinidad Guardian*; Slade Hopkinson and myself in the *Barbados Advocate*).

Apart from the encouragement from our "home" editors, we were stimulated by lectures given under the auspices of the British Council by people like H.A. Vaughan (poet, historian, judge), Judge Chenery, Crichlow Matthews and Frank Collymore himself. Small wonder then that by the end of the war (1945–1946) we felt our region to be a zone of excellence, though not of peace because memories of the war still clung: the Dutch merchant ship *Cornwallis* had been torpedoed in Carlisle Bay, straight across the water from our back door,[24] and the *Oumtata* had gone down spectacularly in Castries harbour, St Lucia.

Yet the boys still played "cowboy and crook" up and down the stairs of the Round House, under the cellar and on the beach. Everybody could swim out to the liners in the bay, but I found it rather scary the one time I tried. Then the boys would come in from the beach to eat and listen to music – jazz, classics, the blues. Kamau had a gramophone and a formidable collection of records (he still has!) by the time he reached sixth form, bought mostly from saved lunch money: Dizzy Gillespie, Harry James, Sinatra, Ella Fitzgerald, Sarah Vaughn, Woody Herman, Charlie Parker. His poem "So Long Charlie Parker" echoes the very notes of the sax itself.[25]

As the movement of the sea has shaped so much in Kamau's poetry, so the music of the sea has influenced his writing – powerful imagery, lyrical beauty, magnificent symphony of

song . song . song
syllable of circle . pellable of liquid
contralto tonnelle of your tone into fire
and the songs of crossing the river and the dead and
sea
of the morning and the brass and bells of the
water.
So that the syllable
the stone
skids full circle and becomes "there in the rise
and rise of the sorrel horizon
and sing . ing
and sing . ing
the song of the morn
ing".[26]

Both Sharon and Doris [27] loved to sing . . .

NOTES

*Mary E. Morgan, the sister of Kamau Brathwaite, originally presented the essay (an abridged form is reproduced here) as a talk delivered at Hostos Community College, CUNY, in October 1992 as part of a programme titled "Kamau Brathwaite and the Caribbean Word". The complete version of the essay was published in *World Literature Today: A Literary Quarterly of the University of Oklahoma* (Autumn 1994), pp. 663–9.

1. Kamau Brathwaite left the island for England by ship, out there in the bay "before they built the deep-water harbour, sinking a whole island to do it", so that we had to go out to the liner by launch; and when we were on board, we could look straight "back to the land and the house where [we] lived" Kamau Brathwaite [*Sun Poem*, (Oxford: Oxford University Press, 1982), p. 17], right there on the beach, and I remember that when our mother discovered that his passport and other important papers had been left behind, I had to run back down the gangway before the launch steamed back to shore, run from the Pierhead up Bay Street to the Round House, to retrieve the folder with the papers, and get back to the ship. But I was lucky getting back. I caught sight of our neighbour, Captain King the pilot (he appears as "Mr. Queen" in *Sun Poem*), on the beach outside, just about to step into the small rowboat that would take him out to his "Pilot Boat". I called out to him, ran down the back steps, and was lifted by his men into the rowboat, and so arrived in fine style back at the gangway of the French ship *Gascoigne*. Ten years later, our brother returned home from England and Ghana, again by ship.

2. James Vinson, ed., "Kamau Brathwaite", *Contemporary Poets of the English Language* (London: Macmillan Press, 1980), p. 129.

3. Kamau Brathwaite, *Mother Poem* (Oxford: Oxford University Press, 1977), p. 115.

4. Brathwaite, *Sun Poem*.

5. Kamau Brathwaite, *Soweto* Mona (Jamaica), *Savacou*, 1979.

6. Brathwaite, *Mother Poem*.

7. *The People Who Came*, the title of a three-part textbook for schools edited and co-authored by Kamau Brathwaite (first published in 1968, 1970 and 1972; revised editions 1987, 1989 and 1993). (Trinidad: Longman Caribbean); p. 3 (unnumbered).

8. Kamau Brathwaite, *Dream Stories* (Harlow: Essex: Longman, 1993).

9. Our mother tended to do her ironing while sitting rather than standing, because even then she was suffering from "her feet", what we now know was a diabetic effect.

10. Kamau Brathwaite, "Rights of Passage", in Norman Hidden, Amy Hollins, eds., *Many People Many Voices* (London: Hutchinson, 1978).

11. See Gordon Rohlehr's, "The Rehumanisation of History: Regeneration of Spirit: Apocalypse and Revolution", in Braithwaite's *The Arrivants and the X-Self*, pp.

163–202 and Stewart Brown's, "Sun Poem: The Rainbow Sign?", pp. 152–62, in *The Art of Kamau Brathwaite* (Bridgend, Wales: Poetry Wales Press Ltd., 1995). In an interview reproduced in the same collection, Kamau Brathwaite explained his technique of "tidalectics", which mirrors "the movement of water backwards and forwards as a kind of cyclic . . . motion rather than linear." See Nathaniel Mackey", "An Interview with Kamau Brathwaite", p. 14.

12.   Brathwaite, *Mother Poem*, p. 113.

13.   This poem was published in Brathwaite, *Rights of Passage.*

14.   "Stone: for Mikey Smith". First appeared in Kamau Brathwaite, *Jah Music* (Mona: Savcou, 1986).

15.   Kamau Brathwaite, *Islands* (Oxford: Oxford University Press, 1969), p. 34; the collection was re-issued as part of Kamau Brathwaite, *The Arrivants: New World Trilogy* (London, New York: Oxford University Press, 1973). I understand that Pam Mordecai is working on a thesis that explores this very image – the stone and pebble.

16.   Brathwaite, *The Arrivants*, p. 48

17.   Brathwaite, *Sun Poem*; Brathwaite, *Mother Poem* p. 90

18.   Barbados has four towns: Bridgetown, the capital; and Speightstown, Holetown and Oistin, which when we were growing up were little more than villages.

19.   Brathwaite, *The Arrivants*, p. 239

20.   Brathwaite, *Mother Poem*, p. 119

21.   "Ogun" in Brathwaite, *The Arrivants*, p. 242

22.   Brathwaite, *The Arrivants*, p. 243

23.   Derek Walcott first appears in *Bim*, 10 (June 1949), with the poem "A Way to Live". Kamau's first publication is in *Bim*, 12 (June 1950), the poem "Shadow Suite". Between 1950 and 1972, when Colly was editor, Kamau published some seventy-five poems in *Bim*.

24.   The *Cornwallis* incident is recorded in George Lamming's book, *In the Castle of my Skin* (London: Longmans, 1953) and in even greater detail in Kamau's unpublished novella, *The Boy and the Sea*, since after the torpedoing, he and his friends used to swim or row out to "the wreck in the harbour". It was there for years, tilted onto the sea floor, and there was this great gaping hole of horror in its side where the torpedo had struck, blowing its way through the submarine nets that stretched on huge buoys right across the mouth of the harbour from Pelican Island to Needham's Point. For months the boys from our beach went out there, diving into that black hole and bringing up cans of corned beef, sardines, and all sorts of tarsticky goodies.

25.   A version of Kamau Brathwaite's poem "Bird" was published in his *Jah Music*, *Savacou*, Mona (Jamaica), (1986), pp. 12–13.

26. Kamau Brathwaite, "Shar" (Mona, *Savacou*, 1990). This poem is dedicated by Kamau to Sharon, his niece (my daughter) who died in July 1990, after a triumphant fight with non-Hodgkins lymphoma and the miracle birth of her second son (born March 1990) after sustaining her pregnancy through chemotheraphy.

27. Doris, was Kamau's late wife. Kamau's account of his wife's death in 1986 is contained in *The Zea Mexican Diary* (Madison: University of Wisconsin Press, 1993).

PART TWO

Creolisation and Creole
Definitions, Meanings and Models Critiqued

O. Nigel Bolland

Chapter 2

CREOLISATION AND CREOLE SOCIETIES

A CULTURAL NATIONALIST VIEW OF CARIBBEAN SOCIAL HISTORY*

The meaning of the term "Creole" varies in different societies and over time. It is used in the British, Dutch, French and Hispanic
Caribbean and also in parts of the North and Central American mainland, in
much of South America and in Sierra Leone. Virginia Dominguez, who has
studied the changing usage of "Creole" in Louisiana since the eighteenth
century, concludes:

> A single definition of the term *Creole* may have been adequate for all of these
> societies during the early stages of European expansion. But as the Creole
> populations of these colonies (or former colonies) established diverse social,
> political, and economic positions for themselves over the years, *Creole* acquired
> diverse meanings.[1]

Generally, the term "Creole", referring to people and cultures, means something or somebody derived from the Old World but developed in the New. In the
United States of America, in accordance with racist pressures in the nineteenth
century, "Creole" came to refer to Caucasian people of French or Spanish descent,
but elsewhere the term was not so racially differentiated. "Creole" refers to locally
born persons of non-native origin, which, in the Americas, generally means people

15

of either African or European ancestry, or both. In Sierra Leone, "Creole" refers to the "westernised" community of descendants of liberated Africans who, in 1787, began to be resettled in the area that became Freetown. In this case, too, "Creole" refers to people who are *culturally distinct* from the Old World populations of their origin. The concept of "creolisation", then, refers to those processes of cultural change that give rise to such distinctiveness.

In common Caribbean usage, "Creole" refers to a local product which is the result of a mixture or blending of various ingredients that originated in the Old World. For example, in an essay on "West Indian Culture", first published in 1961, the late Jamaican anthropologist M.G. Smith wrote:

> Creoles are natives of the Caribbean . . . The Creole complex has its historical base in slavery, plantation systems, and colonialism. Its cultural composition mirrors its racial mixture. European and African elements predominate in fairly standard combinations and relationships . . .
>
> Perhaps this combination of European and African traditions is the most important feature of Creole life.[2]

Smith viewed this "multiracial Creole complex" as a "graduated hierarchy of European and African elements", with a "dominant Creole-European tradition" contrasting with the "'African' Creole culture" at opposite ends of the spectrum. He concluded, on the eve of the collapse of the West Indian Federation, that the connection between culture and nationalism was highly problematic in the West Indies:

> The common culture, without which West Indian nationalism cannot develop the dynamic to create a West Indian nation, may by its very nature and composition preclude the nationalism that invokes it. This is merely another way of saying that the Creole culture which West Indians share is the basis of their division.[3]

In contrast to Smith, other writers have subsequently emphasised the potential of Creole culture for national integration. In the popular view, creolisation is a version of the old "melting pot" hypothesis, which conceives of a new cultural unity evolving from the blending of diverse original elements. For example, a recent book on Caribbean festival arts uses the metaphor of callalou, a local soup made of diverse ingredients, to describe racial and cultural relations and the "pan-Caribbean aesthetic": "The blending of these disparate elements is indicative of the creolisation process."[4] The "flavour of the Caribbean character" is said to be the result of such blending: "The more diverse the ingredients, the sweeter the soup; the more diverse its people's racial and cultural backgrounds, the stronger, the better the nation."[5] As popularly conceived, then, the image of Creole culture and a Creole society emphasises social unity – the new nation as a Creole *community*.

From the perspective of the sociology of knowledge, we may ask why the conception of a "Creole society" emerges at a particular time, promoted by particular people. In the case of Sierra Leone, it has been argued that the "society has always been socio-economically and ethnically divided. However, 'Creole' intellectuals, especially in the 1950s, sought to emphasise social unity and a common culture in order to protect their privileged position."[6] These intellectuals are said to have described Sierra Leone as a "unified and self-conscious community ... which identified itself as Creole". By the 1840s, though,"There is no evidence that at any time during the nineteenth century the society of Sierra Leone either shared a common culture or manifested the solidarity of a unified group."[7] Indeed, it is said that "the Creole community, as it is popularly known today, did not become politically or socially unified even during the period 1940 to 1960."[8] This is an example of "inventing traditions", in Eric Hobsbawm's words, "establishing or symbolising social cohesion or the membership of groups, real or artificial communities",[9] for the purpose of nation-building. The intellectuals of Sierra Leone attempted to create a sense of Creole identity and unity, and claimed that it had existed for over a century, in order to maintain their hegemony as the country prepared for independence.

This brief consideration of the case of Sierra Leone indicates that the promotion of the image of a Creole society is not limited to the Caribbean and that it is linked to the process of decolonisation and nation-building. The subject of this article is, in fact, an example of a much broader problem associated with the role of intellectuals in the creation of images of their societies, particularly during periods of rapid social transformation. Hobsbawm has pointed out that all historians are engaged in inventing traditions "inasmuch as they contribute, consciously or not, to the creation, dismantling and restructuring of images of the past which belong not only to the world of specialist investigation but to the public sphere of man as a political being".[10] This is especially true in connection with the ideologies, symbols and images of nationalism.

The concept of Creole society, as it has been used in the Caribbean, stresses the active role of Caribbean peoples and the importance of African cultural traditions. In many ways it is the antithesis of the old imperialist viewpoint that denies the "natives" a history of their own and asserts that nothing of any cultural value was ever produced in the Caribbean. By insisting on the fact that the common people – slaves, peasants, freedpeople and labourers – were active agents in the historical process, the creolisation thesis has made a major contribution to

Caribbean historiography. This thesis, which reflects the influence of anthropological approaches, has broadened our conception of the scope of Caribbean social
history and reconstituted our ways of looking at the dynamics of social and
cultural change. Caribbean societies and cultures can no longer be thought of as
the result of a one-way process, of the unilateral imposition of European culture
upon passive African recipients. Important as European expansion, slavery, the
plantation system and the deracination of Africans unquestionably are, it is now
generally recognised that the conjoint participation of different peoples, not least
those from Africa, produced from a very early time a distinctive African-American
or Creole culture.[11]

The analysis of creolisation as a process of cultural interaction and synthesis
may be understood as part of a broad intellectual trend among learned humanists
and social scientists towards a global culture history. In this trend the insights of
anthropology are combined with an understanding of the political economy of
the emerging capitalist world-system.[12] But the Creole-society model, as a vision
of Caribbean social history, is not limited in its antecedents and implications to
scholarly debates in the international academe. As the antithesis of the imperialist
view of the Caribbean, this model reflects and enhances the emerging Caribbean
nationalism of the third quarter of the twentieth century. More specifically, the
cultural and populist aspects of the Creole-society viewpoint, with its emphasis
upon the origins of a distinctive *common* culture as a basis for national unity,
constitutes the ideology of a particular social segment, namely a middle-class
intelligentsia that seeks a leading role in an integrated, newly independent
society.[13] The Creole-society thesis, then, is a significant ideological moment in
the decolonisation process of the Caribbean.[14]

Nevertheless, the concept of creolisation has not been adequately defined or
clearly located within a broader theoretical model of culture change. Consequently, the use of the concept is inconsistent and often crude. Here I will argue
that the Creole-society thesis, while drawing upon anthropological theories of
culture change, lacks a consistent and explicit theoretical basis, sometimes taking
a dualistic and sometimes a dialectical form. William A. Green, in a critique of
what he calls the "creolisation of Caribbean history", concludes that the notion
of creolisation satisfies the needs of West Indian nationalists but that it is "in
danger of going awry", unless it is disengaged from dialectical analysis.[15] I will
argue, to the contrary, that the thesis of creolisation and the Creole society, as
exemplified in the work of Brathwaite, is not dialectical enough. The importance
of understanding the process of creolisation in Caribbean history is not merely in
order to broaden the scope of the traditional definition of the subject-matter, so
that we may return to our work with the old methods and theories intact, as

Green seems to suggest. Rather, our understanding of creolisation as a central cultural process of Caribbean history should lead to a reconceptualisation of the nature of colonialism and colonial societies, as social forces and social systems that are characterised by conflicts and contradictions and that consequently give rise to their own transformation. This dialectical view of Caribbean social history is often implied but is inadequately developed in the Creole-society thesis. The purpose of this critique of the Creole-society model from the viewpoint of dialectical theory is to reveal both its essential contribution and its shortcomings and to propose a more adequate theoretical basis for the thesis.

Before examining the theoretical ambiguity of the Creole-society model it is necessary to examine briefly the prevailing images of Caribbean society that preceded it.

THE PLANTATION-SOCIETY AND PLURAL-SOCIETY MODELS

The two most influential models of Caribbean society among English-speaking intellectuals in the 1960s were those of a plantation society and a plural society.[16]

The plantation-society thesis identifies the institution of the plantation and along with it the experience and legacy of slavery, as central in Caribbean social life. The social organisation and culture associated with plantation production is seen as a microcosm of the whole society. The distinguishing features of the plantation – which include mono-crop production for export, strong monopolistic tendencies, a rigid system of social stratification that includes a high correlation between racial and class hierarchies, a weak community structure, the marginality of peasants who engage in subsistence production as well as periodic work on the plantations – make it the nexus of cultural and political, as well as economic, activities.

The plantation has been compared to Erving Goffman's "total institution" in which a new "identity" is imposed upon the inmates.[17] Orlando Patterson emphasises the importance of the plantation as the unit of social organisation during the period of slavery:

> Jamaican slave society was loosely integrated; so much so, that one hesitates to call it a society since all that it amounted to was an ill-organised system of exploitation . . .
>
> Jamaica is best seen more as a collection of autonomous plantations, each a self-contained community with its internal mechanisms of power, than as a total social system.[18]

Other writers, notably George Beckford, stress the persistence of the characteristics of the slave/plantation society in the present period. Among these characteristics is the dependency of the plantation upon inputs and markets in the metropolis, which leads to underdevelopment and so to the persistent powerlessness and poverty of the majority of the population. Beckford emphasises the interrelationship between the "plantation as a social system in the territory in which it is located (the internal dimension) and . . . the plantation as an economic system both in the territory of its location and in the wider world community (the external dimension)."[19] Individual plantations, though relatively isolated as social units, are interrelated through their connections with the political economy of the metropolis and the intra-imperial system as a whole. The model suggests three distinct but interrelated levels of social analysis: the plantation as an oppressive local institution, the plantation society as a weak and dependent aggregation of plantations, and the intra-imperial system that is bound up with the world economy. The plantation as an institution and the plantation society itself are actually conceived as sub-systems that cannot be understood without reference to the place they occupy in relation to the intra-imperial social system.

The plantation-society model emphasises the socio-economic structure of the plantation, perceived as a central institution which has an all-pervasive character, essentially coercive and exploitative in nature, in the dependent society. While it must be said in the model's defence that slavery and the plantation, which have been so central in Caribbean society for so long, continue to have an influence on cultural and social organisation long after they have ceased to be central (or have even ceased to exist), it should also be noted that this model generally underestimates the ability of the victims to influence the system. Susan Craig has observed that "The appealing attempt to derive social structure from the plantation experience is too simple and too reductionist."[20]

The model has also been criticised on the grounds that it identifies the institutional arrangement of production with the entire society in such a way as "to leave the analysis at an institutional level".[21] Although the economic system had distinctive and influential institutional features, it should not be conflated with the social system which includes features other than those identified with the plantation as such. Even when we conceive of the plantation in terms of political economy, that is, as production occurring within political structures, this is still inadequate if it leaves out the cultural issues, such as conceptions of rights and duties, the values and visions, beliefs and ideas, of the various protagonists within the society. These social and cultural aspects are generally influenced by, but are surely not limited to, plantation life.[22]

In fact, the colonial system was never able to guarantee the plantation sub-system for long without recourse to the use of force because it failed to achieve cultural hegemony over the producers, whether they were slaves or legally free labourers. This is why the cultural emphasis of Smith's plural-society model made such a valuable contribution. Smith argues that there was never a consensus of cultural values between Europeans and Africans, and that there is a "cultural pluralism" among the diverse peoples in these Caribbean societies. He focuses on institutions, such as kinship, education, religion, property and economy, as the core of a people's culture and the matrix of their social structure. In an article first published in 1953, which was chiefly concerned with the social structure of St Vincent and Jamaica in about 1820, Smith equated the "plural society" with cultural pluralism. The "three principal sections of colonial society", namely the Whites, the free people of colour and the slaves,

> . . . were differentiated culturally – that is, by their adherence to different institutions . . . In effect the population of a British West Indian colony at this period was culturally pluralistic – that is to say, it contained sections which practiced different forms of the same institutions. Thus the population consti- tuted a plural society, that is, a society divided into sections, each of which practiced different cultures.[23]

Soon after, Smith described contemporary Jamaica, for the first time, as "a plural society of three culturally distinct social sections which could be distinguished as white, brown and black by reference to the modal race of most of their mem- bers".[24]

Later, Smith distinguished between cultural pluralism and a plural society. In his own words,

> . . . having identified pluralism with the condition of institutional and cultural diversity within a given population, I went on to distinguish plural societies as those culturally split societies governed by dominant demographic minorities whose peculiar social structures and political conditions set them apart.[25]

What distinguishes a society exhibiting cultural pluralism from a plural society, then, is the fact that in the latter cultural groups act in the public domain as corporations:

> . . . plural societies are constituted and distinguished by corporate divisions that differ culturally, and . . . these may be aligned in differing ways to create hierarchic, segmented or complex pluralities . . . In short, while the coexistence of culturally distinct aggregates is sufficient and necessary to constitute plural-

ism, to constitute a plural society such divisions must also operate as corporations, *de jure* or *de facto*, within the public domain.[26]

The undoubted strength of the plural-society model is that it draws attention to the cultural and institutional differentiation and complexity of Caribbean societies. However, when the model is applied to particular cases, the racial, cultural and class categories tend to become conflated in a simple social hierarchy. For example, when Smith analyses the political scene in Jamaica in the 1980s, he argues that

> ... different sections of the society pursue and interpret party politics in radically different ways. The murderous 'tribal warfare' between supporters of rival political parties in Kingston and other Jamaican townships is confined to the poorest and least educated strata of the Black population, not all of whom are *lumpenproletariat*, but who live in the most overcrowded and insanitary conditions. At the other end, the directorates of the political parties and industrial unions consisted almost exclusively of the 'brown section' or 'coloured middle class', not all of whom are phenotypically brown ... Beyond and above the brown political elite stand [sic] a tight handful of expatriate and Creole Whites who, by virtue of their economic assets and contacts, are largely able to dictate economic conditions to the people and government.[27]

It appears from this account that all the cultural sections are participating in *the same economy and polity* and that it is differential access to and control over certain key economic and political resources that determine intergroup relations. In other words, although Smith labels the social sections by colour, they are really distinguished in terms of *social class*. Contrary to the plural- society model, these social sections *all* participate in the same political parties and trade unions, although, not surprisingly, they do so in different ways according to their position in the class structure.

Smith adheres to the notion that, in Caribbean societies, "class structures are subsumed within those wider racial and cultural divisions that together constitute the corporate macro-structure of these societies",[28] but he acknowledges that "the decisive structural determinant has been and remains the *distribution of power* among and within institutionally distinct groups and categories having modally different racial cores, numbers, histories, cultures, wealth and prospects."[29] All we can conclude from this is that a discussion of cultural pluralism and racial groups should not exclude a consideration of social classes and power, just as the analysis of the political economy and class structure should not exclude consideration of culture and race. Although Smith conceives of the plural society as inherently unstable, barely held together by one cultural section's monopoly of power, he says little about the nature and direction of social change.[30] He appears to be suggesting that the most important feature of the social structure is the fact that the principal social sections are differentiated culturally, but that the structure is actually determined by the distribution of power.

The problem with the plural-society model is that if it is to have any explanatory power as a theory of social change, rather than being merely a simple and static classificatory scheme,[31] it must account for the distribution of power that determines the social structure. Such an account cannot be in terms of cultural differentiation, but must be in terms of the conditions of inequality and exploitation that are generated by the political economy of colonialism.[32]

THE CREOLE-SOCIETY MODEL

The model of a Creole society, like the plural-society model but unlike the plantation-society model, focuses on the importance of culture in Caribbean societies. However, in contrast to the plural-society model, which stresses the persistence of social segmentation and of conflict between racial and ethnic groups, the Creole-society model draws attention to an evolving cultural unity which "could well support the development of a new parochial wholeness".[33] Unlike the plural-society thesis, then, the notion of the development of a Creole society is predicated on a conception of social and cultural change. This is the concept of "creolisation", a concept that is now widely used to refer to processes of cultural change in the Caribbean and elsewhere. The Creole-society model, as exemplified by Kamau Brathwaite's study of Jamaica between 1770 and 1820, acknowledges the existence of internal cleavages and conflicts in the slave society, but also stresses the processes of interaction and mutual adjustment between the major cultural traditions of Europe and Africa. The central argument of the Creole-society model is that the Europeans and Africans who settled in the Americas contributed to the development of a distinctive society and culture that was neither European nor African, but "Creole".

Brathwaite developed his conception of Jamaican society in reaction to Orlando Patterson's. In a review of *The Sociology of Slavery*, Brathwaite criticises Patterson's "disintegrationist concept of society".[34] In contrast to Patterson, Brathwaite cites Elsa Goveia's study of the Leeward Islands, in which she found a "firmer sense of living wholeness" in the slave society[35]:

> The slave society of the Leeward Islands at the end of the eighteenth century
> was divided into separate groups, clearly marked off from each other by the

differences of legal and social status, of political rights and economic opportunity, and of racial origin and culture. The existence of these separate groups is so striking that it tends to obscure the existence of the community of which they were all a part. But this community did exist, and its fundamental principles of inequality and subordination based on race and status were firmly impressed upon the lives of all its members. It was these basic principles, embodying the necessities of the West Indian slave system which determined the ordering of the separate groups as part of a community and held them all together within a single social structure.[36]

Brathwaite criticised Patterson for "largely ignoring the White group of masters" and the role of the free Coloured population who could be seen "as an integrating force".[37] In conclusion, however, Brathwaite argues that Patterson, "in pointing out that within the system the slave was still able to retain areas of activity, recreation and belief for himself . . . makes his most important contribution to our understanding of the reality of Jamaican slavery".[38] In this review of Patterson's book, published in 1968, lies the essential themes of the *Creole-society* thesis.

In *The Development of Creole Society in Jamaica, 1770–1820*, Brathwaite defines the process of creolisation as a cultural change "based upon the stimulus/response of individuals within the society to their environment and – as White/Black, culturally discrete groups – to each other".[39] And he emphasises that this "intercultural creolisation" is a "two-way process".[40] While acknowledging that one of these groups has power over the other, Brathwaite's purpose is to show the integrative effect this intercultural evolution has in the emerging society. To this end, he draws attention to the importance of the expanding intermediate group that resulted from miscegenation: "the large and growing coloured population of the island, which . . . acted as a bridge, a kind of social cement, between the two main colours of the island's structure, thus further helping (despite the resulting class/colour divisions) to integrate the society."[41]

Brathwaite refers to Robert Redfield's conception of the interdependence in a civilisation of the great and little traditions when he discusses the "folk" culture of the slaves, "the culture of the mass of ex-Africans who found themselves in a new environment and who were successfully adapting to it".[42] He stresses that the "great tradition" of Jamaica's slaves was in Africa, but he deliberately eschews any discussion about African "survivals" or "retentions", nor does he make any distinctions between the varieties of African cultures from which Jamaican "folk" culture was derived.[43] He mentions the importance of the abolition of the slave trade in 1807, which cut off the possibilities of demographic and cultural renewal from Africa and the increasing tendency of the more privileged among the Blacks and Browns to imitate European models.

> But the African influence remained, even if increasingly submerged, as an impor-
> tant element in the process of creolization. European adaptations or imitations
> could never be wholehearted or complete. There might be apparent European
> forms, but the content would be different. There was developing a European-ori-
> ented creole form (Euro-creole) and an African-influenced creole form (Afro-cre-
> ole); and they existed together within, often, the same framework.[44]

Brathwaite's distinction between the "Euro-creole" and "Afro-creole" variants of Jamaican "folk" culture implies that Creole culture and society is only a potential unity, as yet unfulfilled, and that the differences between these variants were "developing" in the early nineteenth century. This image of the divisions in Jamaican culture is similar to that depicted by Smith in 1961, as we saw at the beginning of this essay. Despite the unifying tendencies of the creolisation process, then, Brathwaite understands Jamaican culture to be deeply divided:

> Here, in Jamaica, fixed within the dehumanising institution of slavery, were two
> cultures of people, having to adapt themselves to a new environment and to each
> other. The friction created by this confrontation was cruel, but it was also
> creative. The White plantations and social institutions . . . reflect one aspect of
> this. The slaves' adaptation of their African culture to a new world reflects
> another. The failure of Jamaican society was that it did not recognise these
> elements of its own creativity.[45]

Although this recognition of the "two cultures" appears similar to the view of the plural-society thesis, Brathwaite sharply distinguishes his orientation from that of Smith's:

> [T]he educated middle class, most finished product of unfinished creolisation;
> influential, possessed of a shadow power; rootless (eschewing the folk) or
> Euro-orientated with a local gloss: Creo- or Afro-Saxons. For them the society is
> 'plural' in so far as it appears to remain divided into its old colonial alignments.
> They are 'West Indian' in that they are (or can be) critical of the colonising power.
> But they are also dependent upon it . . . [T]he concept of a 'plural society' would
> appear to be a colonial rather than a Creole contribution.[46]

In this ideologically loaded passage, Brathwaite dissociates himself from the plural-society protagonists and identifies with what he calls, apparently inter-changeably, the Afro-Creole or "folk" orientation. In another passage, he suggests that this identification and commitment is connected with the emerging cultural nationalism of the 1960s:

> Some understanding of the nature of this folk culture is important, not only in terms of the Creole society to which it was to contribute within the time limits of this study, but also because the changes in Jamaican society after 1865 involved the beginning of an assertion of this folk culture which was to have a profound effect upon the very constitution of Jamaican society. This assertion has become increasingly articulate since the gaining of political independence in 1962 and is now the subject of some study by scholars and intellectuals. This 'folk culture' is also being made use of by many Jamaican and West Indian artists and writers.[47]

Brathwaite concludes his study of the development of Creole society in Jamaica between 1770 and 1820 with speculation about "whether the process of creolisation will be resumed in such a way that the 'little' tradition of the (ex-) slaves will be able to . . . provide a basis for creative reconstruction. Such a base . . . could well support the development of a new parochial wholeness, a difficult but possible Creole authenticity."[48] The question, for Brathwaite, is whether the political power that had come into the hands of the Black majority of the population with independence in 1962 could mediate the development of a national culture. His answer is that an understanding of Jamaican history points to the process of creolisation as the source of authentic Jamaican culture, rooted in the descendants of the ex-slaves.

Brathwaite was not alone among Caribbean intellectuals exploring these issues in the post-independence period. I will briefly discuss contributions by three others: Rex Nettleford, Mervyn Alleyne and Orlando Patterson, selecting these, not because they are "typical", but because they have developed interesting variants on the theme of creolisation.

Rex Nettleford, current vice-chancellor of the University of the West Indies, artistic director of the National Dance Theatre Company of Jamaica, former director of the Trade Union Education Institute and former head of the Department of Extra-Mural Studies, clearly longs for a Creole culture in which the African heritage is given its due. He has sensitively discussed the delicate interplay between Old World cultures to "form an organic whole inextricably bound up and expressive of a new and rich phenomenon which is neither Africa nor Europe, yet embodying the two in unprecedented and creative modes of relationship".[49] Noting that Jamaica is officially committed to multi-racialism, Nettleford observes that "Europe's melody" nevertheless predominates in a "lop-sided Creole culture"[50] in which "Africa's rhythm" is largely submerged. In his judgement, claims of "harmonious racial heterogeneity" and of "cultural consensus" are exaggerated. He sees the creolisation process to be more one-sided than does Brathwaite: "Jamaican life has been determined by a process of assimilation with one culture absorbing another rather than by one of mutual acculturation which could produce that new and vital other force after which so many hanker."[51] Nettleford concludes:

> One thing is certain: there must be the liberation of the Jamaican Black, whether he be peasant, proletarian or struggling middle class, from the chains of self-con-tempt, self-doubt and cynicism. Correspondingly, there will have to be the liberation of Jamaican Whites, real and functional, from the bondage of a lop-sided Creole culture which tends to maintain for them an untenable position of privilege. Then the harmony which so many well-intentioned Jamaicans claim to exist will begin to transform itself from fiction into fact.[52]

Nearly two decades later, Nettleford refers to the outcome of the creolisation process as "Euro-African" or "Afro-Creole" culture. Now, like Brathwaite, Nettle-ford stresses the creative contributions of Africans in the Caribbean: "The Afri-canisation of the European was no less important to the creolisation process than the Europeanisation of the African."[53]

Mervyn Alleyne (former professor of Socio-Linguistics at the University of the West Indies in Jamaica) is a student of Creole languages. He argues that the predominant languages in the Caribbean colonies, whether Creoles or non-stand-ard dialects of European languages, were the consequence of a prolonged struggle between enslavers and enslaved over the medium of communication. The out-come of this struggle reflects the metropolitan hegemony, and becomes a further means of maintaining social inequalities. Alleyne reminds us that an important element of cultural imperialism is that the Europeans viewed the cultures of peoples over whom they ruled as "savage" or "primitive", and the Creole cultures of the Caribbean were not considered "culture" at all. The Creole languages developed by Africans and their descendants were evaluated by Europeans as pathological versions of European originals, as " 'deficiencies', 'corruptions', and 'mutilations' ".[54]

Alleyne leaves us in no doubt about the political significance of this evaluation of the development of Creole languages in a colonial society. "An important part of the colonial syndrome is the acceptance by the colonised of the coloniser's interpretation of them. Caribbean people have largely accepted European's views of their language behaviour as part of a more general self-deprecation and negative evaluation of their cultural behaviour."[55] While this is probably overstating and overgeneralising the case for the "internalisation" of the coloniser's norms and values, there is certainly a strong association between the use of Creole languages and low status in Caribbean societies, and elites have used language distinctions as a way of maintaining oligarchic power. Alleyne argues that, just as this pattern of language use has contributed to the existing cultural hegemony, the "use of Creole languages, the mass vernaculars of the Caribbean, is now a vital factor in the democratisation of national life and institutions and in the accessibility of these institutions to the mass of the population".[56]

More recently, Alleyne has emphasised the African contribution to Jamaican culture, particularly in religion, music and dance and language. As in his earlier work, he stresses the continuing struggle in the process of cultural change:

> African surface forms of culture have become progressively diluted in the behaviour of most Jamaicans . . . But the African heritage survives . . . Jamaican culture is indeed a 'degradation' or 'corruption' – not so much of European culture as of African culture. The cultural history of Jamaica is one in which Black people constantly struggled to maintain their African heritage in the teeth of slavery, colonialism, neocolonialism, and imperialism in the guise of modernisation.[57]

In the years immediately after constitutional independence, many West Indian intellectuals, such as Brathwaite and Nettleford, drew attention to and contributed to the revitalisation of their Afro-Creole culture with some self-confidence. But Alleyne warns that today "this culture is under relentless siege", despite the search for African roots and campaigns to preserve the folk culture. "It is ironic", he says, "that British, European, and North American influence in Jamaica is now stronger than it ever was, although today the island is politically independent."[58]

Orlando Patterson, the Jamaican novelist, sociologist and scholar of comparative slavery, believes that the process of creolisation was much less developed during the period of slavery than Brathwaite portrays. Patterson distinguishes between "segmentary creolisation", which resulted in two kinds of culture, namely the Euro-West Indian and the Afro-West Indian (and largely peasant) Creole cultures, and "synthetic creolisation", which

> . . . draws heavily on Euro-West Indian culture for its instrumental components and on Afro-West Indian segmentary Creole for its expressive institutions and symbols. The political, economic, educational, and legal institutions of synthetic Creole are, essentially, slightly modified versions of Euro-West Indian segmentary Creole; whereas its language, theater, music, dance, art, and literature are actively drawn from Afro-West Indian segmentary Creole sources.[59]

Segmentary and synthetic creolisation are basically antithetical, with the latter seeking to unite the segmentary cultures which resist such unification.

The synthetic creolisation period is said to have started in the 1950s,[60] but the process of national cultural unification is far from complete, according to Patterson: "Caribbean societies are, today, best seen as neo-colonial systems with enormous class cleavages."[61] While members of the middle and upper classes identify with a synthetic Creole culture, which some of them self-consciously promote, the majority of the lower classes adhere to the segmentary Afro-West Indian Creole culture. Patterson, more than the other intellectuals cited, reconciles aspects of the cultural analysis of the plural-society and Creole-society models with a strong emphasis on the class character of Caribbean societies, a character that stems from the socio-economic structures of the colonial plantation system.

Having examined some of the chief variants of the Creole-society thesis, I will now explore its theoretical ambiguities, and will seek to develop an alternative, more consistent theoretical basis for the thesis.

A DIALECTICAL VIEW OF CREOLISATION

Caribbean nations were created in the crucible of the prolonged and pervasive experience of slavery and colonialism, and survive today in a fragile state, threatened by external political, military, economic and cultural forces beyond their control. They have a desperate need for a coherent national ideology and cultural identity. The Creole-society thesis offers an approach to national integration by seeking to unite people of diverse origins in an overarching ethnicity based on the recognition and creation of a developing Creole culture. The creation of a Creole identity and the vision of the nation as a Creole community constitute a *synthetic* mode of nationalism.[62]

The idea that the synthesis of new cultural practices emerges from the struggle between conflicting social forces is certainly not new as an interpretation of Caribbean history and society,[63] but the development of the Creole-society thesis gave this idea new urgency and specificity. Implicit in the thesis is a dialectical view of social dynamics and cultural change. Conceptually, however, "creolisation" and the "Creole society" remain ill-defined and ambiguous. On the one hand, the vision of a Creole nation rests on the axiom that the individual is the elementary unit of social life, and hence that "society" is the aggregate of its individual citizens and "cultures" are simply the aggregates of what individuals believe and do in a society. Related to this axiom is the dualistic conception of the "individual" and "society", a portrayal of social dynamics in mechanical terms and a separation of cultural processes from social structures. When the Creole-society thesis leans on this conception of society, for example, the social structure is portrayed simply as a "Black/White dichotomy",[64] and the creolisation process is seen as a "cultural action . . . based upon the stimulus/response of individuals within the society to their environment and – as White/Black, culturally discrete groups – to each other."[65] This dichotomous model of the society becomes modified with the expansion of the intermediate "Coloured" population which "acted as a bridge, a kind of social cement, between the two main colours of the island's structure, thus further helping . . . to integrate the society."[66] Brathwaite refers to "the juxtaposition of master and slave",[67] as if these are individuals who have an existence independent of each other, rather than social roles that are mutually constitutive and defined by their relationship.

This dualistic view of society leads to the portrayal of creolisation as a "blending" process, a mixing of cultures that occurs without reference to structural contradictions and social conflicts. For example, in an overview and analysis of music in the Caribbean, Kenneth Bilby describes the creolisation process as the "blending of two or more older traditions on new soil", resulting in "a broad spectrum of musical forms, ranging from purely European-derived examples at one extreme to what have sometimes been called neo-African styles at the other".[68] This view of a simple "blending" and "spectrum" obfuscates the tension and conflict that existed, and still exists, between the Africans and Europeans who were the bearers of these traditions. The cultural process of music, in other words, becomes isolated from the historical process of domination/subordination in the wider society.

On the other hand, elements of the Creole-society thesis have drawn attention to precisely these conflicting relationships and the tensions that exist in processes of social and cultural change. Brathwaite himself has described the creolisation process in a dialectical manner, as "a way of seeing the society, not in terms of White and Black, master and slave, in separate nuclear units, but as contributing parts of the whole".[69] Alleyne's analysis of the development of Creole languages also implies a dialectical outlook when he characterises Caribbean societies as "contradictory, conflict-prone and insecure, ambivalent in outlook and attitudes, ambiguous in their formation and in their functioning . . . The language situations existing in the Caribbean are mirrors through which the complex cultural history of the region may be observed."[70]

The dialectical analysis of society draws attention to the interrelated and mutually constitutive nature of "individual", "society", and "culture", and of human agency and social structure. Dialectical theory conceives of social life as essentially *practical* activity and of people as an essentially *social* beings. Hence, society consists of the social relations in which people engage in their activities, and is not reducible to individuals. Karl Marx drew attention to the fact that people make their history and society, but under conditions and constraints that they find already in existence: "Men make their history, but they do not make it just as they please; they do not make it under circumstances chosen by themselves, but under circumstances directly found, given and transmitted from the past."[71] Culture and society, in the form of traditions, ideas, customs, languages, institutions and social formations, shape the social action of individuals, which in turn maintains, modifies or transforms social structure and culture. This mutually dependent relationship between social structure and human agency has been referred to as the "dialectics of structuring".[72]

Dialectical theory draws attention, in particular, to conflicts in social systems as the chief sources of social change. Many important social relationships are defined and differentiated in terms of power between the dominant and the subordinate. As the forms of oppression vary from one society to another (indeed, we often distinguish between types of society in terms of these prevailing forms), so do the locations and kinds of social change. Marx focused most of his attention on Western European capitalist society in the nineteenth century and correctly identified the relationship of social class as decisive in the understanding of the dynamics of that society. But that does not mean, of course, that class is the only relationship of domination/subordination. On the contrary, various forms of oppression are based on status inequalities, defined in terms of race, ethnicity, gender, age and legal status, or a combination of these as well as class. Such status-based inequalities may or may not coincide with the class relationship and may vary in the nature of their connections with class, but it was Marx's key insight that no society has been free from the social conflicts and changes caused by relations of domination/subordination, of "oppressor and oppressed". Marx also drew attention to the interrelations between the systems of exploitation that were based upon slave labour in the Americas and wage labour in Europe:

> Liverpool waxed fat on the slave-trade. This was its method of primitive accumulation . . . Whilst the cotton industry introduced child-slavery in England, it gave in the United States a stimulus to the transformation of the earlier, more or less patriarchal slavery, into a system of commercial exploitation. In fact, the veiled slavery of the wage-workers in Europe needed, for its pedestal, slavery pure and simple in the new world.[73]

Oppressive regimes are sustained by the manipulation of consent as well as by force. Antonio Gramsci's work on cultural hegemony has shown how the persistence of a regime of exploitation often depends on the capacity of the rulers to persuade the oppressed of the justice, or at least the inevitability, of the system.

Hence, too, the importance of understanding the political nature of processes of cultural resistance. As Peter Worsley has said:

> . . . the great strength of Marxism is that, analytically, it does focus upon material *interest*, on the economic, power and status rewards enjoyed by those who control society, and the exploitation suffered by the great majority who do the producing, and upon the mechanisms which justify these basic inequalities and which cope with resistance to them.[74]

The work of Michel de Certeau on the "practice of everyday life" offers important insights into the central problem of the Creole-society thesis – namely, how the dominated people in a society can shape their own culture and make their own history. De Certeau rejects the "social atomism" that posits the individual as the elementary unit of society. His analysis of everyday practices "shows that a relation (always social) determines its terms, and not the reverse, and that each individual is a locus in which an incoherent (and often contradictory) plurality of such relational determinations interact".[75] He shows that those people whose status in society is that of "dominee" are neither passive nor docile but, on the contrary, their actions frequently subvert the goals and structures of the dominators. For example, he refers to

> . . . the ambiguity that subverted from within the Spanish colonisers' 'success' in imposing their own culture on the indigenous Indians . . . Submissive, and even consenting to their subjection, the Indians nevertheless often *made of* the rituals, representations, and laws imposed on them something quite different from what their conquerors had in mind; they subverted them not by rejecting or altering them, but by using them with respect to ends and references foreign to the system they had no choice but to accept. They were *other* within the very colonisation that outwardly assimilated them; their use of the dominant social order deflected its power, which they lacked the means to challenge; they escaped it without leaving it.[76]

De Certeau's formulation is appropriate to the study of the historical process of culture formation during the period of slavery and colonialism in the Caribbean, and is also relevant in the post-independence or neo-colonial period today.[77] Although there were many direct challenges to the dominant social order, often courageous in nature, there were also less visible "murmurings" in everyday practices. We should not look just for those "outward", external manifestations that suggest either assimilation (acculturation) or its opposite ("survivals" or "retentions"). For obvious reasons, cultural resistance in social contexts of domination is often not externally manifested and those of subordinate status often conceal their modes of action and their contributions to the formation of culture. Within relations of domination, the subtle art of bricolage enables the oppressed to avoid repercussions while making "innumerable and infinitesimal transformations of and within the dominant cultural economy in order to adapt it to their own interests and their own rules".[78] Hence, the weak must make use of the powerful by ingenious ways, seizing their opportunities on the wing, smuggling in their hidden agendas, infiltrating their own innovations – in these ways, they "lend a political dimension to everyday practices".[79] It is highly significant that Anansi, the spider trickster of West African tales, who "play fool fe catch wise", became the folk hero of slaves and their descendants throughout the Caribbean.

The Creole-society thesis needs a general theoretical framework, incorporating dialectical theory, for the analysis of social and cultural change. Roger Bastide, the French sociologist-ethnologist, articulated such a general framework within which he studied the African religions of Brazil. He stressed the connections between religious beliefs and activities and the conflicts in the wider society, in particular the relationship between religious ideologies and practices, on the one hand, and the issues and relations of domination/subordination, on the other. For Bastide, the process of cultural change is not to be understood as the clash of "cultures", but rather as the activities of individuals who are located in institutions and differentiated by power:

> There are never . . . cultures in contact but rather individuals, carriers of different cultures. However, these individuals are not independent creatures but are interrelated by complex webs of communication, of domination-subordination, or of egalitarian exchange. They are a part of institutions, which have rules for action, norms and organisation.[80]

Bastide's achievement, as Richard Price has said, "is to analyse, within a single conceptual framework, individuals, culture, and social and economic infrastructures, and to clarify the dialectical relationship between the historical transformation of these infrastructures and the religious phenomena in question".[81] The West Indian advocates of the Creole-society thesis have not articulated such a "single conceptual framework" and, as a consequence, their analysis too often fails to make specific connections between social organisation and cultural process. Three brief illustrations of this problem must suffice.

Obeah

First, with regard to the question of African cultural retentions, the practice of magic, or *obeah*, is often cited as an example of continuity. Brathwaite, for example, says, "in African and Caribbean folk practice, where religion had not been externalised and institutionalised as in Europe, the obeah-man was doctor, philosopher, and priest."[82] He contrasts obeah with European religion, but makes no distinction between varieties in the practice of obeah in Africa and the Caribbean. In this view, the individual practitioner is isolated from his social context, a context that differs in Africa and the Caribbean in crucial ways. The specific forms of social organisation to which magical practices are linked in African societies did not exist in the Caribbean slave societies. Among the Ashanti, "witchcraft (*bayi*) is believed to be effective only within the lineage",[83] while among the peoples of the Nuba Hills in the Sudan, witchcraft (*kamerge*) "is powerful only within the clan".[84] In this connection, Bastide observes:

> . . . in moving from Africa to America, magic breaks the bonds that linked it to a certain form of social organisation . . . [I]n America the effectiveness of witchcraft is not determined by affiliation with a lineage or clan or even a 'nation'; the formidable power of the witch doctor serves the struggle of one entire race against another . . .

Thus, magic was detached from its social frameworks, and the detachment was certainly facilitated by the disappearance of the lineages and clans and by the creation of a new solidarity, the solidarity based on the slaves' dependence on their White masters.[85]

In failing to indicate the links between the activities of obeah-men and specific social organisations, Brathwaite fails to note that obeah has taken on a *whole new meaning* in the societies of the Caribbean, a meaning derived from the power structures, the social oppositions, in these societies. So, when Brathwaite states that the shift in the public leadership of slaves from obeah-men to Black preachers following the influx of Baptist slaves to Jamaica after the American Revolution, is "evidence, certainly, of creolisation",[86] he obscures a crucial point – namely, that the activities of obeah-men were *already creolised* when they extended their practices in entirely new ways in Jamaica. Cultural practices such as obeah do not exist, either in Africa or the Americas, apart from the social structures in which they are conducted and to which they relate. In the Caribbean there was, from the earliest days of slavery, "a great deal of syncretistic mixing of variants of West African culture",[87] including obeah, that both reflected and promoted the iden-tity of all Africans vis-a-vis Europeans. One of the consequences of the fact that these practices took place in relation to new social structures is that they promoted new social identities, including that of "Creole", by defining one set of people over and against another. To understand the nature of the changes in these practices, therefore, we need a conceptual framework and general theory that focuses on the dialectics between religious values, beliefs and activities, on the one hand, and social structures, on the other.

Jonkonnu

It is not enough to say simply, as Brathwaite does, that creolisation is a "two-way process" that "worked both ways",[88] or to say that "it was in the intimate area of sexual relationships that the greatest damage was done to White Creole apartheid policy and where the most significant – and lasting – inter-cultural creolisation took place", resulting in the "social cement" of the Coloured population.[89] In his search for historical precedents for an integrated society, Brathwaite obscures the obvious fact that in most of these sexual relationships, "intimate" though they were, there was an overlap between relationships of domination defined in terms of gender, race and legal status – or, more bluntly, that Black women, whether slave or free, were often raped by White men. In other words, consideration of the "inter-cultural creolisation" process must take account of the often brutal realities of power. Elsewhere, Brathwaite does distinguish between two aspects of creolisation:

> . . . *acculturation*, which is the yoking (by force and example, deriving from power/prestige) of one culture to another . . . and *inter/culturation*, which is an unplanned, unstructured but osmotic relationship, proceeding from this yoke. The *creolisation* which results (and it is a process not a product), becomes the tentative cultural norm of the society.[90]

Here he acknowledges the importance of power, but the relations are conceived as being between "cultures" that are reified and disconnected from both individuals and specific social formations.

This aspect of the problem becomes clearer when we examine Brathwaite's account of street processions or festivals, which he describes as "a brilliant fusion of African and European elements",[91] and, specifically, of Jamaican John Canoe or Jonkonnu. These masked bands that danced, and still dance, in the streets during the Christmas holidays, are described in terms of a simple African-European, or "Afro-Creole"-"Euro-Creole", spectrum:

> This process of creolisation from African motif to something local but (externally) European-influenced may be studied in the development of the masked (masque) bands like John Canoe . . . [T]he brown girls . . . were the ones most noticed, representing as they did, the Euro-tendency of this part of creole society . . .

But the African influence remained, even if increasingly submerged, as an important element in the process of creolisation . . . There was developing a

European-orientated Creole form (Euro-Creole) and an African-influenced Creole form (Afro-Creole); and they existed together within, often, the same framework . . . There were also large areas of public entertainment that remained intransigently African or Afro-Creole. Those bands, for instance, who continued to dramatise or satirise aspects of the slave-society – their and their masters' condition.[92]

Brathwaite merely hints at an aspect of these masked bands that is really essential for understanding them, namely their dramatisation of the central relations of the slave society. To picture Jonkonnu only in terms of African influences and European orientations, existing together within a common framework, obscures the fact that the dancers were participants in *political* processes of cultural resistance and self-definition. There are, of course, legacies of the African heritage in Jonkonnu, including the characters with animal masks, cowhead and horsehead, as well as European influences, such as the sailor costumes and the fife and drum music. The English residents often patronised these events and, by lending money or costumes, influenced the African performers. But the evidence of satire, in songs and white face masks, shows that there was more conflict involved in the performances than is suggested when they are described simply as "syncretic forms" of African and English folk theatre.[93] When Jonkonnu is viewed as an activity within a broader political and cultural process, we can understand it as one of the many ways in which individuals drew upon elements from a wide repertoire of cultural traditions in order to express their human, social condition. Their choice of "intransigently African" elements of costume, song and dance, or of satirical expressions of master/slave relations, even in circumstances that were not of their choice, was a contribution to their own social and cultural history, a way of redefining themselves as a new collective identity vis-á-vis the Europeans.

Colonial or Creole?

The conceptual ambiguity of the term "Creole society" may be illustrated with reference to Brathwaite's chapter, "Jamaica: Colonial or Creole?" in *The Development of Creole Society in Jamaica*. He identifies "colonial" as metropolitan and reactionary, and "Creole" as local and creative, a simple dualism in which the interaction between the parts is mechanically conceived: "At every step . . . the creatively 'creole' elements of the society were being rendered ineffective by the more reactionary 'colonial'."[94] Then, in posing an empirical question, Brathwaite reveals his conceptual problematic: "Was the dichotomy already described related only to Jamaica's 'external' (colonial) relationship with the Mother Country; or was the external dichotomy a reflection of a deeper cleavage – of attitude and action – within the society itself?"[95] Brathwaite here appears unsure whether "colonialism" is "external" to Jamaican society, or whether it has somehow penetrated to the nature of the society itself. In a later paper, he continued to conceive of colonialism as an "outside influence" on the Creole society.[96] From the viewpoint of dialectical theory, however, the fact that the metropole is geographically overseas does not obscure the *social* reality that colonialism is *constitutive* of Jamaican society, not external to it. The colonial relationship between Europe and the Caribbean is, by its very nature, neither "internal" nor "external" because it refers to parts of a single social system, not to discrete units, geographically defined.

From the dialectical viewpoint, "metropole" and "colony", "coloniser" and "colonised", like "master" and "slave", are the differentiated parts of a whole, constituting a unity of opposites. They are parts of a system that have no independent existence, but are defined in their relation with each other. Brathwaite's question, "Colonial or Creole?" implies a dualism that obscures the true meaning of colonialism and, hence, of the "Creole society". Rather than thinking in terms of a dichotomy of "Colonial or Creole", we should think in terms of "Colonial *and* Creole", where the phenomena of colonial domination and of Creole responses to such domination are but two aspects of the same system. As Peter Worsley has said, "Despite the political power of the conqueror, each colony was the product of a dialectic, a synthesis, not just a simple imposition, in which the social institutions and cultural values of the conquered was one of the terms of the dialectic."[97] Dialectical theory draws attention, unequivocally, to the elements of resistance that are inherent in the domination/subordination relationship between the metropole and the colony, and shows how resistance and conflict are therefore constituent aspects of the cultures and social and economic structures of the colonial society.[98]

> Karen Judd, in a recent paper on creolisation in Belize, argues that the concept will remain imprecise as long as it is used to describe what are essentially two processes: 1) a retrospectively observed pattern of cultural change over the colonial and postcolonial periods, and 2) an active political process, occurring during periods of social or political crisis, in which individual struggles to define ethnic identity become collective.[99]

This helpful distinction draws attention to the two elements that lie within the Creole-society thesis, as we have examined it. The work of Brathwaite and others has stressed the former while I am stressing the latter. Dialectical theory, by drawing attention to the centrality of relations of domination/subordination, including class relations, provides the explicit and unambiguous theoretical foundation for the analysis of processes of social and cultural change, whereas the Creole-society thesis has generally left these political aspects implicit and ambiguous. As Judd points out, the appropriation of the term "Creole" by different groups in society, is itself affected by "the successive struggles between and among active agents rather than on their cumulative outcome at any given time".[100] Creolisation, then, is not a homogenising process, but rather a process of *contention* between people who are members of social formations and carriers of cultures, a process in which their own ethnicity is continually re-examined and redefined in terms of the relevant oppositions between different social formations at various historical moments.

Among the social formations and relations that the Creole-society thesis neglects is that of *class*. The cultural and political nationalism implied in the Creole-society thesis is based on a populist conception of cultural homogeneity that overlooks class distinctions and hostilities. This populist image of a unified nation emerging from the colonial oppression and cultural pluralism of the past has also been promoted in a number of Caribbean nationalist slogans, such as "Out of Many, One People" (Jamaica) and "All o' we is One" (Trinidad). We need to comprehend the nature of the transition from slavery to post-emancipation society in ways that the Creole-society model does not accommodate. A class analysis is required to understand the nature of the system of domination that followed the abolition of slavery.[101] The Creole-society thesis does not enable us to see how or why the system of domination in the colonies changed from status inequalities during slavery to class inequalities after legal emancipation, as a consequence of both the social dynamics within the colonies and the colonies' relations with the metropoles.

In sum, Brathwaite's vision of the Creole society is an advance on the plantation- and plural-society models in so far as it emphasises the active role of Caribbean people and the importance of African cultural traditions in the development of Caribbean cultures and societies. He asserts that, "for the Caribbean, as elsewhere, the basis of culture lies in the folk, and that by folk we mean not in-culturated, static groups, giving little; but a people who, from the centre of an oppressive system have been able to survive, adapt, recreate."[102] But this undifferentiated notion of the "folk" ignores the complex class character, and hence the continuing conflicts, within post-emancipation, and also post-independence, societies. Brathwaite himself has called for more complex, historical/sociological models to enable us to see "the plural/whole" of the Caribbean, in which cultural orientations and influences are related to "class consciousness and class interests".[103] The Creole-society thesis, however, cannot accomplish this so long as it remains a theoretically ambiguous analysis of Caribbean social history, and this underscores the need to develop an explicitly dialectical model.

CONCLUSION

One of the reasons why the Creole-society model has been so attractive in recent years is its nationalistic insistence on the validity of Creole culture and its potential role in national integration in societies that have recently become independent. What distinguishes the Caribbean intellectuals of the late twentieth and early twenty-first centuries from their African and Creole progenitors is their conscious use of the Creole-society thesis in their claim to a national birthright. The emphasis on a common rather than a plural culture involves an attachment to a "homeland" as well as a sense of social identity, thereby sharply distinguishing Caribbean people from expatriates. It was the innumerable everyday practices of these progenitors, enslaved and freedpeople, Africans and Creoles, throughout the political process of Caribbean history, that made this nationalist claim possible. Their daily struggle was, and continues to be, the central dynamic of Caribbean social history.

The Creole-society thesis has contributed to our understanding of Caribbean cultures and societies by drawing attention to the creative activities of Caribbean peoples. It has encouraged us to look for the various ways in which Africans and people of African descent manipulated the structures of domination of which they were a part and, in so doing, contributed to the development of Creole cultures and societies. However, the recognition of the inherent conflicts and contradictions of colonial societies, both during and after the period of slavery, requires a reconceptualisation of such societies in dialectical terms. Dialectical theory enables us to understand African "continuities" and Creole culture[104] as aspects of the continuing transformations of activities by, and relations between, innumerable individuals in their daily confrontations with the dominant political, economic, social and cultural forces in their societies.

NOTES

*The first version of this essay was written for and presented at a symposium on Intellectuals in the Twentieth-Century Caribbean held at the Centre for Caribbean Studies of the University of Warwick in 1987. I wish to thank Professor Alistair Hennessy, then director of the Centre, for inviting me. The article was first published in *Intellectuals in the Twentieth-Century Caribbean, vol. 1: Spectre of the New Class: the Commonwealth Caribbean* edited by Alistair Hennessy (London and Basingstoke: 1992, pp. 50–79).

I am grateful to several friends and colleagues who have made helpful comments on earlier drafts of this essay, including Salvatore Cucchiari, David Hess, Karen Judd, Michael Peletz, Mary Turner and, especially, Arnold Sio and Gary Urton, whose criticisms have helped me to formulate and clarify my ideas. I also wish to thank Ellen Bolland for helping me to clarify my prose. However, they are all absolved from responsibility for any remaining shortcomings in the essay.

1. Virginia R. Dominguez, *White by Definition: Social Classification in Creole Louisiana* (New Brunswick: Rutgers University Press, 1986), p. 13.
2. M.G. Smith, *The Plural Society in the British West Indies* (Berkeley: University of California Press, 1965), pp. 5–6.
3. Ibid., p. 9.
4. John W. Nunley and Judith Bettelheim, *Caribbean Festival Arts* (Seattle: University of Washington Press, 1988), p. 37.
5. Ibid., p. 31.
6. David Skinner and Barbara E. Harrell-Bond, "Misunderstandings Arising from the Use of the term 'Creole', in the Literature on Sierra Leone", *Africa* 47:3 (1977), p. 305.
7. Ibid.
8. Ibid., p. 314.
9. Eric Hobsbawm, "Introduction: Inventing Traditions", in Eric Hobsbawm and Terence Ranger, eds., *The Invention of Tradition* (Cambridge: Cambridge University Press, 1983), p. 9.
10. Ibid., p. 13.
11. An excellent discussion of this cultural process and the social context in which it occurred is in Sidney W. Mintz and Richard Price, *An Anthropological Approach to the Afro-American Past: A Caribbean Perspective* (Philadelphia: Institute for the Study of Human Issues, 1976). This paper was originally presented at a symposium on "Creole Societies in the Americas and Africa" at the Johns Hopkins University in 1973.
12. On the importance of the concept of culture in world history, see Eric R. Wolf, *Europe and the People Without History* (Berkeley, Los Angeles and London: University of California Press, 1983) and Peter Worsley, *The Three Worlds: Culture*

and World Development (London: Weidenfeld and Nicolson, 1984); and on the world-system approach, see Immanuel Wallerstein, *The Modern World-System: Capitalist Agriculture and the Origins of the World-Economy in the Sixteenth Century* (New York: Academic Press, 1974).

13.   Raymond T. Smith has pointed out that Kamau Brathwaite, a leading exponent of the Creole-society thesis, comes from Barbados, the only ex-British colony that was never subjected to Crown Colony rule, that "retained a resident White upper class, and . . . is the one country that developed a deep sense of national unity and a common 'culture' – even if it appeared abjectly pro-British at times"; "Race and Class in the Post-Emancipation Caribbean", in *Racism and Colonialism*, ed., R. Ross (The Hague, Boston, and London: Martinus Nijhoff, 1982), p. 118. Gordon K. Lewis has drawn attention to the sense of a "colonial aristocracy" that developed among the Barbadian planters in the latter half of the seventeenth century. But this early "Creole" viewpoint was not much more than an "emergent sense of collective planter identity", rooted in their divergence of interest from the British mercantilists, and, as such, is quite distinct from the popular nationalism in the twentieth-century West Indies; see Lewis, *Main Currents in Caribbean Thought: The Historical Evolution of Caribbean Society in its Ideological Aspects, 1492–1900* (Baltimore and London: Johns Hopkins University Press, 1983), pp. 72–5.

14.   The first British Caribbean colonies to become independent were Jamaica, and Trinidad and Tobago, in 1962, followed by Barbados and Guyana in 1966.

15.   William A. Green, "The Creolization of Caribbean History: The Emancipation Era and a Critique of Dialectical Analysis", in *Journal of Imperial and Commonwealth History* 14:3 (1986), p. 164.

16.   Raymond T. Smith described Guyanese history as a sequence of stages, each with a distinct "socio-cultural model": plantation society, Creole society and "open democratic" or modern society. He called M.G. Smith's plural society thesis a "most successful failure". See "Social Stratification, Cultural Pluralism and Integration in West Indian Societies", in S. Lewis and T. Mathews, eds., *Caribbean Integration: Papers on Social, Political and Economic Integration* (Rio Piedras: Institute of Caribbean Studies, 1967), p. 227.

17.   Ibid., pp. 229–32.

18.   Orlando Patterson, *The Sociology of Slavery: An Analysis of the Origins, Development and Structure of Negro Slave Society in Jamaica* (London: MacGibbon and Kee, 1967), p. 70.

19.   George Beckford, *Persistent Poverty: Underdevelopment in Plantation Economies of the Third World* (New York: Oxford University Press, 1972), p. 10.

20.   Susan Craig, "Sociological Theorising in the English-Speaking Caribbean: A Review", in Susan Craig, ed., *Contemporary Caribbean; A Sociological Reader* (Port of Spain: the author, 1982), p. 150.

21. Clive Y. Thomas, *Plantations, Peasants, and State: A Study of the Mode of Sugar Production in Guyana* (Los Angeles and Kingston: Center for Afro-American Studies and the Institute of Social and Economic Research, 1984), p. 9.

22. Marc Bloch made a comparable point when he deemed it important to maintain a distinction between the manor, as an institution, and feudalism, by not equating the manorial system with feudal society; see *Feudal Society* (Chicago: University of Chicago Press, 1961), p. 279.

23. Smith, *The Plural Society*, p. 112.

24. M.G. Smith, *Culture, Race and Class in the Commonwealth Caribbean* (Mona: University of the West Indies, 1984), p. 7; he refers to *A Framework of Caribbean Studies* as published in 1956, but it was actually published in 1955 (Kingston: University College of the West Indies, Caribbean Affairs Series, 1955), and reprinted in *The Plural Society*, pp. 18–74.

25. Smith, *Culture, Race and Class*, p. 29.

26. Ibid., p. 32.

27. Ibid., p. 34.

28. Ibid., p. 141.

29. Ibid., p. 140; emphasis added.

30. "Given the fundamental differences of belief, value, and organisation that connote pluralism, the monopoly of power by one cultural section is the essential precondition for the maintenance of the total society in its current form"; *The Plural Society*, p. 86.

31. Malcolm Cross, "On Conflict, Race Relations, and the Theory of the Plural Society", *Race* 12:4 (1971), p. 484.

32. O. Nigel Bolland, *Colonialism and Resistance in Belize: Essays in Historical Sociology* (Benque Viejo del Carmen, Mona and Belize City: Cubola Productions, Institute of Social and Economic Research and Society for the Promotion of Education and Research, 1988), "Introduction".

33. Kamau Brathwaite, *The Development of Creole Society in Jamaica, 1770–1820* (Oxford: Clarendon Press, 1971), p. 311.

34. Kamau Brathwaite, "Jamaican Slave Society: A Review", *Race* 9 (1968), p. 336.

35. Ibid., p. 333.

36. Elsa V. Goveia, *Slave Society in the British Leeward Islands at the end of the Eighteenth Century* (New Haven and London: Yale University Press, 1965), pp. 249–50.

37. Brathwaite, "Jamaican Slave Society", p. 337.

38. Ibid., p. 341.

39. Brathwaite, *The Development of Creole Society*, p. 296.

40. Ibid., p. 300. This contrasts sharply with the view of Africans, stripped of their cultures, becoming Europeanised: "If Europe dominates West Indian political and economic life, in terms of culture the West Indies are also Old World appendages.

No other ex-colonies are so convinced they are British or French or cling more keenly to their European heritage . . . Englishness, Frenchness, and even Dutchness and Americanness permeate all aspects of West Indian life . . . [I]n the Caribbean, European culture and institutions, artifacts and ideas, are the only generally recognised heritage"; David Lowenthal, *West Indian Societies* (New York, London, and Toronto: Oxford University Press, 1972), p. 5.

41. Ibid., p. 305. (See also Arnold A. Sio, "Marginality and Free Coloured Identity in Caribbean Slave Society", *Slavery and Abolition*, 8 (1987), pp. 166–82.

42. Ibid., p. 212.

43. Brathwaite's tendency to refer to "African culture" in the singular has been justly criticised. Richard Price, for example, has commented that the simple model of cultural interaction between Africans and Europeans pays too little attention to the cultural heterogeneity of the Africans and envisions "culture" as "some kind of undivided whole"; Richard Price, "Commentary" in Vera Rubin and Arthur Tuden eds., *Comparative Perspectives on Slavery in New World Plantation Societies* (New York: New York Academy of Sciences, 1977), p. 497.

44. Brathwaite, *The Development of Creole Society*, pp. 231–32.

45. Ibid., p. 307.

46. Ibid., p. 311.

47. Ibid., p. 212.

48. Ibid., p. 311.

49. Rex M. Nettleford, "The Melody of Europe, the Rhythm of Africa", in *Mirror, Mirror: Identity, Race and Protest in Jamaica* (Kingston: Collins and Sangster, 1970), p. 173.

50. Ibid., p. 211.

51. Ibid., p. 210.

52. Ibid., p. 211.

53. Rex Nettleford, "Implications for Caribbean Development", in Nunley and Bettelheim, eds., *Caribbean Festival Arts*, p. 194.

54. Mervyn C. Alleyne, "A Linguistic Perspective on the Caribbean", in Sidney W. Mintz and Sally Price eds., *Caribbean Contours* (Baltimore and London: Johns Hopkins University Press, 1985), p. 160.

55. Ibid., p. 160.

56. Ibid., p. 175.

57. Mervyn C. Alleyne, *Roots of Jamaican Culture* (London: Pluto Press, 1988), p. 152.

58. Ibid., p. 161.

59. Orlando Patterson, "Context and Choice in Ethnic Allegiance: A Theoretical Framework and Caribbean Case Study", in Nathan Glazer and Daniel P. Moynihan, eds., *Ethnicity: Theory and Experience* (Cambridge, Mass.: Harvard

University Press, 1975), p. 319. For a compatible analysis of the development of two segmentary Creole cultures in nineteenth-century Jamaica, see Philip D. Curtin, *Two Jamaicas: The Role of Ideas in a Tropical Colony, 1830–1865* (Cambridge, Mass.: Harvard University Press, 1955).

60. Patterson, "Context and Choice", p. 334.

61. Ibid., p. 319.

62. See Worsley, *The Three Worlds*, p. 252, and Bolland, *Colonialism and Resistance*, pp. 204–5.

63. Melville J. Herskovits' work on "the amalgamation of cultures" and the concept of "syncretism" was pioneering in Caribbean anthropology; see, for example, *Life in a Haitian Valley* (New York: Alfred A. Knopf, 1937).

64. Brathwaite, *The Development of Creole Society*, p. xiv.

65. Ibid., p. 296.

66. Ibid., p. 305.

67. Ibid., p. xvi.

68. Kenneth M. Bilby, "The Caribbean as a Musical Region", in Mintz and Price, eds., *Caribbean Contours*, p. 185.

69. Brathwaite, *The Development of Creole Society*, p. 307.

70. Alleyne, "A Linguistic Perspective", p. 158.

71. Karl Marx, "The Eighteenth Brumaire of Louis Bonaparte", in Robert C. Tucker, ed., *The Marx-Engels Reader* (New York: W.W. Norton, 1972), p. 437.

72. Philip Abrams, "History, Sociology, Historical Sociology", *Past and Present*, p. 87 (1980), p. 13. This is similar to the theory of "structuration", in Anthony Giddens, *Central Problems in Social Theory: Action, Structure and Contradiction in Social Analysis* (Berkeley and Los Angeles: University of California Press, 1979).

73. Karl Marx, "Capital", in *The Marx-Engels Reader*, pp. 314–15.

74. Peter Worsley, *Marx and Marxism* (Chichester: Ellis Horwood, 1982), p. 67.

75. Michel de Certeau, *The Practice of Everyday Life*, trans. by Steven F. Rendall (Berkeley, Los Angeles and London: University of California Press, 1984), p. xi.

76. Ibid., p. xiii.

77. O. Nigel Bolland, "United States Cultural Influences on Belize: Television and Education as 'Vehicles of Import'", *Caribbean Quarterly* 33 (1987), pp. 60–74.

78. De Certeau, *The Practice of Everyday Life*, p. xiv.

79. Ibid., p. xvii.

80. Quoted in Richard Price, "Foreword" to Roger Bastide, *The African Religions of Brazil*, trans. by Helen Sebba (Baltimore and London: The Johns Hopkins University Press, 1978), p. x.

81. Richard Price, "Foreword", p. x.

82. Brathwaite, *The Development of Creole Society*, p. 219.

83. Meyer Fortes, "Kinship and Marriage Among the Ashanti", in A. R. Radcliffe-Brown and Daryll Forde , eds., *African Systems of Kinship and Marriage* (London: Oxford University Press, 1950), p. 258.

84. S.F. Nadel, "Dual Descent in the Nuba Hills", in *African Systems*, p. 345.

85. Bastide, *African Religions*, p. 400.

86. Brathwaite, *The Development of Creole Society*, p. 162.

87. Alleyne, *Roots*, p. 79.

88. Brathwaite, *The Development of Creole Society*, p. 300.

89. Ibid., pp. 303, 305.

90. Kamau Brathwaite, *Contradictory Omens: Cultural Diversity and Integration in the Caribbean* (Mona: Savacou Publications, 1974), p. 6.

91. Brathwaite, *The Development of Creole Society*, p. 228.

92. Ibid., pp. 229–32.

93. Judith Bettelheim, "Jamaican Jonkonnu and Related Caribbean Festivals", in Margaret E. Crahan and Franklin W. Knight, eds., *Africa and the Caribbean: The Legacies of a Link* (Baltimore and London: Johns Hopkins University Press, 1979), p. 87.

94. Brathwaite, *The Development of Creole Society*, p. 100.

95. Ibid., p. 101.

96. Kamau Brathwaite, "Caliban, Ariel, and Unprospero in the Conflict of Creolisation: A Study of the Slave Revolt in Jamaica in 1831–1832", in Verene A. Shepherd and Hilary McD. Beckles, eds., *Comparative Perspectives on Slavery*, pp. 42–3. Reprinted in *Caribbean Slavery in the Atlantic World* (Kingston: Ian Randle Publishers, 2000), pp. 879–95.

97. Worsley, *The Three Worlds*, p. 4.

98. Bolland, *Colonialism and Resistance*, p. 7.

99. Karen Judd, "Cultural Synthesis or Ethnic Struggle?: Creolisation in Belize", in *Cimarron*, 2 (1989), p. 105.

100. Ibid., p. 105.

101. O. Nigel Bolland, "Systems of Domination After Slavery: The Control of Land and Labor in the British West Indies After 1838", *Comparative Studies in Society and History*, 23 (1981), pp. 591–619. Walter Rodney argued that the indentured Indians in late nineteenth century colonial Guyana were becoming creolised, but that the "existing aspects of cultural convergence were insufficiently developed to contribute decisively to solidarity among the working people of the two major race groups. The obverse of this race-class conjuncture is that the development of class forces and class consciousness was inadequate to sustain unity of the working people across the barriers created by legal distinctions, racial exclusiveness, and the separate trajectories of important aspects of culture. There were, in effect, two semi-autonomous sets of working-class struggles against the

domination of capital – the one conducted by the descendants of ex-slaves and the other by indentured labourers and their fellow Indians. Pursuing their legitimate aspirations, these two ethnically defined sectors of the labouring people could and did come into conflict with each other". *A History of the Guyanese Working People, 1881–1905* (Baltimore and London: Johns Hopkins University Press, 1981) p. 179.

102. Brathwaite, *Contradictory Omens*, p. 64.
103. Ibid., p. 64.
104. See O. Nigel Bolland, "African Continuities and Creole Culture in Belize Town in the Nineteenth Century", in Charles V. Carnegie, ed., *Afro-Caribbean Villages in Historical Perspective* (Kingston: African-Caribbean Institute of Jamaica, 1987), pp. 63–82.

Carolyn Allen

Chapter 3

CREOLE

THE PROBLEM OF DEFINITION

Chief among the ideas that Kamau Brathwaite has elaborated for our benefit is an understanding of the cultural dimensions of Caribbean history as a process in which the arrivants and their progenitors forge a complex dynamic of group identity and interrelations. Choosing "Creole" as the root term, he labelled the process "creolisation", a concept which is receiving increasing recognition in an age highly attuned to indeterminacy and cross-cultural hybridity. Non-Caribbean scholars are turning to the region for tools to decipher global culture – "It is . . . the Caribbean which has been the crucible of the most extensive and challenging post-colonial theory"[1] – as regional scholars like Edouard Glissant look outward to the world.[2]

General interest notwithstanding, "Creole" and "creolisation" hold particular significance for the region. For Sidney Mintz and Sally Price in *Caribbean Contours*,[3] they are first among the aspects of development which suggest the legitimacy of discussing the Caribbean as a unit, despite internal diversity. Some 15 years after defining the concept of creolisation in *Caribbean Cultural Identity*,[4] Rex Nettleford notes its continued importance in *Inward Stretch, Outward Reach*: "Addressing creolisation brings the student of Caribbean affairs closer to the deep social forces as well as the complex, contradictory and dialectical reality of Caribbean life."[5] This interest on the part of social scientists is not accidental, says Jean Casimir in *La Caraïbe Une et Divisible* [*The Caribbean: One and Divisible*].

To paraphrase in English, Creoles and the creolised are fundamental to the network of lasting relationships on which these colonial societies are built.[6] In the 1988 publication *Pidgins and Creole Languages*, Suzanne Romaine observed that Creole studies constituted the fastest growing field in linguistics.[7] Something of the interest of literary theorists – especially in the growth field of postcolonial studies – is indicated in the first quotation above from Bill Ashcroft, Gareth Griffiths and Helen Tiffin. Given the continued attention of historians, "Creole" might logically be considered a useful area of interdisciplinary study of the region as a whole.

Yet one important question immediately comes to mind. Do we all mean the same thing when we say "Creole" and "creolisation"? The "difficulty of defining this word with precision",[8] obliges writers to state the meaning they intend. O. Nigel Bolland (this volume), Mintz/Price and Brathwaite all give brief accounts of its varied applications. In Brathwaite's *Contradictory Omens*, the survey goes from Peru to Sierra Leone via Louisiana, clearly indicating how meaning differs according to location, as it does with historical period[9] and from one discipline to another. "Creole" is, among other things, language type, person, style and culture. Given the range of meanings, it is not surprising to find contradictory claims. According to the late Samuel Selvon, who saw himself as "completely creolized", it is a term used in Trinidad and Tobago "meaning you live among the people, whatever races they are, and you are a real born Trinidadian . . .".[10] With an emphasis on a cultural nationality, racial indeterminacy and implicit social class, this differs from the mutually opposed definitions of Brathwaite and Mintz and Price.[11] How feasible is dialogue in the abstract when the concrete term itself is so unstable?

If the value of the concept is not to be compromised by this variety and contradiction, we must approach an understanding of why this single designation is appropriate in each case. What is the basis of the fundamental commonality among these phenomena? If it is feasible to consider "Creole" a genus (a group having common structural characteristics distinct from those of all other groups and containing several species), then the challenge is to identify its characteristic elements.

This is the aim here, based on an hypothesis born of curiosity. Given the close association between the emergence of the term and the phenomena it names, perhaps we can derive functional principles from an investigation into the very "history" of its use. The undertaking is modest and exploratory, working from a survey of dictionary definitions in three languages (English, Spanish and French) and selected scholarly pieces, primarily on the Caribbean, in a range of disciplines. The concepts extracted as the principles of co-identification in the variety of

Creole-designated phenomena may facilitate dialogue which currently seems hazardous.

> Creole [native to the locality, 'country'; believed to be a colonial corruption of *criadillo*, 'bred, brought up, reared, domestic' . . . According to some 18th C. writers originally applied by S. American Negroes to their own children born in America as distinguished from Negroes freshly imported from Africa; but D'Acosta, 1590, applies it to Spaniards born in the W. Indies] [12]

The origins of the term Creole are obscure. Acknowledging this fact, the *Dictionnaire de la langue française* gives three possibilities: Caribbean origin; an invention of the Spanish conquistadors; a derivation from Spanish *criar*. By most other accounts however, it derives from Portuguese (Brazil), with the Latin root "to create", referring in this context to servants born and brought up in the master's house. Yet, this received opinion does not fully account for what some etymologists have acknowledged as an uncharacteristic suffix.[13] Among available sources, the *Diccionario Crítico Etimológico de la Lengua Castellana* gives the most extensive examination of possible transformations, but is unable to come to any definite conclusion in the absence of systematic study of suffixes in sixteenth-century Portuguese and Brazilian speech. What it is quite decisive about is its earliest use by Blacks in Brazil, a notion also acknowledged by a few other sources. Recent research by Maureen Warner-Lewis reinforces the notion of possible African origin.[14] Among other terms thought to be of Portuguese or Spanish origin, she posits a Kikoongo root for "Creole", meaning "outsider", which coincides with the attitude perceived among Africans towards their locally born offspring, by at least one often quoted source:

> Garcilaso el Inca (Peru 1602): Es nombre que inventaron los negros y así lo muestra la obra. Quiere decir entre los negros, *nascido en Indias*; inventáronlo para diferenciar los que van de acá [es decir, del Viejo Mundo, que incluye Africa], nascidos en Guinea, de los que nascen allá [América], porque se tienen por mas honrados y de mas calidad por haber nascido en su patria, que no sus hijos, porque nascieron en la ajena, y los padres se ofenden si les llaman *criollos*. Los espanoles, por la semejanza, han introducido este nombre en su lenguaje, para nombrar los nascidos allá.[15]
>
> [It is a name invented by the negroes . . . Among the negroes it means born in the Indies; they invented it to distinguish between those born here [that is, in the Old World, which includes Africa], born in Guinea, and those born over there [America], because they consider themselves more honourable and of higher status for being born in their homeland, and not their children who were born

abroad, and the parents are very offended if they are called Creoles. The Spanish, likewise, introduced this name into their language, to identify those born over there.] (My translation.)

The Africans born in the mother country saw themselves as more honourable and of higher quality by virtue of their place of birth.

In both accounts "Creole" is and expresses the result of the Atlantic crossing and colonisation. Evident in the etymology are fragmentation, obscurity, possible invention or corruption, and adaptation. If we take the Warner-Lewis account, the term will have passed from the African to the European – serving the same purpose, if not with the same connotation – a phenomenon which accentuates the dimension of cultural contact and transfer associated with the term. There is also clear evidence of another dimension of cultural contact and transfer across the region, from one colonial enclave to another. The etymological notes suggest a sequence which goes from Portuguese to Spanish to French to English. With closer attention to dates and sources this would no doubt provide an outline to the progressive colonisation of the region. Creolisation is a common pattern.

We also have an indication of its multiplicity. A Creole might be White or Black with no intent or likelihood of co-identification between the two:

> In the West Indies and other parts of America, Mauritius, etc. *orig.* A person born and naturalised in the country, but of European (usually Spanish or French) or of African Negro race: the name having no connotation of colour, and in its reference to origin being distinguished on the one hand from born in Europe (or Africa), and on the other hand from aboriginal.[16]

Here we find a principle of duality consequent upon cross-cultural encounter. The "but" indicates the value of "Creole" as a marker of difference. The New World-born offspring of Old World parents had one identity by blood and another by place of birth, being simultaneously the same and different, colonial "Other". It is worth noting – though the majority of sources do not – that this difference also had a dual quality, distinguishing the Creole from his/her parent on the one hand and from the aboriginal or indigenous population, also locally born, on the other. Originally then, "Creole" was an intermediary category, defined primarily by its relationship to others, rather than by an essence. Retaining this quality, shifts in application occur consequent upon changes in context. The question of race provides a useful illustration.

There is no consensus on whether "Creole" was first applied to Blacks or Whites. While some sources question its legitimacy with reference to Blacks, others (like the *Oxford English Dictionary* [*OED*]) claim it has no racial implication at all. The major debate, however, concerns its application to persons of so-called "mixed blood", European and African in particular. In French, dictionaries of proper usage and special difficulties highlight the (erroneous) practice of not distinguishing between a Creole, of pure White blood, and a "Métis", the accurate term for a person of mixed blood: "Un créole n'est pas un métis, il est né aux Antilles, mais d'origine blanche."[17] (A Creole is not a "métis", he is born in the Indies, but of White origin.) H.W. Fowler's *Dictionary of Modern English Usage* agrees, giving "mulatto" as the appropriate term in English for a person of mixed blood.[18] These efforts, especially noticeable in the nineteenth century, are significantly outweighed by the many sources, which list the mixed-blood definition among Creole's legitimate applications. In *Jamaica Talk*, Frederic Cassidy illustrates how this shift occurred, noting similarly futile attempts at "correction": "The term 'Creole' has no reference to colour, as is commonly supposed by Europeans, but merely means 'native'. We speak of a Creole horse, or of any vegetable or esculent not common to the country."[19] Ironically, Carol Barash claims the opposite: "In England, 'Creole' means Jamaican, outsider; in Jamaica, 'Creole' means a person of mixed race . . ."[20] Here it is the English who perceive "Creole" as implying belonging to the location rather than as a racial term. What both writers maintain however, is a difference between local and foreign usage. The insider/outsider opposition appears once again. It is perhaps inevitable that a term which marks difference should vary with the perspective and context of the user.

"Creole. A term applied with varying connotation to a person of European stock or of mixed blood . . ."[21] These "varying connotations" no doubt include those of visiting Europeans who wrote about the local White population, as well as attitudes perceived among the Blacks. In the case of Jamaica, for example, Edward Long and Lady Nugent suggest that Creole Whites were culturally inferior to their British-born counterparts. (This perhaps corresponds to the Old World superiority noted among the early Africans.[22]) According to at least one writer, Blacks shared this perception of the Creole Whites.[23] Pejorative connotations are also noted in French and Spanish American usage: in the outdated reflexive verb "se créoliser" meaning to take on certain characteristics of a Creole, and in the definition "Nacional, vernáculo, indígena o propio de los países hispanoamericanos y por lo mismo de calidad inferior a lo extranjero, principalmente europeo", meaning indigenous and therefore of inferior quality with reference to that which is foreign, especially European.[24]

Also important historically, is the antipathy between locally born Blacks and new African arrivants. From the vantage point of the coloniser, it was the Creole Black who, quite rightly, thought himself/herself superior:

The Creole Blacks differ much from the Africans, not only in manners, but in beauty of shape, features and complexion. They hold the Africans in the utmost contempt, styling them 'salt-water Negroes', and 'Guinea birds'; but value themselves on their own pedigree.

Les noirs créoles [de Saint-Domingue] professaient [...] le plus profond mépris pour les noirs congos. [The Creole blacks [of Saint-Domingue] expressed the greatest contempt for the Congo blacks.]

The farther back the Negro could trace his Creolism, the more he valued himself.[25]

These attitudes had political implications for movements of resistance against slavery,[26] reminding us forcefully of one effect of the Creole's difference and intermediacy – social tensions, a manifestation of the hierarchical structure of colonial society, the racial and social divisions which made the forging of national identities truly challenging across the region.

Yet, even as it carried the burden of social tensions, "Creole" would become the watchword of nationalistic movements. One reason for this is the importance of nativity within the concept, a role closely associated with the adaptation which made of the Creole a distinctive type. Not unlike the plants and animals which grew differently in the tropical zones, humans were perceptibly modified by climate and surroundings. Habits of behaviour, attitude, speech, cuisine and more, came to be identified with Creole populations:

It is extraordinary to witness the immediate effect that the climate and habit of living in this country have upon the minds and manners of Europeans . . . they have become indolent and inactive, regardless of every thing but eating, drinking and indulging themselves . . . [27]

So closely was this lifestyle associated with Creoles, that a verb form was coined to name their characteristic way of lounging. In both French and English we read of "creolizing":

Radiguet 1923. La marquise y gagna une prostration maladive, qui fit d'elle une créole des images, passant sa vie sur une chaise-longue. [The marquise took on a bad habit of prostrating herself, which made of her the image of the Creole, passing her life away on a lounge chair.]

1818 J. McLeod. The ladies . . . generally creolized the whole day in a delectable state of apathy . . . Creolizing is an easy and elegant mode of lounging in a warm climate.

A word now out of use, but which we have found earliest in Jamaica, is to *creolize* – that is to lounge easily and elegantly, as Lady Nugent learned to do after she had been in the island for a time: After breakfast, the usual routine; writing, reading, and creolizing. This word, obviously, would be used by outsiders, not by creoles, in explanation of the informal dress and relaxed habit, that they adopted because of the climate.[28]

This no doubt contributed to the association of both indolence and grace with Creoleness. In territories across the region, Creole attributes also include nonchalance, cowardice, simplicity, lack of etiquette. Although it is not clear whether these perceptions are consistently those of outsiders, it is fairly certain that they were considered the "trademarks" of a quintessential local type, perhaps as much influenced by climate as by association with the "Other". Franklin Knight's commentary on Creole slaves and their advantages over the Africans, points to a corresponding adaptation: "They were physically acclimatized as well as mentally socialized to the conduct and routine of the plantation and local culture, and in some cases they spoke and understood the local languages."[29] Perhaps more important than race, then, is the Creole's affinity to place, having intimate knowledge of it and being committed to it by experience and/or attachment.[30]

This identification between inhabitant and land, especially in the colonial situation, is an important moment, signalling a turn away from the "mother country" and an embryonic national consciousness which would develop into the anti-colonial movement towards self-possession and definition. Here the duality and intermediacy of the Creole become argument for claiming power. Who better to represent the new, multifaced society? Who was more settled and committed to the future of the country?

> . . . the initial emergence of a national culture and ideology in Caribbean societies, seems to have depended to a great extent on the possibilities for growth of a "creole" group (i.e. of Old World origin, but born in the New World) whose primary identities were with the new society, rather than with their ancestral cultures of origin. Such Creole stabilisation occurred most clearly in the Hispanic Caribbean, where colonists came to stay and, early on . . . began to create genuine insular cultures.[31]

This movement had its parallel on the continent, the locally born population claiming the legitimate right to rule,[32] so that among Creole Whites of Spanish America, *criollismo* became synonymous with nationalism, and the term took on the definition "tendencia a exaltear lo criollo" (a tendency to exalt the Creole). The ultimate success of these movements may be seen in the evolution of Creole into a synonym of "native", especially throughout Latin America, though not exclusively, as we observed earlier in the discussion of race. One Cassidy/LePage source states "A creole is a Jamaican . . .".[33] *The Dictionary of American English* records, "Creole is a word signifying 'native', and applies to all kinds of men and things indigenous to New Orleans."[34] Haitians and Martinicans alike use it to refer to local culture. Since, as the *OED* observes, "local use varies", the specific manifestation of Creoleness will vary from place to place. As a result, though "Creole" may be shared by all the territories of the region, it must be recognised as belonging to each in its own way.

In one respect at least, the nature of this difference has been a source of debate. For the Creole culture of Haiti and Martinique is not that of the descendants of European settlers, as in the Spanish American territories, but rather the culture of the Creole-speaking majority, largely of African descent. The seed of this distinction may be seen in the early dual application of "Creole" to both Blacks and Whites, native-born. It owes something also to the extension of the meaning of the term to apply to languages which emerged typically out of colonial encounters, thus creating an apparent anomaly in its uses.

> L'étymologie indiquée par Littré montre bien que l'emploi de créole pour désigner les Noirs des Antilles n'est pas une faute grossière. Cependant le 'bon usage' a imposé de n'employer créole que pour les Blancs. Il reste que le dialecte antillais, dit, 'créole', est plutôt parlé par les Noirs.[35] [The etymology indicated by Littré clearly shows that the use of creole to refer to Blacks in the West Indies is not a gross error. However, proper usage insists on reserving the term for Whites. Notwithstanding, the West Indian dialect called 'creole' is largely spoken by Blacks.]

This duality becomes controversy when we move from person and language to the abstract, the understanding of the creolisation process out of which our cultures have emerged.

> . . . on the mainland there sprang up a Creole culture in which the American-born Spaniard, the *Criollo*, felt himself different from the Spaniard born in Spain, the Gachupine. In the islands it was the African who gave a distinctive character to the new communities that were to come into existence.[36]

Is it legitimate to consider, to name the latter also, "Creole" cultures? This is where the theorists are divided.

Endorsing Philip Sherlock's distinction between mainland and island culture, Jean Casimir points out the risk of referring to these African-based cultures as "Creole", the risk of confusing the creations of the dominated with the adaptations of European institutions by the dominant.[37] In 1972, Sylvia Wynter held a similar position. For her, creolisation represents a "false assimilation" in which the dominated adopt elements from the dominant culture in order to obtain prestige or gain status. This is in keeping with the perception of the Creole Black of the colonial period, acculturated to European ways and perpetuating prejudices against Africa, denying (and hindering) its energising role in Caribbean culture: "It is the African heritage which has been the crucible of the cultural deposits of the immigrant peoples, transforming borrowed elements of culture into something indigenously Caribbean."[38] Consequently, avoiding the risk of confusion, Wynter calls this process indigenisation. She depicts it as secretive, a kind of maroon activity, by which the dominated culture resists and survives.

It is precisely this activity which other writers call "Creole". David Nicholls, for example, points specifically to Voodoo, in his discussion of stubborn, particularly countryside, resistance to cultural imperialism in Haiti.[39] The Voodoo religion, he says, "is a genuinely *créole* phenomenon", because along with other recognisable Caribbean practices and institutions, it incorporates elements of Christianity within its development of African religions. Nicholls identifies Rastafarianism in Jamaica, with its revulsion against Western civilisation, as another genuinely "créole" phenomenon. For his part, Rex Nettleford uses "creolisation" and "indigenisation" almost interchangeably, giving direct challenge to the Wynter reading:

> The term 'creolisation' is sometimes used in a pejorative sense to denote the tenacious hold that the conceivably superordinate metropolitan forces of Europe maintain over the cultural apparatus of the Caribbean. But more properly it refers to the agonising process of renewal and growth that marks the new order of men and women who came originally from different Old World cultures . . . and met in conflict or otherwise on foreign soil.[40]

It is simple enough to argue that this is merely a disagreement about semantics. Nicholls' use of the French makes it clear that, unlike Wynter, he associates the term with the emergent, local culture of the Creole-speaking, predominantly Afro-Caribbean, community. This endorses its validity as Glissant's choice for the culture of Neo-America, the region in which Africa is predominant in the populations.[41] But Nicholls' italics also suggest that "créole" in English would not be satisfactory since it does not carry similar associations. In territories like Jamaica, it lacks the currency of everyday use. Although its principles of cross-cultural interaction may be expounded on platforms, usually through metaphors like melting-pot and callaloo, it has not become a catchword. Nevertheless, Michael Dash suggests that (some of) the blame for muddling its meaning must be borne by governments, whose "ideological appropriations" of the concept have so emphasised harmony and unity, at the expense of tension and conflict, that "the notion of creolization still remains ill-defined and fraught with ambiguities."[42] Bolland directly addresses this nationalistic exploitation of the Creole-society model, acknowledging its reluctance to deal with sources of conflict and social tension.[43]

Robert Young's reading of Brathwaite might suggest aligning him with the politicians, since fusion is seen as the end result of an organic hybridity set against a conscious, oppositional, open-ended notion of Bakhtin.[44] Yet, even a cursory reading of *Contradictory Omens* would make this difficult to accept, given the doubt it casts on the possibility of synthesis. There is a clear distinction between the syncretic model and the Creole society:

> Based on the concept of interculturation, where the various segments are seen to share certain institutions and tools, though these may/will be used/interpreted differently while the several segments vie for cultural hegemony, and in which external and/or political interference with the process could be disruptive.[45]

We hear echoes in Bolland's definition, which takes us further:

> Creolization, then, is not a homogenising process, but rather a process of contention between people who are members of social formations and carriers of cultures, a process in which their own ethnicity is continually re-examined and redefined in terms of the relevant oppositions between different social formations at various historical moments.[46]

Clearly, academic discourse on the concept of creolisation has moved its definition far beyond Wynter's application. In fact, the recognition which she claims for the active role of Africans, is precisely what the Creole-society model has emphasised, insisting on the active agency of the common people, and offering an "antithesis [to] the old imperialist viewpoint that denies the 'natives' a history of their own . . .".[47]

When we consider the continually extended definitions and applications of the term "Creole" itself, the inconsistencies in the understanding of the concept and the related cultural process are much less surprising. Paradox is almost inevitable. Since attempts to iron out these ambiguities must ultimately meet with frustration, we look instead for underlying genetic characteristics, in the hope of facilitating dialogue among these definitions:

1. A movement away from origin and the difficulty of reconstructing a path back to the source(s) suggested in the etymology of the term.

2. The inescapability of difference, recalling that Creole was introduced to mark the appearance of a simultaneously similar/dissimilar type.

3. With the historical experience of colonialism which gave rise to its use, the primacy of cross-cultural encounter and the location of Creoleness at an intersection, negotiating between identities and forces, and defined by its relations.

4. The consequence, however strongly resisted, of a modification of type involving rejection, adaptation, accommodation, imitation, invention.

5. The value of nativisation or indigenisation, marking the point of recognition of that new type as belonging to the locale.

6. Yet, the difficulty of fully accounting for this type which does not become a fixed form but continues in a dynamic process of interaction with new influences.

7. The multiplicity of Creole forms/types making context and point of view crucial to understanding.

All of these principles can be seen at work in the language definition of Creole which took hold only fairly recently – the first international conference on Creole linguistics was held in 1959 – although its use has been recorded as early as the sixteenth century.[48] Dictionary definitions some decades ago carried the pejorative connotations noted earlier with reference to Creoles. They indicate the perception of Creole languages as inferior, savage corruptions, or merely simplified versions of civilised European languages. Advancements in the field of linguistics have erased these comments from more recent editions, no doubt, another effect of decolonisation.

Encounter, nativity and process are significant elements in the linguistic definition:

> In sociolinguistic terms, [Creole languages] have arisen through contact between speakers of different languages. This contact first produces a makeshift language called a pidgin; when this is nativised and becomes the language of a community, it is a Creole . . . The process of becoming a Creole may occur at any stage as a makeshift language develops from trade jargon to expanded pidgin, and can happen under drastic circumstances.[49]

Note the use of the plural. Here Creole truly designates a genus. There are several Creoles (within and beyond the Americas), derived from a variety of languages, many with individual names at home. The difference between a pidgin and a true Creole is important to note – native tongue and extension. The hybrid language must become the mother tongue of a speech community. This stage is unlikely to be reached until the language has expanded and developed a range and capacity suited to the needs of the community, a process which occurs over an extended period of time. This process of becoming is what they have in common, although the products differ. The multiplicity and relativity of Creoleness being undeniable – since what it means to be Creole in actuality shifts with each context – it is best understood with reference to a specific field of signification. But linguistic studies also provide schematic outlines of the process which may be appropriated to enhance the analysis of other cultural phenomena.

Within this framework, nativisation becomes one important stage, rather than an alternative or other process. Brathwaite's formulation in *Contradictory Omens* actually allows for the inclusion of different kinds of creolisation – Euro, Afro and mulatto – accommodating both sides, Wynter and Nicholls, Casimir and Bolland. In fact, Roger Andersen's definition of nativisation shifts the grounds of the debate:

> . . . it is the individual's mental capacity to construct such a linguistic system that makes it possible for a new 'native' language to arise, as in the case of the creation of a Creole language. Each individual has the potential for creating his own system. New input then must assimilate to *his* system. This process of creating an *individual* autonomous system I call *nativization* . . .[50]

Here assimilation is redefined (in terms somewhat similar to Senghor's) as an active response of the receiver, challenging the presumption of passivity. One might extend this notion to the discussion of the artistic strategies of writers attempting to represent the nature of this culture, their methods of devising a poetics of creolisation:

> [language] is at the crux of the struggle to forge a genuinely indigenous literary idiom. The essence of that idiom . . . must itself be a dramatic example of the dynamic process of creolization, of the cultural confrontation and creation it attempts faithfully to examine and reflect.[51]

In a 1997 article, Jahan Ramazani discusses the significance of the wound in Derek Walcott's *Omeros* as a "polyvalent metaphor", which in its "[k]nitting together [of] different histories of affliction" . . . "exemplifies the cross-cultural fabric of postcolonial poetry but contravenes the assumption that postcolonial literature develops by sloughing off Eurocentrism for indigeneity."[52] The issues considered there are closely linked to those outlined in the seven-point principles of creolisation and the discussion of its "history": "interpretive opacity" "hybrid, polyvalent and unpredictable"; "tropological binding up of seeming antitheses"; "cultural convergence in the Americas [and its] violent genesis"; "the twists and turns of intercultural inheritance"; "[Derek]Walcott's appropriation . . . resembles other well-known indigenisations"; "the metamorphosis . . . is more tangled . . . for it invokes shifts"; "Walcott has spliced a variety of literary genes [sic] and even antithetical cultures to create a surprisingly motley character" with a "multiple and contradictory parentage".[53] Ultimately, the article, not unlike the linguist's definition above, argues for a more complex understanding of nativisation: ". . . the post-colonial poet's seeming capitulation to or subversion of European influences needs to be rethought as a more ambiguous and ambivalent synthesis than is usually acknowledged."[54]

This, we have seen, also applies to the term "Creole" from its etymology to its many definitions varying with period and place, and its extended forms and designations. Variety and contradiction notwithstanding, there is an identifiable, though not stable, group of principles associated with the notion wherever it is found. To the range of metaphors invoked by various scholars to enhance our understanding of Creoleness – melting pot, quilt, rhizome root[55] – we may add yet another, the mathematical formula which involves a "chaos"-producing factor, creating a variety of curves despite the constant relationship among its parts. A grasp of the formula may hopefully facilitate dialogue.

NOTES

1.   Bill Ashcroft, Gareth Griffiths and Helen Tiffin, eds., *The Empire Writes Back: Theory and Practice in Post-colonial Literatures* (London and New York: Routledge, 1989), p. 145. See also J. Michael Dash in "Psychology, Creolisation and Hybridisation", in Bruce King, ed., *New National and Post-Colonial Literatures: An Introduction* (Oxford: Clarendon Press, 1996), pp. 45–58, quoting James Clifford's, *The Predicament of Culture: Twentieth Century Ethnography, Literature and Art* (Cambridge, Mass.: Harvard University Press, 1988) where the Caribbean is seen as a "paradigm for modern syncretic cultures".

2.   In his *Introduction à une poétique du divers* (Paris: Gallimard, 1996), Edouard Glissant also sees the implications of studying creolisation as going beyond the region, to offering a new approach to the spiritual dimension of the humanities (p. 17).

3.   Sidney Mintz and Sally Price, *Caribbean Contours* (Baltimore and London: Johns Hopkins University Press, 1985), p. 6.

4.   Rex Nettleford, *Caribbean Cultural Identity* (Kingston: Institute of Jamaica, 1978), p. 2.

5.   Rex Nettleford, *Inward Stretch, Outward Reach: A Voice from the Caribbean* (London and Basingstoke: Macmillan, 1993), p. 64.

6. Jean Casimir, *La Caraïbe Une et Divisible* (Port-au-Prince: CEPALC/Nations Unies/Henri Deschamps, 1991), p. 27. "La mise en place de groupements et de résaux de relations durables suppose un certain degré de connaissance du mode de fonctionnement de la société. Dans une situation coloniale, cette mise en place est donc l'oeuvre des créoles ou des créolisés. Ce n'est pas par hasard que les spécialistes des sciences sociales de la région, s'émancipant de la tutelle métropolitaine, s'efforcent de mettre au clair ce que sont le créole et le processus de créolisation".

7. Suzanne Romaine, *Pidgins and Creole Languages* (London: Longmans, 1988), p. 1.

8. Noted in entry on "Creole", in *A Dictionary of American English* (Chicago: University of Chicago Press, 1940).

9. See Frederic G. Cassidy, *Jamaica Talk* (London and Kingston: Macmillan Caribbean/Sangster's, [1961] 1982) for changes in Jamaican usage. Also O. Nigel Bolland's reference to Virginia R. Dominguez' study (*White by Definition: Social Classification in Creole Louisiana* [New Brunswick: Rutgers University Press, 1986]) of the meaning(s) of "Creole" in Louisiana since the eighteenth century. See O. Nigel Bolland, "Creolization and Creole Societies: A Cultural Nationalist View of Caribbean Social History", in Alistair Hennessy, ed., *Intellectuals in the Twentieth-Century Caribbean. Vol. 1 – Spectre of the New Class: The Commonwealth Caribbean*, Warwick University Caribbean Studies (London: Macmillan Caribbean, 1992), reprinted in this volume.

10. Quoted by Stefano Harney in *Nationalism and Identity: Culture and the Imagination in a Caribbean Diaspora* (London and Kingston: Zed Books and UWI, 1996), p. 95.

11. According to Brathwaite, "In Trinidad, it refers principally to the black descendants of slaves . . ." See Kamau Brathwaite, *Contradictory Omens* (Mona, Jamaica: Savacou, [1974] 1985), p. 10. Mintz and Price: "In modern settings, it refers in some areas (e.g., coastal Suriname) to Afro-Americans and in others (e.g., Trinidad) to persons of European ancestry." *Caribbean Contours* (Baltimore and London: Johns Hopkins University Press, 1985), p. 6.

12. *Oxford English Dictionary*, vol. 11 (Oxford: Oxford University Press, [1933] 1961), p. 1163.

13. To give just a few examples: *Dictionnaire de la langue française* (Paris: Hachette, 1878). "L'origine de *criollo* est douteuse; si l'on fait venir de l'espagnol . . . la formation est tout à fait irrégulière . . ." Oscar Bloch and Wlather von Wartburg, *Dictionnaire Etymologique de la langue française* (Paris: Presses Universitaires, 1975, 6th ed.) "dér. De criar . . . lat. Creare, avec un suff. peu clair". *An Etymological Dictionary of the English Language*. (Oxford: Oxford University Press, 1987) ". . . a corrupt word made by the negroes; said to be a contraction of creadillo . . .".

14. Maureen Warner-Lewis, "Posited Kikoongo Origins of some Portuguese and Spanish Words of the Slave Period." Paper presented to the Tenth Biennial

Conference of the Society for Caribbean Linguistics, Georgetown, Guyana (August, 1994). For further support and commentary on the African origins of linguistic Creole formation see William Washabaugh and Sidney M. Greenfield, "The Development of Atlantic Creole Languages", in Ellen Woolford and William Washabaugh, eds., *The Social Context of Creolization* (Ann Arbor: Karoma, 1983), pp. 106–19.

15. *Diccionario Crítico Etimológico de la Lengua Castellana* (Berna: 1954).

16. *Oxford English Dictionary*, vol. II (Oxford: Oxford University Press, [1933] 1961), p. 1163.

17. Alexandre Borrot and Marcel Didier, *Bodico: dictionnaire du Français sans faute* (Paris: Bordas, 1970).

18. H.W. Fowler, *A Dictionary of Modern English Usage*, 2nd ed. (London: Oxford University Press, 1965).

19. See Frederic G. Cassidy, *Jamaica Talk*, p. 162.

20. Carol Barash, "The Character of Difference: The Creole Woman as Cultural Mediator in Narratives about Jamaica", in *Eighteenth-Century Studies*, 23:4 (1990), p. 424.

21. *A Dictionary of American English.*

22. See Warner-Lewis extract above. Edward Long, *The History of Jamaica*, 3 vols. (London: T. Lowndes, 1774). Philip Wright, ed., *Lady Nugent's Journal of her Residence in Jamaica, 1801–1805* (Kingston: Institute of Jamaica, [1907] 1966).

23. Southall quoted in F. Cassidy and R.B. LePage, *Dictionary of Jamaican English* (Cambridge: Cambridge University Press, 1967), p. 130. Also see Jean Rhys *Wide Sargasso Sea* (London: Penguin Books, 1966) for a fictional representation. Also discussed by Carol Barash in "The Character of Difference".

24. *Trésor de la langue française: Dictionnaire de la langue du XIXe et du Xxe siècle* (16 vols.), vol. 6 (Paris: Eds. Centre National de la Recherche Scientifique, 1978). Francisco J. Santamaría, *Diccionario de Mejicanismos* (Méjico: Editorial Porrua, 1959).

25. Long, *History of Jamaica*, quoted in Cassidy, *Jamaica Talk*, p. 156; Victor Hugo (1826) cited in *Trésor de la langue française*; J. Ramsay (1788), quoted in the *Oxford English Dictionary*.

26. As Selwyn Cudjoe notes in *Resistance and Caribbean Literature* (Chicago: Ohio University Press, 1980), "Given these divisions, it became impossible for Africans to maintain the sense of cohesiveness necessary to overthrow the Europeans and develop their own national state". For a more extended discussion of Haiti, see David Nicholls, *From Dessalines to Duvalier: Race, Colour and National Independence in Haiti*. Warwick University Caribbean Studies (London and Basingstoke: Macmillan Caribbean, 1988).

27. Wright, ed., *Lady Nugent's Journal*, p. 98.

28. Radiguet (1923) cited in *Trésor de la langue française*; J. McLeod (1818) in *Oxford English Dictionary*; Cassidy, *Jamaica Talk*, p. 153.

29. Franklin W. Knight, *The Caribbean: The Genesis of a Fragmented Nationalism*, 2nd edition (New York: Oxford University Press, 1990), p. 128.

30. Kamau Brathwaite, "Creative Literature of the British West Indies During the Period of Slavery", *Roots* (Ann Arbor: University of Michigan Press, 1993), p. 129.

31. Sidney Mintz, "The Caribbean as a Socio-cultural Area", in Michael M. Horowitz, ed., *Peoples and Cultures of the Caribbean* (New York: Natural History Press, 1971), p. 34.

32. Discussing the racial politics of Mexican independence, for example, Chester Hunt and Lewis Walker state, "Mexican independence and Mexican nationalism were first stimulated to serve the interests of the criollos . . ." *Ethnic Dynamics: Patterns of intergroup relations in various societies* (Homewood: Dorsey Press, 1974), p. 141.

33. Cassidy and LePage, *Dictionary of Jamaican English*, p. 130.

34. Joseph Tregle's discussion of the political importance of Creoleness in Louisiana is instructive, in "Creoles and Americans", in Arnold R. Hirsch and Joseph Logsdon, eds., *Creole New Orleans* (Baton Rouge and London: Louisiana State University, 1992), pp. 131–85.

35. "Créole", *Encyclopédie du Bon Français dans l'usage contemporain*, vol. 1 (Paris: Éditions de Trévise, 1972).

36. Philip M. Sherlock, *West Indian Nations: A New History* (London: Macmillan; Kingston: Jamaica Publishing House, 1973), p. 32.

37. Jean Casimir, La Caraïbe Une et Divisible, 44. My translation of: "Qualifier la culture locale de culture créole fait courir le risque de confondre les créations des ethnies dominées avec les adaptations des institutions européennes par l'ethnie dominante".

38. Sylvia Wynter, "Creole Criticism – A Critique", in *New World Quarterly* 5:4 (1972), p. 14.

39. David Nicholls, *From Dessalines to Duvalier*, pp. 248–49.

40. Rex Nettleford, *Caribbean Cultural Identity*, p. 2.

41. Edouard Glissant, "Créolisations dans la Caraïbe et les Amériques", in *Introduction à une poétique du divers (Paris: Gallimard, 1996)*, p. 14.

42. Dash, "Psychology, Creolisation and Hybridisation", pp. 45–58.

43. Bolland, "Creolization and Creole Societies", pp. 50–79.

44. Robert J.C. Young, *Colonial Desire: Hybridity in Theory, Culture and Race* (New York: Routledge, 1995), pp. 20–2.

45. Brathwaite, *Contradictory Omens*, p. 58.

46. Bolland, "Creolization and Creole Societies", p. 72.

47. Ibid., p. 52.

48. "Creoles and Pidgins", in *The Linguistics Encyclopedia* (London and New York: Routledge, 1991), p. 82. For a more detailed account with quotations but later dates see Peter Stein, "Quelques dates nouvelles de l'histoire du mot 'créole'", *Etudes Créoles*, 5.1–2 (1982), pp. 162–5.

49. *Oxford Companion to the English Language* (Oxford and NY: Oxford University Press, 1992), pp. 270–1.

50. Brathwaite, *Contradictory Omens*, p. 58. Roger Andersen et al. *Pidginization and Creolization as Language Acquisition* (Rowley and London: Newsbury House, 1983), p. 11.

51. Roberto Marquez, "Nationalism, Nation and Ideology: Trends in the Emergence of a Caribbean Literature", in Franklin W. Knight and Colin A. Palmer, eds., *The Modern Caribbean* (Chapel Hill and London: University of North Carolina Press, 1989), p. 330.

52. Derek Walcott, *Omeros* (New York: Farrar, Strauss and Giroux, 1990). Jahan Ramazani, "The Wound of History: Walcott's Omeros and the Postcolonial Poetics of Affliction", in *Publications of the Modern Languages Association* (hereafter *PMLA*), p. 112 (1997), pp. 405–17. Quoting from Abstracts, 536.

53. Jahan Ramazani, *PMLA* 112 (1997), pp. 405–17, passim.

54. Ibid., p. 409.

55. The difficulty of thinking outside the habits of mind which privilege the linear structure makes metaphors both useful and attractive. All three embrace the essential ingredients of multiplicity and encounter or relationship, but each contains a limitation: in the melting pot original identity is lost; with the quilt each element remains discreet, unaltered; the "parts" of the rhizome root may have little relation to each other outside the point of origin.

PART THREE

Class, Gender, Ethnicity and Identity

Paul E. Lovejoy *and* **David V. Trotman**

Chapter 4

ENSLAVED AFRICANS AND THEIR EXPECTATIONS OF SLAVE LIFE IN THE AMERICAS
TOWARDS A RECONSIDERATION OF MODELS OF "CREOLISATION"

Discussions of slave life in the Americas have only just begun to see Africans as wholly human and as peoples whose peculiar histories had resulted in their forced migration across the Atlantic.[1] Each individual arrived with his or her own attitudes, ideas, beliefs and expectations, and as Michel Sobel has observed in her discussion of colonial Virginia, "Africans brought their attitudes towards slaves and masters with them to Virginia, suggesting an important but totally unexplored issue." Sobel notes that "their expectations and reactions may well have been an important factor in shaping the character of American slavery."[2] We agree with Sobel that the individual life experiences of the enslaved affected how people responded to their bondage in the Americas. Our purpose here is to explore the range of possible expectations which enslaved Africans might have had about life in bondage before crossing the Atlantic and also to examine some of the fundamental characteristics of the slave experience in the Americas that differed from preconceived notions of slavery that had been formed in Africa. In this way we hope to comment on the process of "creolisation", as developed by Kamau Brathwaite and others, in relation to the impact of African ideas and expectations on the early culture of slavery in the Americas.

According to Brathwaite, who drew his insights from the Jamaican experience between circa 1770 and the 1820s,

> "Creole" . . . presupposes a situation where the society concerned is caught up "in some kind of colonial arrangement" with a metropolitan European power, on the one hand, and a plantation arrangement on the other; and where the society is multiracial but organised for the benefit of a minority of European origin. "Creole society" therefore is the result of a complex situation where a colonial polity reacts, as a whole, to external metropolitan pressures, and at the same time to individual adjustments made necessary by the juxtaposition of master and slave, elite and labourer, in a culturally heterogeneous relationship.[3]

We follow Brathwaite in defining the cultural action and social process of creolisation as a "response and interaction . . . dictated by the circumstances of the society's foundation and composition – a 'new' construct, made up of newcomers to the landscape and cultural strangers to each other; one group dominant, the other legally and subordinately slaves."[4] Even more specifically, Brathwaite noted,

> . . . here in Jamaica, fixed within the dehumanising institution of slavery, were two cultures of people, having to adapt themselves to a new environment and to each other. The friction created by this confrontation was cruel, but it was also creative. The white plantations and social institutions . . . reflect one aspect of this. The slaves' adaptation of their African culture to a new world reflects another.[5]

The adaptation that was necessary under slavery, which is central to Brathwaite's conception, nonetheless applies to a specific period – from the end of the eighteenth century until emancipation – and therefore not to the whole period of slavery or necessarily to other slave societies in the Americas, without modification.

Our focus is on the period in which enslaved people who were African-born predominated in the population, roughly the first 100 years of colonial settlement in the English and French Caribbean and North America, but including nineteenth-century Brazil and Cuba, when there was a great influx of African-born migrants. In these contexts, there was a significant population of first-generation slaves with roots in Africa, and in our opinion these enslaved Africans, and the periods and places in which they formed a majority or large minority, must be clearly distinguished from the "Creole societies" in which later generations tended to dominate. Taking generations into consideration, the foundations of "Creole society" are to be located in the period in which African-born slaves formed the bulk of the population. Our intention is to explore aspects of the mental map which the enslaved brought with them and subsequently adapted. The contours of those maps relate specifically to the landscape of trans-Atlantic slavery.

Until recently, the tendency has been to homogenise the African experience under slavery and to assign beliefs and actions to an amorphous group without reference to the specific historical circumstances in which individuals found themselves. For Sidney Mintz and Sally Price, the African background became submerged into the "crowds" that filled the slave ships to the Americas, and hence the African background could only have a generalised influence on slave culture, which received its dynamism through the agency of the slaves themselves, responding to the oppressive conditions of slavery.[6]

We contextualise "creolisation" in such a way as to demonstrate the reality and specifics of Africa and the impact that this might have had on the experiences of those enslaved in the Americas.[7] By focusing on the period of heaviest African settlement, and the period in which the African-born predominated in the population, our study attempts to flesh out the African-derived cultural heritage that is crucial to Brathwaite's conception of Creole society. We suggest that many enslaved Africans found ways of extricating themselves from the mentality of the crowded slave ship to reformulate their expectations, adjusting their visions as new experiences challenged their assumptions, whether it was being devoured by cannibals, or whatever. In this way, we suggest that the claim of Mintz and Price that the African background was filtered through the crowd mentality of the middle passage fails to appreciate the extent to which people were able to disengage from the crowd.

In our view, a careful reading of the African context reveals that in the Americas the enslaved were subjected to forms of oppression that were remarkably different in substance from what was generally known in those parts of Africa from which they came, but in our view, a careful reading of the African context reveals that enslaved Africans still interpreted what they confronted in the light of their previous experiences and resulting expectations. We contend that the experience of slavery in the Americas, buttressed by racism, was fundamentally different than what the expectations of the enslaved must have been before leaving Africa. It is possible to assess what people expected in some situations through an examination of the personal histories of individuals who were enslaved. Testimonies of enslaved Africans offer insights into what people knew and what they feared.[8] When we raise the issue of previous experience and expectations, it is not an attempt to suggest that Africans were somehow preconditioned for a life of servility in the Americas. Moreover, African notions of slavery were in sharp contrast to the reality of racial slavery in the Americas. Rather, our attempt is to highlight the possible junctures at which disappointments and oppression would lead to resistance and rebellion.

In virtually every society with which enslaved Africans were familiar, there was a social status and legal category of servility in which people were treated as property and hence could be bought and sold, inherited, or given away.[9] The range of legal and customary obligations varied widely, as did the various terms for different categories of servility in various languages and places.[10] While the different patterns of obligations and responsibilities may or may not have constituted a continuum of relationships, they all included slavery as the extreme form of servility.[11] The available data, and the detailed studies of these data, demonstrate conclusively that virtually everyone who was taken to the Americas as a slave, except the very young, had his/her own understanding of what slavery was supposed to be. Clearly that is not to argue that everyone who crossed the Atlantic was a slave in Africa before their transportation, although many were. Moreover, there was a distinction between recent captives, who might still have hope of being ransomed, and slaves who had been sold on the market. An awareness of the existence of systems of obligations included outright slavery. We contend that the cultural practices of the society from which the enslaved came informed the attitudes and reactions of these individuals to their experience of slavery in the Americas. These attitudes and reactions varied, of course, depending upon the age at which a person was removed from Africa and the extent of exposure to people of similar background in the diaspora, among other factors. The European immigrants to the Americas, although travelling with similar notions of service obligations (serfdom, apprenticeship, impressment, "transportation" of criminals) could expect to use the transition to their "New World" as an opportunity to change their circumstances – for the vast majority of involuntary African migrants this would not be the case. Some did achieve emancipation and even repatriation, but the overwhelming majority found themselves enmeshed in the coils of a system that would require them to plumb the full repertoire of their cultural skills to survive.

Given the large number of children who were taken as captives across the Atlantic, especially in the nineteenth century, the question of age and its relationship to memory and expectations is an important consideration, and a feature that is seldom fully acknowledged in the literature. Although attitudes and expectations were modified, the homeland experiences were never completely removed from the individual's memory bank. The memory of a ten-year-old was significantly different from that of a 24-year-old, but even then children continued to be nurtured within a community that re-enforced traditions of the homeland from where the children had come, or children were effectively adopted and treated as if they were from some other homeland. An Igbo child might well have found him or herself on a plantation in the Americas with a substantial Igbo population, or in a population where Igbo cultural influences might be prominent,[12] or a boy from Mozambique might be adopted by someone who spoke Kikongo or Kimbundu from west-central Africa.

Similarly, gender as well as age also affected the ways in which individuals understood servile status. The range of experiences for enslaved women requires detailed comparison. As the demography of the trans-Atlantic slave trade establishes, enslaved women were more likely to be retained or sold locally in western Africa than sold into the Atlantic trade, and they were quite likely to end up in relationships of marriage or concubinage that were governed by law and custom. Moreover, free females, often girls, could be pawned, which meant that male elders had control over their persons, but not the right to sell them. Instead, marriages could be arranged to cancel debts. Under slavery in the Americas, women seldom ended up in legally constituted marriages with their masters, who might sexually exploit them, but who could also sell them, whether or not they had borne their children. As a slave in western Africa, a woman might well end up in a sexual relationship that was forced upon her, as indeed would likely be her fate in the Americas, too. Her status after bearing children, and indeed the status of her offspring, were carefully regulated but often violated in practice, on both sides of the Atlantic. Unfortunately, there have been few comparative studies of the treatment of women and their offspring that bridge the Atlantic during the period of slavery. In the Americas – certainly Mexico, Brazil, the Caribbean and North America – slaves formed families, but there is virtually no information on slave families in Africa during the same period, only information on the children of enslaved women who inherited the free status of their fathers. A comparison of gender relations and child-rearing in the Americas with marriage customs and residence patterns in western Africa might well demonstrate ways in which trans-Atlantic slavery helped to shape the treatment and therefore the expectations of enslaved women.

In areas where Islamic law prevailed, the status of slave, particular concubine, was clearly defined, and while there was debate and disagreement over how the law should be applied, individuals who were exposed to Islamic law in Africa, whether in countries where Islamic law prevailed or along trade routes controlled by Muslim merchants, people understood slavery in an Islamic setting. The discussion of slavery in this context dates back to the period before the trans-Atlantic slave trade, and the topic remained central to Islamic discourse within West

Africa throughout the whole period of the Atlantic trade.[13] Given the nature of Islamic education, whether in the rudimentary form to which most Muslim children were exposed, or in the more learned discussion of written texts and scholarly traditions that was open to the educated elite, there was ample opportunity to explore well-developed and historic arguments about slavery. Inevitably, a comparison with the real world around them followed from such exposure, and dissatisfaction with the treatment of freeborn Muslims was a major grievance within the Islamic community, at least since the early seventeenth century. Muslims even discussed how to behave and what to expect if they found themselves enslaved to Christians.[14]

In non-Muslim regions along the Guinea coast – where slaves also came from and which was a region through which slaves from the Muslim interior had to pass to reach ports of embarkation for the Americas – there were also clearly understood codes of servility commonly observed to be slavery. A clear distinction in theory, at least, was maintained between slaves and pawns, for example.[15] Slaves were individuals who were purchased and could be sold, while pawns were individuals whose kin were using them as collateral for debts. Whereas slaves were considered to be property, pawns were servile dependents subject to contracts that prohibited their sale. While there were many cases in which these distinctions were ignored and many others where the legal rights of pawns were violated, in theory, nonetheless, the distinction between the practices of slavery and pawnship confirms the fact that enslaved Africans from these areas had preconceived views of the distinctions among different types of servility. The slavery of the Americas was a new type based on race.

Although individuals came from areas where slavery and other forms of bondage were well known, the legal, ideological and practical implications of servile status varied considerably. Africans in the Americas did not confront slavery for the first time, but the nature of the institution in the Americas was fundamentally different from what many people could have expected, although at least some reports indicate that enslaved Africans were sometimes aware that this was so. As Thomas Phillips described, the attitudes of captives on board the *Hannibal*, in 1693–1694, people had "a more dreadful apprehension of Barbadoes than we can have of hell".[16] Certainly in Dahomey, which according to Edna Bay was a country "deeply affected by the slave trade", those directly involved in the trade "knew its brutal nature and understood something of the fate that awaited those sent overseas".[17]

Differentiation in status in western Africa, as elsewhere, was not only common but was often fluid. Individuals might well experience a change in status, either through enslavement or through pawnship, marriage or apprenticeship.

They were aware that these possibilities were part of life experiences and that fortune, Allah or the ancestral spirits might influence their lives. There are numerous examples of Muslim merchants and aristocrats from countries where Islam was widespread who ended up in the Americas as slaves, despite the efforts to protect Muslims. There are also examples of individuals who were sold because they had been convicted of some crime or otherwise were being punished for crimes that they were accused of committing. There are even claims that the number of offenses punishable by enslavement increased as a result of the trans-Atlantic trade. Lt Hugh Dalrymple, who was at Gorée in 1779, learned that

> Every Person who commits any Sort of Crime is sold for a Slave. Crimes [which were] formerly to be punished in different Ways are now punished by this . . . [whereas] formerly the Punishment for all Crimes was commuted for a certain Number of Cattle or Quantity of Grain, which was either paid by the Offender or by his Family, in case of his Incapacity but, since the Introduction of the Slave Trade, not only all Crimes are punished by Slavery, but even the most trivial Offences are punished in the same Manner.[18]

The experiences of merchants, aristocrats and convicts certainly differed, but the evidence demonstrates that people could experience dramatic changes in their status. The gradations of status and the alterations in fortune were common knowledge and must have been the subject of discussion among the enslaved and, indeed more generally, especially among Muslims and at the slave ports along the coast.

Whether for political or other reasons, the idea that Africans had conceptions of slavery before coming to the Americas has traditionally been downplayed in the study of the adjustments of the enslaved to chattel bondage in the Americas.[19] At best, those studies that have broached the subject have argued that slavery was so different in Africa as to have had no impact on the adjustments of Africans to their situation in the Americas. We would suggest that prior knowledge of slavery and other forms of servitude helped in shaping the range of responses of the enslaved. Moreover, the expectations of slaves as to how they should be treated derived from their personal knowledge of slavery in Africa. The forum for debate over expectations and the reality of the Americas was in the fields, mines and manor houses of the Americas, where racial arguments and actions increasingly became the recourse and the discourse of the slave-owning elite in maintaining and explaining their domination. There was pressure from below to conform to expectations, and thereby "soften" slavery. Moreover, individuals came from specific places, not a generic "Africa"; hence to examine expectations and notions of slavery, it is necessary to identify the specific historical circumstances and contemporary attitudes towards enslavement and slavery in those regions of Africa from which the enslaved people originated.

The method of enslavement affected the expectations of individuals.[20] Those who were taken in war might well have expected to be ransomed, although the presence of high-ranking officials and wealthy merchants in the Americas demonstrates that ransoming did not always occur. Frequently, women and children were considered the spoils of war, and while in many cases, soldiers and the political elite might retain many captives, others were still sold as a means of realising the payoffs from war. Those who were too old or too young might be killed, which certainly must have been a greatly feared feature of war. Slave raiding was often connected with on-going political rivalry and friction among states, and hence the harassment caused by raiding must also have shaped the expectations of many people who grew up in western Africa during the height of the slave trade across the Atlantic. Kidnapping, though often considered illegal, is reported to have been common in many places, as for example in Igbo country. Equiano's experience is well known, but there are many other such recollections.[21] Kidnapping even blurred into seizure as compensation for some debt or crime. Thus one teenage girl, who was given the name Eve, claimed that she had been enslaved as compensation for a goat that had deliberately been placed in her father's garden – her father was then accused of theft.[22] Undoubtedly, the uncertainties of an era in which kidnapping was a problem affected people's expectations. The possibilities of enslavement were many, therefore, whether through judicial or religious means, debt-bondage, or capture.

Religious issues, especially in the case of Islam, affected expectations, since Muslims who found themselves slaves to non-Muslims were likely to receive different treatment from those whose masters were also Muslims. Religious or other justification for changes in status also varied, of course, whether or not Islam was a factor. In areas where Islam was not important, slaves might be sacrificed, and hence foreign sale was a source of victims for religious ceremonies. In the Niger delta and the Cross River, areas that were clearly affected by the trans-Atlantic slave trade, slaves were killed at funerals and were also sacrificed at religious rites. To avoid sale and possible execution, outcasts, such as the mothers of twins, became "slaves" of religious shrines, thereby protected from sale or sacrifice but nonetheless ostracised. The possibility of death or total social isolation certainly were known to many people, and this knowledge must have affected the expectations of the newly enslaved and those being sold.[23]

As with other aspects of slavery, we need to consider to what extent the existence of the trans-Atlantic trade became such common knowledge that it formed part of the mental landscape of Africans. While slavery existed before the

Atlantic trade, and slaves had gone across the Sahara, the question is how the Atlantic experience was internalised as one option which the enslaved might be forced to confront. Removal from the social formations of western Africa and sale across the Atlantic were possibilities that faced most people in western Africa because it was impossible to guarantee that people would not be enslaved. It is not always possible to determine when enslavement became a punishment for crimes or the fate of captured warriors and kidnapped women and children, but it is clear that most people could not escape the possibility that they or their relatives might have to be ransomed one day or otherwise be permanently enslaved. It can be assumed that people in the areas that were long in contact with the Atlantic world discussed issues of slavery and the slave trade, just as they responded to the fluctuations in the market, whether in slaves or others goods, and adjusted accordingly.[24] Walter Rodney analysed these changes in terms of the extent and degree of social oppression that can be documented for the upper Guinea coast, and how there seems to have been a correspondence between the scale of the export trade in enslaved Africans and the incidence of slavery, pawnship and other institutions of dependency in those areas affected by the trans-Atlantic market. Rodney's argument has been extended to other parts of Africa.[25] Documenting changes in attitudes and practices is painstaking work, which is far from complete, and it still must be admitted that the degree and timing of change in social institutions is difficult to document, even if trend seems to reinforce Rodney's thesis.

The role of the *ekpe* society in governing master-slave relations and hence in supporting the slave trade has been reasonably well documented.[26] *Ekpe* was a "secret society", as anthropologists have sometimes labelled this graded association of adult males which was controlled by the most influential and wealthiest men in the interior of the Bight of Biafra. The society was only "secret" in the sense that decisions and enforcement of decisions were determined collectively among the members of the highest grade of the society, and hence individuals could not be held responsible for decisions. The spread of *ekpe* in the interior of the Bight of Biafra in the eighteenth century had important implications for the institutions of slavery and pawnship. In overseeing the enforcement of debt repayment, *ekpe* served to protect pawns from enslavement, except in cases of default, when the society could determine who would be executed or otherwise punished and who would be sold into slavery. Hence, *ekpe* was involved in deciding who was enslaveable and who was not, and therefore had a direct impact on distinguishing between slave and free.

The arbitrary powers of *ekpe* developed in the context of the Atlantic slave trade and implicitly reveal that senior members of the society, at least, had full knowledge of the consequences of the trans-Atlantic trade. Indeed, some of these senior members had been educated in England. They were responsible for the development of a "written" language of over 500 signs that was used to announce decrees and enforce decisions of the elite. Despite the difficulty of demonstrating how slavery changed over time, such developments as the emergence of *ekpe* affected how the enslaved viewed slavery, and specifically what they expected as a consequence of their enslavement and their possible sale to different buyers, including those trading to the Americas.

Expectations were also affected by the abuse of power, and the degree to which individuals suffered from such abuse. In many cases, enslavement itself resulted from war, kidnapping or the reduction of debt pawns to slavery, all of which exploited relationships of power. The extent to which the existence of a slave market encouraged such distortions, is reflected in the discussion over "legal" versus "illegal" enslavement.[27] Hence Muslims debated whether or not enslavement was "just"; efforts to define the status of being a Muslim were articulately explored in the works of Ahmad Baba and Muhammad Bello.[28] Similarly, the Kongo civil war raised issues of who could and should not be enslaved in a Christian context.[29] Jose Curto has recently uncovered a case of "wrongful" enslavement in Angola in 1805, in which a Portuguese military expedition raided for slaves among allies and subjects of the Portuguese crown, with the result that the governor freed the prisoners and punished his own soldiers.[30]

We are not suggesting a simple correlation between the growth of the trans-Atlantic slave trade and the corruption of institutions; rather we are suggesting that modifications and adaptations of institutions were complex and ultimately contributed to the ongoing supply of slaves for the Americas.[31] There was corruption and distortion of institutions on all sides of the slave trade. Thus, some members of the British legal system contributed to the corruption of justice in England by manipulating the law to facilitate the transportation of prisoners to Barbados and Jamaica in the seventeenth century; and hence the phrase "to be Barbadoed".[32] Similarly in Africa, there are numerous examples of individuals wrongly accused of crimes and subsequently enslaved, or simply kidnapped, and there was the practice of "panyarring", the specialised term that was used to describe the practice of holding people collectively responsible for debts or wrong-doing, so that anyone considered to be associated with an act could be seized and enslaved. Although it is not always possible to verify whether or not accounts of "wrongful" seizure are truthful, it is certainly likely that the types of cases that are reported did occur.

The controversy surrounding the abolition of the slave trade and the emancipation of slaves in the Americas affected the expectations of the enslaved. It took

Mahommah Gardo Baquaqua only two years to realise the opportunities presented by abolition. From the time he was enslaved near Djougou in circa 1843–1845, until his escape from a Brazilian ship in New York harbour in late June 1847, he had been a slave in Pernambuco and Rio de Janeiro. "Freedom" took on a new meaning once he was under the protection of the New York Vigilance Society and spirited away to Haiti. What is not always recognised is that there was debate on both sides of the Atlantic. Hence in Africa, people debated the meaning of abolition. In Asante, there was general perplexity over the fact that the British, the country with the greatest number of slave ships active on the African coast, should abruptly abolish the trade in 1808. How could a trade that had previously been legal now be illegal? The Asantehene asked one British delegation to Kumasi what was to be expected if slaves could not be sold overseas, other than large-scale public executions?[33] A British mission at the royal court of Benin responded to another set of questions about abolition in 1838. Frustrated by what the Benin government perceived as an "illegal" blockade of the West African coast by the British anti-slave trade patrol, the *oba* attempted to explain the apparently irrational policy of abolition on the basis that Britain had a queen and not a king, or as the *oba* of Benin stated it, "the King of England is a woman."[34] At Old Calabar, Egbo Young Eyambo, the principal merchant in Duke Town, asked Henry Nicholls, who was there in 1805 on a mission from the African Association, to explain his reasons for visiting the town, since he was not a merchant. Eyambo is reported to have asked Nicholls if he "came from Mr. Wilberforce . . . and eyed me with some little ferocity, saying, if I came from Mr. Wilberforce they would kill me."[35] Such hostility was justified later with the repatriation of liberated slaves with abolitionist ideas.

Similarly, in the Americas, as historians have observed, the significance of the American and French revolutions take on new meaning when viewed in Atlantic perspective, both representing the triumph of "Creole society", although in different ways. On the one hand, "Creole" North America became a new nation that institutionalised slavery, while on the other hand, Haitian "Creole" emerged as a new nation in which slavery was terminated. Whether through the uprising in St Domingue or the ongoing struggle against slavery in the United States, the expectations of slaves were clearly affected, but what is sometimes not recognised is that the whole Atlantic was in turmoil in the eighteenth century, at least since 1776. The "creolisation" of the Americas occurred at a time when there was a prevailing mood of resistance and unrest arising from trans-Atlantic slavery. That resistance is first apparent in the baracoons of western Africa and on the slave ships themselves in the form of revolt, suicide and acts of sabotage.[36] Hence the expectations of the enslaved were always set within a framework of resistance and schemes of freedom. Enslavers everywhere worried about what those enslaved might be scheming, but they could not prevent them from learning about ideas of abolition and emancipation. The discussion around the emancipation of the enslaved in British colonies, for example, infected the enslaved with ideas of freedom. Both the 1824 and 1831 slave rebellions in Jamaica followed the spread of rumours of a general emancipation granted by Queen Victoria that was reputedly being subverted by the local slave owners.[37] Rebel leaders used the fact that emancipation was inevitable as a crucial element in the mobilisation of support for the rebellions. We admit that these incidents occurred towards the end of the British trade, but what does it mean for Africans who were still being shipped across the Atlantic at this time? Did news of these rebellions and developments filter back to African societies and thereby inform the expectations of those recently enslaved?

As these cases suggest, the idea of slavery was subject to an ongoing, if often blurry, debate, or rather series of debates, in different parts of the Atlantic world, including Africa. The attitudes of the enslaved who were sent to the Americas were shaped by these discussions. To what extent was the issue of enslavement as justifiable discussed in Africa, so that individuals had some knowledge/experience in the debates over legitimate servitude and protection of the free population from enslavement. This raises the issue of how the "free" population was defined, and by this we mean the population that was recognised to be protected from enslavement. And it is also necessary to explain how people could be enslaved despite such protection, so that we can determine when this happened in a form that was acceptable to local custom and when there was an abuse of power. Here the debate enters the difficult terrain of subtle distinctions over "legitimate" enslavement and the limitations on enslavement. Moreover, discussions of the rights of slaves and the distinctions among servile categories also affected the expectations of individuals. Unlike traditional views of African slavery, therefore, our view posits a complex range of experiences and expectations that were also affected by age and gender and the extent to which people of similar ethnic and linguistic backgrounds found themselves together under slavery. Moreover, attitudes changed over time – slaves from sixteenth-century Kongo were more medieval in their thinking about slavery than nineteenth-century Yoruba escaping from *jihad*.

In the context of slavery, the enslavement of an individual could realise a financial reward equivalent to the profits acquired through theft. Such opportunities for profit weakened the social fabric, as reflected in the collapse of central authority in the Kingdom of Kongo in the last decades of the seventeenth century. Officials might well threaten enslavement in the hope of financial gain and religious shrines came to accept slaves as compensation and retribution. Determining when institutions succumbed to corruption and officials and merchants abused their power, raises issues of context and place, as Rodney demonstrated for the upper Guinea coast.[38] Social oppression and the corruption of institutions were not, of course, only associated with slavery and the trans-Atlantic slave trade, but inevitably there were institutional responses to trans-Atlantic slavery that increased the level of oppression. We are thinking here of the development of the Aro commercial network in the eighteenth century which supplied slaves to Bonny and Old Calabar, the adaptation of the institution of pawnship to accommodate the commercial requirements of British traders at Old Calabar, and the development of similar commercial practices elsewhere that depended on an interplay between the external demand for slaves and local political and social conditions.[39] Where a strong centralised state controlled the ports, as Dahomey and Oyo did in the Bight of Benin, pawnship was not a feature of the transactions between Europeans and Africans;[40] in the Bight of Biafra, the nature of the political structure was entirely different, so that the use of pawns to guarantee debts that were owed to the captains of slavers became common practice.

The impression often given is that the transactions in slaves occurred in a state of silence; that slaves, as commodities, did not have ears or minds that could intercept and interpret the events around them. In fact, there were numerous people involved in transactions – from captors, merchants, guards, people who provided food along the slave routes and at the ports before embarkation, African sailors, and indeed white sailors and ship captains – with whom slaves had to interact and from whom they gained information or misinformation that went into the construction of their fears and expectations. The enslaved had to distinguish among various types of stories and gossip, whether these were myths of white cannibalism, rumours that someone might be freed because of proof of wrongful enslavement, or conspiracies to seize ships. The fact that relatives and friends did occasionally find one another also has to be taken into account. The period of exposure to conflicting information, thereby leading to uncertainty, was at least a few months from time of capture to delivery in the Americas, and often much longer. The existence and extent of wide and interlocking networks of information flows and informants and hence what was known about the trade and slavery are often ignored or under-appreciated. There were Black seamen in all periods of Atlantic history, from the earliest voyages through the eighteenth century when the slave trade was at its height, and they constituted an important network for the trans-Atlantic and circum-Atlantic flow of information.[41] Similarly, the existence of continuous interaction between Brazil and western Africa created an important avenue for the circulation of knowledge and hence the formation of expectations. The deportation of criminals, often slaves and mulattoes from Brazil, to the western coast of Africa as punishment began in the late sixteenth century and was a feature of the Brazilian penal system into the nineteenth century. Hence, many of the rebels in the 1835 Male uprising in Bahia were sent to the Bight of Benin.[42] Similarly, the education of the children of African merchants in Europe and the role of Islam as a network of information both challenge the idea that knowledgeable people along the slave routes in Africa were isolated from and hence ignorant of what was going on beyond the Atlantic.

We are suggesting that the degree of isolation of western Africa has been exaggerated. Certainly there was a gap between what merchants knew and what the enslaved knew, but it cannot be said that merchants and ruling elites were unaware of the likely fate of the deported population, especially not at the ports and along the trade routes that supplied slaves. How long did it take for those enslaved to find out what was going on? Enslaved people who were retained on the coast certainly learned about the significance of export, and the fear of being shipped on a European slaver must have often served as an effective means of controlling captives on the coast. It was difficult to trick slaves on board the French ship *Deux Soeurs* in 1825 because there were on board,

> . . . several slaves who had been employed as labourers and boatmen [in Sierra Leone.] These men were aware of the consequences of being taken to the coast which no doubt induced them to have recourse to force to affect their liberation.[43]

The result was an uprising in which seven French sailors were killed. Sometimes, at least, there was reasonably clear knowledge about the fate awaiting slaves being taken to the Americas, which raises the issue of language and ease of communication, including the importance of "trade" languages and the use of common languages on board ships. The fact remains that many people along the slave routes had to know what was going on, although it is not always clear how they interpreted what they saw and what they heard about.

The incidence of attempted suicide both on board ship and on plantations in the Americas raises questions about how such actions reflected the worst expectations of the slaves.[44] Although a persistent feature of the slave trade and slavery, it is not clear how suicide was conceived in different societies in Africa and how specific "African" notions either supported or proscribed such extreme actions. Since some slaves, at least, believed that "Whites" were cannibals, and it may be that such stereotypes were re-enforced by slave owners in Africa as a means of discouraging their own slaves from resisting bondage through the fear of being sold overseas.[45] Certainly, the autopsies that were performed on board some slave ships must have intensified such fears about the intentions of Whites. As one surgeon, Dr Falconbridge, told the Parliamentary enquiry into the slave trade in 1790 in London, efforts to discover the causes of deaths were easy to misinterpret, which is why he always conducted autopsies at night, by candle light, so that the slaves below deck would not know what was going on, which may only have had the effect of feeding rumors.[46] Captains of slave ships at some point began erecting nets on the main decks to prevent people from jumping into the sea. Moreover plantation owners in the Americas complained frequently that suicide was a form of resistance that was directed at destroying the value of their property. Certain ethnic groups, especially Igbo, became identified with suicide, and hence there were efforts to avoid the purchase of enslaved Africans of this background. More often than not, however, the quest for profits dictated that all available slaves be purchased, so that preferences could not always be satisfied.

Similarly, infanticide also reflects the views of some enslaved Africans that the life under slavery was not worth living. While it is clear that infant mortality rates were high, most scholarship has linked these high rates to the conditions of servitude (diet, the labour regime, disregard for pre- and post-natal care), but we cannot ignore the possibility of induced abortions and deliberate infanticide as part of a pattern of what some have called "gynaecological" resistance.[47] The decision to take the life of an unborn or recently born infant is a serious issue, whose discussion would have been cast in particular moral, religious and political terms reflecting the African background. Unfortunately, we know next to nothing about levels of infanticide and abortion in Africa during the period of the trans-Atlantic slave trade and the corresponding differences in attitudes and beliefs in Africa and the Americas. Those enslaved Africans who made the decision to kill children, and there was a significant minority who did, had to take this step with reference to their previous understandings about the gravity of the act and the likely consequences. While we need to know more about attitudes towards both infanticide and abortion, like suicide, the expectation that conditions of slavery would continue to be intolerable surely shaped the decisions of individuals to commit such acts of desperation.

Our purpose has been to demonstrate the extent to which the enslaved were aware of the world around them and the extent to which movement along the routes that fed the trans-Atlantic trade was a factor in the evolution of slave consciousness. What most enslaved African captives experienced upon being sold to the captains of slave ships was different in ways that were as profound as the crossing of the Atlantic itself. Already along the slave routes, the question of communication had required slaves to learn a common language, and in so doing their identities became tied up with issues of ethnicity and ultimately in religious expression.[48] However, the alteration in the status of individuals who had been enslaved did not make people forget skills or fail to take advantage of situations in which past experience mattered. The new world of the Americas reinforced ethnicity and the use of common languages, often in pidgin form, as a means of overcoming isolation. Hence, the bonding that characterised slavery in the Americas encouraged the development of a sense of community based on common, and often shared, experience and the ability to communicate beyond the hearing of their enslavers. Such bonding must have been based on expressions of widely divergent emotions and expressions that resulted in shared knowledge of the enslaving past.[49] This common memory certainly was important later when enslaved people were separated and sold to different enslavers. We have evidence of expressions of relief because someone was not sacrificed at a funeral; hysteria because of a violation of the underlying principle of debt bondage that prohibited further alienation and outright sale; the grief expressed by those who had suffered from "panyarring" because they belonged to a group that was being punished as a collectivity.[50] Finally, the fate of war prisoners, both combatants and non-combatants, must have been a common subject of discussion during the Middle Passage.

A central issue in understanding how the enslaved adjusted any expectations that they might have had about the nature of slavery and their own plight as slaves to their actual experience and the various warnings that must have been immediately showered on them by other slaves of their new owners in the Americas, relates to what was called "seasoning" and the distinction between the Creole generation and the African-born. It should be noted that in most of the slave societies of the Americas, for most of the period of slavery, the majority of the population had been born in Africa.[51] The growing importance of a Creole population, born in slavery in the Americas, should not distort the importance of African-derived notions of civility and society, and hence we want to make a sharp distinction in periodisation, emphasising the shift in the demography of slave societies. Second-generation slaves had far different experiences than those born in Africa, and their expectations of slavery varied accordingly.[52] Moreover, the second generation also included a mixed, "mulatto", population, almost always the result of unrecognised, even illicit, sexual liaisons between White men and enslaved women. Sometimes such liaisons led to the emancipation, effective or legal, of the women, but more often, the offspring of such unions were born slaves and remained so. The violation of enslaved women was a characteristic of the Atlantic crossing, and hence it is not always possible to discern when mulatto offspring were the result of relations with slave owners and other Whites in the colonies and when pregnancy occurred during transit. How did the mothers of children born of such shipboard rapes react, what did they see as their future and the future of their offspring? For a variety of reasons, the existence of mulatto slaves whose paternity was effectively denied suggests that racial distinctions were defined in specific ways. On the one hand, the prosperous slave colonies of the Caribbean experienced a steady growth in the "free" Black population, which was disproportionately mulatto, although there were also mulatto slaves and indeed mulatto slave owners. Racial distinctions were indeed blurry. Similarly, in many parts of Hispanic America, the racial distinctions also became confused, but in a different, although also racially perceived, manner.[53] The process there has often been referred to as the "browning" of the population, as the demographically-dominant Amerindian population absorbed Spanish and African alike. Mulatto/prado and other designations thereby emerged as forms of categorisation that promoted the "racialisation" of slavery. Ethnic identification appears gradually to have given way to racial categories.

In considering the differences between what happened to men and women under racial slavery and other forms of slavery, it should be recognised that the sexual dimension was regulated and violated in different ways. Women in Islamic and in non-Muslim African societies had the possibility of cohabitation, whether voluntary or not, which often led to improved status for children and the women themselves. In the Americas, what did the racial dimension impose on relationships between enslaved women and free men? Enslaved women in Africa could expect that sexual relationships would alter their status and the status of their children, but in the Americas, the racial dimension imposed a barrier that often thwarted such expectations. When children of slave women were recognised, they often attained a higher status, but very often paternity was not recognised in the Americas and children, therefore, continued in bondage.[54] Because the mulatto/free Black population was descended from such sexual liaisons, this process was imbedded in the society as an ongoing struggle. In the Americas, there were firm lines of racial difference, while under Islam and in non-Muslim African societies, there were no such distinctions. In the Americas, descendants of mixed liaisons between slave and free could aspire to membership in the class of freed Blacks and mulattoes, but not membership in the White class. There were no such restrictions in Africa or Islamic lands based on race.

In the context of the trans-Atlantic slavery, at what point did Africans begin to recognise the racial dimension of their enslavement? In Africa, the enslaved sometimes recognised their subordination, on ethnic, religious and political grounds – but never on racial grounds. J.K. Fynn has expressed the absence of racism on the Gold Coast in the eighteenth century as follows: "There was no racism then; Black Man cheat; White Man cheat; everyone cheat; no racism."[55] In the Americas, subordination was not always racial, especially early in the history of some colonies; hence Irish indentured workers and slaves in Barbados and mainland North America sometimes staged coordinated resistance. In Brazil, generalisations about the nature of slave society in seventeenth-century Bahia do not apply to the nineteenth century. Each major economic development, whether the renewed growth of sugar and tobacco in Bahia, the development of the gold mines of Mineas Gerais or the coffee plantations of Sao Paulo, evolved in a specific context. Each phase in development relied on a distinctive grouping of enslaved Africans, who require identification and correlation with the history of their homelands before it can be fully understood what the newly enslaved thought about slavery and how they expected to survive in captivity. We contend that strategies of servility were not crystallised, and while scholarship has usually examined the shift in attitudes from the point of view of the primarily White enslaving class, the expectations of the enslaved as to differences in treatment for Black and White servile labour have to be reassessed. Our interest lies in examining these shifts from the point of view of the enslaved. Differences in pigmentation meant that individuals experienced servility as racial domination and therefore at variance with the expectations that would have seemed likely in Africa.

The response of enslaved Africans to racial domination reinforced ethnic loyalties. On the basis of ethnic loyalty, Akan became synonymous with Maroon resistance in Jamaica, as Monica Schuler and others have shown.[56] Similarly, John Thornton has drawn attention to the influence of the Kongo civil wars on events in Haiti and in Georgia/South Carolina and the consolidation of Kongo ethnicity.[57] Ethnic identification, while a vital reflection of how people responded to enslavement in the Americas, nonetheless was ultimately subordinated to race, so that over generations the racial dimension superceded and then fully replaced the ethnic. When did slaves perceive maroons, other slaves, freed blacks as racial colleagues and not merely as members of different ethnic communities? Categories of identification recognised by the enslavers reflected a nascent community structure among those enslaved that often began on board ship, or even before, and resulted in the acceptance of languages of communication that frequently carried over into the Americas and thereby helped integrate new slaves into a community that had established an ethnic identity – that is, one based on acceptance of common origins and preserving an autonomous means of communication through a shared language that was not generally understood by members of the slave-owning elite. Shared language and common experience inevitably reinforced a sense of community and confirmed the perceptions of slave owners that slaves recognised ethnic loyalty.

This association of ethnicity with resistance highlights an important transition in the evolution of racialised slavery. The ethnic basis of slave identification is often attributed to the initiative of enslaved Africans themselves, who had to overcome Old World rivalries in order to form pan-ethnic unions to confront New World realities. On the contrary, we understand ethnic identification as a fluid and dynamic process affecting individuals and how they relate to social groups. We are suggesting that what was unique in the Americas was not the development of ethnic associations of slaves but the opposition of such identities with racial categories. In doing so, we are distinguishing between individual resistance and collective resistance, and attempt to examine the differences in terms of what people expected and how they responded when their expectations were not met. We assume that slavery as an institution fosters resistance, but we distinguish the responses of slaves in Africa to bondage from their experiences of the enslaved in the Americas, where racial distinctions became a factor in strategies of accommodation and resistance. We want to know when resistance moved from the individual to the collective, and thereby what roles ethnicity, religion and race played in shaping patterns of resistance. We contend that these questions relate to the issue of the expectations of slaves and how those expectations changed along the slave routes to the Americas.

Africans had expectations of how status could be improved under slavery both in Africa and, by extension, in the Americas as well. In Africa, there were various means by which to achieve manumission. Individuals who had been enslaved were successful in achieving freedom or otherwise escaping from slavery through ransom by relatives or other third parties.[58] Others received redress in future war, in which they were liberated, but there was also self-purchase through private employment and acts of charity. Morover, each of these avenues of freedom was possible on both sides of the Atlantic. In the Americas, however, the intensification of chattel status affected the incidence of emancipation, so that avenues of amelioration and liberation became more difficult. In this regard, the racial factor was of course very significant.

Whereas enslavers in widely separated places and with very different cultural and political views shaped the institution of slavery in increasingly racialist terms, the enslaved themselves came to accept racial characteristics as the basis of a collective strategy of accommodation and resistance. Racialist ideas and practices, which varied widely and changed over time, nonetheless introduced a new and powerful weapon in the subjugation of slave populations and implicitly laid the foundations for the emergence of an "African" consciousness in the Creole societies of the Americas. Because of recent scholarship, it is now possible to determine the specifics of the "African" cultural baggage that was taken across the Atlantic. By examining expectations, our aim has been to individualise the slave trade, and hence to demonstrate the importance of personal histories, whether in the form of profiles, autobiographies or oral traditions. These life stories can be used to examine notions of slavery in western Africa and the reality of racialised slavery in the Americas and thereby informs an analysis of identity and consciousness under slavery and how ethnicity, religion and other factors affected the ways individuals adjusted in the Americas.

Brathwaite's notion of adaptation as a crucial element in the process of creolisation is an important starting point in any discussion of the histories of enslaved Africans; for he assigned them an agency that was lacking in much of the previous scholarship. He rescued enslaved Africans from the ahistorical, non-active, unspecified role of victim. They came to life in his poetry more so than in his writing as an historian, for it is in poetry that he allowed Africans and their descendants to express their vibrancy and creativity. We suggest that their real life historical ancestors/counterparts are better understood and their limitations, possibilities and responses better appreciated with a fuller understanding of their expectations. We can only under these expectations if we ground them in the historical reality of their times. These expectations figured prominently in their adaptation to the reality of enslavement in the Americas. In the process they influenced the system of slavery (even as it influenced them) and over time created Creole societies. Thus, Creole society is not created from the adaptation of a generalised African background but from the specificity of the expectations and actions of identifiable individuals and communities.

NOTES

1. Research for this paper was funded by the Social Sciences and Humanities Research Council of Canada. An earlier version was presented at the conference, "Reunion: La Ruta del Esclavo en Hispanoamérica", Universidad de Costa Rica, 24–26 Feb. 1999.

2. M. Sobel, *The World They Made Together: Black and White Values in Eighteenth Century Virginia* (Princeton: Princeton University Press, 1987), p. 29.

3. Kamau Brathwaite, *The Development of Creole Society in Jamaica, 1770–1820* (Oxford: Clarendon Press, 1971), p. xv. It should be noted that the book is based on his 1968 Ph.D. thesis.

4. Ibid., p. 296.

5. Ibid., p. 307.

6. Sidney Mintz and Richard Price, *The Birth of African-American Culture: An Anthropological Perspective* (Boston: Beacon Press, 1992).

7. See, for example, the accounts in Philip Curtin, ed., *Africa Remembered: Narratives by West Africans from the Era of the Slave Trade* (Madison: University of Wisconsin Press, 1967). For an insightful discussion on this, see Richard Rathbone, "Some Thoughts on Resistance to Enslavement in West Africa", *Slavery and Abolition*, 16 (1985), pp. 11–22.

8. See, for example, the accounts in John W. Blassingame, ed., *Slave Testimony: Two Centuries of Letters, Speeches, Interviews, and Autobiographies* (Baton Rouge: Louisiana University Press, 1977), pp. 225–28, 254–61, 306–20; especially the accounts of William Thomas, John Homrn, Lorenzo Clarke, Maria Rosalia Garcia, Margarita Cabrera, Maria Luisa Macorra, Dolore Real, Luca Martina, and other former slaves from Cuba. Also see the various biographies in Curtin, ed., *Africa Remembered*; and Allan D. Austin, ed., *African Muslims in Antebellum America: A Sourcebook* (New York: Garland, 1984), especially the account of Mahommah Gardo Baquaqua (pp. 585–634). For a general discussion, see Paul E. Lovejoy, "Biography as Source Material: Towards a Biographical Archive of Enslaved Africans", in Robin Law, ed., *Source Material for Studying the Slave Trade and the African Diaspora* (Stirling: Centre of Commonwealth Studies, 1996), pp. 119–40.

9. For a general discussion of slavery in the African context, see Paul E. Lovejoy, *Transformations in Slavery: A History of Slavery in Africa* (New York: Cambridge University Press, 2nd edn., 2000).

10. See, for example, the various studies in Suzanne Miers and Igor Kopytoff, eds., *Slavery in Africa: Historical and Anthropological Perspectives* (Madison: University of Wisconsin Press, 1975); Claude Meillassoux, ed., *L'esclavage en Afrique precoloniale* (Paris: Maspero, 1975); Paul E. Lovejoy, ed., *The Ideology of Slavery in Africa* (Beverly Hills: Sage, 1981); and Claire C. Robertson and Martin A. Klein, eds., *Women and Slavery in Africa* (Madison: University of Wisconsin Press, 1983).

11. Emmanuel Kwaku Senah argues that conditions of servility in West African were fundamentally different from European constructs and did not include the full range of meanings attached to European ideas of slavery; see "What Slave? What Chattel?: A Philosophical Critique of Aspects of Caribbean Historical Literature from the Perspectives of Ga, Ewe-Foh, and Akan Culture and Language", paper presented at the 30th Annual Conference, Association of Caribbean Historians, Suriname, April 1998.

12. Douglas Chambers, "He Is an African But Speaks Plain: Historical Creolisation in Eighteenth-Century Virginia", in Alusine Jalloh and Stephen E. Maizlish, eds., *The African Diaspora* (College Station, TX: Texas A and M University Press, 1996), pp. 100–33; "My Own Nation: Igbo Exiles in the Diaspora", *Slavery and Abolition*, 18:1 (1997), pp. 72–97; and "Tracing Igbo into the Diaspora", in Paul E. Lovejoy, ed., *Identity in the Shadow of Slavery* (London: Continuum, 2000).

13. John Hunwick, "Islamic Law and Polemics over Race and Slavery in North and West Africa, 16th–19th Centuries", *Princeton Review* (1999); Paul E. Lovejoy, "Cerner les identites au sein de la Diaspora africaine: L'Islam et l'esclavage aux Ameriques", *Les cahiers des anneaux de la memoire*, 1 (1999).

14. Sylviane A. Diouf, *Servants of Allah: African Muslims Enslaved in the Americas* (New York: New York University Press, 1998).

15. Toyin Falola and Paul E. Lovejoy, eds., *Pawnship in Africa: Debt Bondage in Historical Perspective* (Boulder: Westview Press, 1994); Paul E. Lovejoy and David Richardson, "The Business of Slaving: Pawnship in Western Africa, ca. 1600–1810", *Journal of African History*, 42:1 (2000).

16. Thomas Phillips, "The Voyage of the Hannibal in 1694–94", in Churchill, *Collection of Voyages and Travels* (London, 1732), vol. 4, pp. 218–19. See the discussion in Rathbone, "Enslavement in West Africa", pp. 17–18.

17. Edna G. Bay, "Dahomean Political Exile and the Atlantic Slave Trade", proceedings of the UNESCO/SSHRCC Summer Institute, "Identifying Enslaved Africans: The Nigerian Hinterland and the African Diaspora", York University, Toronto, 1997.

18. Testimony of Hugh Dalrymple, who served on Gorée in 1779 and made frequent excursions to the mainland; see Sheila Lambert, ed., *House of Commons Sessional Papers of the Eighteenth Century. Report of the Lords of Trade on the Slave Trade, 1789*, part 1 (Wilmington, Del: Scholarly Resources Press, 1975), vol. 69, p. 25.

19. Mintz and Price, *African-American Culture*; Philip Morgan, "The Cultural Implications of the Atlantic Slave Trade: African Regional Origins, American Destinations and New World Developments", *Slavery and Abolition*, 18:1 (1997), pp. 122–45; Morgan and Ira Berlin, *Many Thousands Gone: The First Two Centuries of Slavery in North America* (Cambridge, MA: Harvard University Press, 1998), pp. 102–3.

20. On the methods of enslavement, see, for example, David Northrup, *Trade without Rulers: Pre-Colonial Economic Development in South-Eastern Nigeria* (Oxford: Oxford University Press, 1978); Lovejoy, *Transformations in Slavery*, pp. 66–87, 135–58; and Robin Law, "Legal and Illegal Enslavement in the Context of the Trans-Atlantic Slave Trade", paper presented at Colloque: Les Heritages du Passe: Cinq Siecles de Relations Europe-Afrique-Amerique, Dakar, 1997.

21. James Walvin, *An African's Life: The Life and Times of Olaudah Equiano, 1745–1797* (London: Continuum, 1998). Also see various papers presented at the conference on "Repercussions of the Slave Trade: The Interior of the Bight of Biafra and the African Diaspora", Enugu, Nigeria, July 2000.

22. Account reported by James Arnold, who was at Bimbia in 1787; see Lambert, ed., *House of Commons Sessional Papers of the Eighteenth Century*, vol. 69, p. 50.

23. For an overview, see Lovejoy, *Transformations in Slavery*, and the references cited therein.

24. Bay, "Dahomean Political Exile"; Law, "Legal and Illegal Enslavement"

25. Rodney, "Slavery and Other Forms of Oppression."

26. Paul E. Lovejoy and David Richardson, "Trust, Pawnship, and Atlantic History: The Institutional Foundations of the Old Calabar Slave Trade", *The American Historical Review*, 104:2 (1999), pp. 333–55.

27. Law, "Legal and Illegal Enslavement".

28. Lovejoy, "Situating Identities".

29. John Thornton, "'I Am the Subject of the King of Congo': African Political Ideology and the Haitian Revolution", *Journal of World History*, 4:2 (1993), pp. 181–214.

30. Jose Curto, "An Unlawful Prize: Slave Raiding and Luso-African Relations between the Kwanza and Kwango Rivers, 1805", Harriet Tubman Seminar, York University, 1999.

31. Also see David Eltis, *The Rise of African Slavery in the Americas* (Cambridge: Cambridge University Press, 2000).

32. Eric Williams, *Capitalism and Slavery* [1944] (London: Andre Deutch, 1964 edn.), pp. 9–19.

33. Ivor Wilks, *Asante in the Nineteenth Century: The Structure and Evolution of a Political Order* (Cambridge: Cambridge University Press, 1975), pp. 176–78.

34. John Beecroft, "Account of a Visit to the Capital of Benin, in the Delta of the Kwara or Niger, in the Year 1838", *Journal of the Royal Geographical Society*, 14 (1841), pp. 191–92.

35. Account of Henry Nicholls, 1804–04, in *Records of the African Association (1788–1831)*, ed., Robin Hallet, (London, 1964), p. 197.

36. Antonio T. Bly, "Crossing the Lake of Fire: Slave Resistance during the Middle Passage, 1720–1842", *Journal of Negro History*, 83:2 (1998), pp. 178–86.

37. Williams, *Capitalism and Slavery*, pp. 197–208; Michael Craton, *Testing the Chains: Resistance to Slavery in the British West Indies* (Ithaca: Cornell University Press, 1982); Mary Turner, *Slaves and Missionaries: The Disintegration of Jamaican Slave Society, 1787–1834* (Champagne-Urbana: University of Illinois Press, 1982); and Emilia Viotti da Costa, *Crowns of Glory, Tears of Blood: The Demerara Slave Rebellion of 1823* (New York: Oxford University Press, 1994). Also see Eugene Genovese, *From Rebellion to Revolution* (Baton Rouge: Louisiana University Press, 1979) Gary Okihiro, ed., *In Resistance. Studies in African, Caribbean, and Afro-American History* (Amherst: University of Massachussetts Press, 1986).

38. Rodney, "Slavery and Other Forms of Social Oppression on the Upper Guinea Coast in the Context of the Atlantic Slave Trade", *Journal of African History*, vol. 7, no. 4 (1966), pp. 431–43.

39. Lovejoy and Richardson, "Old Calabar Slave Trade", pp. 353–55; Lovejoy and Richardson, "Business of Slaving"; and Ugo Nwokeji, "The Biafran Frontier:

Trade, Slaves, and Aro Society, c. 1750–1905". Ph.D. thesis, unpublished, University of Toronto, 1999.

40. Robin Law, "On Pawning and Enslavement for Debt in the Pre-Colonial Slave Coast", in Falola and Lovejoy, eds., *Pawnship in Africa*, pp. 55–70.

41. W. Jeffrey Butler, *Black Jacks: African American Seamen in the Age of Sail* (Cambridge, MA: Harvard University Press, 1997).

42. Pierre Verger, *Trade Relations between the Bight of Benin and Bahia, 17th–19th Century* (Ibadan: University of Ibadan Press, 1976); Bellarmin Coffi Codo, "'Les Bresiliens' en Afrique de l'ouest: Hier et aujourd'hui", *Les Cahiers des Anneaux de la Memoire*, 1 (1999); João Reis, *Slave Rebellion in Brazil: The Muslim Uprising of 1835 in Bahia*, trans. Arthur Brakel (Baltimore: Johns Hopkins University Press, 1993).

43. Commissioner of Sierra Leone to Canning, April 1825, as quoted in Rathbone, "Enslavement in West Africa", p. 18.

44. See the testimony of Mark Cook, reporting on Jamaica in 1791, in Lambert, ed., *House of Commons Sessional Papers, Slave Trade 1791 and 1792*, vol. 72, p. 194; also comments of Isaac Wilson, surgeon, who examined slaves who had hung themselves on board ship at Bonny in 1788; in ibid., p. 567. Also see Rathbone, "Resistance to Enslavement", 14; and John Saillant, "Explaining Syncreticism in African-American Views of Death: An Eighteenth Century Example", *Culture and Tradition*, 17 (1995), pp. 25–41.

45. William D. Piersen, "White Cannibals, Black Martyrs: Fear, Depression, and Religious Faith as a Cause of Suicide among New Slaves", *Journal of Negro History*, 62 (1977), pp. 147–59; Barry Higman, *Slave Populations of the British Caribbean, 1807–1834* (Kingston: UWI Press, 1995), pp. 295, 343–46. For a reference to the fear that Europeans were cannibals, see William Bosman, *A New and Accurate Description of the Coast of Guinea* [1705] (London: Frank Cass, 1967 reprint), pp. 363–65.

46. Testimony of Falconbridge, in Lambert, *Sessional Papers*, vol. 72, pp. 581, 626.

47. Barbara Bush, "Hard Labour: Women, Childbirth and Resistance in Caribbean Slave Societies", *History Workshop*, 36 (1993), pp. 83–99; Todd L. Savitt, "Smothering and Overlaying of Virginia Slave Children: A Suggested Explanation", *Bulletin of the History of Medicine*, 49 (1979), pp. 400–4; Michael P. Johnson, "Smothered Slave Infants: Were Slave Mothers at Fault?", *Journal of Negro History*, 62 (1977), pp. 147–59.

48. Rathbone, "Enslavement in West Africa", pp. 21–22, n. 17, n. 25.

49. See various studies in forthcoming volume on slavery and memory, edited by Ralph Austen.

50. See the various testimonies in Lambert, *House of Commons Sessional Papers*.

51. For the ratio of African-born to American-born in the slave population, see Eltis, *Rise of African Slavery in the Americas*.

52. Hilary McD. Beckles, *Centering Woman: Gender Discourses in Caribbean Slave Society* (Kingston: Ian Randle, 1999).

53. Colin Palmer, "From Africa to the Americas: Ethnicity in the Early Black Communities of the Americas", *Journal of World History*, 6:2 (1995), pp. 223–36. Also see Teresa Castello Yturbide, "La Indumentaria de las Castas del Mestizaji", *Artes de Mexico*, 8 (1998), pp. 72–80.

54. Hilary McD. Beckles, "Female Enslavement in the Caribbean and Gender Ideologies", in Lovejoy, ed., *Identity in the Shadow of Slavery*, pp. 163–82; Beckles, "Sex and Gender in the Historiography of Caribbean Slavery", in Verene A. Shepherd, et al., eds., *Engendering History: Caribbean Women in Historical Perspective* (Kingston: Ian Randle, 1995), pp. 125–40.

55. *The African Trade*, BBC Timewatch, November 1997.

56. Monica Schuler, "Akan Slave Rebellions in the British Caribbean", *Savacou*, 1:1 (1970), pp. 8–31; and "Ethnic Slave Rebellions in the Caribbean and the Guianas", *Journal of Social History*, 3 (1970), pp. 374–85.

57. Thornton, "Subject of the King of Congo"; and *Africa and Africans in the Making to the Atlantic World* (Cambridge: Cambridge University Press, 2nd edn., 1998).

58. Paul E. Lovejoy, "Murgu: The Wages of Slavery in the Sokoto Caliphate", *Slavery and Abolition*, 24:1 (1992), pp. 168–85; and Lovejoy, "Muslim Freedmen in the Atlantic World: Images of Emancipation and Self-Redemption", conference on "From Slavery to Freedom: Manumission in the Atlantic World", paper presented at the Conference on Manumission, College of Charleston, 4–7 October 2000.

Percy C. Hintzen

Chapter 5

RACE AND CREOLE ETHNICITY IN THE CARIBBEAN

CARIBBEAN IDENTITY

Caribbean identity occurs within the discursive space of the "Creole". To be "Caribbean" is to be "creolised" and within this space are accommodated all who, at any one time, constitute a (semi)-permanent core of Caribbean society. Creolisation brought with it notions of organic connections across boundaries of ethnicised and racialised difference. It was the mechanism through which colonial discourses of difference, necessary for its legitimation, were accommodated. Everyone located in its discursive space, whatever her/his diasporic origin, becomes transformed in a regime of identific solidarity. At the same time, the Creole construct is integrally inserted into a discourse of exclusion as a boundary-maintaining mechanism. Maintaining a strict and rigid boundary between "Caribbean" and "non-Caribbean" (local versus foreign) has functioned strategically as a mechanism for manipulation in the maintenance of order and control.[1]

From this perspective, Caribbean ethnicity is constituted by its créolité. In their panoptic gaze, White colonisers imposed créolité to render invisible the racialised division of labour and the racial allocation of power and privilege. Historically, the discourse of racial difference has been shifted to distinctions between the Creole and non-Creole. The result has been a valorisation of White

The sot as restage

purity, located outside Creole space. This valorisation, at the root of White supremacy, became the foundation principle of colonial power, privilege, honour and prestige. Créolité went hand-in-hand with the symbolic capital of Whiteness.[2] It offered the possibility of "whitening" while demonstrating the consequences of descent into the world of savagery represented, in European discursive construction, by the colonised.

Nationalism, according to Benedict Anderson, is to be understood in terms of "the large cultural system that preceded it, out of which – as well as against which – it came into being".[3] And culture constitutes the representations and practices of ethnicity. As its precedent, créolité has imposed upon Caribbean nationalism European aspirations that have become hidden behind the veil of anti-colonialism. It has served to hide commonalties in social practice that could have formed the basis of counterdiscursive challenges to North Atlantic power. The visualisation of similarities located outside of European constructs could have come with "new possibilities for struggle and resistance, for advancing alternative cultural possibilities".[4]

Creole discourse has been the bonding agent of Caribbean society. It has functioned in the interest of the powerful, whether represented by a colonialist or nationalist elite. It is the identific glue that bonds the different, competing and otherwise mutually exclusive interests contained within Caribbean society. It paved the way for the accommodation of racialised discourses of difference upon which rested the legitimacy of colonial power and exploitation. Difference was rendered invisible in a cognitive merger created and sustained by its impositions. Competing interests and relations of exploitation and privilege became socially organised in a fluid clinal system of racial and cultural hierarchy. This was the observation of Caribbean sociologist Lloyd Braithwaite in what has been termed a "reticulated" colour-class pattern of social stratification by anthropologist Leo Despres.[5]

Look of Braithwal

To be Caribbean, then, is to occupy the hierarchical, hybridised, "Creole" space between two racial poles that serve as markers for civilisation and savagery. It is to be constituted of various degrees of cultural and racial mixing. At the apex is the White Creole as the historical product of cultural hybridisation. The Afro-Creole is located at the other end of the Creole continuum. The "creolisation" of the latter derives from transformative contact with Europe's civilising influences and from physical separation from Africa. Valorised forms of European racial and cultural purity become unattainable ideals in Creole representation and practice. Distance from the ideal European phenotype and from Europe's cultural practices determines and defines the Creole's position in the social hierarchy.

Thus, the principles of hierarchisation of Caribbean-Creole society are intimately tied to notions of European civilisation and African savagery. When applied to Europeans, creolisation implies the taint of savagery. When applied to Africans it implies a brush with civilisation. The Caribbean is the location where civilisation and savagery meet and where both become transformed. In this regard, Creole nationalism becomes a quest to be fully European.

The discourse of purity is one of the means through which disciplinary power is imposed upon Caribbean society. Under colonialism, White purity came to be represented as symbolic capital in the practices of the colonial administrators. This was contrasted with the hybridised practices of the White Creole. In the English colonies these different regimes of representation were concretised in colonial institutional practices of the nineteenth century. In the administration of governance, White Creole practices were represented in a merchant-planter-dominated financial college, which became the representative arm of the local White population. British colonial interests came to be signified and represented in the practices of a Court of Policy that served, in effect, as the legislative arm of government. Executive power was exercised through a colonial administration centred on the governor and comprising civil servants appointed by the Crown.[6] This development in political representation and practice contributed significantly to the process of White creolisation. It paralleled the development of divergent material interests between local and metropolitan capitalists. It differed across territory, irrespective of colonial jurisdiction, and presaged differences in the presence and significance of White Creoles in the development of Creole identity across the region.

THE DISCOURSE OF PURITY

The hybridised reality of Creole society left little room for accommodation of claims to cultural and racial purity. It is important to emphasise here that purity, like race, is socially constructed. It emerges out of discursive regimes of representation and practice. In Dominica, for example, despite a long history of racial intermixing with Blacks, cultural conversion, and the practice of Creole forms of social organisation, discourses of purity still exclude the putative descendants of the indigenous Kalinago ("Caribs") from Creole society. Purity emerged as a boundary defining and maintaining principle separating Creole society from the external world. It is a central principle in the discourse of difference that separates the "local" Creole White from the foreign "pure" European. This distinction is quite important in the assertions by the national elite of cultural claims to the new global order of North Atlantic universalism. These assertions have been made possible by nationalist rejection of White supremacy. As symbolic and cultural capital (acquired knowledge, skill and capabilities) such assertions have come to embody the new European aspirations of the nationalist elite.

To be "genuinely" White in the Caribbean is to be culturally and racially pure, untainted by absorption into the society of the former enslaved Blacks. This taint of impurity, forged out of cultural and sexual contact with the African, became the basis for exclusion of White Creoles from colonial power and privilege. Paradoxically, the organic connection to the "territory", which was at the root of such exclusion, assured the White Creole a position of privilege in nationalist construction. White inclusion in the nationalist space suggests the need for a much more nuanced view of the nationalist movement. The embrace of representations and practices of the racialised European mirrors precisely, the position of the nationalist movement toward European institutional and cultural forms. Many of the latter were adopted wholeheartedly after independence.[7] Whiteness, however tainted, retains its valorised position in Creole-nationalist construction.

The rights of White Creoles to social and economic privilege and preference in the territorial space were retained, and even enhanced, with the departure of the colonial power. In many instances, White Creoles are used as international brokers in the new regimes of sovereignty. At the same time, their representation as cultural and racial hybrids and their organic claims to the territory served to protect their social and economic privilege in the crucible of anti-colonial nationalism with its anti-European and anti-White implications. Such representations rendered their "Whiteness" invisible in the face of a nationalist rejection of White supremacy. In this way, White creolisation became the mechanism for the non-problematisation of Whiteness. It legitimised a post-colonial version of racial capitalism and explains the continued domination of Whites in the private sector of the post-colonial Caribbean.

Thus, the nationalist movement was neither anti-White nor anti-European. Rather, it was a contestation of the claims of Whites and Europeans to supremacy and superiority. Its various assertions of Africanity in national expression must be understood in these terms. The meaning of such assertions continues to be subject to debate among scholars and writers in the Francophone Caribbean under conditions where nationalist ambitions have been frustrated. Rather than a shift to sovereign independent status like their Anglophone counterparts, the French Antilles have become incorporated into the administrative and jurisdictional structure of the French state as *départements*. Frustrated nationalist ambitions have fuelled the development of a Créoliste movement "agitating for the local culture and language of the French West Indies".[8] This has supplanted earlier nationalist expressions framed around notions of Négritude. Leading members of the movement have rejected Négritude's notions of Africanity that were integral to Caribbean nationalism. They consider claims to an African past to be an "illusion of Europe with that of Africa".[9] They have painstakingly pointed out the contradictions in the Négritude movement in the support provided by its leadership, headed by Aimé Césaire of Martinique, for *département* status and in Césaire's firm embrace of the party-politics of France. In all of this, what clearly emerges is the rejection of Africa and an embracing of Europe. It is an embrace that is firmly implanted in Caribbean nationalist representations and practices. Its themes are more convincingly evident in the competing versions of nationalist expression in the French Caribbean. They are not so obvious in its Anglophone versions. The necessity of challenging the authorial power of Britain rendered invisible the latter's fundamentally European character.

Creole discourse locates all with claims to purity outside of the territorial community of the Caribbean. This is the point of the Créolistes charge of African and European illusion. Indeed, they go a step further by valorising hybridity as "the vanguard of a world-wide movement".[10] In other words, créolité portends the racial and cultural hybridity of a new North Atlantic that is at the forefront of neoglobalisation. Such hybridity is essential to the notions of Creole nationalism and to the European aspirations contained within them. It substantiates the self-location of the Creole at the centre of a new globalisation of the Europeanised North Atlantic. Thus, Patrick Chamoiseau, one of the movement's leading ideologues, describes creolisation as a "great poetics of relation, which allows people to express their newfound diversity, to live it fluidly. In creolisation, there never comes a time of general synthesis, with everyone beatifically at one with one another."[11]

Thus, claims to purity, essentialised around geographic discourses of origin, cannot be accommodated in Creole discourse. This is the basis of the Créolistes' discomfort with "illusions of Africa and Europe". It is why the North must first undergo a *métissage* transformation to accommodate the European aspirations of Creole nationalism. Thus, firmly embedded in nationalist aspirations is the goal of the conversion of Europe into the pregnable, transitory and open space that is the Caribbean. This is very much what has occurred in the French Antilles. The assertion of créolité is very much a declaration of the hybridisation of European space occupied exclusively by Whites. Indeed, the term Creole, before its hybridisation, signified the representations and practices of White French Caribbeans known as *Békés*. It referred specifically to "a White person of pure race born in the Antilles".[12]

Post-emancipation indentureship imposed its own legitimating regime of exclusion. Its legitimacy rested upon the "racial" and cultural location of the new indentures outside of the European-African continuum of Creole society. But the new rationality of exclusion also applied to European and African post-slavery indentures. Portuguese indentures, imported from Madeira, were unable to make immediate claims of racial affinity with the White Creoles in Trinidad and British Guiana (now Guyana). They remained for a time outside of Creole society. For post-emancipation African indentures, the boundary maintaining distinction between African and Afro-Creole, typical of slave systems, prevailed. Once inserted into plantation society, however, Portuguese and Africans became quickly amalgamated. For the African, creolisation came with location at the lowest rung in the colour-class hierarchy.[13] The Portuguese took over from Coloureds in small-scale retailing. They followed a trajectory of incorporation into Creole society by Whites and near Whites as "trading minorities".[14] This was also the path followed by the small migrant population of Lebanese, Syrians, Jews and post-indenture Chinese who, with the Portuguese, were able to establish themselves in the retail sector, particularly in Trinidad and Jamaica.

Amalgamation has become integral to the historical reproduction of Creole identity. It calls for an abnegation of purity through sexual and cultural immersion. The Creole space "swallows everything up . . . remaining permanently in motion, pushing us headlong in a movement of diversity, of change and exchange."[15] "Blending and impurity" stand as its fundamental values.[16] With the exception of the Syrians and Lebanese, whose cultural forms disappeared with their creolisation, immersion has acted, historically, to modify the African-European continuum in the Anglophone Caribbean. Rituals and practices of Creole transformation can include racial immersion through miscegenation. Cultural immersion can occur through marriage, religious conversion, association and adoption of the tastes and styles of Creole society. Cohabitation has become quite important in individual practices of creolisation. For the offspring of the ensuing unions, Creole parentage negates any claim to purity. It brings with it automatic location within the White-Black continuum. To some degree, cohabitation with White Creoles has offered the most acceptable means of immersion into Creole society for those located outside of the European-African space. As the most "desirable" of the Creoles, cohabitation with Whites serves to lessen the social opprobrium of creolisation with its implications for impurity. Thus, with the exception of the Whites who were pushed "downward" into Creole space, the thrust of creolisation has always been upward to the European end of the racial and cultural spectrum. The quest of the nationalist movement was to penetrate the barrier of racial purity by hybridising European space.

Exclusion and Incorporation

Symbolic exclusion is the instrument of disciplinary power wielded historically against diasporic communities functionally integrated into Caribbean political economy. It rendered legitimate the systematic denial of any claims non-Creoles might make upon the resources of Creole society. This became the basis for exclusion from opportunities provided through access to these resources. While historically pervasive, the discriminatory and exploitative consequences of symbolic exclusion were not always universal. With exclusion came also the benefits of freedom from the normative strictures of Creole society. It created opportunities unavailable to those located in the colour/class hierarchy of Creole social space. The discourse of purity served historically, until well into the twentieth century, to confine Asian Indians to rural agriculture and to justify their semiservile status. At the same time, however, Asian Indians have managed to use peasant agricultural practices as a springboard for upward mobility through business and the professions. In the process, they were able to eviscerate the social stigma of agricultural labour. Their agricultural background did not prefigure in social evaluations of their fitness for business and higher education, as it would have been for Creole subjects. As "outsiders", these standards of evaluation were rendered irrelevant.

The benefits of exclusion were evident, also, in the ability of Chinese and Portuguese (coming in as nineteenth-century indentures), Syrians, Lebanese and the small number of Jews (all arriving after World War I) to exploit economic opportunity. Their exclusion from Creole society freed them from the strictures of colour imposed by their light complexion. As such, they were able to ignore the principles of behaviour and association implicated in the colour/class hierarchy of Creole society. They established themselves in petty trade by developing highly personalised relationships with customers lower down the colour/class hierarchy. From here, they created niches in small-scale retailing, particularly in Trinidad, Jamaica and British Guiana (now Guyana). Their activities, and the pattern of associations and practices engendered by them, became the springboards for the structural and social insertion of their members into colonial Creole society. Once located in Creole space, they were able to combine symbolic capital (derived from their colour) with economic capital to move up the social hierarchy. Many came to occupy positions identical with or just below Creole Whites. What became most evident in their upward mobility was the importance of the symbolic capital of Whiteness. This pattern of amalgamation and upward mobility was not available to the over 40,000 post-emancipation Africans brought to the Caribbean between 1834 and 1867 for plantation labour.[17] Their amalgamation occurred at the lowest rung of the colour/class continuum of Creole society.

It is through racial and cultural incorporation that the transitory nature of Creole society is preserved. Incorporation allows Caribbean society to respond to the constantly changing pressures and demands from outside its borders. These must be accommodated for the very economic survival of the territories of the region. Practices of amalgamation have changed the racial and cultural character of Creole society. They have produced new forms of racial hybridity involving, particularly, Asian Indian and Chinese post-slavery additions to plantation society. Similarly, new emergent forms of cultural hybridity have become integrated into Creole practice. Thus, cultural and racial insertion has contributed to an historical reformulation of Creole identity. It has produced, over time, a modification of its racialised construction. Dark skin continues to retain the signifying power of inferiority. However, its exclusive association with African diasporic origin is no longer a firmly entrenched principle. Thus, a White-Black polarity based on colour has replaced Europe and Africa at opposite ends of the Creole continuum. This has been particularly the case as new diasporic communities with origins in Asia, the Middle East, and in the indigenous population of the region have become immersed into Caribbean reality. "Blackness", however, continues, by and large, to retain its association with Africa in an ongoing counter discourse to Creole construction. This is quite evident in the regional spread of the Rastafarian movement that originated in Jamaica[18] and in the Orisha religious movement in Trinidad.[19]

For the most part, the indigenous and diasporic communities with cultural and racial origins outside Africa and Europe remain, in representation and practice, outside Creole reality. For members of these communities, amalgamation is available through individual practices of cultural and sexual immersion. For Asian Indians, individual practices of racial miscegenation with Afro-Creoles have been significant enough to produce a distinctive Creole variant identified as "Douglas" in local lexicon. As the products of Afro-Indian unions, "Douglas" have become integral to the construction of Creole identity in Guyana and Trinidad. They have also come to symbolise the threat posed by creolisation to Asian Indian purity. The theme of "Douglarisation" emerges persistently in Asian Indian narratives of purity. It has become emblematic of the polluting consequences of sexual contact with Africans. "Douglarisation", therefore, is the process of transformation of Asian Indians into racial Creoles through miscegenation. Another route to Asian Indian creolisation is through cultural amalgamation. Asian Indians may enter the social space of Creole organisation through practices of inter-marriage, religious conversion, Creole association (including location of residence) and through the adoption of Creole style and tastes.

The representations and practices of créolité are responses to the deployment of symbolic power at the disposal of the constituents of its various segments and of those located outside its symbolic space. Each is engaged in a constant struggle to define Creole reality. Creoles activate honour and prestige as symbolic power, they activate resources of economic, social and cultural power available to them, and they activate the privilege of belonging in order to maintain créolité's existing integrity. Those excluded from créolité definition are perpetually engaged in efforts to redefine its character or to challenge its centrality in national conceptions of belonging. These struggles produce constant reformulations over time of the cognitive schemata that inform Creole identity and out of which its representations and practices are fashioned. They have also produced territorially specific manifestations of Creole constructs.

Trinidad provides an example of the complexities and idiosyncrasies of Creole construction and its implication for nationalist discursive formation. The European cultural component of Trinidadian society has been shaped quite significantly by Spanish colonialism (the former colonial power) and by the presence of a French merchant plantocracy (via Haiti after the Haitian revolution). As "local Whites", French and Spanish Creoles were historically differentiated from the administrative class of the British in colonial representation and practice. As a result, Creole identity in Trinidad became heavily infused with French and Spanish representations and with Roman Catholicism. It has also been influenced by the presence of Asian Indian, Chinese, Portuguese, Syrian and Lebanese diasporic populations and by the various racial and cultural hybridities produced in social interaction among all these groupings. In particular, hybridised rituals and symbols of Asian Indian representations and practices are gaining considerable visibility in Creole construction. This is despite the latter's historical exclusion from the creolised space of Trinidadian identific discourse. At the same time, Trinidadian créolité has amalgamated the representations and practices of "Douglas" (the products of miscegenous unions between Africans and Indians), Portuguese (by giving up their claims to Whiteness), and Chinese, Syrians and Lebanese (through cultural amalgamation and miscegenation).

At over 40 per cent of the population, the size and functional integration of East Indians in Trinidad have had profound consequences for the reproduction of Creole society. Their strategic presence has produced considerable challenges to the central role that créolité has played in nationalist construction. The fundamental contradiction between the structural integration of Asian Indians in Trinidad's political economy and their symbolic exclusion from nationalist space has produced an increasing crescendo of national conflict as well as persistent contestation of nationalist discourse. Access to Creole society has been available only to those members of the Asian Indian community prepared to reject representations and practices of purity on cultural grounds or to those who are prepared to reject patterns of racial solidarity and marriage endogamy. One avenue for rejection is through conversion to Christianity. For the smaller population of Muslim Asian Indians (which constitutes less than 25 per cent of the total Asian Indian population), religion poses less of a barrier to creolisation given their monotheism and the common foundation of beliefs that they share with Christianity. As a result, Muslims have been much more visibly included in the representation and practices of Creole nationalist expression. However, discourses of purity continue to locate the large majority of Asian Indians, as Hindus, outside the national space. Members of the Asian Indian middle classes, particularly its economic, social, and political elite, experience most profound pressures for creolisation. This derives from their high degree of functional integration into the "Creole" segments of Trinidad's political economy. To this is added their own predispositions toward creolisation as they seek to realise the benefits of nationalism that have accrued to their Creole counterparts in the post-colonial era. The pressures and predispositions have resulted in the incorporation by many Hindus of more universal western forms into their religious practices and the opening up of their religion to Creole practitioners. It has produced a form of creolisation that comes with little sacrifice to Hindu identity.[20]

Notwithstanding the pressures placed upon the Hindu middle classes and their own predispositions for Creole incorporation, there is mounting resistance to creolisation among the Hindu cultural elite. In their campaign, they activate the symbolic power of purity to petition for inclusion in the nationalist space as Asian Indians. Hindu purity is deployed as a symbolic resource by these leaders to delegitimise "polluted" Creole discourse. The leaders reject the central role that Creole representations occupy in notions of national belonging. Such rejection is organised around narratives of cultural degradation directed, particularly, at the cultural ascendance of Afro-Creole forms in nationalist discourse. There is mounting contestation of the claim made by Afro-Creoles of their own central role in nation building. Asian Indians are beginning to present themselves as the true builders of the nation. Their cultural elite has constructed an historical narrative of Asian Indians as redeemers who have, time and again, delivered the country from the abyss of Afro-Creole degradation.[21] The Asian Indian challenge to Creole nationalism is not merely a quest for nationalist inclusion. Rather, it is an attempt to retain representations and practices of cultural purity while resisting "Douglarisation". It represents a redemptive counter-discourse to Afro-Creole nationalism and presents a fundamental challenge to Trinidadian créolité. It remains a rejection of the "blending and impurity" of the form of hybridity that occupies the critical centre in the value framework of Creole's discourse.

Despite Hindu challenges, the fundamental thrust of creolisation is deeply embedded in the historical development of Trinidadian national identity. Créolité occupies the critical core of the country's national psyche. This is evident in the mythic representation of the "Spanish". As a social construction of the ideal-typical Trinidadian, it has emerged as a means of managing the complexities and conflicting pulls of disaporic identity. But "Spanish" identity is instructive in another important way – it exposes and externalises the European aspirations that exist at the root of Creole discourse and that are integral to the country's nationalist expression. It is a narrative of a simpler time in Trinidad colonial history before the introduction of plantation slavery (and hence of the complexity of the African presence). The "Spanish" construct embodies all the positive elements of the various ethnic groupings that occupy the country's territorial space (creolised or otherwise). As such, it is a trope of hybridised harmony in the face of multiple and competing representations and practices of difference.[22] But it is a harmony forged out of idealised "European" qualities, devoid of notions of ethnic, cultural and social exclusivity.

In Trinidad, the struggle for the nation occurs in the field of symbolic production and reproduction. Representations and practices of purity are raised as challenges to Creole nationalism. In Guyana, symbolic representations of nationhood that valorise Creole cultural forms are less important than practices of institutional solidarity. This is related partly, to an historical absence of White Creoles in the colour class order of Guyanese social construction. Nationalist discourse did not have to accommodate a White Creole presence through the activation of colonial notions of cultural and biogenetic hybridity. The absence of Creole discourse left a cultural vacuum in the nationalist movement that was filled by competing racial claims to the state. Such claims were activated after 1955 through deployment by competing political elites of institutional resources under exclusive racial control. This occurred in the wake of a breakdown in the multi-racial nationalist movement. It set the stage for development of an integral association between nationalist organisation and existing racialised practices of institutional inclusion and exclusion.

Between 1957 and 1964, racial claims to the state by Asian Indians were held in check by colonial overlordship and by colonial predispositions to countenance the demands of the Creole elite for control of national power and privilege. But the efforts of the British colonial office to place this elite in power through fiat collapsed after an uncertain tenure between 1964–1967. Creole elite ascendance was stymied in the face of a successful effort to place a more Africa-centred stamp on Guyanese nationalist expression. During the 1960s, the African Society for Cultural Relations with Independent Africa (ASCRIA) had become highly integrated into the structure and organisation of the Black nationalist People's National Congress (PNC) that had run the country since 1964. ASCRIA's leaders enjoyed powerful positions in the government and saw their role as ensuring the location of the Black lower class at the centre of the country's nationalist agenda. In the colour-class hierarchy of Creole society, this grouping's historical location at the bottom of the socio-cultural ladder facilitated and reinforced identific notions of its own African origin. The Black lower class comprised Afro-Guyanese rural own-account peasantry and urban proletariat, many of whom were migrants from rural villages. ASCRIA was the organisational arm of its membership. The Association's leadership mounted challenges to Creole discourse with narratives of African belonging. Under its influence, the country's foreign relations shifted to an emphasis on the development of close relations with the African continent. At its insistence, elements of the state's national policies were adopted, almost wholeheartedly, from Tanzania's version of cooperative socialism.

The emphasis on Africa conflicted with the culturally rooted aspirations and practices of the country's Creole middle classes, a significant proportion of whom were Coloured. By 1971, middle-class opposition forced the ruling party to abandon its ideology of Africa-centred nationalism. In response, ASCRIA leaders resigned their government posts and began a scathing campaign against the ruling PNC. Added to rejection of an African-centred nationalism by the Black and Coloured middle classes was strong and organised opposition from an Asian Indian population that exceeded 50 per cent of the country's total. As a means of neutralising Asian Indian challenges to its nationalist agenda, the PNC was forced to embark upon a strategy of co-optation of the most strategic sectors of the Asian Indian political economy, particularly its businessmen, professionals and educated elite. This received added impetus from the ruling party's quest for institutional control of the public space. In turn, the Asian Indian elite came to rely upon the protection and patronage of a ruling party in control of the overdeveloped Guyanese state.

The absence of a legitimate historical cultural claim to nationhood, rendered Afro-Creole assertions of nationalism in Guyana quite problematic. Asian Indian opposition produced a need for co-optation of the Asian Indian elite. Co-optation combined with middle-class opposition to dilute Afro-Creole nationalist expression.

Through its strategy of co-optation, the ruling party exercised considerable control over the public activities of strategic sectors of the Asian Indian population. It was able, also, to neutralise the effects of Asian Indian opposition. East

Indians are strategically located in all the major institutional sectors of the political economy, much more so, in most cases, than the Creole population. This is particularly true of the local private sector, where ownership and control is almost exclusively Asian Indian and is reinforced by the type of racially en-dogamous patterns of recruitment and hiring that typifies every sector of Guyanese political economy. There is also a significant presence of East Indians in the professional sector. They enjoy an almost exclusive racial presence in the country's agro-productive sector as cash crop producers and plantation labour.

By 1975, the international relations of Guyana's ruling party shifted to a close alliance with Eastern Europe. This occurred in the wake of state take-over of the foreign private sector and of many large local merchant and trading enterprises. In the process, the "nation" came to be constituted by the institutions of the state. The latter began to play pervasive roles in almost every aspect of public behaviour. The justifying ideology of socialism displaced cultural notions of Creole national belonging from the centre of nationalist discourse.

Socialism, a Euro-Communist orientation in foreign policy, and co-optation of the Asian Indian institutional elite all combined to produce a form of nationalist expression that was less integrally tied to créolité than was the case in Trinidad. Guyanese nationalism began to take the form of state-centered institutional cooperativism. It became identified with the institutions of governance and with the domestic institutional interests represented by and identified with the governing elite and its allies.[23] In Trinidad, competition for the national space occurs over issues of its ethno-cultural character. In Guyana, competition for the national space occurs over access to the institutional resources of power. In both cases, however, challenges to nationalist construction emerged from within the Asian Indian population. In Guyana, they were mounted by representatives of East Indian working-class interests.

Nationalist expression in Guyana has come to incorporate the symbolic capital of the governing elite and the interests it represents. In popular consciousness, these continue to be understood in racial terms despite efforts at cross-racial co-optation. The result is a racialised struggle over control of the national space that takes place in the political arena. The struggle is objectified in political competition for control of the governing institutions of the state and takes place among competing racialised political organisations – these include political parties and trade unions. In 1992, the Asian Indian political elite, organised since the 1950s in the People's Progressive Party (PPP), regained the executive and legislative power that it lost in 1964. It proceeded to redefine the national space using the control it exercises over the executive and legislative branches of the state. In response, the campaign for control of the nation has shifted to the bureaucratic apparatus of government (including the country's police and security forces) and to the judiciary. Both remain largely under the control of a Black and Coloured bureaucratic elite.[24] These have become the locomotive centres of Afro-Guyanese challenges to an East Indian take-over of the institutionalised national space.

Asian Indians in Trinidad and Guyana have employed different strategies to challenge nationalist constructs and to redefine national identity. In Guyana, challenges have been mounted also by the Black lower classes. Each challenge represents a specific instance of the incorporation over time of multiple and competing claims to the national space. Each is a particular response to colonial and post-colonial discourses of exclusion, legitimised in the historical production and reproduction of Creole reality. Each challenge presents itself as an assault against the rituals, symbols, and institutions of Caribbean self-representation. In the final analysis, each represents a counter-discourse to the complexity of cultural and racial representations and practices constitutive of Creole identity and to the honour and prestige that underlie Creole claims to privilege and power. In Trinidad, créolité remains visible as the critical component of nationalist expression. In Guyana, it is rendered invisible by the institutional construction of national space. At the same time, it continues to be pervasive in the representations and practices of all the racialised groupings of elite. Its non-problematisation in Guyana has intensified the process of Asian Indian creolisation, producing a Creole elite distinguished from its Afro-European counterparts only by the racialised sources of its institutional power.

Creole discourse is so integral to national identity in the Caribbean that nation-state contestation seems to lead, inevitably, to the intensification of the process of creolisation for those located outside of Creole space. Efforts aimed at dislocation from the state seem to be capable of producing a more successful result. In Dominica, the Karifuna descendants of the indigenous Kalinago ("Caribs") are engaged in a struggle for autonomy against the Creole nation-state. The struggle is a manifestation of the developing organisation of indigenous peoples in Latin America and the Caribbean. It has emerged in response to colonial and post-colonial practices of exclusion and displacement organised through historical containment of the Karifuna in a Kalinago reserve. Ironically, these very practices have become bases for rejection of Creole nationalism. During colonialism, they facilitated the super exploitation of the Karifuna as they became structurally integrated into the Dominican political economy.

Karifuna contestation of nationalist authority occurs through rejection of the historical practices of marginalisation and displacement. They have engaged the legal system to make a claim for exclusive right of occupation of the very "Carib Territory" that was developed for their exploitation. In the process, the "Territory" has become transformed into the symbolic objectified centre of Karifuna identity. The demand for autonomy is accompanied, periodically, by ritual acts of purification. Such as the explusion of non-"Caribs", particularly Afro-Creole males and their Karifuna female partners, from "Carib" territory.[25] What is significant here is that Karifuna claims to territory are based on notions of prior occupation. The contestation of Creole nationalist practice is organised by groups with putative claims to indigenous identity – this provides them with consider-able moral legitimacy. Such legitimacy is transformed into symbolic power in the deployment of the honour and prestige that attaches to the rights of prior occupation. As such, Dominica provides an example of the strategic deployment of symbolic power in the contestation of Creole domination. This form of contestation is not confined to Dominica alone – parallel movements have emerged among "Carib" populations in St Vincent and the Grenadines.

Creole nationalism has been negotiated differently by the much larger indige-nous population of Guyana. "Amerindians" occupy a much more ambiguous position in Guyanese nationalist space compared with the Karifuna in Dominica. They do not have at their disposal a single territorial location that can be converted into a symbol of identific separation from Creole society. Rather, they are scattered throughout the hinterland of the country in numerous small communities under the disciplinary authority of Creole administrators and functionaries. Their integration into Creole society and into national institutions varies with geographic location and is not uniform. This is accompanied by an uneven pattern of economic integration into the Guyanese political economy. Amerindian communities display varying degrees of cultural hybridity: most of their members have been converted to Christianity and there are varying experi-ences of miscegenation across the several geographic communities. "Amerindi-ans" experience differing degrees of co-optation in the institutional arena of politics and have differing degrees of access to the institutionalised national space.

The absence of a definitive identific boundary between "Amerindian" and Creole societies has diluted demands for autonomy from nationalist repre-sentations and practices. Their indeterminate relationship to Creole practice and to nationalist expression has produced less of a predisposition to nationalist rejection than their counterparts in Dominica. This is despite participation in international and local organisations of indigenous peoples.[26]

In Barbados, Creole society has deviated little from its original colonial con-struction. In its historical reproduction, much of the European-African roots in its colour-class hierarchical social formation has been retained. The persistence of this ideal-typical form can be explained by a history of uninterrupted British colonial rule. There was no importation of labour for post-slavery indentureship and this minimised the possibility of counter-discourses to Creole formulation that appeared in countries like Guyana and Trinidad. A certain idiosyncrasy has emerged in the historical reproduction of Creole society. The Barbadian historical process of creolisation was fashioned much more from cultural rather than bio-genetic syncretisation. Practices of cohabitation between Europeans and Africans were significantly less than in the other territories and this is reflected in the relatively small number of persons classified as mixed. At 2.6 per cent, these "Coloureds" constitute an even smaller proportion of the population than Creole Whites who number around 3.3 per cent. Thus, the colour-class continuum is far less smooth and far more abrupt in Barbados. There is a considerably greater discernible distinction between White and Afro-Creoles in representation and practice. This distinction is only minimally mitigated by the presence of the small intermediary grouping of Coloureds. The local White Creole had considerable access to power and privilege in colonial organisation. White settlement and identification with the territory was fostered historically by colonial practices of White Creole governance. This was accompanied by a great degree of institutional exclusivity in economic, social and cultural practices. The local merchant-plantocracy, together with the colonial administrators, dominated the politics of the colony until the introduction of representative government in the mid-twentieth century. Since then, power has been shared with the Coloured and Black Creole middle classes.

Creole discourse has rendered almost impossible the accommodation of any diasporic community existing outside the European-African continuum in Barbados. The latter part of the twentieth century has seen immigration of a merchant class of South Asians that has grown to 0.5 per cent of the population. Despite an initial period of intermarriage within the local community, the social location of members of this grouping remains strictly confined to a position outside Creole nationalist space. There, they retain their cultural and racial distinctiveness as "foreign". This has contributed to the reinforcement of identific rituals of purity as Hindus and Muslims. These rituals are accompanied by strict practices of endogamy in marriage. Community organisation is tight and closed and there is an enforced social seclusion of women.[27]

The Euro-cultural aspirations of Creole nationalism are least hidden in Barbadian nationalist discourse. Anglophilia continues to be strong in Barbadian popular consciousness and is evident in the generalised pride expressed in the idea of the country as a "Little England". There has been little challenge mounted against the economic, social and symbolic power of the Creole Whites.

CONCLUSION

The representations and practices of Creole nationalism differ significantly across the territories of the Anglophone Caribbean. Such differences reflect the varying compositions of colonial and post-colonial societies and the different ways in which the diasporic communities have become inserted into political economy. Ultimately, they reflect, in all the manifestations of créolité, differences in the technical and social conditions of capitalist production over time and space. Conceptualisations of White purity continue to reinforce and legitimise a system of globalised dependency. Domestically, Creole nationalism continues to hide the reality of racial capitalism. Aspirations to cultural purity have prevailed in the face of hybridity and have been at the root of an endemic conflict over identity and nationalism in the region. They have also foreclosed opportunities for regional integration. Creole nationalism in the post-independence era has foreclosed possibilities for development of a social construction that can serve as an alternative to the cultural and social legacy of Europe. It has wedded the former colonies to patterns of international relations characterised by an uncritical acceptance of the North Atlantic as the center of the social, cultural, political and economic universe. This has been the tragedy of the current colonial construction of créolité in the Caribbean.

NOTES

1.   For an elaboration of the ideas discussed in this paper and their application to race and ethnicity in the Caribbean see Percy Hintzen, "Race and Creole Ethnicity in the Caribbean", in David Golberg and John Solmos, eds., *The Blackwell Companion to Racial and Ethnic Studies* (Oxford: Blackwell Publishers, 2001).

2.   The use of the term "symbolic capital" is taken from Pierre Bourdieu and pertains to the accumulation and display of symbols of honour and prestige that renders "unrecognisable" the true exploitative nature of relationships of economic exchange. It is "denied capital recognised as legitimate". See Pierre Bourdieu, *The Logic of Practice* (Stanford, CA: Stanford University Press, 1990), pp. 118 and 112–21.

3.   Benedict Anderson, *Imagined Communities* (London: Verso, 1983), p. 19.

4.   Arturo Escobar, *Encountering Development* (Princeton: Princeton University Press 1995), p. 155.

5. See Lloyd Braithwaite, "Social Stratification in Trinidad", *Social and Economic Studies*, 2 (1953), pp. 5–175, and Leo A. Despres, *Cultural Pluralism and Nationalist Politics in British Guiana* (Chicago: Rand McNally, 1967)

6. Vere T. Daly, *A Short History of the Guyanese People* (Georgetown: Daily Chronicle, 1966), p. 214.

7. The point here is not that White Creoles should not be included in the nationalist definition. Rather, it is to point out the paradox of this embrace by a nationalist movement rooted in challenges to White supremacy.

8. L. Taylor, "Créolité Bites: a conversation with Patrick Chamoiseau, Raphael Confiant, and Jean Bernabé", in *Transition*, 74 (n.d.), p. 124.

9. See Taylor, "Créolité Bites", p. 128.

10. Ibid., p. 141.

11. Ibid., p. 136.

12. Ibid., p. 132.

13. Maureen Warner-Lewis, *Guinea's Other Suns: the African Dynamic in Trinidad Culture* (Dover, Massachusetts: Majority Press, 1990).

14. D.G. Nicolls, "No Hawkers and Peddlers", *Ethnic and Racial Studies*, 34 (1981), pp. 422–26.

15. See Taylor, "Créolité Bites", p. 142.

16. Ibid., p. 137.

17. J. Asiegbu, *Slavery and the Politics of Liberation, 1787–1861* (London: Longman, 1969), pp. 189–90.

18. Barry Chevannes, *Rastafari: Roots and Ideology* (Syracuse: Syracuse University Press, 1995).

19. J. Houk, "Afro-Trinidadian Identity and the Africanisation of the Orisha Religion", in K. Yelvington, ed., *Trinidad Ethnicity* (Knoxville: University of Tennessee Press, 1993), pp. 161–79.

20. See Morton Klass, *Singing with Sai Baba* (Boulder: Westview Press, 1991).

21. Kevin A. Yelvington, *Producing Power: Ethnicity, Gender and Class in a Caribbean Workplace* (Philadelphia: Temple University Press, 1995), p. 77

22. Isha Khan, ed., "What is 'a Spanish'?: Ambiguity and Mixed Ethnicity in Trinidad", in K. Yelvington, ed., *Trinidad Ethnicity* (1993), pp. 180–207.

23. See Percy C. Hintzen, *The Costs of Regime Survival* (Cambridge and New York: Cambridge University Press, 1989), pp. 169–71

24. Percy C. Hintzen, "Democracy on Trial: The December 1997 Elections in Guyana and its Aftermath", *Caribbean Studies Newsletter*, 25 (1998), pp. 13–16.

25. C. Gregoire, P. Henderson and N. Kanem, "Karifuna: The Caribs of Dominica", in Rhoda E. Reddock, ed., *Ethnic Minorities in Caribbean Society* (St Augustine, Trinidad: University of the West Indies, Institute of Social and Economic Research, 1996), pp. 107–71.

26.   D. Fox and G.K. Danns, *The Indigenous Condition in Guyana* (Georgetown: University of Guyana, 1993).

27.   P. Hanoomansingh, "Beyond Profit and Capital: A study of the Sindhis and Gujaratis of Barbados", in Reddock, ed., *Ethnic Minorities in Caribbean Society,* (1996).

Rhoda Reddock

Chapter 6

CONTESTATIONS OVER CULTURE, CLASS, GENDER AND IDENTITY IN TRINIDAD AND TOBAGO

"THE LITTLE TRADITION"*

"Like monkeys pleading for evolution, each claiming to be whiter than the other, Indians and Negroes appeal to the unacknowledged White audience to see how much they despise one another. They despise one another by reference to Whites; and the irony is that their antagonism should have reached its peak today, when White prejudices have ceased to matter."[1]

Studies of social stratification, race, ethnicity and pluralism have characterised Caribbean social science since its inception, so to speak, in and around the 1950s. The Caribbean, of course, is a complex construction comprising in various definitions, the island archipelago, the Guianas on the north-east of South America, the islands north of the southern continent and various Central American countries, most frequently Belize, depending on the definition.

One of the defining characteristics of this region has been its experience of plantation, slave and/or bonded labour in a colonial context and the importation of diverse peoples to provide labour in the wake of the decimation or marginalisation of the indigenous peoples. Not surprisingly, therefore, next to family, the issues of race, ethnicity and social differentiation generally have been central to scholarship and indeed to everyday life in this region. In spite of these common-alities, the experience of social differentiation within the region has much that is similar and much that is different. Yet Caribbean scholars have sought to develop broad theoretical and conceptual frameworks which have relevance to the entire region.

The two most famous of these formulations are those of Jamaican sociologist the late M.G. Smith and Barbadian historian and cultural studies scholar Kamau Brathwaite.[2] To summarise, from as early as 1959, Smith developed a theory of plural society based on the earlier work of the Dutch economist, J.S. Furnivall. In Smith's own words: "For my part, although convinced by the contrast between Caribbean societies and others, I then knew of the relevance of Furnivall's concepts for Caribbean sociology."[3]

For Smith, plural societies were basically political units characterised by "cultural plurality" in relation to their social institutions such as "marriage, family, property, religion, economic institutions, language and folklore".[4] He defined cultural plurality as:

> . . . a condition in which two or more different cultural traditions characterise the population of a given society . . . Where cultural plurality obtains, different sections of the total population practise different forms of these common institutions; and . . . differ in their internal social organisation, their institutional activities, and their system of belief and value. Where this condition of cultural plurality is found, the societies are plural societies.[5]

In this definition, the salience attributed by Furnivall to economic structures in the maintenance of plural societies was rejected by Smith and replaced by an emphasis on culture. In the words of Glenn Sankatsing: "Smith who considers Furnivall's conceptualisation of pluralism as a general theory . . . purged it of its economic dimension and elaborated it into a social scientific model based on culture to understand and explain the complex Caribbean societies."[6] For some this was a reflection of Smith's rejection of Marxism and his continued reluctance to give "class" a central role in the analysis of Caribbean society.

What is interesting is that Smith developed this concept for the Caribbean based on research in what his critics see as some of the least plural societies of the region – Jamaica, Grenada and Carriacou. It is not surprising, therefore, that this theory is more often used in relation to the complex societies of the southern Caribbean such as Trinidad and Tobago, Guyana and Suriname,[7] than to the predominantly Afro-Creole societies of the rest of the region for which it was originally developed. In later writing and largely in response to criticism, Smith differentiated between what he defined as homogenous, plural and complex plural societies, and between the characteristic of pluralism (social and cultural) in contrast with an actual plural society.

The other competing theoretical approach, that of "Creole society", has been most fully developed by Kamau Brathwaite, based on the earlier writings of historian Elsa Goveia and anthropologist Dan Crowley. This concept is most fully developed in Brathwaite's *Contradictory Omens: Cultural Diversity and Integration in the Caribbean*. Here he articulates most sharply his conceptualisation of a "Creole" society and the process of "creolisation" as the result of the twin processes of "acculturation", the absorption of one culture by another and "interculturation", a more reciprocal and spontaneous process of enrichment and intermixture on both sides.[8]

In other words, Brathwaite saw Caribbean society as emerging both from the forced assimilation of Blacks to the dominant European colonial norms and behaviours and from the inadvertent interculturation of Whites into African-derived norms and behaviours and vice versa. This creolisation process was facilitated through socialisation – for example, through the seasoning process during the slave period – as well as through "imitation, native creation or indigenisation, language, sex and amorous influences".[9] This process, however, was uneven and the degree of Euro-Creole dominance in relation to the Afro-Creole varied within the population and over time, providing a continuum ranging from the Euro-Creole plantocracy and business elite to the rural folk. Central to this perspective was the recognition that New World Africans had not simply adopted European cultural norms and behaviours but in their forced assimilation transformed or indigenised them, creating Caribbean Creole culture and society. The concept of "creolisation" has had different responses in different parts of the region. Whereas it has been embraced in most of the northern Caribbean, including the Hispanic areas, it has had a more contentious response in the southern Caribbean. This is so because of the more complex nature of ethnic group relations in these societies. To a large extent, this approach, like most others prior to the 1980s, tended to concentrate on the overarching dominant/subordinate relations between Whites and Blacks/mixed (Coloureds), and to pay less attention to subordinate group relations between and among subordinate cultural/ethnic groups. This is expressed by Jamaican historian Verene Shepherd when she notes:

> Race relations studies in Jamaica show an overwhelming concern with Black-White relations, with only a few dealing in any detail with the interaction of other race groups in a situation of multiple-ethnic contact. Indeed though the subject has for long engaged the attention of historians and sociologists, most of

the studies which have emerged have tended to focus on the relations between dominants and subordinates, ignoring, for the most part, the subject of subordinate group relations.[10]

I expressed similar sentiments in relation to explorations of race/ethnicity, class and gender when I noted that:

> In the international literature on race, class and gender, little input has been made of the Caribbean experience. Indeed, most of the debate has centred around the experience of Afro-American women or Afro-British women in the metropolis, African women in South Africa and Indo-British women in Britain. Within that context, race, like class and gender becomes a basis of exploitation, discrimination and oppression of non-European (non-White) groups. No contribution to these discussions have [sic] yet been made on, for example, the issue ... in a situation where two or more non-White groups have antagonistic or non-antagonistic relations, albeit within a context of overall Euro-American imperialist domination.[11]

Creole-society theory has been particularly problematic in its application to the southern Caribbean, although in *Contradictory Omens*, Brathwaite attempts to deal with this complexity. The problem emerges in the differential understandings and usages of the term. Although, like plural-society theory it was developed in relation to other Caribbean societies, it is central to an understanding of problems of national identity and national culture in Trinidad and Tobago, Guyana and Suriname.

Originally, the term "Creole" was used to refer to all persons born within the region but with an external origin. Today in Trinidad and Tobago, for example, it is used in three senses: (1) to refer to an amalgam of descendants of Europeans who still dominate the local economy, known locally as French Creoles; (2) primarily by Indians to refer to persons of African descent, also referred to by a Hindu derivative "kirwal" and (3) to refer to cultural artifacts of the dominant culture such as Creole food, Creole bacchanal, and so on.[12] The term "Creole", therefore, for Indians is strongly identified with Afro-Creole culture and creolisation is seen by many as a process of cultural domination.

This rejection of or ambivalence towards Creole culture is to a large extent only recently being understood by Afro-Creole Trinidadians, largely as a result of action by Indian cultural activists. In an earlier paper, I examined the ways in which the definition of a national culture had become a contested terrain in post-independence Trinidad and Tobago where, until the 1970s, indigenous and African-derived art forms, belief systems, names, ways of life, language, dress and even foods were not accepted by the dominant Euro-Creole culture.[13]

As I noted earlier, the increased acceptance of Afro-Creole culture within the national culture, therefore, has to be seen first as the result of years of class struggle, as it was the poorest and working-class who were most creative and persistent in their creation and indigenisation of cultural forms. Second, it has to be seen as a cultural struggle, as it was a struggle by African-derived groups for the valorisation and acceptance of their creation by the European-dominated colonial and post-colonial societies. Afro-Creole dominated nationalist governments, since 1956, in response to grassroots pressure, have to some extent succeeded in valorising a national culture based on Creole norms and behaviours.[14] The question to be considered now is, what has been the relationship of other ethnic/cultural groups to the economically subordinate but culturally dominant Creole groups and culture? And herein lies the complexity of class, ethnicity and, as we shall see later on, gender. What is problematic here is the reality that this cultural dominance does not in the present instance in the Caribbean reflect a commensurate economic or political dominance even though it can certainly influence them.

THE CONSTRUCTION OF ETHNICITY AND IDENTITY IN TRINIDAD AND TOBAGO

Over the last ten years the parameters of the discourse on social differentiation in this region have shifted immensely. The discussion has shifted from one of the relationship among racial groups to one of the social construction of "ethnicity" and social identity, the "racing" or "deracination" of various groups and the processes through which group boundaries are constructed and reconstructed. These discourses are interesting as they present new and exciting insights into the understanding of these complex phenomena. In addition to a marked increase in research on Caribbean ethnic minorities, most notably Indians and to a lesser extent, Chinese, Portuguese, Lebanese and indigenous peoples, a renewed interest in subordinate group relations has been generated albeit within the context of continued Euro-Creole cultural and economic domination.

As noted by Daniel Segal, immigrant groups are all assumed to be "pure" and to have had a prior existence in their host countries before settling in Trinidad and Tobago;[15] nevertheless, local conditions in Trinidad and Tobago shaped their experiences thereafter and affected their ethnic classification and identity. What is also important is the fact that this construction took place within the context of European colonial and cultural dominance, which to a large extent shaped the process of ethnic definition. Thus, we have from very early the construction of the "Negro" or "Black" at the lower end of the social hierarchical continuum with the "European" or "White" at the other end. In between fit other ethnic groups, latecomers to the process as well as the results of racial "mixing" between the groups at the opposite ends of the spectrum. Of course one's position on this continuum depended on a number of interrelated factors including skin colour and phenotype (especially hair quality), economic status and educational attainment. The stereotypical construction of the "Negro" owes much to the resistance to slave labour characteristic of that historical epoch. According to David Trotman, "The idea of the congenital laziness of the African and those of African descent was one of the major pillars of the justifications of slavery and died hard in the 19th century."[16] Much was made of the luxuriant flora and fauna of the region which facilitated this indolence as people could survive without resorting to work on the plantation. This stereotype was of course central to the nineteenth-century cries of labour shortage and the call for large-scale immigration from overseas.

Not surprisingly, the entrance of large numbers of Indian immigrants occasioned the creation of new ethnicities and new stereotypes. The new "East Indians" (to be distinguished from "West Indians"), were defined in opposition to their labouring predecessors both internally and externally as they sought also to define themselves. In contrast, "East Indians" were constructed as hard-working and thrifty, common characteristics of immigrants anywhere, including present-day African-Caribbean migrants to New York. These analyses, however, could be taken much further, for nowhere is the differential construction as clear as in relation to women. Indian women have been defined in opposition to African women. "She" is everything the African woman is not. Through a combination of male violence and state legislation,[17] a localised "East Indian woman" was constructed in many ways as an essentialised and orientalised Indian woman, as described by Rishee Thakur.[18]

Along with the process of distinct ethnic group formation, of which a great deal has been written,[19] was the continuing process of "interculturation". R.K. Jain, developing on Brathwaite, identifies the twin processes of acculturation and interculturation as opposing forces in the history of group relations in Trinidad and Tobago. The former he sees as a reactionary force based on the imitation and privileging of Euro-Creole norms and behaviour (the Afro-Saxon) which opposes the spontaneous indigenous and creative interculturation which has been taking place continuously since the nineteenth century.[20] This formulation is interesting, as scholars in the region have for some time sought to explain the basis of ethnic tension and difference in Trinidad and Tobago. Their main arguments can be summarised as follows:

1. At the point of the arrival of the Indian immigrants, African ex-slaves had already inculcated European values of "civilised" and acceptable behaviour and lifestyle. They accepted, for example, the lower value of dark skin, the superiority of Christianity over other religions and belief systems, the barbarism of indigenous practices and the unacceptability of indigenous foods. In the same way that they devalued their own African cultural survivals, and their African phenotype, they also devalued the heathen and "backward" practices of uncivilised "coolie culture".

2. Indians were also seen as "scab labour", depressing the relatively high agricultural wages and removing the labour advantages now being sought by the ex-slaves.

3. In the case of most Africans and their descendants, 400 years of brutal enslavement had resulted in the transference of culture memory from the conscious realm to the subconscious or unconscious realm; however, for Indians, Hindus and Muslims, their diverse practices, more present in their consciousness, were re-codified and continued as part of their daily lived experience and through regular infusions from India. The experience of a small but significant number of "free Africans", who arrived after the abolition of slavery, had a negligible impact on this reality. Nevertheless, in the post-1970 period there has been some re-valorisation of African and African-derived forms.

4. In relation to Indians, whereas in the past it was assumed that the caste system had lost its significance when faced with the realities of the plantation, and lower sex ratios in the nineteenth century, it is now being realised that the caste values (*varna* ideology), for example, in rules of hierarchy and status – continue to exist although in a new reconstructed form in keeping with the realities of the new situation. I have argued elsewhere that values of purity and endogamy, discourage ethnic intermarriage and sexual relations in a circumstance in which other "ethnic" and/or religious groups – for example, Africans, Europeans, Christians, Hindus and Muslims – take up new places as pseudo-castes or sub-castes in a new Caribbean-derived hierarchy.[21]

5. More generally, there is also the view that in the context of colonial aggression and control, the African/Indian Other became a more accessible target for rivalry and attack than the dominant European coloniser – a similar displacement as that suggested for working-class male aggression against subordinate females.

Central to much of this discourse has been the failure to engage with issues of class and gender. As we have seen, most groups are assumed to be monolithic and the specific constructions of female identity or of female working-class identity, for example, are only now beginning to be explored.

Jain, following K.N. Sharma, identified two early periods of Indian-African relations in Trinidad and Tobago. The first period 1845–1870, which Sharma saw as one of "deinstitutionalisation", Jain identified as one of the initial interculturation. During this relatively short period of time he noted that:

> The caste system disintegrated, the marriage institutions were in ninepins; the customary system of social control through the panchayat was swamped over by the constituted plantation authorities; and the religious system of the folk in the Indian village, which was always bound up with the tap-roots of the "great tradition" now existed like fish out of water.[22]

However, according to Jain, this "disintegration" was accompanied by a "restructuration" of a Caribbean Indian "culture" and it was in this context that he saw the process of interculturation taking place. For example, this restructuration encompassed the coming together of the diverse little traditions of the various Indian groups which were brought to the region – this coming together of course took place within the context of the dominant processes of acculturation and subordinate processes of interculturation.

In recent times, there has been the identification by some Indian nationalist groups of a dominant Afro-centric culture in Trinidad and Tobago. This has recently been criticised by Thakur who, like Jain, seeks to differentiate between the dominant colonial and racist Afro-Saxon culture and the working-class indigenous, African-derived folk culture which has never been dominant in the region.[23] According to Jain:

> This incipient middle-class élite was fervently European in its attitudes, orientations and aspirations; hence the emergence of what has been called the Afro-Saxon model of acculturation. Simultaneously the seeds of racism . . . were deliberately sown in the already fertile soil of racist stereotypes.

Jain also points to:

> . . . the upsurge of racism in the new "colonial" rather than "Creole" ethos to buttress White domination . . . Such events created conditions in which interculturation [creolisation] went underground and phenomena such as Afro-Saxonism and "plural society" cultural segmentation and racial stereotyping moved to the centre of the stage. It has been conventionally held that acculturation to [White Anglo-Saxon norms] replaced interculturation as the cultural dynamic in the Caribbean.[24]

Most Indian cultural resistance therefore has to be seen as resistance to this dominant Afro-Saxon acculturative mode and less to the subordinate African-derived mode.[25] But even this "resistance" has often necessitated the subtle incorporation of Euro-Creole practices. This was probably inevitable within the structured context within which all groups were forced to operate. For example, much Brahmanical-controlled Hindu worship and rites of passage, such as marriage, take place in centralised temples and Sunday worship (services) and Sunday school are increasingly being officiated by ordained pundits. On the other hand, the basis for the subordinate level interculturations where they have taken place has been either where parallel root-traditions occur (the two best examples of this are in the bitterly contested and non-Brahmanic and working-class dominated activities of Muharram Festival and the Orisha and Kali worship/belief systems) or where significant numbers of women, sometimes unconsciously, find spaces of solace and respite from the wider patriarchal system.

In an earlier work I examined the contestations which have taken place over the content and definition of "national culture" in Trinidad and Tobago.[26] These struggles are still taking place and will continue to be significant for sometime. What I would like to examine in the rest of the article, however, are two examples of subordinate level interculturations.

THE MUHARRAM OR "HOSAY FESTIVAL"

From as early as the 1850s, just five years after the arrival of the first Indian immigrant ship, the *Fatel Rozack*, African-Trinidadians (then called Negroes) were reported to be involved in the Shia Muslim Muharram or Hosein (Hosay) festival. This festival, according to Kelvin Singh, comprised a re-enactment of the death of Hosein and Hassan, the grandsons of the Prophet Mohammed, during the Battle of Kerbala in what is now modern-day Iraq. In India this festival had, according to Singh, probably been syncretised with the Hindu Khrishnalila celebration and in its Indian form comprised the construction of large temple-like structures known as *tazias*.[27]

This festival and aspects of its celebration were taken by immigrants to Trinidad and it became the largest Indian festival, celebrated annually in the holy month of Muharram, the first month of the Muslim calendar. Many of its characteristics – the creation of huge ornate structures, the playing of drums, in this case the *tassa*, and dancing in the streets – had much in common with "root traditions" of the African working-class as noted by Jain. In his own words:

The Indian (Muslim) festival of Hossey (known in India as Taziya) has been observed jointly by the East Indians and Negroes at least since 1850. Two cultural characteristics of the celebration – the beating of drums (tassa) and the playing with sticks (gadja) – form the nuclei on which East Indian and Negro root traditions converge.[28]

The festival itself was of great concern to the upper classes, Christian church leaders and colonial officials. In addition, Sunni Muslim leaders in the nineteenth century, and still today make an annual call for the festival to be banned. One area of concern for the former groups, however, was the large participation of African-Trinidadians in this festival. It is interesting that African-Jamaicans also participated in this festival which was celebrated during indentureship, although the dispersal of Indian immigrants and their relatively small number did not facilitate the reconstruction of a distinct Indian sub-culture as in Trinidad, Guyana and Suriname.[29]

Colonial resistance to this festival culminated in the Hosay "disturbances" on the October 30, 1884 when colonial police, supported by a detachment of British soldiers, shot into a Muharram celebration in San Fernando. Sixteen people were killed and over 100 wounded. This act stymied the development of this festival in the south and central of the country but it continues today mainly in the north-western town of St James with even greater African participation than before. African males in particular participate in the production of Tadjahs and in the drumming from early ages and today young girls are seen from time to time on the drums or in the procession.

In spite of its popularity, this festival continues to be contentious. The religious leadership of the numerically dominant Sunni, recently with increased vigour, justify their call for its banning by deriding the non-Muslim and "impure" aspects of the festival. These are most notably the participation of non-Muslims (mainly Africans), the accompaniment of dancing and drumming and alcohol consumption in what is after all supposed to be a religious festival. In the renewed religiosity of the time, this festival is being forced to recreate itself as a religious Muslim festival as opposed to the popular "people's" festival which it always has been in this country. In the new religious and conservative context, working-class African participation (as in carnival) is seen as a polluting factor, one which introduces decadence, unbridled enjoyment and open sexuality – factors from which respectable religious and other leaders (Christian and non-Christian) have sought to distance themselves. Interestingly, in spite of the ambivalence shown by many Indians and Indian cultural and religious leaders to the steelband and other aspects of the Afro-Creole culture, it is suggested that the steelband, the national instrument of Trinidad and Tobago, which developed in the 1930s owes much to the *tassa*. Stephen Steumple, notes the influences between the *tassa* and the early steelband put forward by Trinidadian cultural activist Noor Kumar Mahabir in 1984:

> . . . the shells of the Indian bass drums used to be made from biscuit drums (as were the early steelbands); tassa drums are heated to stretch the skins and raise their pitches, and the drums in the ensemble are suspended around the neck and played with two sticks as steelbands still are today.[30]

ORISHA / KALI WORSHIP

The African population in nineteenth-century Trinidad comprised the following: Creole ex-slaves, mainly descendants of those imported from Africa before 1838 (many migrants from other islands); liberated Africans from various Caribbean societies after 1841; descendants of Black soldiers (including many native Africans) demobilised from the Third West India Regiment in 1815; and descendants of freed United Slaves who had fought for Britain in the 1812 war and who were settled in company villages in 1816. By 1861, therefore, seven per cent of the African population in Trinidad was African-born and a larger proportion only one or two generations removed. It should not be surprising, then, that African survivals and reinterpretations[31] were of particular significance in shaping the Creole culture of Trinidad and Tobago. One of the areas in which this has been most apparent has been in relation to religion and belief systems. Throughout the Western hemisphere, wherever African enslavement took place, religious ritual and experience were profoundly affected. Melville Herskovits, the famous United States Africanist, identified certain components of African religion that were transferred to the New World. These included: its connection with everyday life and integration into the daily round of activities; the ever-present forces of the universe; democratic organisation; local autonomy reflected in independent churches/temples; ritual expression in song and dance with possession by the god as the supreme religious experience and the association with water, including total immersion in natural bodies of water.[32] In the case of Trinidad and Tobago, the most important expressions of African-derived religion have been the Shango or Orisha belief system and the Shouters or Spiritual Baptists. These have usually been seen as acculturative religions based on syncretisms of West African religious traditions and Christian (Catholic and/or Protestant) traditions. The Shouters or Spiritual Baptists is the most prevalent stream, developing in the later days of the nineteenth century among ex-slaves who under the force of being Christianised sought to re-establish and continue their West African religious traditions. In this development where for example in 1883, the colonial government introduced a "Music Bill" which was eventually codified into law, the playing of drums, tambours and chac chacs (rattles) was prohibited from 6:00 am to 10:00 pm.[33] The Shouters therefore developed other methods of reflecting their Africaness. As noted by Herskovits, this is seen: . . . in Africa or in the New World, wherever African patterns of worship have been preserved. Drums and rattles, forbidden in Christian rite, are naturally absent. But the deficiency is compensated for by handclapping and the improvisations of rhythm taking the form of a vocal "rum-a-tiddy-pum-pum" sung in the bass by men who have the power needed to make their contribution heard above the blanket of singing.[34]

The importation of Africans after the abolition of slavery contributed further to African folk culture. The introduction of Yoruba, Ibo, Congo and Hausa peoples directly from Africa meant that traditions that were not as heavily mediated through the slave experience could develop. The impact of the Yoruba has been particularly strong and this has been documented extensively for other countries in the region, such as Cuba and Puerto Rico (Santeria) and Brazil (Condomble). Orisha or Shango worship, as it is more commonly referred to in Trinidad, is a Yoruba-derived belief system which no doubt owes some of its continued vitality to the arrival of free Africans in the years immediately after the abolition of slavery.

According to Maureen Warner-Lewis, the Yoruba was the dominant African group in Trinidad and provided the basis for a unified African tradition offering cohesion and cultural dynamism to the whole African population. The Yoruba, she argues, had a distinct impact on the development of Trinidadian Creole culture and this is reflected in the Shango/Orisha belief systems, the Shouters, in calypso and the traditional rotating credit schemes such as the *susu*.[35]

The Shango belief system as it developed in Trinidad has been and continues to be primarily a working class and peasant phenomenon. Middle-class participation, although increasing, has always been limited. Shango worship is characterised by veneration of and possession by a range of deities or Orishas; maintenance of shrines to various powers; initiation through a period of seclusion known as "mourning"; large annual rituals including animal sacrifices and feasts; feeding of children and immersion in water.[36] Shango, according to Warner-Lewis, is "the Orisha manifest in the thunder and the hurling of thunderstones as well as in lightening". She notes also that the Shango religion originated in Oyo state religion in present-day Nigeria and was transferred to Trinidad by Yoruba immigrants.[37]

One characteristic of all Afro-Christian religion in the Caribbean has been the participation of women at levels that are not evident in Christianity, Islam or other mainstream belief systems. This participation is both as members and participants as well as leaders. George Eaton Simpson in his fieldwork in Trinidad in 1960 found that:

> . . . the cult leader is called Mother, Pa, Queen or Aunt etc . . . The six women leaders known to the writer are dominant figures and with one exception, each has a mild, passive husband who is involved in the "work", and who believes in it as strongly as his wife.[38]

Throughout Simpson's work, references to leaders of churches or *chapelles* (Shango places of worship) were primarily female. Similarly, he noted that in the participation in the big annual ceremonies women usually outnumbered men three to one.[39]

The African-derived religious systems reflected a remarkable ability to be acculturative and interculturative; to incorporate those aspects other belief systems which were in concert with theirs, whether these were forcibly introduced like Christianity or more subconsciously incorporated as with aspects of Hinduism.

In 1960 Simpson found that in Trinidad "Quite a number of East Indians have joined Spiritual Baptist groups, but relatively few have become Shangoists." In spite of this, he found that of the 63 powers' identified, "two of these, Baba and Mahabil were described as East Indian powers. One Chinese power Wong Ka was also identified."[40] The inevitability of this interculturation, however, was signalled by one female informant who noted that "What a person is afraid to do, he does when possessed." She continued "I never liked Indian people, but when I went to mourn and Mahabil came . . .". Similarly, on another occasion, "Baba" ordered her to go to Blanchisseuse Mountain and four people went with her.[41]

Simpson also noted the limited presence of Indian men as active participants in the Orisha worship in 1960 and the use of *deeahs* (small clay pots filled with coconut oil and wicks) at the outdoor shrine of Baba. Since then, the incorporation of Indians and symbols and practices of Hinduism into Shango worship increased. In the 1980s, according to James Houk, close to 10 per cent of participants in 18 Orisha feasts were Indian. He noted:

> One Indian, for example, is a popular and respected drummer. Another Indian is one of the most prominent and respected figures in the religion and is himself a shrine head who annually holds one of the most popular feasts on the island . . . Leader Scott, a well-known and respected Orisha priest and Spiritual Baptist

leader, and other worshippers noted that it was not until the 1960s or so that they began to notice Hindu elements in Orisha compounds. In the sample of 37 Orisha compounds discussed above, it was found that 10 to 27 per cent contained Hindu flags and shrines for up to six different Hindu deities.[42]

In an insightful article entitled "Hindu Elements in the Shango/Orisha Cult of Trinidad", Noor Kumar Mahabir and Ashram Maharaj provide interesting insights into the syncretism of this African-derived system and the Kali Mai cult which enjoys a similar subordinated status in relation to the established religious bodies.[43] The latter, originally practised by the South Indian Madrassi-descended Indians, according to Stephen Vertovec, was "selectively suppressed by White colonial authorities and Hindus themselves".[44] The article suggests that the basis of interculturation has to do with the similar root traditions that are characteristic of the rural folk and working-classes of both ethnic groups. Additionally, these grassroots religious experiences provide greater scope for women's religious expression as celebrants, unlike more mainstream patriarchal religions. Interestingly, among the similarities of the working-classes of both groups is the eclectic approach to religion and the lesser adherence to the maintenance of religious boundaries. In the words of the authors:

> The integrated complex of drum, chant, dance, liturgy, shaped ritual, spirit possession and animal sacrifice which mark the worship of gods in the Orisha cult are akin to the Kali-Mai (Black Mother) cult of Hinduism in Trinidad . . . Some items are common to both Kali worship and Orisha ("Parallel tradition") from inception; others are absorbed through the process of transmutation. Both the East Indian Kali Mai and African Orisha cults are lower-class forms of folk culture with a tradition of White-collar unemployment, familial property-holding, apolitical participation and little formal organisation.[45]

They continue, "Forms of Orisha worship in Trinidad find counterparts in the procession, broom dance, reverence to ancestors and use of certain ritual paraphernalia in the Indian Shia Muslim festival of Hosay."[46]

What is interesting is not only the participation of Indians in the Orisha ceremonies but the integration and syncretism of Indian gods and "powers" within the local Shango pantheon. Ogun, Yoruba god of war, the hunt and iron, is syncretised with the Hindu monkey god Hanuman, while as early as the 1950s, anthropologist Dan Crowley noted that Osain, a Yoruba god of medicine, was syncretised with Husain, the martyred grandson of the prophet Mohammed. In other words, on the local scene these two are considered to be Indian powers.[47]

Until the 1970s, the activities of both these groups were shrouded in mystery – they were considered forms of devil worship and *obeah*. Even the Hindu leadership in an effort to gain respectability from the colonial Euro-Creole dominated society sought to distance itself from what was regarded as "extreme forms of heathenism" and in both instances their significance was declining. This, however, has been changed with the renewed interest in indigenous forms and belief systems, although they are also under threat from United States (and increasingly also European) derived pentecostalism.

This recent challenge of pentecostalism (more acculturative than intercultu-rative) in rural Trinidad and Tobago raises new questions about the maintenance of Indian and Afro-Creole religious traditions. Pentecostalism, unlike Presbyteri-anism, the earliest Christian proselytiser among the Indians, makes no attempt to syncretise its rituals and practices with Indian or African practices, but like the earlier Christian denominations, campaigns actively against all strains of "heathenism".

Mahabir, in some ways, suggests that the attraction of pentecostalism, espe-cially to the rural working class and women, lies in their alienation from the Hindu hierarchy.[48] Women, he notes, predominate in all the religious functions but are not accorded any leadership roles commensurate with their numbers, professional training and educational levels.[49] The growing number of conver-sions, a slight majority of them female according to Kumar, reflect an increased willingness of working-class Indians to associate with working-class African-Trinidadians which Kumar suggests would not have taken place earlier.[50] He concludes: "The picture that emerged here is one of radical, social and religious behaviour by many working-class Indians and a complex correlation between social class, gender and religious affiliation."[51]

The move to pentecostalism is also paralleled to a lesser extent by a re-connec-tion with indigenous religions especially among the middle-classes. Among the African and mixed groups, this has led to a new interest in Orisha/Shango and a trend towards its re-Africanisation.[52] James Houk notes that in the wake of the 1970s Black Power revolution, concerns with Africa and African derivations became important and efforts to develop a purer religion (now known more as Orisha than Shango) emerged with closer links to Nigeria and other Orisha communities, for example, in Brazil. In this context, efforts to remove all evidence of syncretisms, whether Catholic, Protestant (including Spiritual Baptist) or Hindu, have become evident.

Houk sees this as a reflection of both a re-connection with Africa and things African as well as concern with the increasing involvement of Indians in the religion. He sees this as a "revivalist response to that threat".[53] We find a situation, therefore, where as sections of the Indian middle and professional classes move more towards various continental Indian gurus such as Sai Baba and Ravi Shankar for an experience of Hinduism more in keeping with modern times and western values,[54] significant sections of the Indian working-class, and female working-class in particular, move more towards religious identification with fundamentalist Christianity – a move which contributed greatly to the recent intensification of the militant Indian identity movement.

CONCLUSION

For radical scholars there is need for much greater critical analysis and insight into the socio-cultural context of contestation and accommodation among subordinate ethnic and cultural groups in our societies. There is also a need to comprehend the dynamic social reality and its political implications.

As noted in an earlier paper, there is much in the "little tradition" of Africans and Indians in the Caribbean which lends itself to interculturation and the development of common cultural practices. These aspects, however, are the aspects of the national culture, which are questioned, have low status and are carried out mainly by the rural and urban working class and folk. It was to these groups that Brathwaite attributed the creativity that led to the indigenisation of the dominant culture, which we now know was true both for Indians and for Africans. Interestingly, the discourse on ethnicity is once more shifting or expanding, in addition to the recent emphasis on the construction of group identity in relation to but more often in opposition to the other. There is also recognition that these differential levels of ongoing interaction, acculturation and interculturation are deeply affected by class and gender. In creating an alternative mode of inter-relations among subordinate groups, we need to understand more fully the processes of indigenous grassroots interculturation and accommodation which have developed over time in our societies as well as the bases of difference.

NOTES

*This paper in many ways complements an earlier (1993) one entitled, "Intersections of Ethnicity, Class and Gender in Trinidad and Tobago: Contestations Over National Culture", in which I examined the struggle over the definition and content of national culture using the three components of the dominant Afro-Creole artforms, Mas (carnival), Pan (steelband) and Kaiso (calypso).

1.   Vidia Naipaul, *The Middle Passage* (London: Andre Deutch, 1962), p. 80.
2.   Kamau Brathwaite, *The Development of Creole Society in Jamaica, 1780–1820* (Oxford: Clarendon Press, 1971), Brathwaite, *Contradictory Omens: Cultural Diversity and Integration in the Caribbean* (Mona: Savacou Publications, 1974), and M.G. Smith, *The Plural Society in the British West Indies* (Kingston: Sangster's Book Store, 1965).
3.   J.S. Furnivall, *Netherlands India: A Study of Plural Economy* (Cambridge: Cambridge University Press, 1944); Smith, "Pluralism and Social Stratification", in Selwyn Ryan, ed., *Social and Occupational Stratification in Contemporary Trinidad and Tobago* (University of the West Indies, Trinidad: Institute of Social and Economic Research [I.S.E.R.], 1991), p. 10.
4.   Smith, *The Plural Society*, pp. 14–15.
5.   Ibid.
6.   Glenn Sankatsing, *Caribbean Social Science: An Assessment* (Caracas: Regional Unit for the Social and Regional Sciences for Latin America and the Caribbean, 1989).
7.   From now on referred to as the Southern Caribbean.
8.   Brathwaite, *Contradictory Omens*, p. 11. See also Elsa Goveia, *Slave Society in the British Leeward Islands at the end of the Eighteenth Century* (University of Puerto Rico: Institute of Caribbean Studies, 1965) and Dan Crowley, "Plural and Differential Acculturation in Trinidad", *American Anthropologist*, 59:5 (1957), pp. 817–24.
9.   Brathwaite, *Contradictory Omens*, p. 19.
10.   Verene A. Shepherd, "Indians and Blacks in Jamaica in the 19th and early 20th Centuries: A Micro-Study of the Foundations of Race Antagonisms", in Howard Johnson, ed., *After the Crossing* (London: Frank Cass, 1988), p. 95.
11.   Rhoda Reddock, "Primacy of Gender Within Race and Class", in J. Edward Green, ed., *Race, Class and Gender in the Future of the Caribbean* (Mona, Jamaica: I.S.E.R., 1993), pp. 47–73.
12.   Rhoda Reddock, "Douglarisation and the Politics of Gender Relations in Trinidad and Tobago", in R. Deosaran, N. Mustapha and R. Reddock, eds., *Contemporary Issues in Social Science: a Caribbean perspective*, vol. 1 (University of the West Indies, Trinidad: Department of Sociology, 1994), p. 7.
13.   Rhoda Reddock, "Intersections of Ethnicity, Class and Gender in Trinidad and Tobago", paper presented at the Rockefeller Humanities Center, Hunter College, 1993.

14. Ibid., p. 8.

15. Daniel Segal, "The European: Allegories of Racial Purity", in *Anthropology Today*, vol. 7:5 (1991), pp. 7–9.

16. David Trotman, *Crime in Trinidad: Conflict and Control in a Plantation Society* (Knoxville: University of Tennessee Press, 1986), p. 207.

17. Rhoda Reddock, "Indian Women in Trinidad and Tobago, 1845–1917: Freedom Denied", *Caribbean Quarterly*, 32:3, 4 (1986), pp. 27–49.

18. Rishee Thakur, "Orientalism Revisited", *Caribbean Issues*, vol. 6:2 (1993), pp. 11–15.

19. Morton Klass, *East Indians in Trinidad: A Study of Cultural Persistence* (Illinois: Waveland Press, 1961; 1988 reprint); Klass, *Singing with Sai Baba: The Politics of Revitalisation in Trinidad and Tobago* (Boulder: Westview Press, 1991).

20. Ravindra Jain, "The East Indian Culture in a Caribbean Context: Crisis and Creativity", *Indian International Centre Quarterly*, vol. 13 (1986).

21. Reddock, "Douglarisation and the Politics of Gender Relations in Trinidad and Tobago".

22. Jain, "The East Indian Culture in a Caribbean Context".

23. Ibid.

24. Ibid., pp. 154–55

25. Kusha Haraksingh, "Structure, Process and Indian Culture in Trinidad", in Howard Johnson, ed., *After the Crossing*.

26. Reddock, "Intersections of Ethnicity, Class and Gender in Trinidad and Tobago".

27. Kelvin Singh, *Bloodstained Tombs: The Muharram Massacre, 1884* (London: Basingstoke: Macmillan, 1988), pp. 4–5.

28. Jain, "The East Indian Culture in a Caribbean Context", p. 158.

29. Shepherd, "Indians and Blacks in Jamaica in the 19th and early 20th Centuries", p. 101.

30. Stephen Steumple, "The Steelband Movement in Trinidad and Tobago: Politics and National Identity", Ph.D. Dissertation, University of Pennsylvania, 1990, p. 57.

31. Melville Herskovits and Frances Herskovits, *Trinidad Village* (New York: Alfred Knopf, 1947); Melville Herskovits, *The Myth of the Negro Past* (Gloucester: Mass: Peter Smith, orig. pub. 1958, 1970 edn.).

32. Herskovits, *The Myth of the Negro Past*, pp. 207–33.

33. This Bill also sought to curb the "noise" emanating from the Moharram or Hosein festival. According to Brereton, ". . . officers at the St James Barracks were annoyed by drum-beating by Indians in Coolie Town, St James". See Bridget Brereton, *Race Relations in Colonial Trinidad, 1870–1900* (Cambridge: Cambridge University Press, 1979), p. 161.

34. Herskovits, *The Myth of the Negro Past*, p. 223.

35. Brereton, *Race Relations in Colonial Trinidad*; Maureen Warner-Lewis, *Guinea's Other Sons: The African Dynamic in Trinidad Culture* (Massachusetts: Majority Press, 1991).

36. George Eaton Simpson, "The Shango Cult of Trinidad", in G.E. Simpson, ed., *Religious Cults of the Caribbean: Trinidad, Jamaica and Haiti* (San Juan: Institute of Caribbean Studies, 1960).

37. Warner-Lewis, *Guinea's Other Sons*, pp. 133, 137.

38. Simpson, *Religious Cults*, p. 79.

39. Ibid., p. 80.

40. Ibid., p. 21.

41. Ibid., pp. 21, 125.

42. James Houk, "Afro-Trinidadian Identity and the Africanisation of the Orisha Religion", in Kevin Yelvington, ed., *Trinidad Ethnicity* (Knoxville: Macmillan/University of Tennessee Press, 1993), p. 174.

43. Kali, the "Black Mother" is often seen as the "evil incarnation" of the good mother deity Durga. This information was gleaned from personal interview with Paula Morgan.

44. Stephen Vertovec, *Hindu Trinidad: Religion, Ethnicity and Socio-Economic Change* (London: Macmillan, 1992), p. 218.

45. Noor Kumar Mahabir and Maharaj Ashram, "Hindu Elements in the Shango/Orisha Cult in Trinidad", in Frank Birbalsingh, ed., *Indenture and Exile: the Indo-Caribbean Experience* (Toronto: Tsar Press, 1988), pp. 192–93.

46. Mahabir and Ashram, "Hindu Elements in the Shango/Orisha Cult in Trinidad".

47. Noor Kumar Mahabir, "Finding Neutral Grounds in a Plural Society", *Caribbean Issues*, 6:2 (1993); Reddock, "Primacy of Gender Within Race and Class"; Simpson, *Religious Cults*, p. 127, and Crowley, "Plural and Differential Acculturation", and "Cultural Assimilation in a Multiracial Society", *Annals of the New York Academy of Sciences*, 83 (1960), pp. 850–54.

48. Mahabir, "Finding Neutral Grounds in a Plural Society", p. 19.

49. Ibid. Today, for example, while the first female pundit (*pandita*) is being severely challenged by the Hindu leadership of virtually all traditions, a few Indian women Pentecostalists and Evangelicals have large congregations, often preaching strongly against Hinduism and other forms of "heathenism".

50. Mahabir, *Finding Neutral Grounds*, and Margaret Rouse-Jones, "Changing Patterns of Denominational Affiliation in Trinidad and Tobago", in S. Ryan, ed., *Social and Occupational Stratification in Contemporary Trinidad and Tobago*, p. 362.

51. Mahabir, "Finding Neutral Grounds in a Plural Society", p. 19.

52. Houk, "Afro-Trinidadian Identity and the Africanisation of the Orisha Religion".

53. Ibid., p. 177.

54. Klass, *East Indians in Trinidad*.

Patricia Mohammed

Chapter 7

THE "CREOLISATION" OF INDIAN WOMEN IN TRINIDAD[1]

INTRODUCTION

"Creolisation" is a troublesome but useful term. Troublesome because there are so many interpretations of the word; useful because it confronts the issues related to ethnicity and ethnic relations in a multi-racial society. It is a daring, perhaps even an offensive word to use in reference to Indian women in Trinidad, for it was used popularly to refer to those women who mixed or consorted with people of African descent, especially men – Indian women who changed their eating and dress habits and who adopted non-Indian social customs. But this perhaps draws on a more popular interpretation of the term. A derivative of the word "Creole", used in Trinidad to refer to descendants of African slaves to distinguish them from indentured Indian immigrants, "creolisation" was viewed as synonymous with the absorption of Black culture at the expense of one's own – a process referred to as "acculturation". Anyone appreciative of the history of the relations between the two majority ethnic groups in this society – Blacks and Indians – understands immediately the anathema which greets the suggestion of acculturation, especially from the Indian population.

The term creolisation, however, has a vastly richer meaning that that suggested above, and it is in the more expansive framework of the concept that I want to discuss the changing status of Indian women in the post-independence period in Trinidad and Tobago. I am drawing first on the original Spanish sense of the word, from *criollo*, which meant born in and committed to the area of living. In Trinidad and Tobago we have been accustomed to using it in this sense – for instance, when we refer to French or Spanish Creoles. Creole societies emerge in the context of a colonial arrangement with a metropolitan power, so that there is the additional dimension of an internal reaction against external metropolitan pressures. There is, simultaneously, a process of internal adjustments taking place between the cultures interacting in the society. This is a more reciprocal relationship between cultures, an "intermixture and enrichment, each to each", as it has been formulated by Kamau Braithwaite[2] – or, in other words, interculturation as opposed to acculturation. Included in the latter process is also the acceptance of the values inherent in Creole society – in this instance, its preoccupation with class and colour. My discussion is focused on these ongoing and dynamic processes – acculturation, commitment to one's country of birth, reactions against external cultures and interculturation.

There, however, are two other concerns though which are central to any consideration of movement and cultural change in society: first, the impact and influence of political movements on attitudes and practices among competing ethnic groups; and second, the effect of "modernisation" on the competing cultures.

Where and how do Indian women fit into this matrix of cultural change? How do they contribute to the process and how are they affected by it? That they comprise a significant proportion of the population is a demographic fact worth noting. In the 1980 census of the population, Indian women accounted for 39.6 per cent of the total female population of Trinidad and Tobago, while women of African descent comprised 39.9 per cent. They therefore account for just under one-quarter of the total population of the country. It is also important to recognise that Indian is not synonymous with Hindu: in fact, in 1980 Hindu women comprised 24 per cent of the total female population, while Muslim women comprised six per cent, Presbyterians four per cent and other Christians just under six per cent. Although Hindu women predominate, there are subtle differences to be found between Indian women of different religions, differences which transcend their ethnic similarity.[3]

THE PRE-INDEPENDENCE PERIOD

We need to start at the very beginning. Post-independence changes are clearly meaningless if they are not matched against the pre-independence era. From all accounts, Indian women's introduction into the new society was dramatic to say the least and made for the rather paradoxical situation in which the first Indian female immigrants found themselves in the new society – a paradoxical situation of being at the same time more free yet less free. First of all, consider the sexual imbalance between Indian males and females that existed for the entire period of indenture 1845–1917, and well into the post-indenture period. Between 1881 and 1891 there were 2,117 males to every 1,000 females. Not given to celibacy, Indian men found the situation unsatisfactory. Planters were also concerned about accretions to their labour supply, especially when it seemed that the system of indenture would be discontinued. Thus, efforts to increase female immigration resulted in a ratio of 1,354 males to every 1,000 females by 1911. Despite these efforts, at no time during the indentureship system did the number of females equal that of the number of males imported into the colony. By 1931, there was still an imbalanced ratio of 1,135 men to 1,000 women.

Second, consider the type of woman who was indentured. Rhoda Reddock has suggested that those women who came would have already been a more independent breed; it is calculated that two-thirds of the women who were recruited were either single, widows who would have been forbidden to remarry in India, women who had separated from or been abandoned by their husbands or other women of "easy virtue".[4] Though more conclusive research is needed, the fact remains that under new and more promising conditions, the Indian woman could challenge her former role in India. She was now in the enviable position of being a scarce and valuable resource. She was also, like her male counterpart, a wage earner on the estate.

These two factors obviously created conditions for a more independent and less passive role for Indian women. This, however, was more easily said than done. Indian men could no longer rely on the rules, which entrenched patriarchy in India in both Hindu and Muslim families. On the estate they could not make recourse to the rules governing Hindu life, as the doctrines of karma and dharma, while glorifying womanhood, also placed femininity in a passive role as chattel to masculinity, ensuring female subservience and passivity. Indian men in Trinidad violently coerced their women into submission. Bridget Brereton notes that between 1872 and 1900, 87 murders of Indian women occurred, of which 65 were wife murders.[5] This legacy of institutionalised violence persisted and appears to have been one of the features of the relations between Indian men and women when they were married, such as those typified in the cruel and dehumanised relationship between Pa and Ma in Tola Trace in 1905 in Harold Sonny Ladoo's *No Pain Like this Body*.[6]

Yet in the face of this kind of coercion, it is believed that Indian women were the keepers of the culture, establishing in the new society as many of the traditions and cultural practices of the motherland. It is strangely ironic that Indian women would voluntarily recreate a pattern of life which would be restricting and oppressive to them. We need to ask, as sociologist Kim Johnson has done, if Indian women sought independence in the first place, then who was it from? His explanation appears to me to be a logical one. He suggests that, like Indian men, Indian women clung to their remembered culture as the only solace and strength: there was nothing in the new culture which replaced the old. It was possible, proposes Johnson, that Indian women were not "struggling for chimeric independence but for an altered balance of power within the family",[7] a balance which was altered in their favour.

Certainly neither Indian men nor women attempted at first to become integrated or even familiar with the new society. Loyalties were first to India, to which they hoped to return some day. They lived culturally apart from the rest of the "Creole" society. Geographical and occupational separation, combined with mutual contempt and misunderstanding, kept the various races apart. For their part, Blacks, who had internalised the values of Creole society had contempt for this group of immigrants who spoke "barbarous" languages, dressed differently, and worked for cheaper wages than they did. Indians, on the other hand, regarded the Blacks as untouchables and polluted as they ate the flesh of pigs and cattle and engaged in occupations which they considered ritually impure. Despite the scarcity of Indian women, sexual relations between Indian men and African or Creole women were extremely rare. Twenty-six years after Indian indenture had begun, the Protector of Immigrants could note that there "was not a single instance of an indentured immigrant who cohabits with one of the negro race".[8]

The last 30 years of the nineteenth century marked a turning point in Indian integration into the wider island community. The sugar market became depressed, more and more Indians were still being introduced and improved technology in the sugar industry lessened the availability of jobs in the factories. Indians sought jobs that were formerly held by Africans. In addition, Crown lands were being sold to them instead of repatriation to India. They began to recreate Indian villages on these settlements – something they were unable to do under conditions on the estates.

This movement out of the estates into little villages, and the knowledge that they would no longer be returning to Mother India must clearly have had an impact on the way in which Indians began to relate to the wider non-Indian community. Certainly, the movement out of cloistered estates and housing settlements and intermixing as a result of job diversification led to greater contact between the Indians and non-Indians. While our sociologists may have been less observant on the subject of acculturation, as early as 1939, some calypsonians had begun to notice and comment on the changes which were taking place among, at least, some Indian women.

In 1939, in a calypso entitled *Marajh Daughter*, Invader sang:

I want everybody to realise
I want a nice Indian girl that is creolise
I don't want no parata or dhal water
I want my potato and cassava

Gordon Rohlehr comments, and accurately so, that this calypso does not provide a true portrait of the Indian woman, revealing instead the rejection of Indian women's culture.[9] We can also deduce though, that there must have been a growing tendency on the part of Indian women to become "creolised" in order for this calypsonian to begin to comment, in less than complimentary fashion, on the phenomenon. By the 1940s, however, we see more conclusive evidence of cultural change among Indian women. Killer, leader of the Young Brigade, commented:

. . . But I notice there is no Indian again
Since the women and them taking Creole name

Long ago was Sumintra, Ramnawalia . . .
But now is Emily, Jean and Dinah . . .

Long ago you hadn't a chance
To meet an Indian girl in a dance
But nowadays it is big confusion
Big fighting in the road for their Yankee man
And see them in the market they ain't making joke
Pushing down nigger people to buy dey poke
And see them in the dances in Port of Spain
They wouldn't watch if you call an Indian name[10]

Reference to the Yankee men in this calypso is very significant. The expansion of employment opportunities on the American bases provided an option for some Indian women to find jobs and also mix with men who were thought, perhaps especially by their parents, to be more acceptable than men of African descent.

But movement out of the rural villages and socialising with non-Indian men created gaps between the expectations of the older generation of Indians and their daughters.

From 1957–1958, Morton Klass carried out anthropological fieldwork in Amity, a fictional name for an existing Indian village in Trinidad. If we view this village as generally but not entirely representative of Indian attitudes and lifestyles in other parts of Trinidad, especially rural Trinidad where Indians were largely concentrated, a brief look at some aspects of its social organisation is very revealing of the prevailing condition and status of Indian women in the society at the time. Klass subtitled his research, "A study of cultural persistence", and this is precisely what he found.[11]

Kinship relations were still as binding and observed. In fact, Klass was struck by what he termed the "East Indian capacity for indefinite extension of kinship" and by the important observance of the rules and regulations that governed kin relations.

A major concession had been made in the area of marriage. Boys and girls were now introduced to each other before the marriage and had a right to veto the proposed match. While a boy was considered of marriageable age from the time he was 16 until around 30, and even over 30 he was still very eligible, the Indian girl was really only marriageable between the ages of 15 and 17. An unmarried girl over age 18 became a serious problem for the father if not a disgrace to the entire family – no one wished to have an unmarried daughter in the house. Apart from being an economic liability, it was feared that she would lose her virginity or become pregnant before she could be married or, worse yet, consort with the dreaded polluted race of Black men bringing utter shame and disgrace on the family. Indian men used the notion of an untrammelled female sexuality as another rationale for the close vigilance of Indian girls and women. On this Klass noted "It is a generally held assumption in the village that no female has any capacity to resist sexual advances. Only the continually watchful eyes of her family can protect her." This clearly had the effect of restricting the freedom which Indian women could otherwise have had, but it also had the contradictory effect of allotting them a vibrant women's culture based on the freedom of female libido, a factor which perhaps, despite their subservient and passive role, undoubtedly made for greater female self-confidence. The ritual of *lawa* in the *maticore* ceremony before the Hindu marriage is illustrative of this point. In this ceremony there is a frank and ribald sharing and enjoyment between older women with the younger ones, of the joys or otherwise of the sexual experience. In addition, the bride (and separately the groom) is anointed with a mixture of yogurt and tumeric to prepare their bodies for the first nights of their sexual union. I speculate that on such bases Indian women were geared for better adjustment to the mixed and multi-racial society when they attained greater freedoms in the society of Trinidad in the decades that followed.

Restrictions had been imposed before marriage to ensure their purity while they were schooled in the art of pleasing their menfolk. This schooling clearly did not entail education outside the home and by this time only a small proportion of Indian women – mainly those who had been converted to Christianity – had had access to any formal schooling. For many young Indian brides in both the Hindu and Muslim households, marriage represented simply a changing of the guards. The bride was now under the protection of a new extended household in which other oppressive conditions were the norm – while the *doolaha* or bridegroom could expect to be served by his new *doolahin* in addition to his mother. The new *doolahin* was expected to shoulder the full burden of the household chores, with greater acceptance into the new family only coming with the birth of her first child. She was also expected to display ample evidence of her fertility by producing many sons, another activity which ensured her total domestication and restricted her involvement in any activity in the wider society. It was not uncommon, for instance, to find Indian women in the rural areas at the age of 21 already with five or six children. Jack Harewood has found that the level of fertility in Trinidad and Tobago's women of Indian descent was for a long time appreciably higher than that of non-Indian women as a group, and more specifically than that of women of African descent – so much so, that in the analysis of fertility in this society, demographers often separated the rest of the female population from women of Indian descent. Between 1946 and 1960, the completed fertility of Indian women was still in the vicinity of 40 per cent to 50 per cent higher than that of women of African descent.[12]

While this unfolding picture for Indian women can be generalised across Indian women of different religions, there were subtle differences between Hindu and Muslim women and women converted to Christianity. For instance, in Amity, Klass noted that the Muslim young people, being in the minority, exhibited some indication of a sense of alienation from the community. Two young Muslim girls who had become converted to Presbyterianism professed a certain distance from the community in terms of its "backwardness" and the "ignorance of its inhabitants". And in Amity, between those who had been converted to Christianity and those who had not, there was a feeling of mutual contempt. Clearly, the process of creolisation whether acknowledged or not, had started. The Indian population had begun to embrace the values inherent in Creole society.

Although we have begun to see qualitative changes in the relationship of Indians to the wider community, on the political front, if conditions under the period of indentureship ensured separatism between the dominant cultures and a certain degree of hostility, other features which emerged in the society up to the period of independence also kept much of this distance alive. These data are highly schematised and so omits much of the detail of the underlying political struggle between the two dominant cultures. But it is interesting to note that the period of decolonisation in Trinidad and Tobago did not also coincide with a growing nationalist consciousness among the majority of peoples of Indian descent. Selwyn Ryan notes for instance, that between 1919 and 1939, the bulk of the Indian population did not identify with the nationalist movement,[13] while Marianne Ramesar makes the point that the development of a group consciousness among Indians during the period 1921 to 1946 in fact contributed to friction with other groups developing similar nationalism. In addition, the movement to self government and the coming to power of the Peoples National Movement (PNM) was characterised by differences and rifts among the Indian community itself, and certainly not wholehearted support for a party which they felt would take advantage of them when in power.[14] Apart from a few urbanised Muslims and Christian Indians, the Hindu population was largely anti-PNM.

Evidence of Indian integration, though limited, could be seen in the greater occupational diversification among the Indian population. Although the Tyson report shows that in 1931 only a small percentage of Indians comprised the non-agricultural work force in Trinidad, we see evidence of both male and female inroads into various professions. There is no question that there is a clear predominance of Indian men over Indian women in the gainfully occupied work force – for instance, of the 637 men and women recorded under the category, professions, only 72 were women and these were all teachers. In fact, women comprised 29.2 per cent of the total work force of Indians and, of this, 25 per cent were in the lowest paid, lowest status jobs, and were either agricultural labourers or domestic servants.[15]

Despite their increasing integration of one sort or another in the wider community, actual racial intermixing was very limited. A crude indicator of the degree of intermixing with non-Indians is seen in the following figures. In 1911 there were 1.47 mixed Indians to every 100 unmixed Indians. In 1921 this figure had increased to 1.87 per 100 unmixed Indians and, by 1946, to 4.29. On the other hand, intermixing in the urban areas was greater for the 1946 census calculated at a rate of 21.37 Indian Creoles per 100 unmixed Indians in the main city of Port-of-Spain.[16] This leads one to conclude that another factor that contributed to the gap between the two major cultures was the geographical separation from each other.

When greater integration into the community developed for Indian men and especially Indian women, it came in through educational and employment opportunities away from the home or family farm. Initially, education was mainly for boys. It was thought unwise to educate girls. In Seepersad Naipaul's *Adventures of Gurudeva* (written in the 1940s) we see some of the reasons why. Gurudeva is impatient with his new child bride Ratni's proclivity to answer back and seeks advice from his father Jaimungal:

Gurudeva: I have not patience with her. She is rude and crude and gives me back-answers.

Jaimungal: I know that. But she is only a woman and will ever be foolish, no matter what you do: but you must keep your temper, for you can read and write, and know good from bad . . . But she – well to her letters are like dirt.[17]

Indian women had not been given early opportunity of the rudimentary education system available then. In 1899, after 30 years of Canadian missionary schooling, girls comprised only 28 per cent of total enrolment in primary schools and were mainly kept at home to do domestic chores. Even where and when the Canadian missionaries educated them, this was initially meant to prepare them to make good wives for the converted Indian men who had become teachers in the Presbyterian schools. Illiteracy rates were relatively high compared to the rest of the population. A look at the proportions of females of various ethnic groups in Trinidad and Tobago who were illiterate according to the 1946 census gives a very good idea of the extent of the problem. 65.7 per cent of Indian females ten years and older were illiterate, compared with 10.1 per cent for women of African descent, 3.4 per cent for women of European descent and 8.3 per cent for women of Chinese descent.[18] By the 1950s there was an organised attempt to catch up with the rest of the population and by this time too it had become more acceptable to educate daughters as well as sons. The Indian Centenary Review of 1945, for instance, includes entries of 16 women in professions or business and, of those, one Gladys Ramsaran was a barrister. It is again significant that these women were all Christians and most came from families that had attained professional status a generation before.[19] The Muslim and Hindu communities opened their own schools or expanded existing facilities to include secondary education. With the easier acceptance of education offered by the Presbyterians, very soon the effects could be seen on the female Indian population.

Given their delayed entry into the education system, it is interesting to note the effects of these developments among Indian girls five years before independence. In 1957, Vera Rubin and Marisa Zavalloni carried out a survey among a relatively large sample of secondary school students on their aspirations in the developing society of Trinidad and Tobago. In correlating university orientation with expectations of becoming full-time housewives, they found that only 17 per cent of the Indian girls compared with 50 per cent of the White girls intended to make home a post-career focal point. The researchers concluded from other indicators as well that, whereas higher education had become a normative expectation for middle- and upper-class girls as preparation for marriage, for Indian girls, securing an education entailed greater sacrifice and more of a break with their culture and consequently was seen as a channel to a career and personal independence rather than as preparation for a housewife's role.

It is again ironic, or on the other hand, perhaps perfectly understandable and inevitable, that in a culture which has suppressed women for so long, Indian women would readily embrace opportunities to engage with the rest of the society. Consider, for example, the aspirations of one Indian girl in Rubin and Zavalloni's study:

> I will go in for the Legislative Council Elections.
> If I am successful I can then help the people of my country
> most of all whether I am the Minister of Health or not,
> though I would be extremely happy if I am the Minister of
> Health or Education.[20]

To my knowledge, there were no Indian women involved in politics at the time. Even within this striving for individual expression and ambition, one sees evidence of those qualities that characterised the traditions expected of Indian women in the society. As another young Indian girl writes:

> I want to be a doctor, yet everything is against me ... I get no real encouragement. They think it is foolish that a girl should sacrifice so many years to study and then at the end of it she'll get married. And even if I decide to go ahead with this idea there is the very real difficulty of finding fees. My father has four children to provide for, two of them are boys who really need a good start in life.[21]

This epitomises the role which Indian women were expected to perform in the Indian community. They were keepers of the culture, they were passive and submissive, they were expected to sacrifice their own ambitions for the benefit of their brothers and husbands. Despite all of this, we can see that some Indian women had begun to commit themselves to goals which identified with the national interest. These aspirations are clear indications, though, that at least some Indian women had begun to become integrated into the Creole society and outside the arena of their erstwhile-restricted domain.

THE POST-INDEPENDENCE YEARS

Independence itself meant very little to most Indians. An interview with a woman who had had the experience of a rural Indian girl, who had come from a small village and had won a scholarship to a prestige grammar school in Port-of-Spain, was insightful: she said quite frankly, that for most of the Indians she knew, independence appeared to be another victory for the Blacks.

Despite indifference from some Indians, guarded participation from others and outright support from few, certain values had become common to the various ethnic groups in the larger society, especially to people of African and Indian descent. One of these was the importance of education as a means of attaining social mobility. Developments in various areas of the economy and society were to benefit all groups even if they benefited some more than others. Developments in the education system and economic expansion in the post-independence period in fact accelerated the integration of Indian women into Creole society.

The rapid expansion in the provision of free secondary education for both rural and urban Trinidad and Tobago was clearly important for Indians, a large percentage of whom still lived in rural Trinidad. For instance, of the total Hindu population in 1960, 68.3 per cent lived in rural districts. The introduction of the Common Entrance Examination, which offered equal chances to boys as well as girls, created major differences in the attitudes to the education of girls and in attitudes to their later employment out of the home. The establishment of the Junior Secondary and Senior Comprehensive school systems later on also contributed to changing attitudes and practices between young people of different ethnic groups, perhaps through contact with each other at earlier ages. And free university education, albeit limited in its offering, also became available to the local population.

The second factor which was of major importance was the opening up and expansion of the cash economy in the 1960s and 1970s. New developments in the economy, especially from the 1970s, which made available jobs in the various sectors – commercial, petroleum and other industrial and public sectors – also involved a greater geographical shifting and displacement in the Indian female population. Indian women began to enter the Public Service as well and mix with the Black men and women who predominated in the public sector. Many Indian women joined the teaching profession, a profession in which they were encouraged as it was regarded as an extension of their nurturing role. Indian women who had had access to a university education began to move into other professions, with the legal profession proving to be one of the most attractive. The main outcome of all of this were the changes which began to occur in the traditional Indian family setting. In the shift to a greater consumer economy, the women's wage or salary earning contribution was now being viewed as important.

Changes, which occurred in the Indian family in the post-independence period, appear to be more sudden than they in fact were as these were evolving over the last few decades. Certainly the extended family network had become eroded over time and replaced by the nuclear family. Researchers and other insightful observers now freely commented on the somewhat oppressive nature of the extended Indian family, despite the glorified notions of support and security which it purported to offer. Pariag's extended family network dominated by a rich uncle in Earl Lovelace's *The Dragon Can't Dance* illustrates the relations of economic dependence which ensured kin allegiances.[22] Some research has revealed a shift to more nuclear-type families among Indians in urban settings – for instance, in San Fernando in 1980, 88 per cent of Indian families were nuclear; in Arouca and El Dorado 48 per cent and 44 per cent of the families were extended and these were based primarily on economic cooperation.[23]

A study on social and cultural change in the Indian community of El Dorado from 1960–1980 is also useful. Sharmatee Sieunarine finds this Indian community not at all homogeneous either by religion or by generational attitudes and practices. With regard to the question of marriage, most of the older women she interviewed between the ages of 50 and 60 indicated that they were married by the age of 12. One woman recounted that she had never seen her husband before the wedding and she only knew she was going to be married on the Sunday when on Thursday her mother took her to town to buy some new clothes. The situation had changed drastically by the 1980s. There was a significant decrease in arranged marriages, and the unmarried girls above 20 felt and said there was no disgrace attached to being unmarried at that age.[24]

Where changes have occurred though, some of them have shown a startling shift for only a few decades. For instance, Jack Harewood has measured a remarkable reduction in the Crude Birth Rate among Indians, from 45.9 per cent to 29.1 per cent from 1960 to 1970. This appreciable decline among the Indian population was due in part to the greater availability and accepted use of contraceptive practices, lower fertility among more educated women and later and deferred childbearing among women who also deferred their age of marriage. It might be pointed out here that despite many changes in mating and fertility practices of Indian women, there is still little acceptance for unmarried pregnancies, especially for women resident in their parents' homes.

At some point we need, however, to differentiate between creolisation and modernisation. In the post-independence era the two are necessarily linked. Creolisation has been interpreted to mean a commitment – political and social – to the new society, as well as physical engagement with the society so that the existent cultures are mixed and enriched in the process; modernisation is taken to mean the intrusion of the external and metropolitan. V.S. Naipaul in *The Middle Passage* is incisive on this: modernity in Trinidad means more than the trappings-air-conditioned bars and supermarkets, night clubs and restaurants, "It means a constant willingness to change, a readiness to accept anything which films, magazines and comic strips appear to indicate as American."[25]

Modernisation and petroleum revenues have been the major democratising agents in the society in the last twenty years or so. The creolisation process becomes interlocked with modernisation as new values are formed and shared between and among the various groups.

To speak of the "creolised" Indian woman at present is to employ both concepts at the same time. If we compare some of the obvious changes in the pre-independence and post-independence periods the picture is a more vivid one.

For instance, the staple diet of Indian women or the meals they prepare in Indian households can no longer be said to be comprised of a traditional cuisine but includes many other "Creole" dishes as well as the more modern North-American fast food. Certainly one wonders also whether the objection to pork and beef is still as strong.

It is very uncommon to see even older Indian women wearing their *ohrnis* – the traditional muslin cover which it was incumbent on them to wear as a form of respect – in the presence of menfolk or the public. In fact, like the *sari*, the *ohrni* and forms of Indian dress have become traditional wear for religious or ceremonial functions. Among younger Indian girls I can detect little difference in their trendy style of dress from women of other ethnic groups. Similar findings, but always with exceptions for age, class and location, can be stated for linguistic patterns, musical preferences and leisure-time activities.

To gauge the extent to which there have been changes among Indian women, I thought a useful exercise would be to assess my theory against the views of some younger women of Indian descent who were born in and are products of the post-independence era. I asked fourth and fifth-form girls from two secondary schools, one school predominantly Indian and the other mixed, to write short essays on growing up in the multi-racial society of Trinidad and Tobago. The responses were encouraging yet troubling. The early paradox which Indian women faced had now been replaced by other paradoxes and in the more complicated society today by a series of growing contradictions. One Indian girl of 14 writes:

> As an Indian girl I feel fairly well adjusted to being in a multi-racial society. I don't consider myself as being superior to anyone else. Although at times I tend to feel a bit inferior when I hear people say "look a coolie", but I don't let this keep me down. Being an Indian has given me a fairly good opportunity to break the tradition that my grandmother and mother followed. I mean I don't have to quit school at an early age for the purpose of learning to handle a household so that I can get matched for marriage. But quite differently, I can pursue a career ahead of me. I think having a career is important because then I would be less dependent on a man.[26]

This independence of thought and action is a source of conflict between many younger and older women as this youngster's predicament tells us:

> Anytime I get into a quarrel with my mother, she gets into a rage and says its time for me to get married . . . anytime I want to go somewhere, for example to the cinema or a bazaar, my mother has to bring up some "nancy" story and say that when she was my age, she never wanted to go anywhere or she never quarrelled with her parents. I know I can't cook, but I try and then at that moment my mother begins her "nancy" stories again, and says that when she was my age she already knew how to cook, wash and take care of a house. She totally hates to see me talking to a boy in person or talking to him on the phone . . . then and there she starts to talk about marriage again. While I am on the topic of marriage she says she doesn't mind who I marry as long as he's rich, has a good job, does not smoke or drink and is not a Muslim.

Young Indian girls today are also keenly aware of the conflicts in male/female relationships which have arisen from greater female autonomy, but it seems that they are also ready to deal with these situations. Another young girl writes:

> A lot of Indian women today are working women. The Indian men, however, do not like the idea of this because they like to be the superior one. I think that people expect too much from an Indian woman and that they have a lot of changes to make in their lives. Indian women have to have the right to their say!

CONCLUSIONS

It has obviously not been possible to deal with every factor or every qualification in presenting these arguments for the creolisation of Indian women in Trinidad and Tobago. In fact, I know I have run the risks of over-generalisations and over-simplifications. I would like, however, in summarising my conclusions to incorporate some observations about the present trend which this process has taken.

My first conclusion is that there has been a tremendous shift in the status of Indian women in this society from their early introduction to the present time. The stereotype of Indian woman as primarily keeper of the culture, sacrificial and passive, can no longer apply to all Indian women. They have become more integrated into the society, a process accelerated in the post-independence era by the increased opportunities available to them in education and employment out of the home. Indian women who embraced Christianity fairly early were among the first to become creolised, but there is a distinct and growing trend for women of the Hindu and Muslim faiths to assert their presence in the society.

The second conclusion I would draw attention to is that contemporary creolisation has been a selective one. While it has involved a necessary degree of interculturation, there is also a qualitative change. Indian women's affirmation of their national identity does not automatically mean a negation of ethnic or religious identity. On the one hand, there is a greater political "national" con-sciousness among both Indian men and women. This is, perhaps, especially evident in political events over the last decade of the twentieth century – although it is clear that women are grossly under-represented in national politics. But a growing confidence in national assertiveness, encouraged by an Indo-Trinidadian prime minister governing the society for the first time, has also reinforced a confidence in ethnic and religious identity. This might explain, for example, the recent attention being paid by the more fundamentalist Hindu groups to the roles expected of Hindu women in this society. Even those Indian women and men who do not subscribe to the Hindu faith, or blindly follow the path of ethnic politics, are reluctant to relinquish the source of their cultural strength. And rightfully so, for it is not clear that the answer to the ethnic problems of plural societies is that of cultural homogenisation.

Finally, what has this meant for Indian women themselves? A process of change, which was in my view, inevitable, has created a number of severe contradictions for Indian women today in their relationships with the rest of the society.

Accustomed to the stereotype of the passive and submissive female role, Indian men have reacted to the growing confidence of Indian women in confused and sometimes violent fashion. This violence is not always manifested physically but can take the form of vicious, degrading or obscene insults slung at Indian women who choose to be friendly with men outside their ethnic group. Without fail, all of my interviewees repeated the theme "Indian men are traumatised by the new and assertive Indian woman they are now seeing." Several felt that the phenomenon of a relatively large proportion of professional Indian women, who were unmarried today, was a result of their increasing outspokenness and assertiveness. The reasons for this reaction on the part of Indian males certainly need to be researched to complete this picture.

Several respondents also hinted at the uneasy relationship which existed between Indian women and women of other ethnic groups in the society. They suggested that this was due to their growing assertiveness in the professions, in an area in which they were historically lagging compared to non-Indian men and women. I cannot claim to substantiate any of these statements, as they can only be subjective and impressionistic at the moment. They reveal, nonetheless, the new contradictions and paradoxes faced by Indian women who have become "creolised".

One can only be optimistic about change which creates possibilities for developing the potential of a group or a sex. I think that the qualities traditionally ascribed to Indian women are being turned in the direction of becoming virtues. Indian women have not become embittered by their history, thus subservience becomes discipline, submissiveness, passion and sacrifice, diligence. Wedded with intelligence, these virtues have only served to propel those Indian women who are prepared to challenge the imposed limits fast forward into a rewarding future.

NOTES

1. This paper was originally published in Selwyn Ryan, ed., *Trinidad and Tobago: The Independence Experience 1962–1987* (St Augustine: ISER, 1988). The changes to this original paper have been deliberately few, although my own work on the area of gender relations in the Indian community has grown substantially in the last decade in both scope and depth. On rereading I feel convinced that it captures a sentiment and component of creolisation, which, if I were to adjust, would not convey the mood, or the moment which the paper expresses at this time. After one decade, I also still agree with most of what I wrote as a younger, more callow scholar

2. Kamau Brathwaite, *Contradictory Omens*. Savacou Publications. Monograph 4. Mona, (1985).

3. *Census of the Population of Trinidad and Tobago, 1980* (Port of Spain: Central Statistical Office, 1982).

4.   Rhoda Reddock, "Women Labour and Struggle in 20th Century Trinidad and Tobago 1898–1960". Ph.D. Thesis. ISS, The Hague, (1984).

5.   Bridget Brereton, *Race Relations in Colonial Trinidad, 1870–1900* (Cambridge: Cambridge University Press, 1979).

6.   Harold Sonny Ladoo, *No Pain Like This Body* (London: Heinemann, 1972).

7.   Kim Nicholas Johnson, "Considerations on Indian Sexuality", paper presented to the Third Conference on East Indians, 29 August – 4 September, 1984, University of the West Indies, St Augustine, Trinidad.

8.   Bridget Brereton, *Race Relations in Colonial Trinidad, 1870–1900* (Cambridge: Cambridge University Press, 1979).

9.   Gordon Rohlehr, "Images of Men and Women in the Calypsoes of the 1930s on the Sociology of Food Acquisition in the Context of Survivalism", in Patricia Mohammed and Catherine Shepherd, eds., *Gender in Caribbean Development* (Trinidad and Tobago: Women and Development Studies, 1988), pp. 232–306.

10.   Raymond Quevedo, *Atilla's Kaiso* (Trinidad and Tobago: Extra Mural Department, University of the West Indies, 1983), p. 88.

11.   Morton Klass, *East Indians in Trinidad: A Study of Cultural Persistence* (New York: Columbia University Press, 1961).

12.   Jack Harewood, *The Population of Trinidad and Tobago*, CICRED Series (St Augustine: ISER, 1975).

13.   Selwyn Ryan, *Race and Nationalism in Trinidad and Tobago* (Kingston: ISER, UWI, 1974).

14.   Marianne Ramesar, "The Integration of Indian Settlers in Trinidad after the Indenture Period", *Caribbean Issues* 11.3 (December 1976), pp. 52–70.

15.   Tyson Report, 1938–1939 (London: HMSO, 1939).

16.   *Census of the Population of Trinidad and Tobago, 1946* (Port-of-Spain: Central Statistical Office, 1948).

17.   Seepersad Naipaul, *The Adventures of Gurudeva and other Stories* (n.p.: Andre Deutsch, 1976), p. 33

18.   Patricia Mohammed, "Women and Education in Trinidad and Tobago, 1938–1980", M.Sc. Thesis, Department of Sociology, UWI, St Augustine, 1987

19.   Jeremy Poynting, "East Indian Women in the Caribbean: Experience and Voice", in D. Dabydeen and B. Samaroo, eds., *India in the Caribbean* (London: Hansib Publishing, 1987), pp. 231–63.

20.   Vera Rubin and Marisa Zavalloni, *We Wish to be Looked Upon* (New York: Teacher's College Press, 1969), p. 89.

21.   Ibid., p. 91.

22.   Earl Lovelace, *The Dragon Can't Dance* (London: Heinemann, 1972).

23.   Adita Mohandaye Maharaj, "The Changing Pattern of the East Indian Family in Trinidad", Caribbean Studies Thesis, University of the West Indies, St Augustine, (n.d.).

24. Sharmatee Sieunarine, "The Social and Cultural Change in the East Indian community of El Dorado in 1960–1980", Caribbean Studies Thesis, UWI, St Augustine, (n.d.).

25. V.S. Naipaul, *The Middle Passage* (London: Penguin Books, 1962), p. 48.

26. This and subsequent quotes were taken from essays written by fifth-form students of the San Juan Senior Comprehensive School. I would like to thank Vasanti Boochoon, a teacher of this school who carried out this exercise for me when writing this paper.

Veronica *M. Gregg*

Chapter 8

"YUH KNOW BOUT COO-COO? WHERE YOU KNOW BOUT COO-COO?"

LANGUAGE REPRESENTATION, CREOLISATION AND CONFUSION IN "INDIAN CUISINE"[1]

[I]t is possible that like an ancient piece of history my presence will leave room for theories.[2]

– Jamaica Kincaid

It is almost impossible to read or write the term creolisation without warnings, caveats, provisos, explanations, reworkings and even scare quotes. Within the Caribbean, the slipperiness of the term can be productive in that it can allow for layered, supple and often contradictory readings of the region. More importantly, this surface slipperiness is but a symptom of the deeply entrenched struggles for and about language and representation in terms of Caribbean identities. No deployment of its meanings in our context, however, can usefully ignore or fail to contend with the centrality of Kamau Brathwaite's thesis which itself was forged out of conflicts about the interpretations of British Caribbean history. His achievement does not only lie in his contribution to knowledge production; but it lies even more in the fact that through his power-fully imaginative reworkings of ideas about Jamaican/Caribbean cultural history, he opened a door where there had appeared to be an impenetrable brick wall. He made available a discursive space within and through which scholars on the Caribbean could *think* differently. In complicating, interrogating, or defying Brathwaite's position, writers and scholars underscore its force.

In one of its most fundamental meanings, Brathwaite suggests creolisation has to do with sex, sexuality, gender and race. *The Development of Creole Society* proposes that what embeds the creolisation process most deeply in the Jamaican socio-cultural order is the intertwining – literal and figurative – of heterosexual sex and race: "... it was in the intimate area of sexual relationships where the most significant (and lasting) inter-cultural creolisation took place."[3] There is much that is problematic in this key concept because of what it simultaneously assumes and overlooks about the constructions of sex, gender and race in terms of power. But it is a valuable proposition to think with because it helps us recognise how these constructions shape our understanding of Caribbean identities.

When the theory of creolisation travels to Trinidad packed within Patricia Mohammed's analysis of the locational identities of the Indian-Caribbean woman, she applies scare quotes, calling attention to the uniquely Trinidadian meanings and anxieties embodied in terms such as Creole, creolisation, Indian, Indianness. She writes:

> It [creolization] is a particularly daring, even offensive word to use in reference to Indian women in Trinidad for it was used popularly to refer to those women who mixed or consorted with people of African descent, especially men, Indian women who changed their eating and dress habits and who adopted non-Indian social customs. But this draws on a more popular interpretation of the term . . . "[C]reolization" was viewed as synonymous with the absorption of black culture at the expense of one's own . . . Anyone appreciative of the history of the relations between the two majority ethnic groups in this society – Blacks and Indians, understands immediately the anathema which greets the suggestion of accul-turation, especially from the Indian population.[4]

Mohammed identifies these concepts of creolisation as rooted in common knowl-edge and a settled system of values. Leaving them intact, her study moves away and goes on to argue for a "richer meaning".[5] The implications and effects of these cultural attributes, however, are made more – not less – potent by distancing. Instead of being left in their place, the premises upon which these embedded assumptions rest must be opened up for examination. They too invite analysis and inquiry.

It is necessary to call attention to the way in which the prevailing interpretations of creolisation and Indianness are constitutively entangled within the terms of a cruelly conceived binary logic. One of the major themes in the dominant narratives of the Indian in the Caribbean, dating back to the nineteenth century, has been an almost surgical separation from the African Caribbean Other.[6] Within these narratives, which have bolstered vastly different ideological projects, Indianness is construed through such terms and tropes as cultural richness and depth, Brahminical purity, family values, rigid patriarchy, female beauty, diligence, thrift, economic saviours of the Caribbean, fear of absorption, marginalisation as a result of envy, hostility or misunderstanding. What is most striking in this concept of Indianness is its reliance on synecdoche and the production of difference. This construction achieves its illusion of security – and indeed, can only be enabled – through and by the implicit and explicit construction of African-Caribbean culture as simultaneously lacking, open, degraded, and of African-Caribbean people as emblems of both promiscuity and sexual undesirability, laziness, chaos, irresponsibility and inferiority.[7]

It is also necessary to note that what is termed the "popular interpretation" of creolisation and Indianness in Trinidad depends, like Brathwaite's, upon the construction of gender and heterosexual sex through racial differentiation. The discursive regulation of the "Indian" woman is a key part of this project. Therefore, regardless of the interpretations that are privileged, common knowledge or "richer meaning", there is no way to address the concepts of creolisation and Indianness without working through the critically enabling roles that are assigned to gender and female sexuality within these definitions.[8] In her reading of Lashmi Persaud's *Sastra*, Paula Morgan observes that the Indian's "anathema" to assimilation and creolisation is articulated, in important ways, through the ascription of gender roles:

> Persaud seeks to construct a 'pure' cultural and ethnic space, an island apart, from the hurly burly of multicultural Trinidad . . . Men and women enjoy peaceful and divinely ordered relationships . . . Even the very young draw comfort and a sense of deep assurance from familial and caste prescriptions . . . The women are the quintessential preservers of the domestic culture – pictures of grace, beauty and subservience . . . creators of nurturing environments . . . As repositories of the tradition – their charm and beauty . . . their ritual acts of obeisance, speak of an enchanted space to which the men can retreat from the despoilation of the broader society . . . Persaud's protagonist locates herself . . . outside of the framework of Caribbean nationalism.[9]

Of course, Caribbeans of Indian ancestry do not speak with one voice. Furthermore, the social and discursive construction of Indianness in terms of the

Caribbean remains a dynamic and contested site. Some writers and scholars insist upon the Caribbeanness of the Caribbean Indian, pointing to the necessity and importance of negotiating an identity from within these still troubled waters.[10]

In the midst of all this contestation, can there be a Caribbean reality that encompasses us all? Ramabai Espinet believes there is; and it is that from which her writerly self is spawned: "[A] Caribbean reality exists and because we have been nurtured within its fold, we know its depths as naturally and intimately as we know the sound of our mother's voice."[11] Espinet does not overlook or minimise the historical, cultural or racial divisions. Instead, her work insists that the imperatives of understanding what divides and unites Caribbeans of different races and both genders require that we all till the ground from which the dominant narratives, ideas and experiences have sprouted:

> [T]he experience of Indo-Caribbean people should not remain within their relatively isolated community. It is part of the general historical movement of peoples into this archipelago and as such belongs to all, impacts on all and should be known by all . . . The argument goes that if [the] intellectual knowledge is to be enlarged then Indians must begin to do it for themselves. Why? Is the Indo-Caribbean experience not part of our common heritage as Caribbean people?[12]

Not only does the Indian identity go into the making of the Caribbean, but this identity itself is a distinctly Caribbean product; it is made in the Caribbean. The protagonist of Espinet's short story "Indian Cuisine" omnivorously consumes cookbooks, which eventually allows her to become a "designer of cuisine" and produce elaborate recipes.[13] In this way, the cuisine of the Trinidadian woman becomes both Indian and something else. That this is part of Espinet's understanding is clear:

> I feel free to take, or make, or break and to mix anything from anywhere if it's right. In a way, this is my sense of being Caribbean and essentially a hybrid . . .
>
> [I]n the poem, 'Merchant of Death,' I use Rasta talk . . .
>
> I have been pounded by some Indo-Caribbean friends for this. One . . . insists that it takes away from the 'purity' of the Indian experience . . . A Brahminical sense of 'purity' certainly operates in the Indian sphere at the level of the ideal – but not at the level of daily experience . . . There is also within that concept of 'purity' a fixedness which denies the evidence of creolisation.[14]

"Indian Cuisine", which can be read as a fictional reworking of the concepts of Indianness and creolisation, deftly explores the concerns with sex and gender, race and culture, by which these terms are enabled.

Yet another way in which we can enter into a discussion of this short story is through Espinet's own response to the fictive Indian Caribbean woman in "Arrival of the Snake Woman" by the non-Indian Jamaican writer, Olive Senior. Espinet's response provides insights into the perils and possibilities that are implicit in her charge to us that we all take responsibility for studying the Indian-Caribbean presence as part of our common heritage. She observes:

> In an ethnically diverse region like the Caribbean, it has begun to strike me forcibly just how people write . . . as if they live in a homogeneous society. Well, maybe they do . . . [An] example is Olive Senior's story, "The Arrival of the Snake Woman." I know that [Senior] was aware that she was venturing into unknown regions and opening up something unspoken . . . in Jamaican culture . . .
>
> Yet, "coolie" is an incredibly loaded racist epithet in the Caribbean for Indo-Caribbean people. It speaks of contempt and low-status . . . [I]n the '80s and '90s can we write a story about a character named Miss Coolie? Coolie is as offensive to Indians as "nigger" is to Afro-Caribbean people. Had the tables been turned and an Indo-Caribbean writer turned out a similar story about cultural confrontation featuring a character called "Miss Nigger" by Indians in a largely Indian community, there would have been instant recognition of the work as racially offensive . . . [Yet] Miss Coolie exists unchallenged. I use this example to show the degree of disdain that still exists in mainstream Caribbean society, on the whole for its citizens of Indian descent.[15]

Terms such as "coolie" and "nigger", Espinet is right to insist, are never neutral and cannot be taken for granted. They secrete violence in their very being. These are verbal acts loaded with hostile intentionality; designed to mark, reduce, distance. The offense they give must not be trivialised, overlooked or evaded.

My desire, therefore, is not to justify Senior's use of the term nor to evade the criticism, but to offer a way of reading that suggests a striking continuity between Senior's and Espinet's portrayal of the Indian-Caribbean woman in terms of creolisation. Both writers are attempting different parts of the same project: enlarging the possibilities of Caribbean language and identity, while courageously confronting the obstacles these impose. They know that the meanings of the symbolic past and the historical past are dispersed and impalpable in the culture but that they are very definite. They go in search of the cultural markings that contribute to the making and positioning of identities. One writer explores the coming of the Indian woman in nineteenth-century Jamaica; the other, the identity of the "Indian" woman in twentieth-century Trinidad. The latter text demonstrates that the Indian-Caribbean woman, and therefore all Caribbean people, are bound still by the same constrictions explored in the former.

Senior is at pains to make clear that the short story "The Arrival of the Snake Woman" is an emblem of the mysteries, the enigmas of everyday life. In writing about the Indian-Jamaican woman who has remained invisible and silent in the literary and historical discourses, Senior refrains from attempting to speak for her or even to tell her story. What the narrative does is to carefully articulate the presence of the space assigned to the Indian woman – as a "coolie" and "Snake Woman" – without encroaching on her subjectivity. The story simultaneously focuses on her presence as an enigma and on the effects that this enigmatic presence has on the society: "Although I tell so much about everybody, everything else, the story doesn't answer the fundamental questions about the 'Snake-Woman' herself, questions that are posed at the end of the work."[16] The story marks the location that the "Snake Woman" occupies in the collective minds of the Black and White people who live in the community. For them, she exists not as a self, but as a topic and catalyst. Some in the rural community even "knew" the "Snake Woman"/"coolie" before she arrived. The naming preceded the arrival.[17] Indeed, terms like "coolie" and the even more dehumanising though less charged "Snake Woman" are meant to mark the demonstrable distance between the Indian woman as object of others' discourse and the Indian woman as historical subject. In the end, the Indian woman reconfigures and thereby escapes these imposed definitions; and her presence and actions effect important shifts in the shape of the community and in others' self-perception. This is most clearly suggested in her attainment of the high status of "Mother" in the hearts and minds of the members of the community.

And yet . . . she enters as an enigma and when the story closes she remains an enigma wrapped in a mystery, producing a puzzle. Senior's narrative is profoundly ironic. In the telling of the tale, the Black narrator reconstructs the world he knew as a child when "Miss Coolie" mysteriously entered. It is his story in which she is almost always silent. When she does speak to offer him advice, he does not take it. Although he tells of her actions and the lessons that she has taught him, he fails to learn from them. She, according to him, actively makes choices to become a part of the community in which she finds herself and ultimately becomes successful and accepted. The narrator also succeeds, but by separating himself from that very community into which she assimilates herself and thereby restructures. In the end, he misperceives the meanings of and the reasons for Mother Coolie's success. With respect and restraint, the Senior short story meditates upon the problems of misnaming and misperception.

If we lay side by side Senior's, "The Arrival of the Snake Woman" and Espinet's "Indian Cuisine", the spirit that imbues the latter story contradicts, in complex ways, its author's critical assessment of Senior's characterisation. What is more, a clear line of continuity emerges between the two narratives. The one is articulating the cultural dogmas that define the Indian-Caribbean woman; the other shows her subjectivity probing these in order that she may speak herself. Senior's narrative describes the location assigned to the "Snake Woman" in the symbolic and social order of nineteenth-century Jamaica and her negotiation of that space. Espinet's shows the Indian-Trinidadian woman coming into representation. Significantly, we see that even when she does attempt to speak (for) herself, as I demonstrate later, the cultural codes by which the Indian-Caribbean woman is defined continue to impose a silence upon her. Both short stories leave questions about the language through which the Indian-Caribbean woman, *as subject and object*, is imagined. These narratives, together and apart, are asking us to question, to go beyond the boundaries imposed upon her identity.

Ramabai Espinet and Olive Senior belong to a group of contemporary Caribbean women writers and scholars who exhibit an imaginative empathy in their bid to come to terms with the complex societies that produced them.[18] Both writers, too, share a common adherence to the concept of creolisation. And the writing of both teaches us that as long as the Indian woman, or any other group, remains trapped within others' definitions, then all Caribbeans are also trapped. They compel us to confront the often ugly and painful ideas that have become encrusted in our culture and, therefore, in our identities. The ways of thinking about (which shape ways of interacting among) Caribbean people of African and Indian ancestry have hardened into an accumulation of matter in the social and cultural body. This hardened matter, which is often erroneously defined as stereotyping, must be lanced in order to be examined. To ignore, selectively use or take it for granted, as I suggested earlier, is to reproduce and make it stronger. But what is most challenging is the realisation that the process of bringing to light commonly held assumptions, subjecting them to scrutiny, is necessarily painful because it requires an apparent repetition of these very ideas. Although this repetition appears to reproduce or reinforce the assumptions, it is meant to do the opposite – to expose the principles by which they are activated.

Studying the systemic violence that structures the language and history of Caribbean identities is the difficult and dangerous work that we must do, if we are to honour Espinet's charge to us. In this regard, as with the ideas about creolisation, the figure of Kamau Brathwaite has much to teach us. He is a still embattled survivor, some say winner, of the culture wars of the 1960s and 1970s which took place mainly in Jamaica and Trinidad.[19] If this was a period of extraordinary ferment and creative discussion about the meanings of Caribbean identity and Caribbean literary critical practice, it was also a time of lacerating quarrels and divisions. In large part, this was because unacknowledged or unexamined anxieties and conflicts about race and colour, sex, sexuality and gender (the last three, being the most deeply repressed) were projecting themselves as discussions about literature. The profound effects of these quarrels continue to resonate today in very interesting ways even outside the region. As someone who was, and is, in the very eye of this fierce and still gathering Caribbean storm, Brathwaite cautions us to learn from those "uncivil civil wars with/in Caribbean culture".[20]

Caribbean-born writers and scholars of succeeding generations, whether this is acknowledged or not, were formed within this crucible. If we are to take responsibility for trying to work out the meanings of our collective identity, we must bring to the surface the hard questions that fester beneath our analyses and responses, and which so often derail our best intentions: What precisely is at stake? What investments do we have in these ideas about Indianness, Africanness, creolisation in the Caribbean? What do these ways of thinking give us? What do they promise? From what do they protect us? To what do they blind us? Is it possible to hold fast to those cultural values that provide us with agency or seem to enhance us, while condemning the ones that assault us? At what point does identity-in-language become inseparable from the "real" African, Indian, in-between (or none of the above) Caribbean person? When and where does the examination of culturally encoded values of race and identity become too close for comfort and start giving offence? What turns the emancipatory gesture of seeking to identify our communal selves into a weapon of assault? Or worse, much worse, when does this gesture feel like an obdurate insensitivity toward our deepest vulnerabilities? Are "Indians" comfortable when "Africans" explore the meanings of Indianness in the Caribbean; or, is it construed as the violence of being named by an Other, being spoken for? Are they more, or less, comfortable when Whites do the same thing? How do Blacks feel when Indian-Caribbean writers and scholars speak (about) blackness? What do we believe, really believe, about ourselves and others? What must remain unspeakable and unspoken? What are the silences, the secrets that our words deny?

Part of the gift of "Indian Cuisine" is the subtle intelligence, the probing sensibility that incarnates the "I" of the Indian-Trinidadian woman who understands that she is formed by the definitions of Indianness, femaleness, Caribbeanness and creolisation; without being wholly determined by these. The narrator probes these ways of ordering reality and compels the reader to do the same. The story offers us no easy certainties, no safe knowing. If the narrative is concerned with questions of Indianness, creolisation and mixing, it achieves its effects primarily through a meditation on the problems of language, representation, and identity. The protagonist/narrator, in recalling the taste of fruit cocktail at Christmas, evokes from her lover the response that she must have enjoyed "a childhood of privilege". She knows it as its opposite, a childhood of poverty. This lover is an intimate stranger, someone who is near yet far. Someone who should understand her but does not. She also understands that the meaning he produces for her story is "wrong, all wrong. And how to begin to excavate the difference from where his head had already settled it?"[21] Her reluctance to correct him, to tell him the true situation, derives less from shame at her past poverty but more from her reluctance to use the language (names/words) that would expose too much:

> Strange, isn't it, that what stops me from telling him about all of this is not the fact of poverty, nor uncertainty, worry or any of those things, but the familiar home-names of everybody – Muddie, Da-Da, Papa, Sonia. Just calling those names would be to expose myself completely. It stayed at fruit cocktail privilege.[22]

The narrator's decision to let it remain at "fruit cocktail privilege" calls up the hydra-headed paradoxes that are secreted in the constitution of self and language. If she wishes to be understood by her lover, the opposite desire to keep herself hidden (perhaps protected?) is also strong, even stronger. She wants to correct his misconceptions about her past but does not want to reveal too much about that past. The desire to be known without self-exposure, to be understood while maintaining one's private self, means that she must keep from him the very thing that she wants him to know, that would make him understand. Within the concealment lies a revelation or a plea: the protagonist shows, that is, points toward, that which she wants to conceal. The secrets that must be kept, the desire to be known; fear of exposure, wanting to be heard – such are the contradictions that produce and impede the self-representation of the "I" of this Indian-Trinidadian woman. The impossibility of effective communication shifts the emphasis to language as a condition of self-exploration and as a prime instance of the culture that produced her. The narrator observes that she is left "alone to sort out the discomfort of my privilege".[23] But this enterprise, inescapably, is fraught with difficulties too. If language can expose too much, it can also be full of silences and secrets. It lacks the transparency that would make access to self and self-exploration fully possible. The arrangement of the story compels us to pay attention to many layers of contradictions at once. The narrative moves forward and backward in a dance of exposure and concealment.

"Indian Cuisine" does not use either/or, or even both/and, in terms of Trinidadian Creole and the formal discourse of Standard English. It mixes things up. Espinet ranges across, up, down and around the linguistic continuum with sure-footed elegance and precision, and sometimes to dazzling effect. Such a technique challenges the notion that the everyday language is more secure in its grasp of realities, a truer record of the way things are. If Caribbean people had come to believe that words could "refashion our futures"; that when we found our language, we would find ourselves and our truths, then this short story asks us to reconsider.[24] Language, whether words used at home or in formal discourse, can lead to duplicity, opacity and constant movement. Creating truths that are lies and lies that are truths, "Indian Cuisine" shows how words confuse and confound. Words are lifted out of one context and placed in another in ways which allow them to crosscut and cross out meanings. Along a kind of semantic drift, words acquire different and contradictory meanings. Each meaning leaves accretions and residue, which instead of helping to clarify, lead to concealment. At the same time, the different contexts and meanings of the key words overlap and sometimes form concentric circles in ways that make languages and "realities" partial and precarious.

Some of these key words are "privilege", "agriculture", "gambler". The narrator meditates on the word privilege: "... now that I think of it, [privilege] is a fabulous Bajan dish made of rice and ochroes, salt meat and saltfish, all cooked-down together. Why did they name it 'privilege'? ... Belize had serre, Trinidad had pelau and Barbados had privilege ... And it was all poor-people Caribbean food."[25] In recalling her own life in Trinidad as one of the poor people, she observes: "It's possible that my only real privilege was that our house was packed with old books. And that made me a reader of everything."[26] Side by side with the old books which she read voraciously existed the constant gnawing hunger of never having quite enough to eat. The remembered life is of poverty and privilege, lack and knowledge.

The grammar of the history and culture, within which she comes to understand her identity and to gain knowledge, is also revealed to be fraught with complexity and contradiction:

> Once Sonia was staying at our house for a while when her parents were on long-leave in England. When we filled out the forms at school for the Government examination the teacher asked where our fathers worked. Uncle Samuel worked at the Ministry of Agriculture so Sonia wrote "labourer" on her card. My father worked at a big supermarket in the downtown area of San Fernando. He was always counting and parcelling up money and one day I was waiting for him in

the office when Mr. Jones dropped in to see him. Jonesie saw him counting out the bills with that swift downward movement that I loved to watch . . . and exclaimed, "If ah didn't know yuh was a gambling peong I woulda guess by de way yuh handling dem bills. Yuh really should be casa man." I had heard talk about gambling at home. I wrote "gambler" on my examination card . . . Their anger at home took us by surprise. Sonia got a good stiff boof. I got a cut-arse.[27]

Sonia's conflation of the meanings of "labourer" and "agriculture" makes sense in terms of the history of agriculture and Indian indentured labour. Yet, long leave in England suggests that her father is a highly placed civil servant and that her family belongs to the professional middle classes. The history and its enabling discourses of Indianness, indentureship and agriculture are more powerful than the "reality" of her family's present existence. Their prevailing might erases the child's knowledge and lived experience when she is asked to write within the formal institution of the school. Conversely, the protagonist's mistake derives from what she believes she knows empirically, based on her senses and her everyday, familial reality. That her father's real job was gambling appeared self-evident because of the praise for his dexterity with handling bills, her mother's complaints about their precarious financial situation, and his returning home too late at night. The young girls' ignorance and their surprise at being punished underscores the disjunction between a supposedly representational language and the "reality" it purports to describe, the painful gap between language and experience.

The duplicitous nature of "reality" in terms of the extended family and of gender hierarchy is also forcefully demonstrated. When her family moves to the suburbs, they must continue to eat "poor people food", a sign of poverty not yet completely transcended. Their relative, under the guise of benign observation, mocks them: "Auntie Semoy . . . asked in her friendly way, 'How your mother always picking ochros so, eh? All yuh like ochro, eh!' She followed this up by asking Muddie who confirmed that we were almost passionate in our taste for ochroes."[28] Pretence and denial also surround the need for her mother to work outside the home:

> Da-da was ashamed of having his wife work, especially as a low-paid store clerk, so he pretended that she wasn't working at all. She pretended she wasn't working too so everything in the house was supposed to run as usual. All of the cooking fell on me although I was twelve years old and had to go to school like everybody else.[29]

The protagonist's experience with cooking derives, in large measure, from the fissures in a world where the desired order is far removed from the lived reality.

It is her practicing with a cookbook that allows the protagonist to learn that her father's gambling does not mean simply his "job", as she had earlier (mis)understood it. She notes that when she prepares the Barbadian dish, coo-coo, from a Caribbean cookbook which she found hidden away, the rest of her family refused to eat it.[30] (Their refusing to consume a Creole dish may be read metaphorically as a resistance to or disdain of absorption of the Creole culture. At the same time, though, the narrative tells us that the protagonist's mother had prepared a dish for the family using some of the same ingredients – "ochroes stirred in cornmeal batter with a whisper of saltfish" – in a different way.[31])

It was Da-da who saved me. His gambling job finished late that night and he came home hungry. He ate and ate and ate. Muddie must have been watching him suspiciously because I heard the hiss in her voice, "Yuh know bout coo-coo? Where you know bout coo-coo? "I . . . listened attentively. I had heard a neighbour whispering to Muddie that Da-Da had a Creole woman and that it wasn't really the gambling job that took up so much time. When he had finished eating, Da-Da called me and gave me a big hug. That was my licence to practise."[32]

The father's late night gambling is simultaneously clarified as well as re-defined to mean his extra-marital affair with a Creole woman – his sexual gambolling. His eating elsewhere whets his appetite for Creole food. This tangle of identities, or to continue the culinary metaphor, the stew into which her father gets himself, encourages the daughter in her cooking, and extends her horizons in ways which she will later articulate as "privilege". The exploration of questions of race, gender, culture and creolisation is enacted through the melding of sexual and culinary practices. In this detour into kitchens and bedrooms, "Indian Cuisine" reveals how the entanglements of everyday life defeat the claims of "Indian" isolation and difference, which, perhaps, makes the insistence on this difference all the more urgent.

The narrative produces less of a story and more of a destabilising effect in terms of language, identity and reality, in that it demonstrates how language can deny the very thing of which it purports to give an account. In its playful and serious exposures, its slipping and sliding, the language exhibits itself in a kind of exuberance even as it displays its camouflages and distortions. What "Indian Cuisine" reveals is not the "truth" or even a truth, but the making of a subjectivity out of the complications of history and culture, race and gender, language and silences: a life shaped by indentureship; sexual and social interaction – denied and unspoken – among African- and Indian-Trinidadians; duplicitous familial relationships; gender hierarchy; fissured "realities"; a focus on social mobility. All this is too much to tell. The protagonist would have needed to explain too much – to give too much of herself away – in order for her lover to understand the histories of contradictions and interpenetrations that are contained in and mobilised by the seemingly transparent word "privilege".

In varying contexts, "privilege" has different and competing meanings: eating fruit cocktail at Christmas; a Barbadian dish usually eaten by poor people; book-learning, that is, reading some of the classics of Europe, but also swallowing a cookbook, and reading the Caribbean cookbook that helps to expose her father's gamble/gambol. But it is within the shape of the narrative itself that "privilege" yields its most complex meanings. In her attempt to explore the family, culture and history that created her, the narrator points to several key events in her life that did not suggest privilege, but indeed its opposite. At the same time, the narrative process calls forth privilege from its lack. That is to say, this reflection on her life, through an immersion in the complexities of language, leads the narrator to understand that she has managed to hew privilege out of its absence.

There remain, however, further complications. She says, "Privilege is the life I lead now. I can do just about anything in this city because I earn enough and am my own woman."[33] A sign of this privilege is that the work she had to do as a child has now become a hobby of sorts. However, the contradictions of "privilege" do not reside in her past. Her present situation raises questions about her ability to authorise her own usable past and to install it as truth. In other words, to define and speak (for) herself; to be truly, as she claims, her own woman, inhabiting her own privileged space:

> The other day one of my wealthy client/acquaintances asked where I was trained. I laughed.
>
> "Well," I said, "when I was twelve years old I went through periods of excruciating hunger. So I swallowed the biggest cookbook I could find."
>
> We both laughed.
>
> "No, really," he insisted.
>
> I answered with a straight face, "I received most of my training at the school of Indian Cuisine in La Plata. It was a real privilege to be trained there."
>
> He nodded, satisfied.
>
> So privilege it really was, fruit cocktail and all.[34]

In the same way that she cannot/will not explain to her lover, the familiar stranger, what "privilege" (or its lack) means, when she is able to explain why she produces such exciting meals, her "truth" is refused. She, therefore, has to tell a lie that makes sense; that is, which is understood as truth by her hearer. Without doubt, the narrator creates something worthwhile ("privilege") and wrests meaning out of the distortions of her life. But does she occupy a position of privilege?

A necessary pre-condition of privilege is a self-identity endowed with the power or immunity to speak and to have that utterance heard and accepted as legitimate.

We are left at the end with questions: First, what of the obstacles still faced by the emergent narrating "I" of this Indian-Trinidadian woman? Her own ambivalence about revealing too much; remaining silent when she wants to be understood by her lover; having her words refused by an acquaintance; all suggest a kind of voicelessness. Still, if the storytelling "I" of this Indian-Caribbean woman remains, in some senses, subject to self-policing and to others' assumptions and desires, is the articulation of this conflict itself a mark of resistance? Second, if the quest for knowledge depends, in an important sense, on acceptable wording and if that wording is required to give the illusion of security, what are we to make of "Indian Cuisine" in which words unhinge our knowing? For it is significant that the process of creolisation exists side by side with a language that disguises as it confers meaning, obscures even as it clarifies.

In showing how contradictions resolve themselves into paradoxes, Espinet prepares a rich banquet of "Indian cuisine", that shows how Caribbean identities are intermingled, interdependent and intercultural. She explores the permeability of boundaries and identities within a shifting multi-racial society. The Asian-Trinidadian author's reworking of the African-Barbadian Kamau Brathwaite's influential theory helps us to understand that creolisation is not yet a settled explanation of an aspect of Caribbean societies. It is the name of a problem whose solution is our promise.

NOTES

1. This essay is a revised version of the one that appreared originally in *Caribbean Quarterly*, vol. 44, nos. 3 and 4 (March/June 1998), pp. 83–92. I wish to thank Ramabai Espinet for her gracious and thought-provoking response to a draft of my first effort. This does not in any way imply that she agrees with, or endorses, my interpretation of her work. I am solely responsible for the points of view herein expressed.

2. Jamaica Kincaid, "Wingless", *At the Bottom of the River* (London: Pan Books, 1984), p. 24.

3. Kamau Brathwaite, *The Development of Creole Society* (Oxford: Clarendon Press, 1971), p. 303

4.   Patricia Mohammed, "The 'Creolization' of Indian Women in Trinidad", in
     Selwyn Ryan, ed., *Trinidad and Tobago: The Independence Experience 1962–1987* (St
     Augustine: University of the West Indies, 1988), p. 381. A version of this article is
     published in the present collection.

5.   Ibid.

6.   One of the exemplary texts in the formation of this discourse is J.A.G Froude, *The
     English in the West Indies: or The Bow of Ulysses* (London: Longman's Green 1888).

7.   Several commentators, within a growing body of scholarship, have elaborated on
     the reasons for the formation and reproduction of "stereotypes" among African
     and Indian Caribbeans. Some recent volumes in which different essayists address
     these issues include David Dabydeen and Brinsley Samaroo, eds., *Across the Dark
     Waters* (London: Macmillan, 1996); Frank Birbalsingh, ed., *Indo-Caribbean
     Resistance* (Toronto: Tsar Press, 1993); David Dabydeen and Brinsley Samaroo,
     eds., *India in the Caribbean* (London: Hansib Publishing, 1987).

8.   The space for a critical inquiry of the contradictory locations of the
     Indian-Caribbean woman within Trinidadian culture was, in a sense, opened up
     by Gordon Rohlehr's influential *Calypso and Society in Pre-Independence Trinidad*
     (Tunapuna, Trinidad, 1990). Another more recent and very valuable reading of the
     claims of Indianness in the Caribbean is that of Indian (South Asian) critic,
     Tejaswini Niranjana, "'Left to the Imagination': Indian Nationalisms and Female
     Sexuality in Trinidad", *Small Axe* 2, (September 1997), pp. 1–18.

9.   Paula Morgan, "East/West /Indian/Woman/Other: At the Crossroads of
     Gender and Ethnicity". Unpublished paper presented at the Sixteenth
     Annual Conference on West Indian Literature, University of Miami,
     April 13–17, 1997.

10. Several Indian-Caribbean women scholars and writers, in addition to Mohammed,
     previously cited, with differing perspectives and emphases, have offered readings
     of gender and sexuality in terms of the Indian-Caribbean woman. These are
     designed to interrogate or modify the prevailing assumptions about Indianness
     and West Indianness. See, for example, Ramabai Espinet, "The Invisible Woman
     in West Indian Fiction", *World Literature in English* 29.2 (1989), pp. 116–25;
     Espinet, "Representation and the Indo-Caribbean Woman in Trinidad and
     Tobago", in *Indo-Caribbean Resistance*, ed., Frank Birbalsingh, pp. 42–61; Nesha Z.
     Haniff, "The Stereotyping of East Indian Women in the Caribbean", (WAND
     Occasional Paper. Adapted from Conference on the 150th Anniversary of
     Indentureship. St Augustine, UWI, 1995); Rosemary Kanhai-Brunton, "The Queer
     One in the Family: Creative Expressions from Caribbean Lesbians". Unpublished
     paper presented at the Sixteenth Annual Conference on West Indian Literature,
     University of Miami, April 13–17, 1997.

11. Ramabai Espinet, *Creation Fire* (Toronto: Sister Vision, 1990), p. xxii. (A CAFRA Anthology of Caribbean Women's Poetry).

12. Ramabai Espinet, "Ramabai Espinet Talks to Elaine Savory: A Sense of Constant Dialogue: Writing, Women and Indo-Caribbean Culture", *The Other Woman: Women of Colour in Contemporary Canadian Literature* (Toronto: Sister Vision, 1995), pp. 106–11

13. Ramabai Espinet, "Indian Cuisine", *Massachusetts Review* 35 (Autumn/Winter 1994), p. 352.

14. Espinet, "A Sense of Constant Dialogue", p. 110.

15. Espinet, "A Sense of Constant Dialogue", p. 108.

16. Olive Senior, "An Interview with Olive Senior by Charles Rowell", *Callaloo* 11:3 (Summer 1988), p. 481–83.

17. This exploration of the space that the Indian occupies in the consciousness of the Black Caribbean is also part of Espinet's concern in the short story, "Barred". The narrative collates the voices of unnamed, but identifiably Black Trinidadian communal voices defining "Indians" as smart and dishonest; hardworking and money grabbing, suicidal and murderous; spineless and ambitious. In *Green Cane and Juicy Flotsam: Short Stories by Caribbean Women*, eds., Carmen C. Esteves and Lizabeth Paravisini-Gebert (New Brunswick: Rutgers University Press, 1991), pp. 80–5.

18. Some of the Caribbean women writers and scholars, of African ancestry, who explore the history and meanings of Indianness include, Maryse Conde, Merle Hodge, Rhoda Reddock, Olive Senior and Verene Shepherd.

19. In an interview with Stewart Brown in 1989, Brathwaite talks feelingly about the personal price he has paid for having "won" the debates:

     "I get the sense that you feel yourself rather an embattled figure in Caribbean literature? I've always been, for some strange reason. I mean I've never consciously found myself encouraged by the environment and the community in which I live . . . I have never had any conscious on-going encouragement from my peers . . . and that has always puzzled me. For instance, other than [Gordon] Rohlehr, the critics who have written about the development of dub poetry don't mention my name, when in fact I would have thought that dub poets come out of my work. When people ignore that I believe they are damaging not only my work but the whole development of the literature.

     "Does it all go back . . . to that debate . . . in *Savacou* (1971). And the last big Caribbean literature conference here in '72 when this sense of "factions" within the literary community really became apparent?

     "Yes it goes back to that. That was the division point. But a lot of other people who were also in that battle have been, let us say, forgiven, but I seem to remain the man who they go on struggling against."

"Is that not perhaps because you're seen to have 'won' the argument."

"I don't get the feeling I've won at all, but it could be. A lot of things have happened since then which have been on the side of what I was saying." Indeed some of the people who seemed to be on the other side of that battle, so far as it was a battle, are now championing the kind of material that they then seemed to condemn. But not including my work in the championship. Strange."

(Kamau Brathwaite, Interviewed by Stewart Brown. *Kyk-Over-Al*, 40 (December 1989), pp. 84–93.

20. Laurence Breiner also notes, "(In the 1990s) within the region, younger writers seem more engaged with Kamau Brathwaite's poetry." The critic also points to "Brathwaite's pervasive influence on recent West Indian poetry." In Bruce King, ed., *West Indian Literature* (London: Macmillan Education, 1995), p. 77.

21. Kamau Brathwaite, "A Post-Cautionary Tale of the Helen of our Wars", *Wasafiri*, 22 (1995), p. 75. Brathwaite suggests that the culture wars in the West Indies and the ensuing divisions have aided and abetted the process by which all West Indian writers and scholars, even the culture itself are denigrated by non-West Indian critics.

22. Espinet, "Indian Cuisine" p. 563

23. Ibid., p. 565.

24. Ibid. In reflecting on the dilemma of narrating the self, Espinet observes: "I do think there is a contradiction between needing to speak and becoming known. Finding a voice is important, but one loses privacy and anonymity, which are still the ultimate freedoms . . . I think writing enables one to feel a sense of constant dialogue, but with whom I don't know . . . [T]he risk of writing is that of becoming known and losing anonymity because words are keys to so much of one's self. The question is: do I want revelation? I don't think so." ("A Sense of Constant Dialogue", p. 104).

25. I annex this term from Gordon Rohlehr, *Pathfinders: Black Awakening in the Arrivants of Edward Kamau Brathwaite* (Tunapuna, Trinidad: 1981), p. 238

26. "Indian Cuisine", p. 565

27. Ibid.

28. Ibid., p. 567

29. Ibid., p. 569

30. Ibid., p. 570

31. For an analysis of the cultural significance of this particular dish in West Indian fiction, see Edward Baugh, " 'Cuckoo and Culture', *In the Castle of My Skin*", *Ariel* 8 (July 1977), pp. 23–33.

32. Ibid., p. 566.

33. "Indian Cuisine", p. 570.

34. Ibid., p. 572.

35. Ibid., p. 573.

PART FOUR

Creolisation and Caribbean Economy, Society and Politics in Slavery and Freedom

Verene A. Shepherd

Chapter 9

QUESTIONING CREOLE

DOMESTIC PRODUCERS IN
JAMAICA'S PLANTATION ECONOMY*

In his seminal work, *The Development of Creole Society in Jamaica, 1770–1820*, Kamau Brathwaite noted that one of the effects of the American War of Independence of 1776 was to make elements in colonial Jamaica become more supportive of the idea of diversification away from the dominant, export-oriented sugar industry and towards the production of more goods locally. This would help the island to survive the break in trade and supplies and the rising cost of imports from the Thirteen Colonies.[1] Jamaica, like other territories in the British-colonised Caribbean which had a significant sugar-planting sector by the mid-eighteenth century, had developed a dependence on outside sources, among them the North American colonies, for plantation supplies like timber, barrel staves, hogsheads, livestock, material for slave clothing and food. As colonial outposts, Caribbean economies were constrained by the mercantilist system and had developed tight connections to international capital, which deepened their underdevelopment.

The view that Jamaica's dependence on North American suppliers in particular, and external sources in general, had to be reduced, had been proffered by the pre-eminent pro-slavery planter-historian, Edward Long, in his multi-volume history of Jamaica published in 1774. Long's solutions for the crisis of supply were, first, for Jamaica to diversify its supply sources by increasing its trade with Britain and Ireland for plantation provisions, and second, for Jamaican producers to increase their efforts to provide some inputs locally and deviate even further from the "classic" plantation system. According to Long,

> . . . how strange, and inexcusable is it, that we should pay so much money every year for their [North American] horses, when those of our own breed are so incomparably more beautiful and serviceable! Great quantities of hoops, heading, and shingles, might be provided in the island, were proper methods taken to encourage our own settlers.[2]

One of the local industries that he believed should be encouraged was the livestock industry. Indeed, he regarded the restoration of the local livestock industry (practically destroyed by the English invading forces in 1655), as so essential a project that he urged legislative action,

> . . . to encourage the island breed and throw gradual restraints upon . . . importation; by which means, beef might possibly, in course of a few years, return to a more moderate price . . . thus might be saved many thousand pounds now paid for foreign salted beef, which is neither so wholesome, nutritious, nor pleasing . . . as fresh meat.[3]

Long's "blue print" for diversification included the expansion of the coffee industry, the settlement of the interior by small settlers engaged in non-sugar crops and, above all, for the White Creole population to be less conservative in its attitude toward locally-produced goods.[4] Some members of the Jamaican House of Assembly seem to have, if temporarily, taken the matter of import substitution seriously; for in 1775 a sub-committee of the House was established to investigate the possibility of producing local supplies of grain, staves, board and other lumber, and food provisions. Several Resolutions and Acts of the Assembly passed between 1775 and the early 1800s provided for the encouragement of local production of plantation supplies, the expansion of coffee cultivation, the removal of the restrictions on new (white) settlement in the interior, the encouragement of immigration and settlement of loyalists from North America, the Bay of Honduras and the Mosquito Shore, and for new experiments in sugar refining and production and other industries.[5]

In 1779, some grazers responded, (perhaps out of economic self-interest rather than out of patriotism) to the need to increase local supplies of meat, especially to supply British troops quartered in the island, and work animals for the estates, in the wake of the American War of Independence. By 1782, according to W.J. Gardner's estimate, the island had 300 pens[6] as more small settlers responded to the need to increase the local supply of animals and as some sugar planters established their own satellite, livestock-producing unit. As testimony to their efforts, in 1783, the local cattle farmers, in a petition to the Assembly, stated that many of them ". . . [had], of late years, employed their time, labour and little capitals in establishing pens of 'breeding stock' with the result that 'new roads of communication [had] been opened, [and] large tracts of woodland cleared'".[7] This, the cattlemen felt, showed "a spirit of improvement, which, if not checked, would soon penetrate into the very heart of the country".[8]

Despite such local/Creole responses to the crisis of the late eighteenth century, Brathwaite has questioned their degree of success and the extent to which they brought about any changes in the nature of the Jamaican economy. Like Long, he believed that Jamaican planters were conservative and were loath to dismantle the traditional economic relations dictated by the mercantilist system. In fact, it is clear that while some locally born Whites participated in non-sugar production, such economic activities remained marginal to sugar production and subject to the imperatives of sugar production. White settlers were not attracted to interior locations and looked to the sugar industry, not alternative husbandry, for upward social mobility. Instead of supporting local efforts at diversification, many among the sugar-planting elite class lobbied for the restoration of traditional trading relationships with North America, rejecting local products as inferior and alternative lines of trade as expensive. The result, as Brathwaite points out, is that "at every step . . . the creatively 'Creole' elements of the society were being rendered ineffective by the more reactionary 'colonial'."[9]

This essay seeks to engage with Brathwaite's vision of what he termed (in a very narrowly defined sense), a "Creole economy" (that is, the local production of goods and services traded internally), and to participate in the debate over the existence of a colonial versus a Creole mentality, using the example of the livestock farmers, arguably among the best example of local producers seeking to provide some alternative to imports. The article supports Long's and Brathwaite's view that Jamaican planters' commitment to external sources of estate inputs undermined local producers; but demonstrates that as far as the livestock industry was concerned, the commitment to the use of imported animals was less towards North America (or even Britain) as they have suggested, and more towards the Spanish Caribbean, a perennial source of competition with local livestock producers. Thus, while it is true that an insufficient number of small White settlers developed land unsuitable for the cane in activities like pen keeping and thus deepened the island's dependence on external suppliers, sugar planters' own commitment to imported supplies of livestock (in keeping with the nature of the plantation system) impeded the attempts of local producers to help to make the Jamaican economy viable in local autonomous terms. The result was the existence of relatively small pens with low livestock densities incapable of meeting the island's total livestock needs and unable to compete with external suppliers. Finally, the essay seeks to answer some fundamental questions: did engagement/participation in "Creole economy" imply a commitment to "Creole society"? Was there really a dichotomy between colonial and Creole? Did the social behaviour of livestock farmers suggest that their participation in the local livestock industry was a reflection of a Creole mentality?

THE HISTORICAL DEVELOPMENT OF STOCK REARING IN JAMAICA

The livestock industry in Jamaica pre-dated the establishment of sugar as the dominant export commodity in the island around 1740, and occupied an important role in the economy even after the island switched to sugar. Facilitating this was the island's varied physical environment, which permitted the production of non-staple commodities, the presence of small settlers who could invest in the less capital-intensive livestock industry but not in sugar, the continued demand by the sugar estates for working animals and the willingness of some sugar planters to support the local producers.[10]

Livestock farming expanded in the late eighteenth and early nineteenth centuries as the need for work animals for the sugar estates increased. For, although using wind and waterpower by the nineteenth century, estates still maintained a large number of animal-drawn mills. Mules, oxen and horses were needed as draft animals, as means of transportation for the army and estate personnel, and cattle were needed to provide meat for a mostly White consumer market. The expense of importing animals from Britain and North America, and the high mortality rate among the animals, were factors which encouraged some producers to engage in stock rearing in the hope of capitalising on the needs of the estates.

THE ECONOMIC POTENTIAL OF THE INTERNAL TRADE

The existence of local livestock-producing units expanded the internal marketing system, more specifically, the inter-property trade. A variety of goods found their way into the internal system of exchange between Jamaican properties. The primary product was livestock, comprising working steers, spayed heifers, breeding cows, mules, horses, bulls, calves, asses, fat cattle (sold to butchers), old worn-out estate cattle and small stock. Other goods included food provisions, grass, milk, bricks, white lime, shingles, fresh beef, fish, timber and staves. Of these goods, livestock was the most lucrative for pens. According to Bryan Edwards, an eighteenth-century estate spent a minimum of £300 per annum to replace stock.[11] The majority, indeed, spent far more. In 1782, Simon Taylor, the attorney for Golden Grove estate in St Thomas-in-the-East, reported that that estate needed 100 working steers annually.[12] Sugar planters expended a significant portion of their working capital to purchase livestock. At around £30 each in 1820, this would cost an estate with an annual need of 100 working animals £3,000 per annum. Estates also bought mules and spayed heifers annually. Around 1820 the price of a mule was £40 and for a young, spayed heifer, £22.10s. to £26 each. J.B. Moreton recorded that an estate with even as little as 100 acres of cane needed to buy 40 mules annually and maintain 100 always on the estate.[13] Pens thus stood to gain considerably from the internal trade in animals.

The volume of livestock being sold in the island can be partially ascertained from the Accounts Produce. In the first return made in 1740 when pens were not as numerous as later on, these units supplied only 34 head of working stock to estates. In that year, few pens were monocultural livestock units, and St Catherine's units, in particular, sold more sheep and small stock than cattle and mules. By 1780, 21 out of the 266 returns were pens. The latter were involved in the sale of 942 head of livestock. This represented 50.7 per cent of the 1,881 sold by the 120 units, such as estates and coffee plantations, involved in local trading. By 1820, when the total number of livestock traded internally was 14,134 head, pens were responsible for 8,267 or 54.49 per cent, an improvement over their 1780 level.[14]

Yet the numbers available from the local pens were never sufficient to meet the total livestock needs of sugar estates, estimated at over 700,000 in the late eighteenth century; and the potential earning power of such units was undermined by the behaviour of the sugar planting elite. Sugar estates squeezed pens onto marginal lands, restricting their pasture space; some planters produced their own livestock on their estate or satellite pen, or bought from cheaper Spanish-American suppliers.

NUMBERS, SIZE, LOCATION AND DIVERSIFICATION ON PENS

A fundamental condition for the viability of the local livestock industry was the availability of adequate land for pasture in order to maintain a certain livestock density to meet the needs of the sugar estate market. According to some estimates, the island's 710 sugar estates in the eighteenth century needed between 56,000 and 710,00 oxen alone, not counting other types of work animals like mules, horses and spayed heifers.[15] However, climatic and other physical environmental factors restricted the expansion of pens in the period of slavery. Additionally, pens were not necessarily allowed to develop on lands eminently suitable for pasture. The greater commitment to the sugar industry meant that estates tended to develop on the flat, coastal lands and the interior plains. As the sugar economy expanded and created competition for land space between agrarian units in the island, pens were unable to maintain the required acreage of pasture and livestock population to supply the market. Pens were, sometimes, confined to marginal interior lands. Even where estates went out of production due to changes in the climate (as in St Catherine where deforestation caused extremely dry conditions), abandoned estates lands were not necessarily turned over to pasture.

Even with restricted space, the absolute numbers of pens in Jamaica – around 400 by the end of slavery – may have been sufficient to supply the total livestock needs of the island's sugar had they devoted all land space to pasture or maintained larger herds. The mean size of pens was 824.58 acres in the period 1780–1845 (with a range from 300–3,750 acres). This was large by island standards; but not all of this land was suitable for pasture.[16] Of the total of 1,248 acres comprising Shettlewood Pen, for example, 68.26 per cent was devoted to grass; and the average in grass for most pens was even lower.[17] Pens were organised as self-sufficient units, much like sugar estates, and so had land devoted to buildings, provision grounds and forestland for timber.

Although they had maintained an independent economic dynamic in the pre-sugar era, by 1740, pen keepers were heavily dependent on the sugar sector. Livestock farmers relied on the sugar planters to purchase their output such as animals and ground provisions. The section of the sugar estate market to which independent pen keepers had access, however, fluctuated according to the state of the market for sugar. This precariousness of the market caused many livestock farmers to diversify their economic activities in an effort to cushion the effects of a low demand and thus a low price for working animals. The instability of the sugar market, particularly in the nineteenth century, caused many pens to intensify their diversification efforts, often incorporating pimento, logwood, coffee and food production. This contributed to the comparatively low livestock density and drew off enslaved labourers for activities unconnected with livestock husbandry. The lack of a larger number of monocultural pens, therefore, had important implications for the supply of livestock in the island. Furthermore, the need to maintain a larger number of enslaved people than was usual for livestock husbandry (usually a ratio of one ednlaved to 50 head of livestock was adequate, but in Jamaica the ratio was higher) increased the production costs on the pens. The estates had a high import co-efficient in foodstuffs; some planters established their own supplementary food-producing units, and the existence of the provisioning system controlled by enslaved people combined to limit the portion of the food market to which independent pens had access.

ECONOMIC BEHAVIOUR OF THE SUGAR PLANTERS AND THE TRADE WITH SPANISH AMERICA

The attitude of the dominant sugar planters and the maintenance of external trading links with Spanish America must be recognised as essential factors explaining the failure of anything like a "Creole economy" to thrive. It has already been demonstrated that although, theoretically, the sugar economy afforded a relatively substantial market capable of acting as a dynamic factor for the development of the island, such potential dynamism was not directed entirely towards the pen sector which in turn was unable to respond adequately to the market opportunities represented by the sugar economy. This dictated a continued dependence on imported supplies, particularly from Spanish America as opposed to North America and Britain. Only occasionally were livestock imported from Britain and Europe because of the high cost involved and the high level of mortality of the animals. The greater portion of the money spent on imported stock was paid out to non-British territories.

This trade with Spanish America may seem surprising in an age of mercantilism and during the existence of the English Navigation Acts. According to the tenets of mercantilism, colonies were primarily sources of supply for the metropole. In turn, they were expected to import their necessities from the "Mother Country".[18] National self-sufficiency was the goal desired by this mutual commerce and thus such valuable possessions required a strict commercial control, which would effectively exclude foreign trade. The Navigation Acts of 1660 sought to impose such control. By these Acts, the staple produce from the British-colonised Caribbean – sugar, rum, molasses, indigo, pimento, ginger and coffee – were to be carried in English ships. These were to be manned by a majority of British crewmen, and their goods were to be consigned solely to English ports.[19] Such policies under the Restoration contrasted with the virtual free trade of Oliver Cromwell's day during which the Spanish trade to Jamaica had developed and, not surprisingly, such laws were virtually ignored.

The importance of the Spanish trade to Jamaica had, however, been long recognised and moves were made to legalise it, despite Spain's opposition to free trade. Nevertheless, successive governors, from Thomas Modyford on, encouraged a clandestine Anglo-Spanish trade, granting licenses to traders to sell slaves and other goods to Spanish America and to import livestock.[20] Spain did not reciprocate by granting similar licenses. On the contrary, the illegal nature of the trade was emphasised in the Anglo-Spanish Treaty of Madrid in 1670. Article 8 of that treaty stated that:

> Subjects of the King of Great Britain shall on no account direct their commerce or undertake navigation to the ports or places which the Catholic King holds in the said Indies, nor trade with them. Reciprocally, the subjects of the King of Spain shall not send to or trade in the places that are possessed there by the King of Great Britain.[21]

However, articles 9, 10 and 11 opened up certain loopholes, which were fully exploited and facilitated the continuation of the contraband trade. These provided that if for any reasons – whether pirate attacks, storms or revictualling – ships of either nation found it necessary to enter the other's ports, such ships should be allowed in.[22] Furthermore, it was stated that if in the future "either king shall deem it convenient to grant any general or special license or any privileges to the subjects of the other for navigating and trading . . . the said navigation and commerce shall be practiced and maintained . . ."[23]

The passing of the British Free Port Act of 1766 had further opened up Spanish trading to Jamaica. This Act sanctioned a branch of colonial trade, which had hitherto been conducted in a clandestine manner. It facilitated the importation and exportation of certain types of goods at certain ports in the British West Indies by small vessels from neighbouring foreign colonies. This did not, however, represent a departure from the Navigation Acts, which still attempted to control the trade of staple commodities and English manufactures. The Free Port Act was designed to allow only trade in goods, which did not compete with the products of Britain and her colonies. The European-directed trade in African captives, North American supplies and the carrying trade between the mother country and her colonies remained firmly in British hands. In Jamaica, Lucea, Savanna-la-mar, Kingston and Montego Bay were declared Free Ports in 1776 and with the passing of the Act and the opening up of ports other than Kingston, the Spanish trade with Jamaica was revived.[24]

The existence of the Spanish trade was a controversial issue in eighteenth- and nineteenth-century Jamaica. The opponents of the trade blamed it for the failure of a larger number of small settlers to engage in pen keeping. The proponents argued that its continuation was vital to the better regulation of the price of beef and plantation stock. At first, the numbers imported were small. Between 1729 and 1739, for example, 124 horned cattle, 1,500 horses, 4,285 mules, 243 asses, 129 horses and 825 sheep, or an annual average of 711 animals had been imported, primarily from Cuba and Puerto Rico. A total of 14,456 animals were imported in the following decade and averaged £111,000 sterling per annum. The same level of importation in 1773 was estimated at £16,000.[25] By 1825, the annual number imported cost £11,836.[26] The largest share of the total expenditure on imported livestock in the eighteenth century was spent on mules. Between 1729 and 1749, a total of 10,477 mules were imported. In 1774, when 745 mules were brought in, the cost to the island was £11,175.[27]

Long also elaborated on two of the reasons that necessitated the importation of animals and emphasised that once these were removed, the trade would end. The first obstacle was a lack of ". . . a sufficient stock of industrious inhabitants to have been employed in breeding the number of these animals proportioned to the annual consumption".[28] The second was the absence of:

> . . . the patriotic endeavours and subsidies of the Assembly, as well as for encouraging such breeding farms, as for making good roads in every district, at the public charge, whereby the internal parts of the country must have been settled and improved with greater facility and the waste of cattle in great measure prevented.[29]

One of the reasons put forward by Long for the failure of more settlers to engage in pen keeping was the fear of overproduction and a consequent price fall.[30] In addition, a "Creole consciousness" and the lack of prejudice against local products which were vital to encourage the local industry, were clearly absent; thus Long's view that ". . . most men have a prejudice in favour of foreign articles, despising their own far superior in value"[31] might not have been too far off the mark. However, he fails to recognise the economic fact that import substitution cannot be feasible where local producers are unable to produce goods competitively, and where government policies protect foreign suppliers.

The pen keepers themselves echoed Long's sentiments. In a petition to the Governor in 1790, the pen keepers in the St Ann vestry complained of "the distressing Prospect arising in the Community in general . . . and this Parish . . . in Particular of the trade carried on between the Spaniards of Cuba and a few of the trading or commercial Persons of this country . . ."[32] Like Long, they stressed that the trade posed an obstacle to the expansion of the pen-keeping industry, "which is being partly discontinued by the Introduction of Spanish Horses, mules, mares, and neat cattle, subject to no Impost or Duty whatever".[33]

As the Spaniards were underselling local producers, Spanish cattle, horses, and mules were generally about one-third to one-half cheaper than local breeds. Spanish American horses could fetch as low as £10 sterling each, for example. Local breeds cost much more as their cost of production was higher. A further request was that livestock be removed as an allowed article of trade under the Free Port Act. This was particularly crucial at a time when, according to the petitioners, the local supply of stock exceeded current demand.[34] In their defence, planters complained that the form of payment demanded by pen-keepers was at variance with the existing method. Pen keepers required immediate payment in cash upon delivery of their livestock to sugar or coffee estates, whereas importers gave credit and demanded payment at the end of 12 months, charging 6 per cent interest. However, the scale of operation of importers was far greater than that of pen keepers who could not, under the best circumstances, afford to wait a year for payment.

The drain of capital occasioned by the import trade from Spanish America was a matter of concern towards the end of the eighteenth century. According to Long, ". . . vast amounts of our small hammered silver rials [ryalls] and pistorins are constantly exported together with dollars for purchasing mules and cattle."[35] Planters even sold some of their rum internally in order to obtain cash to purchase Spanish stock. This ". . . in every respect", said Long, ". . . seems to be a traffick extremely pernicious to the island and it is from this consideration probably that it has been more connived at by the Spaniards than any other."[36] He urged that immediate steps be taken to end this "pernicious trade". Two solutions were for the Assembly to impose a tax on imported stock and for local pen keepers to give credit – say six or nine months – to enable the poorer proprietors to defray the cost of their purchase out of the rent or succeeding crop.

Up to 1816, however, neither solution seems to have been adopted. The matter of taxation was especially problematic and Long's call for a tax to be imposed on foreign stock was echoed by pen-keepers all over the island. In 1816, for example, the pen keepers of St Elizabeth and Manchester petitioned the House of Assembly to impose a tax on imported stock on account of the hardships they suffered from the allowance of foreign imports.[37] The St Elizabeth grazers, supported by those in Manchester, complained that:

> . . . from late large importation of horned or neat cattle, mules and horses, the stock of the native breeder and grazier has become almost unsaleable, more particularly in respect of mules, there having been scarcely a spell of mules disposed of this season in the whole [pen] district . . .[38]

The complaints of the pen keepers were referred to a committee of the House of Assembly and in 1817, "An Act for laying a duty on all horses, mares, geldings, mules, and horned cattle, imported into this island, except from Great Britain and the United States of America" was effected. The duty initially levied on each head of cattle was £11.70s. but this was increased to £12 in the 1830s after repeated agitation by the pen keepers that the stock duties be raised. By 1843 the duties seemed to have been lowered, with those on neat cattle being once more just around £11 per head.[39]

Members of the House of Assembly continued to disagree over the cattle duty and even towards the end of the century, the matter was still not satisfactorily settled; but it should be stressed that the very imposition of an import tax on imported stock in the nineteenth century was testimony to the changing political situation among which was the declining power of the sugar interests in the Jamaican Assembly.

QUESTIONING CREOLE: SOCIO-POLITICAL ISSUES

The attitude of the sugar planters towards the import trade in livestock and their luke-warm support for the local livestock industry provides a hint of the socio-economic marginality of the livestock farmers; and such marginality cannot be ignored as a factor affecting the expansion of the industry. The lack of a high social standing in White society (in contrast to the sugar planters), of political power and an effective lobby in the House of Assembly clearly worked to their disadvantage. Indeed, the economic relations between planters and pen keepers, while reciprocal in some regards, nevertheless contained an exploitative element. Sugar planters who, naturally, advanced their economic self-interest dominated the House; this explains their failure to acquiesce to the growing petitions of the grazers for an increase in the duty imposed on Spanish livestock. They responded to economic imperatives rather than any blind support for local producers. This is clear from their argument that there was a great price differential in the horses, mules and cattle purchased from Spanish America, even after adding the profits of the middlemen merchants. They sought the cheapest markets when procuring these. Indeed, the very nature of the sugar plantation system, despite Jamaica's slight deviation from the classic model, made any non-economic considerations unviable. The sugar industry was primarily export-dependent; it needed to control operational costs, and sugar planters naturally sought plantation inputs from the cheapest sources.

Finally, not even the pen keepers themselves evinced any blind adherence to Creole society. Jamaica's colonial society, despite its diversified landholding class, was also culturally dominated by the planter-class. Despite the obvious development of a Creole society to which Brathwaite refers, White norms prevailed among the island's European and free-Coloured elements. Some resident White and free-Coloured pen keepers aspired to the values of white elite society which aped English, metropolitan culture. This was reflected in their lifestyle, the education of their children in the metropole and their trek to Britain as soon as their financial circumstances permitted. Thus, the ownership and operation of livestock farms, while generating goods for the local, "Creole" market, did not necessarily imply a commitment to Creole (as opposed to White metropolitan) ideals on the part of pen keepers. Indeed, as soon as financial circumstances permitted, some pen keepers themselves became a part of the absentee proprietary class in Britain.

The internal differences among the resident proprietors also served to reinforce the divisions in Creole society. Small settlers remained scattered, separate and without any consciousness of themselves as a group. They lacked political power and were increasingly marginalised in Creole society.[40] The internal class and ethnic diversities even among particular groups of small settlers were other crucial factors. Pen keepers, for example, comprised traditionally antagonistic sections – Whites and free-Coloureds, Creole-born and metropolitan-born, small entrepreneurs and larger more profitable proprietors – among whom there was no common social goals outside of the context of their similar aspirations to the socio-economic status of the sugar barons. Furthermore, resident sugar planters and resident pen keepers were economically linked, yet socially separated, with the latter aspiring to the social status of the former. Consequently, to have been born in Jamaica and to participate in the production of locally-produced plantation inputs and to display a colonial mentality at the same time was entirely possible in colonial Jamaica; there was no necessary dichotomy.

CONCLUSION

This essay has been located within the context of the discourse on a "Creole economy" in colonial Jamaica and the reasons self-sufficiency in livestock production was not achieved. While it has supported explanations relating to the economic dictates of the imperialist project in the Caribbean which precluded support for anything approximating a domestic/Creole economy and small-settler enterprises, planter conservatism, colonial elite and metropolitan interests, small settler behaviour and custom, the essay has sought to highlight other factors to be considered: the contradictions in the very notion of a "Creole economy" within a plantation system which was export-dependent; the inadequate numbers, small size, (sometimes) less than ideal location and diversified (instead of monocultural) nature of livestock farms. Additional explanations touched on are the absentee status of some "pen keepers", their lack of commitment to any Creole ideal, the high cost of local livestock (in comparison to external supplies), the precariousness of dependence on the sugar estates for a market, and the lack of political clout of the local pen keepers; so that, in the end, Jamaica failed to realise its potential of developing a viable and independent livestock industry capable of meeting its total local needs.

NOTES

*An extended version of this essay appeared in *Caribbean Quarterly*, vol. 44., nos. 1 and 2 (March–June 1998), pp. 93–107.

1. Kamau Brathwaite, *The Development of Creole Society in Jamaica, 1770–1820* (Oxford: Clarendon Press, 1971), p. 80.
2. Edward Long, *History of Jamaica*, 3 vols. (London, 1774), vol. 1, p. 541.
3. Ibid., vol. 11, p. 20, and Brathwaite, *The Development of Creole Society*, p. 81.
4. Long, *History of Jamaica*, vol. 1, p. 437.
5. Brathwaite, *The Development of Creole Society*, pp. 82–4.
6. W.J. Gardner, *History of Jamaica* (London, 1909 edn.), p. 161.
7. *Journal of the House of Assembly of Jamaica* (hereafter *J.H.A.J.*), vol. vi, pp. 609, 21. Nov. 1783; Brathwaite, *The Development of Creole Society*, p. 82.
8. Brathwaite, *The Development of Creole Society*, p. 82.
9. Ibid., p. 100.
10. See Barry Higman, *Slave Population and Economy in Jamaica, 1807–1834* (Cambridge: Cambridge University Press, 1976), p. 16 and Verene A. Shepherd, "Pens and Penkeepers in a Plantation Society", Ph.D. Diss., University of Cambridge, 1988.
11. Bryan Edwards, *History . . . of the British Colonies in the West Indies* (2 vols., London, 1798), vol. 11, p. 259.
12. Taylor to Arcedeckne, 29 Oct. 1782, Cambridge University Library, Vanneck MSS, Jamaica Estate Papers (hereafter J.E.P.).
13. J.B. Moreton, *Manners and Customs in the West Indian Islands* (London, 1793), p. 57.
14. Jamaica Archives, Accounts Produce 1740–1820.
15. Rough estimates of livestock purchases by estates as indicated in the Crop Accounts in the Jamaica Archives. Some indication is also given in the correspondence between Simon Taylor, Attorney, and Chaloner Arcedeckne, 29 Oct. 1782, J.E.P., Cambridge University Library.
16. Verene A. Shepherd, "Pens and Penkeepers", 51–68.
17. Ibid., p. 91.
18. A.P. Thornton, ed., *West India Policy under the Restoration* (Oxford: Clarendon Press, 1956), pp. 1–2.

19. L.A. Harper, *The English Navigation Laws: A Seventeenth Century Experiment in Social Engineering* (New York: Octagon Books, 1939), pp. 30–58.

20. Thornton, ed., *West India Policy*, pp. 78–80, and National Library of Jamaica (hereafter N.L.J.), "Extension Treaty Spain, Ms 450, and "Illicit Trade, 1740", Ms. 1,049.

21. F.G. Davenport, ed., *European Treatises Bearing on the History of the United States and its Dependencies*, 4 vols. (Washington: Carnegie Institute of Washington, 1917), 11, 1929, 1650–1697, p. 195.

22. Ibid., see also, Naula Zahedieh, "The Merchants of Port Royal, Jamaica, and the Spanish Contraband Trade, 1655–1692", *William and Mary Quarterly*, 3rd series 43 (1986), p. 574; and W.A. Claypole and D.J. Buisserret, "Trade Patterns in early English Jamaica", *Journal of Caribbean History*, 15 (1972), p. 1–19.

23. Davenport, *European Treatises*, p. 195.

24. See F. Armytage, *The Free-Port System in the British West Indies: A Study in Commercial Policy, 1766–1822* (London: Longman, Green, 1953), for an elaboration of the Free-Port Act. See also R. B. Sheridan, *Sugar and Slavery: An Economic History of the British West Indies, 1623–1775* (Barbados: Caribbean Universities Press, 1974), ps. 42, 460.

25. Long, *History of Jamaica*, Additional Manuscript (hereafter Add. Ms.), 12, 404, British Library, folio 330.

26. *J.H.A.J.*, 1815–1825.

27. Edward Long, Add. Ms. 12, 404, folio 330.

28. Ibid., folio 329.

29. Ibid.

30. Ibid.

31. Ibid.

32. Letter of Petition to His Excellency the Duke of Effingham from the Custos, Magistrates and Vestry of St Ann, 29 June, 1790. Jamaica Archives, St Ann Vestry Minutes, 2/9/1.

33. Ibid.

34. Ibid.

35. Long, Add. Ms. 12, 404, folio 331.

36. Ibid., folio 330.

37. "Petition of Stock Breeders and Graziers of St Elizabeth", 27 Nov. 1816, and "Petition of the Pen-Keepers of Manchester", 1816, *J.H.A.J.*, 1816.

38. "Petition of the Stockbreeders and Graziers of St Elizabeth", p. 114.

39. Public Records Office, London, C.O. 142/57, Blue Books of Jamaica, 1845.

40. Brathwaite, *The Development of Creole Society*, pp. 146–50.

Hilary McD. Beckles

Chapter 10

CREOLISATION IN ACTION
THE SLAVE LABOUR ELITE AND
ANTI-SLAVERY IN BARBADOS

The slave plantation, a core institution of Atlantic capitalism, was as responsive to market forces and the development of class and community identity as any other part of this mode of production. As a social microcosm, the Caribbean plantation slave community became differentiated over time by inequalities in the distribution among workers of economic and social benefits. Such inequalities were as real as they were paradoxical, and served to highlight the existence of group identity, interests and ideological plurality. The notion of a homogenous slave consciousness was contradicted by deep-seated conceptual differences and political fragmentation. Slave groups were starkly differentiated initially by African-derived ideas about ethnicity, and later by production-based stratification that highlighted occupational status. These differences created a complex identity system among the enslaved that propelled them to pursue betterment in diverse and often self-divisive ways.[1]

The labour politics of specific occupational groups was not always consistent with the wider social interests of the slave class. Rarely was there consensus on a strategic vision for the attainment of collective social freedom. Those who envisaged wholesale changes in the structural organisation of society did not win easily the approval of those who sought material and social improvement within mainstream colonial mechanisms. As a result, the slave class generated consistently a stream of self-contested projects of liberation and social alleviation.

The evidence produced by these contradictory designs suggests the need to adopt discursive devices, such as the concept of a "slave labour elite", in order to penetrate the thinking that informed the survival and empowerment strategies used by the enslaved.[2] Inequalities among enslaved people generated differences in reward levels and created differentiated social, cultural and political behaviour in matters as varied as access to leisure and legal freedom. At different moments across space most of the enslaved concerned with social betterment focused fastidiously on the supply of food and the attainment of cultural, domestic and recreational freedom. While this majority may have fantasised about the unfettered fellowship of legal freedom, only a minority seemed always willing to cast caution to the wind in violent pursuit of it.

In spite of the argument advanced by Michael Craton, Kamau Brathwaite, Monica Schuler, Mary Turner, C.L.R. James, Orlando Patterson, Barry Gaspar, myself and others, that anti-slavery rebellion was endemic to these slave systems, most of the enslaved, particularly those in the English Lesser Antilles, never participated in, witnessed or experienced directly, an armed protest.[3] The revolutionary overthrow of the property-owning elite was essentially the active intention of a few, as was also the case in the decades after the abolition of slavery. That the majority of those enslaved, however, desired freedom from bondage can be seen in the extensive joyful celebrations and religious expressions of gratitude witnessed throughout the region with the final passage of emancipation legislation.

Enslavers, then, had good reason to be painfully aware, (and they entered this in their records) that plantation yards and urban tenements were inhabited by enslaved persons with potential for revolutionary action. They were also aware that the ranks of the few could be joined by the many if changes in the objective circumstances tilted the balance of power, terror, or ideological authority in its favour. As business managers, nonetheless, they had no choice but to proceed with operations in the hope that a flexible policy of administering concessions, controls and punishments would be effective in maintaining an acceptable mixture of social stability and profitability.

The specific culture of enslaver-enslaved relations, of course, varied significantly across space and through time – although general patterns and trends were discerned. As societies moved further away from their frontier scaffold and metamorphosised into creolised formations, enslaved people in the Lesser Antilles, particularly those in colonies with flat, open terrain that did not facilitate guerilla-maroon style resistance, seemed more acutely sensitive to the high levels of danger (and death) involved in unrelenting anti-slavery militancy. At the same time, the benefits of negotiated social and working arrangements became more attractive to a larger number. Africans, and first generation Creoles at the frontier, had suffered very heavy losses in violent anti-slavery contests. A resultant tendency among Creole majorities in the eighteenth century was to seek ways to mitigate the harshness of their condition, while maintaining the ideological posture, or belief, that sooner or later general emancipation would come by law or by war.[4]

Barry Gaspar and J.R. Ward have found it phenomenal that during the "long" eighteenth century the enslaved of Barbados and the Leewards (Antigua, Nevis, Montserrat and St Kitts), the oldest English sugar colonies, did not implement any collective military assaults on their enslavers. Records however, do attest to the discovery of conspiracies, and rumours of the same. The 1736 aborted revolt of Antigua, one such event, has been examined by Gaspar. Jerome Handler, and Hilary Beckles, have commented on the background to rumours of a plot by enslaved people in Barbados in 1701. These events were small-scale in both demographical and geographical terms.

This pattern of resistance when placed against the overall record for the eighteenth century suggests the need to avoid generalisations about anti-slavery strategies and mentalities. Gaspar calls for a "serious study" and indicates that it should "take into account the immensity of the task slaves faced".[5] The intention here is to comment on the social and demographic processes that underpinned the retreat from violent contests, the apparent peculiarity of the enslaveds' non-violent resistance politics, and to suggest a conceptual framework within which Gaspar's concerns may be partly addressed.

Building upon analytic premises found in the historiography of slave resistance, Woodville K. Marshall, O. Nigel Bolland, Verene A. Shepherd, Swithin Wilmot and others, have shown that with respect to the socio-economic goals and political consciousness of Blacks in post-slavery reconstruction, progressive change was conceived by them in terms of the attainment of a range of social and material benefits and privileges that facilitated the creation of a "life of their own".[6] Armed revolt was but one type of strategic response; others were negotiable on a daily basis, perhaps less adventurous, but systematic and consistent with an ideology of freedom. Non-violent approaches, however, were interim – perhaps preparatory – but illustrative of the belief held by Blacks that slavery was ultimately a transitional social condition.[7]

The manifestation of a reformist ethos among the enslaved, then, signalled much more than a propensity towards acquiescence – it reflected a stage in the development of socio-political consciousness in the slave community through which they gave shape to a relevant ideology that was sensitive to social conditions and economic environments. This was seen in their changing strategic reactions to opportunities for social mobility, economic accumulation, self-pur-chased freedom, miscegenation and supportive kinship formation. In these ways, the politics of enslaved people in Creole society suggests that they engaged free classes with a sophisticated dialogue that targeted liberty as the central and ultimate objective.

Barbados, the most demographically creolised sugar-plantation society in the age of abolitionism (1780–1833), can be used as a case study to explore the extent to which this hypothesis is supported by evidence drawn from the culture of everyday life. Specific references are made to Newton plantation for which there are extensive records for the eighteenth century. The colony was the most densely populated and settled of the English-colonised sugar colonies. The slave registra-tion records for 1817 show that the island had a population density of 581 inhabitants per square mile in contrast to Antigua's and Jamaica's density of 140 and 80 respectively. The economic success of the plantocracy reinforced its social commitment to the colony. A consequence of this identity politics was the relatively high level of stability in landownership patterns. Most families who owned estates during the slave registration exercise held them 50 years earlier. The concept of a plantation as the family home in Barbados was well established among Whites, and resident ownership was the norm.[8]

By 1800 at least 90 per cent of Whites and Blacks in Barbados were locally born, by far the largest of the relative Creole populations in the English-colonised Caribbean. Populations were also largely female. The 1680 island-wide census indicated a sex distribution among the enslaved population of approximately 48 per cent males and 52 per cent female; by the early nineteenth century these ratios had settled at 46 per cent and 54 per cent respectively. With respect to the White population the census of 1715 shows that 51.3 per cent of the total were female and 48.7 per cent male; this ratio remained more or less constant throughout the century.[9] These demographic trends, enslavers believed, were significant with regard to shaping the politics of anti-slavery.

Against the background of creolisation and community development a par-ticular type of labour politics emerged. Planters intimated, for example, that enslaved peoples born in Africa were more committed to violent anti-slavery activities than Creoles, and attributed much of the enslaved community's rejec-tion of organised armed violence to their rapidly diminishing numbers. Enslaved Creoles were considered more responsive to negotiable arrangements and patron-age. In 1788, a survey of 22 of the island's plantations with a total enslaved population of 3,112 showed that only 429 (13.7 per cent) were African-born. By 1817, the island-wide percentage had fallen to 7.1 per cent (see Table 10.1). In 1806 when Caribbean proprietors pondered on the effects of the Slave Trade

Table 10.1:   African-born Slaves as a Percentage of Total Slave Population, ca. 1817

Colony	Per cent
Barbados	7.1
St Kitts	1 6.1
Nevis	14.5
St Vincent	38.8
Demerara-Essequibo	54.7

Source: B.W. Higman, *Slave Populations of the British Caribbean, 1807–1834*
(Kingston: UWI Press, 1995 edn.), p. 116.

Abolition Act, many prominent Barbadians, such as John Beckles, Speaker of the House, supported the measure for African exclusion on clear domestic socio-political grounds. One member of the Assembly, stated: "for my part I sincerely rejoice at the abolition . . . I sincerely wish the trade had been totally abolished twenty years ago."[10]

In many respects, Newton plantation's demographics mirrored those of the colony, and suggest its typicality. This is seen in its long history of family ownership, sex ratios among the enslaved population and the degree of their creolisation.[11] An estate of over 400 acres, it was owned by the Lane family for several generations, and practised sugar monoculture during the age of abolitionism.

In 1796, only three of the 50 enslaved women (6 per cent), and five of the 39 men (12.8 per cent) were African-born. Only 8.9 per cent of Newton's 89 enslaved adults in that year were African-born.[12]

Against this social, demographic and economic background it is possible to identify and examine the general development of anti-slavery labour politics. The key to this analysis, however, is an understanding of the precise social origins, growth and maturity of the enslaved labour elite. In the formation and early development of this social group we see in action a firm ideological commitment by the enslaved to the principles of social mobility and economic accumulation. In the early part of the age of abolitionism (1780–1804) it moved into its second stage of development. It was during this stage that the enslaved labour elite expanded and consolidated its position within the plantation system through its facilitation of high productivity. Commentators who witnessed its clearly differentiated lifestyle also noted its assumption of comprehensive political leadership within the enslaved community. The period is associated, furthermore, with a break from African forms of ethnic self-representation, and the adoption of a modernist status model based upon occupation and material consumption. Gaspar points to this development in his study of creolisation in Antigua and emphasised its significance to the forging of new Black identities.[13]

Occupational differentiation as a distinguishing feature of demographic creolisation meant that the elites among the enslaved considered their general interests best served most of the time by the accumulation of rights, social liberties and material privileges. Using their dominant role within slave yards, they legitimised this ideological approach by pointing to tangible, sustained achievement, such as greater opportunities for manumission, improved nutrition, literacy, better medical and material care, right to "respected" family life, access to skilled/supervisoral work, wage remuneration, socio-sexual relations with free persons, possession of property, unsupervised off-plantation movements and greater socio-cultural autonomy.

Altogether, these rights, liberties and privileges allowed the elite among those enslaved to live a life, according to late eighteenth-century reports, which seemed more "free than slave". William Dickson described their condition as follows:

> (A)lthough slavery, properly speaking, admits of no distinctions of rank, yet some slaves live and are treated so very differently from others, that a superficial observer would take it for granted they belong to classes of men who hold distinct ranks in society, so to speak, by tenures essentially different. The porters, boatmen, and fishermen, in the towns and on the coast; the black drivers, boilers, watchmen, and other black officers on estates; the mechanics, and above all, the numerous and useless domestics, both in town and country, all these comparatively. . . really live in ease and plenty; nor can they be said to feel any of the hardships of slavery, but such that arise from the caprices of their owners . . . To these I may add most of the slaves who work out, as it is called, that is, find employment for themselves, and make their owners a weekly return out of their earnings . . . On the other hand, truth obliges one to say, that the great body of the slaves, the field people on sugar plantations, are generally treated more like beast of burden than like human creatures.[14]

The Rev. Henry Husbands supports Dickson, and points towards their distinct socio-political consciousness as an elite group:

> The principal Negroes . . . who have a surprising influence over their inferiors, and who enjoy several privileges and advantages above them, are for the most part so attached to their owners that strange as it may seem, they would if occasion require it, readily sacrifice their lives in the defence of them and their property.[15]

Husbands' emphasis on the political effects of the privileges and liberties elite slaves enjoyed should be understood within the context of Dickson's analysis of the demographic and sociological characteristics of the creolisation process.[16]

The labour elite, Dickson explained, had its general origins within the rapidly advancing process of demographic and cultural creolisation. In specific cases, he tells us, enslavers made conscious decisions based on perceptions of their socio-economic interests to "promote" and privilege certain people among the enslaved population with rewards and incentives. In 1812, when the Barbados Agricultural Society established a committee to report on effective methods for "the regulation of plantations with a particular reference to the treatment of slaves",[17] the slave labour elite as a distinct group was already socially consolidated and recognised. The committee's report, furthermore, recommended measures for the further advancement of the process of slave differentiation by occupation, and reiterated commonplace views about slaves' positive responses to the ideals of social mobility and property accumulation.[18]

The committee noted, in addition, the importance of effective governance for the enslaved, particularly if entrusted with responsibilities, "to feel that it is in his interest to be a good member of the plantation to which he belongs" and to "awaken his mind to those objects of ambition" that free people enjoy. Many enslaved people, the committee concluded, are persons with "ambition and vanity" that require recognition and skillful management.[19] Since the differential treatment of the enslaved was essentially a function of variation in employment, the committee recommended that measures be put in place to diffuse the "depression" among "lesser slaves" caused by "inequality". The principal action recommended was that enslavers should curtail the social and work authority of elite slaves over the rank and file (field hands), and devise ways to promote in this "defected" category ambitions and interests of their own. [20]

John Mayers, Barbadian enslavers' political agent in London during the age of abolitionism, echoed his employers' view that the labour elite reproduced itself primarily within the context of relations between elder, "respected" slaves and their owners. Young slaves, he stated, were selected and put to instruction in skilled trades in order "to gratify the well-conducted parents and reward them for their good conduct".[21] The ambition of parents, then, was to secure for their children, sons in particular, access to a "profession" as a strategic response to hardship alleviation and social betterment. The rooting of social mobility prospects for young slaves within the conduct and character of parents served to reinforce enslavers' control over the process – as well as the conduct of beneficiaries. In this way, social elitism and group identity were reproduced over generations within families. As a consequence, many slave families came to see themselves as "better" than others by virtue of a long-standing association of their interests with the goodwill of plantation management.

Across imperial lines, and over time, the slave labour elite on plantations was largely male, and comprised, on the supervisoral side, head drivers (first gang), stockkeepers, watchmen and housekeepers; artisans were the dominant category in the technology and commodity production sector. In the latter group, special occupational prestige was conferred on sugar technologists (boilers and distillers in particular), but carpenters, coopers, masons, mechanics, fishermen, seamstresses and transport workers also consolidated privileged status around their crafts. In towns, a wider range of skills were marketed, and urban artisans were recognised as an important part of the slave elite. Barry Higman has shown that "in the sugar colonies females accounted for only about 7 per cent of tradespeople", and that artisans were generally recruited as young people for training in the manner identified by John Mayers. "Apprentice carpenters, coopers, masons, and wheelwrights", Higman noted, "distinguished in the Barbados registration returns, were aged between eight and eighteen years."[22]

The youthfulness of apprentices and the domestic circumstances of their selection, indicate the existence of a bias towards Creoles within the slave system. Dickson's explanation for group formation recognised this as a principal social feature. "Creole slaves were generally regarded by planters as more 'intelligent than Africans'", Higman argues, and this contributed to their advantage in the scramble for scarce skilled occupations.[23] Also, enslaved Coloured people – probably the most Creolised of all – had a disproportionate hold on skilled jobs and in their numerical representation in the slave elite.[24] Colour in itself did not always secure privileges, but it certainly facilitated access and in this regard was an important asset in the competition. The general belief that "Mulattoes" were physically weaker than Blacks, and the custom of removing those considered "near White" from field gangs, created constraints within the system that worked in their favour. Considerations of parenthood, colour, age and sex, then, determined the social making of the slave-labour elite.

The capacity of elite slaves to accumulate knowledge, wealth and social reputation varied between the groups. Many travelled overseas with owners, and some were allowed secure settled family lives. Most possessed some property, including the use of slaves for their own purposes. Some of those who were positioned to "work out", or were given autonomy to find paid employment for themselves, paying their owners a percentage of incomes, often accumulated sufficient money to purchase their freedom – and that of their kin. It became normal for artisans on plantations to receive a wage in the form of money for "special" services. Account books reveal these transactions clearly, and the term "salary" was in common use with respect to such payments. In 1798, for example, the accounts of Newton estate in Barbados show that the manager gave "the drive-man as an encouragement for his good behaviour and attention to the Negroes a salary of £10 (200 shillings)". At Codrington estate, less than five miles away, first gang drivers received an annual cash award of 6s. 6d, (six shillings and sixpence) for the same purpose.[24]

The sustained development of the slave-labour elite, however, had as much to do with the rising productivity of the overall enslaved labour force as it did with social processes. Increases in labour productivity enabled enslavers to design and implement ameliorative reforms during the second half of the eighteenth century, which in turn facilitated further efficiency gains in commodity production. Between 1750 and 1830, according to Ward, "Planters in Barbados increased the production of sugar per slave three fold and that of food by a third."[25] An important element in this growth of productivity, and the technical innovations that accompanied it, was a "more thorough trained slave labour force".[26] The effectiveness of Black lower-level management (drivers, watchmen, housekeepers) and artisan professionals incurred financial costs to estates, but these were more than offset by increases in economic output and the value added to slave capitalisation.[27]

Dickson argued, furthermore, that the social benefits to White society which followed this economic development should not be understated. He was convinced that the relative social stability (measured in terms of an absence of armed slave revolts) of Barbados in the second half of the eighteenth century should be understood in terms of the slave elite promoting the perceptions that for the first time enslaved people were benefiting materially from their labour investment in the plantation sector. Elite slaves certainly were, and references to their superior housing and clothing, improved health care and nutrition, and greater access to freedom by manumission and self-purchase attest to it. White society seemed relatively less threatened, and made much, for example, of slaves' loyalty and support during and after the devastation caused by the 1780 hurricane.

The direct relationship between increasing labour productivity and advancing demographic creolisation determined the pace and pattern of slave elite development. Property evaluations for Barbados in the second half of the eighteenth century show that Creole slaves were typically worth in excess of 22 per cent more than African-born slaves of the same age even when put to identical tasks. The percentage of Creoles in the enslaved population of Barbados increased from about 45 per cent to 93 per cent between 1750 and the 1817 slave registration exercise, the most advanced process in the Caribbean, if not plantation America.

Table 10.2:   Average Prices of Sugar and Slaves, 1749–1807

Year	Barbados/Leewards		Jamaica	
	Sugar Price (£/cwt)	Slave Price (£s)	Sugar Price (£/cwt)	Slave Price (£s)
1749–1762	1.14	29	1.05	36
1763–1775	1.16	39	1.13	42
1776–1782	1.02	41	1.66	44
1783–1791	1.54	42	1.50	48
1792–1798	2.20	55	2.08	55
1799–1807	1.72	70	1.64	70

Source: J.R. Ward, *British West Indian Slavery, 1750–1834: the Process of Amelioration* (Oxford; Clarendon Press, 1988), p. 210.

This development was accompanied by sharp increases in the average price of enslaved people as well as the price of sugar (see Table 10.2).

When William Fitzherbert arrived in Barbados to take up the management of the family estate in 1780, like other elite slave-owners he immediately sought a concrete understanding of his own interests as they related to the management of the enslaved. On Turners' Hall estate he indicated a willingness "to give up something to ease" the enslaved as an ameliorative policy designed to improve their productivity. Enslaved skilled workers were given better housing and as well as money wages for "additional" labour; head-drivers of the first gang were encouraged to feel a part of his household.[28]

Using evidence from Newton's plantation it is possible to test the validity of Dickson's hypothesis.[29] From the mid-eighteenth century to the closing of slavery the family of Doll, a retired housekeeper matriarch, dominated elite occupations on the estate (see Table 10.3). Manager's reports speak to issues such as their levels of material and social achievements, the nature of social and sexual relations with free persons, pursuit of freedom and the fears which informed their group judgements and decisions. Doll's family acquired substantial social standing, literacy and some property of their own. The threat of losing it all by the dishonour of relegation to the fields, however, loomed constantly over their heads. Their behaviour was typical of that associated with the labour elite. They rejected arduous manual labour and socialised with free persons, both Black and White. Also, they recognised the need for family solidarity in their dealings with

Table 10.3:   Elite Slaves at Newton Plantation, 1796

Men in Office		Women in Office	
Name	Occupation	Name	Occupation
Saboy	Driver	Old Doll	Retired Housekeeper
Great Tobby	Smith	Mary Ann	(Doll's sister) Housekeeper
Little Tobby	Smith	Dolly	(Doll's daughter) Housekeeper
		Betsy	(Doll's daughter) Housekeeper
Mulatto Daniel	Carpenter	Jenny	(Doll's daughter) in the house
Jack	Carpenter	Kitty	(Doll's niece) in the house
William Saer	Joiner	Mary Thomas	(Doll's niece) in the house
Hercules	Mason		(Doll's son)
George	Head Cooper		(Doll's step-brother)
Bob	Cooper		(Doll's step-grandson)
Toby	Boiler		
Gloster	Basket maker		
Cuffy	Smith		
Hillos	Cooper		
Cupid	Cook		
Ned	in the house		(Doll's nephew)

Source: Inventory of Newton plantation, 1796, Ms 523/225–92; Newton Papers, Senate House Library, London University.

Whites, in order to secure occupational privilege and to capitalise on their authority within the slave yards.

When Elizabeth Newton handed over the estate to her cousins, Thomas and John Lane, in the early 1790s she had requested that Doll's family continue to enjoy the standard of living to which they had been accustomed under her management. This, in fact, meant that the women would continue as the housekeeping elite and the men keep to artisan crafts. None of them were to work in the fields, nor perform any degrading manual task. The new owners made a conscientious effort, in spite of complaints from their managers, to comply with these requests, and Doll's family became a permanent centre of social and labour contests on the estate.

In a 1796 report, Manager Wood outlined the problem of keeping Doll's daughters, Dolly and Jenny, and her niece Kitty Thomas, "in high office", yet not idle. If we "can just catch at a little employment now and then for them", he stated, "we do so, such as cutting up and making the Negro clothing, but this is but once a year and but for a few days". "Dolly", he added, attended him in sickness and "is a most excellent nurse", for which he had some "obligation" to her. Doll, and her mulatto sister, Mary Ann, must also be excused from labour, he stated, on account of their long service to the estate.[30]

Manager Wood recognised the constraints imposed by his employers and added that Doll's daughters and niece "have been so indulged" that any hard work on the estate "would kill them at once". He reported that on one occasion William Yard, his predecessor, had put two of them into "the field by way of degradation and punishment", which caused the entire family to resist his management and try their best to undermine it. During this time, "they were absolutely a nuisance in the field and set the worse examples to the rest of the Negroes".

Under Wood's management the two women were brought back into the household. Mrs. Wood, mistress of the estate, put Dolly to needlework and Jenny to the more prestigious occupation of housekeeping. Kitty was also kept in the house, but no account was given of her precise role. Manager Wood subsequently expressed disgust when Dolly had told him that neither she nor Kitty Thomas ever ". . . swept out a chamber or carried a pail of water to wash" since Doll had other slave assistants do that sort of work. In exasperation at their arrogance, Wood asked his London-based employer: "What think you Sirs, of the hardship of slavery!"[31]

Not only did Doll's family have access to enslaved attendants, they also "possessed" their own enslaved workers who waited on them. As social owners of enslaved people (not allowed to do so legally), Doll's family won the recognition of its elite status among Whites. Nat Saer, the White sexual mate of Mary Ann (Doll's mulatto half sister), had willed her an enslaved female named Esther. By the time of Wood's 1796 report, Esther had five children alive, two boys and three girls who, although legally belonging to Newton estate, were, by custom, in Mary Ann's possession. Esther's children slaved for Doll's family, and this relationship meant that Jenny, Kitty and Dolly were raised to consider themselves "more free than slave". The plantation house, then, was the only place they could work on the estate that was consistent with their social consciousness.

Like free Coloured women, enslaved females in Doll's family aspired to socio-sexual relations with free men, particularly Whites, and considered success in this project symbolic of personal achievement and status. It was an index by which society, Black and White, would judge them, and also a way to minimise the possibility of their (and their children's) relegation to field labour. By the systematic "whitening" of children through a conscious practice of miscegenation, these women sought to concretise their social advantage. Mary Ann's two grandchildren (Kitty's Sam and Polly) who had a White father, were described by Wood as being "as white as himself". Their colour immediately absolved them, Wood stated, from field labour. The boys were put to artisan work at an early age. Wood also stated that the girls "either have or have had White husbands, that is, men who keep them".[32]

Literacy was a prime status symbol in colonial society, and was projected by Whites as evidence of their "right to freedom". Doll successfully negotiated some formal education for her daughters under Elizabeth Newton's management; in 1795 she pressed Manager Wood to allow her grandsons to attend school. Wood's 1796 report states:

> Doll wants me to put two of her grandchildren (Jenny's children) to school to learn to read and write. I told her I should put them to some trade as soon as they were set for it, but as to putting them to school to read and write I must consult you about it, which I do now. If you ask my opinion about it I shall tell you that I shall be very glad to add to the little stock of knowledge of anyone whatsoever, and it is almost a cruelty when it is in our power to indulge them, or to withhold it from them. But inclination must give way to policy, and I think it is a bad one in their situation to bestow on them the power of reading and writing. It is of little good, and very frequently producer of mischief with them.[33]

The career path chosen for Jenny's boys was settled when Uncle George Saers, the estate's head cooper, took them as his apprentices. George had already done the same for his own son and three nephews. With severe competition for the few highly prized occupations on the estates, it was to be expected that elite families would close ranks and reinforce their advantage. Dickson's interpretation of the creolisation process as promoting a pacifying effect upon slave communities through the influence of elite slaves, did not take into consideration the general development and evolution of new Creole identities and mentalities; it is therefore ahistorical and static. Successive generations did not share the same set of social values nor offer identical strategic responses to their enslavement. Rather, new demands were made upon the system for additional concessions.

Ward recognises this, and his analysis of ameliorative processes at the end of the eighteenth century takes into consideration the nature of slave consciousness over time. He asks the question: "Turning aside from the subject of material conditions, is it likely that creolization caused unrest?" Only part of the question, however, is answered when he states that "Creolization is likely to have given the slaves a greater coherence and sophistication of purpose, offering a more serious challenge to the slave-holding regime, not least through their capacity to evoke a sympathetic metropolitan response." At the same time, he recognises the ambivalence of the assertion against the background of an absence of recorded revolts during the age of revolution (1789–1815) that witnessed slave rebellions, Maroon Wars and Amerindian revolt in the neighbouring Windward islands. Furthermore, he adds, most colonists continued to believe that creolisation improved security, and gave reassurance against alarming examples elsewhere.

H.M. Waddell observed during his early nineteenth-century visit to the English-colonised Caribbean that generational differences existed among Creole slaves on the topical issue of their responses to amelioration policy and emancipation discussions. These differences, he intimates, were sufficiently stark to produce significant contests and tension within the slave community. He recognised that younger Creoles, particularly those in the skilled labour elite, seemed unwilling to accept terms and conditions of slavery negotiated at an earlier time by their parents and elders, and were more aggressive in demanding a discourse on full freedom as the mandate of their time. He wrote:

> The Creoles – young, strong and giddy with the new born hope of liberty, which they said the King had given them and their masters withheld – resolved to stand out for wages of free labour, and, if needful, to fight for their rights. The old people discouraged the attempt. They had seen worst times, and were sensible of a growing amelioration of their condition. The experience also of former insurrection taught them to dread the consequences of failure. [36]

While Ward is sensitive to the social implication of this observation, and placed it within the context of the wider debate on reform and abolitionism, he concluded, nonetheless, that "as a rule amelioration worked to strengthen the white man's authority . . ."[37]

The year 1804 was a critical juncture for all slaves. It witnessed the rise of Haiti as an independent nation, but for the enslaved in Barbados it marked the moment when the Legislature made it a criminal offence (with capital punishment) for a White person to murder an enslaved person. It signalled the beginning in Barbados of a new social dispensation. Elite slaves had now maximised the privileges and rights that seemed possible, and were more determined to remove remaining obstacles that stood in the path of full freedom. The abolition of the trade in enslaved African captives in 1807 was also a significant development in this regard. Elite slaves were now in possession of organisational skills, political confidence, and the social authority with the villages, to prepare for self-liberation.

External and internal developments, therefore, contributed to the maturity of social and political conditions that were suited to the transformation of anti-slavery strategies. The imposition of far-reaching ameliorative measures upon the Colonial Assembly by the Imperial Government, especially that which made Whites liable to capital punishment for the murder of an enslaved worker, had a significant impact upon the psychological texture of enslaver-enslaved relations. John Beckles, Speaker of the House when the bill was first debated, stated in opposition to it that such a measure would encourage slaves to see themselves in a different light and to overestimate their own importance. An estate manager subsequently commented that the reform led enslaved people to assume arrogance with respect to their importance. The ameliorative actions, furthermore, formed the basis of the strongly held view of the enslaved that the slavery system was nearing its end, and that enslavers' final acceptance of legislative reform was part of an attempt to keep afloat the sinking ship. This situation was new and was understood by slaves to be heading towards widespread social crisis.

The Haitian Revolution and the increasingly effective imperial abolitionist movement placed additional pressure at all levels of the slave system. Enslavers were forced to justify, almost daily in public fora, the slave system with a range of contradictory and unconvincing moral, cultural and economic arguments; indeed, they found it increasingly burdensome attempting to legitimise their rule and neutralise the increasing anti-slavery anxieties of their slaves. An independent Haiti and a persistent Wilberforce represented the slaves' panacea; for the masters, however, they symbolised the beginning of the end of an old order. For the first time in more than a century Creole society in Barbados was faced with the great possibility of fundamental structural change and upheaval. It appeared to many colonial observers that the Imperial Government would soon free the enslaved. The enslaved themselves believed this to be true and were convinced by 1815 that enslavers were withholding their freedom as stipulated by the Crown. These circumstances greatly altered social attitudes and opinions among Blacks in Barbados. Ideologically, Whites were on the defensive, and the Blacks knew this. Planters became more politically aggressive in defence of the old order, both in relation to the Imperial Government and the slaves. The colony, then, was in deepening crisis; it was within this context of diminishing planter hegemony that elite slaves organised for their overthrow by violent means.

The courses of action opened to elite slaves during this period were either to press for genuinely radical ameliorative measures, such as the right to give testimony in courts against Whites, to legally own property, or to organise armed rebellion. Planters declared the former option off the agenda in 1811–1812 when they rejected aggressively the requests of the free Coloured and free Blacks for a similar package of civil rights. Explicit in the language of this rejection was the idea that there were no more elements of the old slave system which were dispensable. Not only were the free Coloured and free Blacks snubbed, but also they were threatened with a possible reduction in civil rights if they persisted with further petitioning.

The planters' expressed intransigence lay, therefore, at the base of the enslaveds' decision to take up arms during this period. The reactionary, rigid and inflexible nature of their slave management after 1812 helped to exacerbate, rather than rectify, the increasingly disynchronised social order. As the slave system came under increasing pressures from metropolitan forces, slaves saw themselves as the final catalyst. By rebellion, they would assume the role of midwife to the free order, which was slowly but painfully coming into being. The political circumstances for revolt came during the period 1814 to 1816 when the Assembly debated and rejected the Imperial Registration Bill that called for compulsory listing of slaves on all properties. It was not difficult for elite slaves to mobilise field slaves with the argument that the bill was intended to be part of the legislative emancipation process, and that its rejection by slave-owners illustrated their determination to resist freedom in any form.

The rebellion began on Sunday, 14 April, 1816. It was crushed within the week by resident imperial troops and, to a lesser extent, the local militia. One planter suggested that close to 1000 of the enslaved population lost their lives. Evidence produced by prominent members of the White community suggests that the uprising was sudden and unexpected. Whites generally believed that the enslaved, not having attempted any insurrections since the minor aborted Bridgetown affair in 1701, were more prone to running away, withholding their labour in protest, petitioning estate owners, attorneys and managers concerning conditions of work and leisure, than to armed insurrection.

Enslavers claimed that the enslaved were given "liberties" which planters in the other islands could not dare to even consider. The ability of most of the enslaved in Barbados to travel the island extensively in pursuit of social and economic activity was held up by the planters as proof of the long-standing mildness of race relations and plantation management on the island. This attitude seemed to have been widespread throughout the White community. Governor Leith, aware of this long-held complacency which he had never shared, informed the Secretary for Colonies at the end of April:

> [The] planters of Barbados who have flattered themselves that the general good
> treatment of the slaves would have prevented them resorting to violence to

establish an elusion of material right, which by long custom sanctioned by law has been hitherto refused to be acknowledged, had not any apprehension of such a convulsion.[38]

The rebellion was organised and led almost exclusively by elite slaves. For sure, the slave system had given them more rewards than the masses of the enslaved, who, during the heat of battle, according to one report, had to be cajoled and threatened into action. This observation is very significant. It signals the persistence of ideological fracture within the slave community, and offers a perspective on the enormity of the task of political mobilisation.

Commanders in the field were drivers, rangers, masons, carpenters, coopers and a standard bearer. Among them were two prominent African-born slaves, including Bussa – the principal military leader – the driver at Bayleys plantation. Joseph Gittens, a plantation manager, told the Assembly's Commission of Inquiry into the revolt that the leaders were those very slaves to whom "great indulgences were granted", and who had "assumed airs of importance, and put a value on themselves unknown amongst slaves of former period". [39] *The London Times* read these developments correctly and reported:

> . . . the principal instigators of this insurrection, who are Negroes of the worst dispositions, but of superior understanding, and some of whom can read and write, availed themselves of this parliamentary interference and the public anxiety it occasioned, to instil into the minds of the slaves generally a belief that they were already freed by the King and Parliament . . . [40]

The alleged sudden shift in anti-slavery strategies took enslavers by surprise. Robert Haynes, attorney for Newton plantation, who considered himself a supporter of elite slaves in their search for privileges and rights, expressed dismay at the movement in mentality and turn of events. In the immediate aftermath of the revolt he stated:

> The night of the insurrection I would and did sleep with my chamber door open, and if I had possessed ten thousand pounds in my house, I should not have had any more precaution, so well convinced I was of their ['the slaves'] attachment . . . [41]

In this assessment, Haynes indicated that he spoke for the majority of enslavers.

The evidence, then, points to the need for a general sociological approach in which the degree and pace of demographic creolisation, and its relation to economic and social developments, are emphasised in shaping slave relations and attitudes. Creolisation can be understood as a process of demographic and social formation that produced, among other things, distinct group stratification within the slave community. A prominent feature of this process was the emergence of an elite slave group that assumed community leadership and promoted a complex anti-slavery ideology within the slave yards. Changing political circumstances and the evolution of consciousness within the slave labour elite are also critical to an understanding of the strategic politics of anti-slavery. While this group played an important role in enslavers' search for higher productivity and efficiency gains, they constituted a new mentality that contradicted the reproduction of the slave system. It was within the context of rebellion that enslavers recognised the contradictory nature of the reform process but were powerless to effect any social reversals.

Notes

1. See Robert Miles, *Capitalism and Unfree Labour: Anomaly or Necessity* (London: Tavistock Publications, 1987), pp. 71–94; E.D. Domar, "The Causes of Slavery or Serfdom: A Hypothesis", in *Journal of Economic History*, vol. 30, (1970), pp. 18–22; S. Engerman, "Marxist Economic Studies of the Slave South", in *Marxist Perspectives*, vol. 33, (1973), pp. 43–65; H. Kellenbenz, "The Modern World-System: Capitalist Agriculture and the Origins of the European World Economy in the 16th Century", in *Journal of Modern History*, vol. 48, (1976), pp. 682–92; J.R. Mandle, "The Plantation Economy: an Essay in Definition", in *Science and Society*, vol. 36, (1972), pp. 49–62; K. Marx and F. Engles, *On Colonialism* (Moscow: Progress Publishers, 1968); S.W. Mintz, "Was the Plantation Slave a Proleteriat?", in *Review*, vol. 2, no. 1 (1978), pp. 81–98.

2. The concept of a "labour aristocracy" has been used productively with respect to analysing social divisions within the English working class during the Industrial Revolution. See R.J. Morris, *Class and Class Consciousness in the Industrial Revolution 1780–1850* (London: Macmillan, 1979); G. Crossick, "The Labour Aristocracy and Its Values: A Study of Mid-Victorian Kentish London", *Victorian Studies*, xiv, (1976); John Foster, *Class Struggle and the Revolution: Early Industrial Capitalism in Three English Towns* (London: Macmillan, 1974); Robert Gray, *The Labour Aristocracy in Victorian Edinburgh* (Oxford: Oxford University Press, 1976).

3. Barry Gaspar, *Bondsmen and Rebels: A Study of Master-Slave Relations in Antigua, with Implications for Colonial America* (Baltimore: John Hopkins University Press, 1985); Gaspar, "The Antigua Slave Conspiracy of 1736; A Case Study of the Origins of Collective Resistance", in *William and Mary Quarterly*, vol. 33 (1978), pp. 308–24; Mary Reckord-Turner, "The Jamaican Slave Rebellion of 1831", in *Past and Present* (July 1969), no. 40, pp. 108–25; Michael Craton, *Testing the Chains:*

Resistance to Slavery in the British West Indies (Ithaca: Cornell University Press 1982), pp. 19–51; Hilary Beckles, *Black Rebellion: The Struggle Against Slavery, 1627–1838* (Bridgetown: Antilles, 1984), pp. 1–8; also Beckles, "Caribbean Anti-Slavery: The Self Liberation Ethos of Enslaved Blacks", in *Journal of Caribbean History*, vol. 22, nos. 1 and 2 (1990), pp. 1–20. See also Orlando Patterson, "Slavery and Slave Revolts: A Socio-Historical Analysis of the First Maroon War, Jamaica, 1655–1740", in *Social and Economic Studies*, 19:3, (1970), pp. 289–325; Michael Craton, *Sinews of Empire: A Short History of British Slavery* (New York: Doubleday Books, 1974), pp. 289–325; Kamau Brathwaite, "Caliban, Ariel and Unprospero in the Conflict of Creolisation: A Study of the Slave Revolt in Jamaica, 1831–1832", in V. Rubin and A. Tuden, eds., *Comparative Perspectives on Slavery in New World Societies* (New York: New York Academy of Science, 1977), pp. 41–62; Barbara Kopytoff, "The Early Political Development of Jamaican Maroon Societies", in *William and Mary Quarterly*, 35:2 (1978), pp. 287–307; "The Development of Jamaican Maroon Ethnicity", in *Caribbean Quarterly*, 22 (1976), pp. 35–50; Monica Schuler, "Akan, Slave Rebellion in the British Caribbean", in *Savacou*, 1: 1 (1970); also Schuler, "Ethnic Slave Rebellions in the Caribbean and the Guianas", in *Journal of Social History*, 3 (1970), pp. 374–85.

4.   For an earlier version of this theme, see Hilary Beckles and Karl Watson, "Social Protest and Labour Bargaining: The Changing Nature of Slaves' Responses to Plantation Life in 18th Century Barbados", in *Slavery and Abolition*, vol. 8, no. 3, (1987), pp. 270–93.

5.   J.R. Ward, *British West Indian Slavery, 1750–1834: The Process of Amelioration* (Oxford: Clarendon Press, 1988), pp. 226–31; Gaspar, *Bondsmen and Rebels*, p. 255; Beckles, *Black Rebellion*, p. 52; Jerome Handler, "The Barbados Slave Conspiracies of 1675, and 1692", in *Journal of the Barbados Museum and Historical Society*, vol. 36, no. 4, (1982), pp. 313–14; Handler, "Slave Revolt and Conspiracies in Seventeenth Century Barbados", in *New West Indian Guide*, vol. 52, (1982), pp. 5–42.

6.   Michael Craton, "The Passion to Exist: Slave Rebellions in the British West Indies, 1650–1832", in *Journal of Caribbean History*, vol. 13, (1980), p. 18; O. Nigel Bolland, "The Politics of Freedom in the British Caribbean", in Frank McGlynn and Seymour Drescher, eds., *The Meaning of Freedom: Economics, Politics and Culture After Slavery* (Pittsburgh: University of Pittsburgh Press, 1992), pp. 113–46; also Bolland, "Systems of Domination after Slavery: The Control of Land and Labour in the British West Indies after 1838", *Comparative Studies in Society and History*, vol. 25, (1981), pp. 591–619; W.K. Marshall, "Apprenticeship and Labour Relations in four Windward Islands", in David Richardson, ed., *Slavery and Its Aftermath: The Historical Context, 1790–1916* (London: Frank Cass, 1985), pp. 203–24; also Marshall, "'We be Wise to Many More Things': Black Hopes and Expectations of Emancipation", UWI, Mona (1990): Verene A. Shepherd, "The Effects of the

Abolition of Slavery on Jamaican Livestock Farms", in *Slavery and Abolition* 10:2 (1989) pp. 187–211; Swithin Wilmot, "Emancipation in Action: Workers and Wage Conflict in Jamaica, 1838–1848", paper presented to the *Tenth Annual Conference of Caribbean Historians, 1984*; Wilmot, "'Not Full Free': The Ex-Slaves and the Apprenticeship System in Jamaica, 1834–1838", in *Jamaica Journal,* 17 (1984), 11, pp. 2–10, and Wilmot, "Race, Electoral Violence and Constitutional Reform in Jamaica 1830–54", in *Journal of Caribbean History,* 17, (1982), pp. 1–23.

7.   See Beckles and Watson, "Social Protests", p. 285.

8.   See Karl Watson, *The Civilised Island, Barbados: A Social History, 1750–1816* (Bridgetown: Caribbean Graphics, 1979), pp. 34–40.

9.   Jerome Handler and Frederick Lange, *Plantation Slavery in Barbados: An Archeological and Historical Investigation* (Cambridge, Mass: Harvard University Press, 1978), pp. 67–8; The Census of Barbados, 1715, CO. 28/14, Public Records Office (PRO) London; Richard Dunn, *Sugar and Slaves: The Rise of the Planter Class in the English West Indies, 1624–1713* (Chapel Hill: University of North Carolina Press, 1972), p. 87; Barry Higman, *Slave Populations of the British Caribbean, 1807–1834* (Baltimore: Johns Hopkins University Press, 1984), p. 116.

10.   William Dickson, *Mitigation of Slavery* (orig. pub. London, 1814: Westport, Conn: Negro Universities Press, 1970), p. 205; Robert Haynes to Thomas Tane, 16 Sept. 1806, Newton papers, Ms. 523/620. Senate House Library, London University.

11.   Handler and Lange, *Plantation Slavery*, p. 68

12.   Newton Papers, Ms. 523/292.

13.   Gaspar, *Bondsmen*, p. 256.

14.   William Dickson, Letters on Slavery (London, 1789), p. 6.

15.   See Beckles, *Black Rebellion*, p. 74.

16.   Dickson, *Mitigation of Slavery*, pp. 439–41.

17.   Higman, *Slave Populations,* p. 119

18.   Minutes of the Barbados Agricultural Society, 14 Nov. 1812, pp. 129–30.

19.   Ibid.

20.   Ibid.

21.   Cited in B.M. Taylor, "Our Man in London: John Pollard Mayers, Agent for Barbados, and the British Abolition Act, 1832–1834", in *Caribbean Studies*, xvi, nos. 3–4, (1976–1977), p. 7.

22.   Higman, Slave Populations, p. 192.

23.   Ibid., p. 197.

24.   Ibid., p. 203.

25.   Ward, *British West Indian Slavery*, p. 192.

26.   Ibid., p. 193.

27.   Ibid., p. 206.

28.   Ibid., p. 215.

29. These quotations are drawn from the Newton papers, Ms. 523/620.
30. Ibid.
31. Ibid.
32. Ibid.
33. Ibid.
34. Ward, *British West Indian Slavery*, p. 226.
35. Ibid., p. 219.
36. H.M. Waddell, Twenty-Nine Years in the West Indies and Central Africa, 1826–1848 (London: T. Nelson and Sons, 1863), p. 51.
37. Ward, *British West Indian Slavery*, p. 232.
38. CO 28/85, folio 8, Gov. Leith to Lord Bathurst, April 1816.
39. Deposition of Joseph Gittens, Report from a Select Committee of the House of Assembly appointed to Enquire into the Origins, Cause and Progress of the Late Insurrection, April 1816, (Barbados: 1818).
40. *The London Times*, 5 June 1816.
41. Robert Haynes to Thomas Lane, 23 September 1816.

Glen Richards

Chapter 11

"DRIBER TAN MI SIDE"[1]

CREOLISATION AND THE LABOUR
PROCESS IN ST KITTS-NEVIS, 1810–1905

The study of creolisation in the Caribbean has usually focused on the process of cultural change and the growing cultural unity between the disparate ethnic elements that make up the Caribbean population. The impact of creolisation on, and its physical manifestation in, the working world of Caribbean peoples has remained largely unstudied or the subject of only incidental discussion. Yet, as early as 1976, Sidney Mintz and Richard Price pointed to the critical connection between creolisation and the labour process, the central point of encounter between the two main parties in Caribbean plantation societies, the European enslavers and their enslaved Africans.[2] Creolisation as a functional feature of plantation society began in the working world in the interaction between European enslavers and their agents and enslaved Africans largely in the canefields of the Caribbean. Thus, the general absence of specific Caribbean research on the historical evolution and social manifestations of creolisation in the labour process itself, particularly during the period of African enslavement, is somewhat puzzling.[3]

One of the most striking features of enslaver-enslaved relations on the plantations of the Caribbean was the speed with which the enslaved population, with little prior experience of plantation labour and coming from markedly different economic backgrounds, adopted mechanisms of labour bargaining and utilised channels of mediation and conflict resolution which were recognisable and acceptable to their "New World" enslavers. In the process of creolisation, through the means of acculturation and interculturation, the contending parties, enslaved and enslavers, developed means of conflict resolution which allowed the enslaved to find redress for grievances and secure minor but lasting improvements while leaving the labour system based on African enslavement intact. The historical record reveals, again and again, the successful attempts of the enslaved population in different Caribbean settings to negotiate conditions of work with their oppressors through chosen delegates from among them or through the intercession of trusted mediators.

The active and voluntary participation by enslaved Africans and their free descendants in the creation of institutional models, customary or constitutional, which provided them with a means for expressing their industrial grievances as well as their early acceptance of a system of "collective representation" is a feature which sets the Black labouring population of the Caribbean apart from many other similar colonial populations. Marjorie Nicholson, former secretary of the Fabian Colonial Bureau, contrasted what she described as the "parliamentary" impulse of workers in the Commonwealth Caribbean who sought to use representational channels to negotiate their grievances to the practice of workers in some sections of British colonial Africa who insisted on meeting with their employers *en masse* rather than in selecting delegates who they believed would be subject to victimisation.[4] This "parliamentary" impulse, or the use of representational channels to resolve disputes with their owners, can be seen among the enslaved population of the Anglophone Caribbean at least as far back as the eighteenth century.

In her pioneering study of labour bargaining on Caribbean sugar plantations, Mary Turner has shown that enslaved peoples both engaged in collective bargaining with their owners over their conditions of work and employed the weapon of collective strikes in support of their demands for an extension of their customary rights. Turner has noted that:

> . . . all categories of worker in the Americas practised forms of collective bargaining customarily identified with industrial wage labourers. Procedures which included collective withdrawal of labour and appeals for mediation were established by slave workers and developed with varying degrees of success by their heirs and successors.[5]

The study of these features of plantation work and life has helped to deepen our understanding of plantation society. Although the institution of the slave-worked sugar plantation reflected what Mintz and Price have described as "the monopoly of power vested in the European master classes", plantation work norms and production patterns, and the wider plantation society itself, must be seen as the outcome of protracted contests and negotiations between, if not the joint creation of, enslavers and the enslaved.[6]

The very survival of plantation economy required a level of cooperation and accommodation between enslaver and enslaved which meant, in effect, that the "masters' monopoly of power was constrained not only by the need to achieve certain results, in terms of profit, but also by the slaves' clear recognition of the masters' *dependence* upon them."[7] This inter-dependence of all sections of the plantation population was recognised by William Green when he observed that "all elements of the [Caribbean] population were locked in a painful but symbiotic set of economic relationships from which they could not escape without enduring ever greater social and material hardship."[8] It was this need for economic cooperation and accommodation between the contending parties, enslaver and enslaved, which lay at the heart of the creolisation process. Creolisation, as Mintz and Price have reminded us, is not only about the adoption and adaptation of European mores by enslaved Africans, nor is it solely the reconstituting of poorly transmitted and barely remembered African traditions.[9] For African populations in the Americas, with no realistic way of returning to a distant homeland, creolisation meant the forging of a new world and a new life, new memories and new identities. It also meant the development of a commitment to the new societies they had become a part of, a cherishing of the new skills they had learned and of the new possessions that they had acquired or were in the process of acquiring. One notes developing among Caribbean enslaved populations, as in enslaved populations elsewhere in the Americas, a proprietorial attachment to their work and technical know-how.[10]

The labour-bargaining techniques which developed in the Caribbean were by no means unique to the region but can be seen among enslaved African populations (and, of course, free and indentured labourers) in Brazil, the United States and throughout the Americas.[11] Labour bargaining provided a ready means for the enslaved populations of the Caribbean, as elsewhere in the Americas, to shape and remodel their working world and, thereby, maximise the resources available for their survival while, at the same time, adjusting their expectations and demands to fit within the disciplinary constraints imposed by plantation production. Where labour bargaining was engaged in between enslavers and enslaved, work norms and the size of tasks, payment for overwork and the wage rates for such payments, days off, and responsibility for medical expenses all became the subjects of negotiation.[12]

THE ORIGINS OF LABOUR BARGAINING AMONG
CARIBBEAN ENSLAVED POPULATIONS

Where and how did enslaved Africans, most of them strangers to European industrial societies and to the concept of wage labour, learn these methods of labour bargaining? One possibility is that these techniques were learned through exposure to the industrial activities of other workers in the plantation community, most specifically the small but significant population of indentured servants, which up to the 1650s formed the bulk of the plantation labour force in most Caribbean sugar colonies. Indentured servants, although bonded to their employer for the duration of their indenture, remained legally free persons and retained certain legal rights, particularly the right of appeal to a magistrate against excessive punishment and non-payment of their "freedom" dues.[13]

In the early phase of colonisation, on both tobacco and sugar plantations, White indentured servants often worked side by side with the enslaved in the tobacco and cane fields. There was room for association, if not open combination, between both sets of bound plantation workers and the passing on of industrial knowledge. Some historians have even pointed to instances of apparent cooperation between enslaved peoples and indentured servants in open resistance against their owners.[14]

But Donald Akenson, in his study of Irish settlement in Montserrat, has provided us with a timely reminder that White indentured servants, Irish or not, never forgot the legal distinction between themselves and the enslaved Africans and, in their quest to achieve their goal of upward social mobility, aimed someday to become themselves owners of slaves.[15] Many indentured servants invested their "freedom" dues in the purchase of slaves, a very mobile and easily accessible form of investment. In seventeenth-century Montserrat, after the large European plantation owners, the section of the community that was most likely to own purchase human chattel were White, small, independent cultivators, many of whom would have been former indentured servants.[16]

The social and, increasingly, the occupational distance then between enslaved Africans and White indentured servants was great and, with the passage of time, grew greater. The introduction of large-scale African slavery in Barbados in the 1650s led to the removal of White female labour from the canefields and to the gradual withdrawal of White male labour. By the 1680s, most indentured servants in Barbados were employed in the sugar mills.[17] The White indentured servants readily acknowledged their economic and cultural identity with the European planter class and recognised that intractable division between them would only, in the words of Hilary Beckles, "lead to the 'common ruin of the contending parties' and provide a chance for black ascendancy".[18]

It could be expected that the common social oppression and physical exploitation and abuse of enslaved Africans and White indentured servants alike would have promoted an industrial alliance between both groups of workers and joint violent resistance against their common enemy. But evidence for such joint resistance appears to have existed only in the fevered minds of the plantation owners. Hilary Beckles, who was formerly most receptive to the idea of joint resistance by enslaved Blacks and White indentured servants, has since revised that position and points out that in seventeenth-century Barbados the two strongest cases for such an alliance prove on closer investigation to be exceedingly weak.[19]

There exists a possibility, of course, that the African labouring population could have learned their labour bargaining strategies indirectly by observing the industrial conflicts between White indentured servants and their masters. Servants did have the right to petition the court for redress of their grievances but, in fact, few servants actually made use of the legal rights that they had. In Barbados, where the indentured servants were perhaps the most militant in defence of their rights, "servant petitions were few in number".[20] The local courts, presided over by magistrates who were often themselves planters or members of planter families, were more often used to discipline servants than to guarantee their legal rights. Planter magistrates were unlikely to decide court cases in favour of indentured servants if such a decision threatened to undermine plantation discipline. This was even more true of the colonial government, the local representative of the Crown, as witnessed in the notorious case of Governor Jonathan Atkins of Barbados who, in 1677, dismissed the case brought against Charles Grimlin, a leading planter, for murdering one of his Irish maidservants.[21]

The largely disastrous experience of indentured servants before the law could scarcely have provided encouragement for enslaved workers in their contests with their enslavers and, in any case, the legal rights enjoyed by indentured servants were based upon their legal status as free people. Enslaved Africans, having no legal personality, had no right to appeal to the local courts and the rights that they secured were won through their own industrial actions and secured by custom and constant vigilance. White indentured servants were the least likely tutors in industrial relations and techniques of collective bargaining for enslaved Africans.

Another possibility is that these patterns of labour bargaining represented an attempt by enslaved Africans to reconstruct some of their customary rights of appeal to their kings, chiefs and elders in traditional African societies. The European plantation owners, resident or absentee, in their role of *buckra* or *mbakara*, would now take on the status of divine leader of the community.[22] Paul Lovejoy points to the existence of slave plantations long before 1600 in Northern Africa as well as their growth, shortly before or after 1600, in Western and Central Africa.[23] Enslaved Africans brought to the Americas having this background of plantation slavery in Africa could have sought to re-institute their customary privileges in their "New World" situation. However, this use of the word plantation by Lovejoy and others remains open to debate for it is not clear whether the term is being used to describe a large-scale agricultural unit depending on tributary agricultural labour service or a productive enterprise engaged in commodity production under competitive market conditions and based upon the systematic exploitation of slave labour.[24] The former case would, for the most part, give rise to individual or family strategies aimed at manipulating the established patron-client relationship rather than the collective labour-bargaining strategies that are here the subject of discussion. In any case, much of the detailed research conducted on plantation slavery in Western and Central Africa focuses on the nineteenth century long after the labour-bargaining strategies identified among enslaved plantation workers in the British-colonised Caribbean had emerged.[25] Although this line of thought remains an interesting possibility and deserving of further scholarly inquiry, the fact remains that the detailed ethnological research needed to support this argument has not yet been carried out and until this is done any such theoretical postulations would have to remain largely speculative.[26]

"DRIBER TAN MI SIDE": THE SLAVE HIERARCHY AND THE EVOLUTION OF LABOUR-BARGAINING SYSTEMS

But there is, perhaps, no need to turn to external agencies or to an African past to explain the origins of labour-bargaining strategies among Caribbean enslaved peoples. Indeed, the insistent and almost hysteric emphasis on explaining every aspect of the lifestyle and worldview of Africans and African descendants in the New World by reference to European models or African survivals constitutes, in large part, a denial of the human creativity and agency of African peoples. There is evidence that some African agricultural practices were continued by enslaved Africans and incorporated into "New World" agriculture and their African cultural inheritance did help to shape the social and economic world of enslaved African plantation workers and their descendants.[27] But enslaved Africans and their descendants, as rational human beings, also responded to their enslavement in the Americas by evolving new social forms, customs and practices based upon their existing human condition.

The material basis, and indeed the institutional logic, of labour bargaining lay within the very command structure of the Caribbean plantation itself. In acknowledging the centrality of this command structure to the social encounters between owner and enslaved in the creolisation process, Sidney Mintz and Richard Price observed that "the principal avenue of encounter, then, was that created by the communication and delegation of command. . ."[28]

The efficient operation of the plantation required the delegation of authority over the enslaved to persons who would be in regular, direct contact with them. The gangs of enslaved peoples, which were widely employed on Caribbean sugar plantations by the 1650s, were headed by "slave drivers" who were chosen from among the enslaved population. In the interest of promoting labour discipline and increased productivity, planters selected as drivers individuals who had a high social standing among fellow slaves and the criteria used in their selection closely reflects their leadership role in the slave communities. In his *magnum opus*, *Searching for the Invisible Man*, Michael Craton shows that, in 1793, drivers and headmen on Worthy Park estate in Jamaica had an average age of 54.7 years compared to an average age of 26.7 for the entire estate slave population.[29] Notably the ethnic background of slave drivers changed in line with demographic changes in the general enslaved population. The high preponderance of African-born drivers during the eighteenth century, when the population was still predominantly African, suggests that drivers depended not only on the authority vested in them by their owners but also on the social standing which they inherited by virtue of the slaves' continued attachment to African traditions. The almost total reversal of this picture by the 1810s, when the enslaved population had become predominantly Creole and conscious efforts were being made by some of the enslaved to distance themselves from any association with an African past, further strengthens the view that the drivers' social standing in the slave community was a decisive factor in their ability to exercise their occupational function.[30]

Caught between the conflicting demands of the disciplinary role imposed upon them by the plantation labour regime and the social commitments to the communities which they led, slave drivers invariably played a dual role. The slave drivers were, in their occupational function, the creature and the representative of the owners but the criteria for their selection rested on their capacity to exercise a social authority which was accepted and recognised by their fellow slaves making them "natural leaders as well as drivers".[31]

The dual and intermediary role of slave drivers and other slave headmen on the estates, along with the upper echelons of the enslaved community in general, including skilled slaves and trusted domestics, provided a natural impulse to engage in labour bargaining. As community elders and social benefactors, the enslaved at the top of the slave-labour hierarchy would be called upon by their fellow slaves to intercede with their enslaver, or his/her agents, on their behalf. Mary Turner provides a well-argued explanation of the historical evolution of this process writing:

> Crucial to this development were the confidential slaves, the headmen and drivers who mediated between the demands of the owners and managers and the workers they organised and punished. They acted in part out of necessity since their functions as agents of management could be fulfilled only with the cooperation of the work force. They were the sounding board for work-place grievances and had to decide when best to unite with their fellows to confront management, or when it was worthwhile to lend their authority to some spontaneous acts of protest [32]

But drivers of gangs of enslaved workers remained ultimately subject to the enslaver's authority and were compelled to take seriously their role as disciplinarians of their fellow slaves. The incentives that they received, in the form of extra rations, larger provision grounds, the ability to utilise the labour of their fellow slaves and a better standard of housing, gave them every inducement to fulfill their occupational responsibilities. One could question then their readiness to participate in labour bargaining at the probable cost of their privileges. But the engagement by slave drivers and the privileged slave elite in labour bargaining was a rational calculation designed to add to and widen the range of their material benefits and, by containing and channeling the discontent of their fellow slaves into peaceful currents of conflict resolution, increase their owners' dependence on their intermediary role. Participation in labour bargaining by slave drivers and the slave elite, as well as by the general enslaved population, expressed an acceptance of, if not an identity with and commitment to, the new socio-economic relations into which slavery had forced them. Such participation was a function of the creolisation process through which enslaved Africans and their descendants sought to transform their social relations and build a new world for themselves. But labour bargaining also helped to keep the world of the plantation intact.[33]

It must be noted, however, that the position of slave driver was no sinecure and the holders of the position were subject to frequent and, at times, arbitrary changes. It is this occupational reality combined with a tendency of some enslavers to punish slave drivers as an incentive for others to work that cemented the slave drivers' collective identity with their fellow slaves. [34]

It is this collective identity that made slave drivers, and the trusted slaves at the top of the plantation labour hierarchy, the perfect instruments for implementing labour-bargaining strategies. Their intermediary positions and the confidence invested in them by both sides of the labour divide made them perfect mediators and go-betweens. Their role as slave leaders, however, also meant that in moments of crisis, when their material living standards and social standing were under threat, they could also be the agents for transforming peaceful methods of labour bargaining into violent confrontation and open rebellion. The preponderant role of drivers and other members of the slave elite in the leadership of slave rebellions and conspiracies was evident before the abolition of the trans-Atlantic trade in enslaved Africans, but even more present after.[35]

CREOLISATION AND THE LABOUR PROCESS: THE CASE OF ST KITTS AND NEVIS

Situated in the north-eastern arc of the Caribbean archipelago, the islands of St Kitts and Nevis have long been associated with both slavery and sugar production. Among the earliest sugar-producing colonies established by the English in the Caribbean, the sugar economy of both islands progressed rapidly during the late seventeenth century and, by the mid-eighteenth century, the island of St Kitts was, as described by one historian, in proportion to its extent, the single richest colony in the British empire.[36] Sugar production continued to dominate the economic landscape of both islands throughout the nineteenth century but the rocky terrain of the island of Nevis imposed high production costs on the local sugar industry and led to its abandonment after 1900. Up to 1834, however, the planter class in both islands remained fully committed to both the maintenance of slavery and to plantation production of sugar.

One of the most intriguing cases of labour bargaining occurred in the island of Nevis in 1810 shortly after the abolition of the British slave trade. In that year, Edward Huggins, a leading Nevisian resident planter, took possession of Mountravers estate from its absentee owners, the Pinney family, up to that time the most important planter family in the island. Huggins, who had a reputation as a cruel slave master, appointed one of his younger sons, Peter Huggins, as the new estate manager. The enslaved on the estate, who had hitherto been accustomed to the fairly "humane slave regime" under the Pinneys, immediately began testing the new management. A major dispute soon developed between the estate slaves and Peter Huggins over his insistence that they cut grass for the livestock at night. Some of the enslaved began running away, six and eight at a time. Huggins sent the trusted estate slaves, probably including drivers and headmen, after the runaways and the trustees interviewed the runaway slaves but did not bring them back as ordered. When Huggins threatened to punish the trusted slaves, they also ran away. With the escalation of the dispute, the enslaved took further collective action – 20 to 30 at a time would go to the sick house claiming to be ill. When the younger Huggins tried to correct a slave driver in the cane field as to the proper way to stake the ground for holing, the driver insisted on staking the ground according to his method and cursed Huggins when he tried to correct him further. Peter Huggins' attempt to punish the recalcitrant slave driver was met by a hostile attack by the slave gang who surrounded him. The young manager threatened to kill any enslaved worker who laid hands on him and the enslaved slowly returned to work. After this incident, Peter Huggins imposed collective punishment on the field gangs by ordering them to do more night work. On this occasion, all of the estate's enslaved workers ran away *en masse* and sent a delegation to complain Huggins to a nearby planter. The role of the trusted slaves, first in refusing to arrest the original runaway and then by running away themselves, as well as the response of the driver, suggest that, if not the leading organisers, the slave elite was deeply implicated in the dispute. Although the records do not state this, it is most likely that they were also the leaders of the slave delegation to the nearby planter.

The consequence of the dispute is also instructive of the nature of enslaver-enslaved relationships on Caribbean plantations. On 23rd January 1810, Edward Huggins Snr., refusing to endure this challenge to his honour as a White man and a planter, unilaterally ended the dispute and restored order to his newly purchased property by taking 20 of the estate slaves (ten men and ten women) to the public market in Charlestown, the principal town of the island, and inflicted a public whipping. Each of the enslaved received in excess of 47 lashes and one enslaved female received as many as 291. One of the women died after the whipping but a Grand Jury investigation found that she had died of "natural causes". Three of Edward Huggins' sons were members of the Grand Jury.[37]

The dispute on Mountravers estate exhibited, on a small scale, all of the characteristic strategies employed by the enslaved, and their descendants, in the course of labour bargaining. The negotiation of industrial demands, the peaceful withdrawal of labour and the appeal to outside mediation, all modern strategies of industrial conflict, were fully evolved in the slavery period and established a model of industrial dispute resolution which was employed by former slaves and their descendants during the period after emancipation. The institutionalisation of these strategies represented a Creole adaptation to the reality of plantation life and work. By 1817, only 14.5 per cent of the enslaved population in Nevis, and 16.1 per cent in St Kitts, was African born.[38] This meant that the vast majority of plantation labourers knew no other home but the islands and no other living reality but the plantation. Labour bargaining, then, was a collective policy of defending, and extending, existing customary rights and negotiated industrial norms on the plantation while leaving the command structure of the plantation largely intact. But while this strategy failed to threaten the survival of the plantation as an institution, it was, at the same time, a bid to transform the economic relations between plantation workers, enslaved or free, and their masters. Enslaved Africans and their descendants were not simply accepting, and accommodating themselves to, a historical reality thrust upon them. They were trying to reshape the world around them, to create a new industrial order which recognised them not as property and productive units of labour, but as human beings.

LABOUR BARGAINING IN POST-EMANCIPATION ST KITTS AND NEVIS

The end of slavery in St Kitts and Nevis consequently saw a marked rise in the self-assertiveness of the newly freed class of plantation labourers who insisted upon their rights as free subjects and sought to negotiate their terms and conditions of work with their former masters and mistresses on a basis of equality. John Nixon, Lieutenant Governor of St Kitts, observed "a jealousy between some of the managers or overseers on estates and the work people, the former not recollecting that slavery no longer exists, and the latter forgetting themselves, and behaving in a very insolent and provoking manner towards their superiors."[39]

The first major post-emancipation industrial dispute engaged in by the ex-slave populations of St Kitts and Nevis arose over the introduction of the apprenticeship system as a transitional period before the implementation of "full freedom". This failure to implement the full promise of emancipation set the stage for a series of major industrial conflicts between the planters and ex-slaves in both islands. The planters in St Kitts and Nevis, as in the British-colonised Caribbean as a whole, refused to dispense with the traditions of domination and command which they had established during slavery. The opportunity to have free and unhindered negotiations of work contracts between workers and their employers which the end of slavery promised did not materialise in the British-colonised

Caribbean as employers were provided with a new instrument for the compulsion of labour by the passage of a wide range of masters and servants legislation throughout the sub-region.

The 1849 Masters and Servants Act passed by the planter-dominated legislature in St Kitts remained in force until 1922 when it was replaced by a slightly less restrictive Masters and Servants ordinance which was not repealed until 1938. Like the other colonial labour legislation passed in the British Caribbean during the immediate post-emancipation period, the St Kitts act was modelled upon contemporary English legislation which regulated relations between employers and workers, particularly the statute of 1823, 4 Geo. Iv c 34.[40] Early nineteenth-century British and colonial labour legislation entrenched in law the inequality between workers and employers by making a breach of contract by a worker a criminal offence punishable by imprisonment while limiting the liability of an employer who broke his contract with his employee to civil action for damages or wages due. Under the St Kitts act, labourers or employees who withdrew their labour from an employer, after having entered a labour contract, signed or unsigned, before the termination of the contract would be guilty of a criminal offence and were subject to forfeiture of any wages due. They could be sentenced to a fine of up to 50 shillings or to imprisonment for one months' hard labour. A labour contract was deemed to last for one month in the case of non-agricultural workers and one week in the case of agricultural workers.[41] The one week duration of a praedial contract ensured that the estate worker could not respond immediately to any real or perceived injustices and would have to serve out the contract despite any grievances which may appear during the period. It also ensured that a worker had no claims upon an employer which would last beyond the one week duration.

CREOLE STRATEGIES AND TACTICS OF LABOUR BARGAINING

Although strategies of labour bargaining and peaceful conflict resolution were evident among Caribbean enslaved populations when they were still predominantly African-born, these strategies were elaborated on and became more prevalent during the period of the creolisation of the enslaved population, particularly after the abolition of the British slave trade in 1807. Some labour bargaining tactics developed during the period of slavery gained legal sanction and received wider application after the abolition of slavery. But the post-slavery period also saw the development and application of new tactics such as the submission of written petitions addressed to the local government and the Crown. While this could be seen as an extension of the slave practice of appealing for mediation by neighbouring planters and government officials, the writing and submission of formal petitions was a celebration of the ex-slaves new status as freed people. The predominantly Creole labouring population regarded themselves as British, fully entitled to all the rights of British subjects, and the exercise of this quintessentially British right to petition the Crown marked their full acceptance of, and partial integration into, British Caribbean Creole society. Another right that their new status as free persons gave them access to was the right to appeal to the magistrates court. However, when it came to disputes between themselves and the planters, the labourers lacked all confidence in courts that were presided over by planters or close relatives of planters whose main legal role was to enforce plantation discipline by enforcing the legal provisions of the Masters and Servants Act. As with the White indentured servants before them, the right to appeal to the courts was seldom exercised by the free labouring population as a way of resolving industrial disputes with their employers.

PETITIONS AND REPRESENTATIONS

The right to petition the Crown was entrenched by law and was a widely practiced custom among both the White and Coloured population during and after slavery. The enslaved, as property and with no legal personality, had no such rights but after slavery, as legal subjects of the Crown, the ex-slave population throughout the British Caribbean exercised their right to petition the Crown with astonishing regularity. When immediate appeals to planters and other employers for improvements in wages or working conditions failed, the labouring population almost invariably took their petitions to the local government. Petitions of this sort, in St Kitts and Nevis, were often undertaken in response to planter combinations to reduce wage rates or to enforce cuts in the labour force in the face of falling sugar prices. In 1896, after universal wage reductions had been implemented by employers in both St Kitts and Nevis in response to a sharp fall in the international price for sugar, 12 Nevisian workers representing the "(estate) labourers, porters and boatmen of Nevis" presented a petition to the governor calling for an increase in wages which should "be paid at such an hour on payday, as to enable us to procure our daily necessaries". The petition also called on the government to increase the tariff paid to the porters and the boatmen and to fix a schedule which the merchants would be obliged to honour.[42] In a subsequent 1903 petition by Nevisian labourers to the then Secretary of State for the Colonies, Joseph Chamberlain, the labourers complained that at the "slightest displeasure, whim and caprice" of the estate management, land occupied by labourers on estates could be repossessed by the estate and their crops sold or destroyed.

Labourers' livestock which was pastured on estate land could be impounded and were only redeemable upon payment of an impounding fee to the estate.[43]

Labourers in nearby St Kitts also utilised the tactics of petitions and representations. In 1905, the St Kitts planters responding to further falls in sugar prices imposed another unilateral wage reduction and the workers took their case to the public. At the commencement of the sugar crop, the leaders of the estate workers sent a letter to the editor of one of the local newspapers stating their demands regarding wages and working conditions. On individual estates, workers selected delegations to negotiate wage increases with their respective employer and, in face of planter resistance, a joint deputation of the island's estate workers met with the island administrator to represent their case.[44]

In none of these instances did the workers' collective action win the desired results. The unilateral wage reductions imposed by the planter combinations were supported by both the local and Imperial governments as essential economic measures in the face of a deteriorating competitive position for the colonies' main export staple.

LITIGATION

The system of apprenticeship provided for the appointment of stipendiary magistrates to adjudicate in disputes between former enslavers and their apprentices and to protect the worker. While the stipendiary magistrates courts were regularly used to discipline the apprentices and to ensure that they fulfilled their work obligations, the protective role of the courts was seldom exercised and workers made no attempt to appeal for the court's intervention in disputes with their masters. One Methodist missionary in Nevis during the period of apprenticeship observed that the Nevisian planters made no effort to pass on "information to the apprentices relative to the privileges the law secures for them". He added: "I have you to judge of the effects upon the minds of the labourers, to see their masters driving about the magistrate in their carriages to hear complaints against themselves."[45]

The 1849 Masters and Servants Act also empowered the local district magistrates to hear wage disputes between employers and their workers and to award such pay claims as were deemed just. The adjudication of labour disputes by district magistrates who were themselves employers, or were closely related to other employers by blood or marriage, tilted the balance of colonial justice firmly in favour of the employee class.

Few workers believed that they could receive justice in the courts in which they were usually on the receiving end of the courts' punishment. Francis Wigley, the senior magistrate in St Kitts in 1897 who was himself an estate proprietor, testified before the 1897 West India Royal Commission that while there were frequent cases of breach of contract brought by planters under the Masters and Servants Act, there had been none brought by workers.[46]

GENERAL STRIKES AND MASS DEMONSTRATIONS

Where petitions, representations and other channels of protest failed, plantation workers, slave and free, resorted to overt and, at times, violent protest. Such collective actions, sometimes extending over the entire colony and involving large sections of the labouring population, were infrequent but periodic, taking place during times of great economic distress or in response to grave social injustices meted out by the planters. Strikes on individual estates, usually in the form of mass desertions as in the case of the slaves on Mountravers estate, were reported during slavery. These strikes were usually in response to immediate grievances and were undertaken by slaves on isolated plantations with limited and specific aims. But there were also colony-wide general strikes during slavery as in the case of "Bussa's Rebellion" in Barbados in 1816 and the Demerara slave revolt of 1823. But perhaps the most notable and widely organised of these slave general strikes occurred in the Jamaican slave rebellion of 1831–1832 with a collective refusal by the participating slaves to carry out their tasks on the plantations in support of their demand that wages be paid for all labour performed on the plantations. The rebel slaves, led by Sam Sharpe, declared their readiness to end their strike, however, if "Buckra would pay them".[47]

General strikes occurred in St Kitts in 1834, 1896 and 1905. The general strike of 1834 expressed the general refusal of the island's recently freed slaves to serve a period of apprenticeship as stipulated by the Emancipation Act. It was marked by collective refusals to work and mass desertion of the sugar estates with order finally being restored by the landing of marines and forcing of runaway apprentices down from the mountains to recommence work on the estate.[48] The general strike of 1896, which affected both St Kitts and Nevis, was accompanied, primarily in the island of St Kitts, by mass rioting and widespread popular disturbances leading once more to the declaration of martial law and the restoration of public order by the landing of naval marines.[49] The 1905 general strike broke out after the workers' peaceful representations for a wage increase (described above) had failed and when the sugar estate proprietors, pointing to further declines in sugar prices, had instead imposed a collective 25 per cent reduction in wages. The threat by Francis Wigley, the senior magistrate, to jail any striker who was brought before him for breach of contract, coupled with the concerted stand of the employers, convinced the workers to end the general strike.[50] It is notable that these general strikes all occurred during periods of great social change or deepening economic distress. Additionally, as Bonham Richardson has pointed out, these post-slavery general strikes also occurred at a time when workers were forced to remain at home because of a temporary halt to emigration due to external conditions.[51]

These strikes were usually accompanied by mass public demonstrations and processions, moving from village to village and culminating in the urban centre, which adopted the form of the traditional Christmas masquerades, with the playing on drums, blowing of fifes and conch shells, and frenzied dancing and shouting. The largely anonymous leaders of these general strikes and street demonstrations were most probably estate headmen, who were often themselves Christmas masquerade captains, and were possibly the same individuals who had been selected to lead the representative delegations to the planters or the colonial administrator.[52]

It should be noted that, as with the use of petitions and representations, none of these general strikes or public demonstrations enjoyed any success. Where, as in 1896, the outbreak of the strikes and public disorder led to an initial concession to the labourers demands, once order had been forcibly restored, the original wage reductions were re-imposed. Notably some sections of the planting community in 1896 were open to the idea of peacefully negotiating their workers' wage demands. F.A. Hall, managing attorney of an absentee-owned estate, proposed that, in future, delegates be chosen from the mass of workers and a meeting between these delegates and planters be convened to agree on wage rates. Another planter, James Adamson, argued in a letter to one of the local newspapers that a conciliation board be created along British lines to which disputes which could not be settled by the estate management and the "head of the labourers" could be sent. Adamson's letter openly acknowledges the leading role of estate head-men in the resolution of labour disputes on individual estates. These liberal proposals proved too much for the general planting community of both islands and were rejected as unworkable.[53]

In the case of St Kitts and Nevis then, the workers' labour-bargaining strategies, and the tactics employed to achieve them, had only limited, if any, success. Their continued employment, however, suggests an entrenched working-class belief in the possibility of improvement within the existing economic structures and an abiding faith that their masters and employers would respond to their reasonable industrial demands in a just and rational manner.

CONCLUSION

The development of labour-bargaining strategies by the enslaved populations of the Caribbean, and their free descendants, reflects both their acceptance of their historical reality and their concerted efforts to change that reality by transforming the economic relations that bound them to their enslavers and employers. The actions of these workers were motivated by a belief in the possibility of self-improvement within the existing socio-economic structures, the personal objective of bettering material conditions for themselves and their children and the social aim of upward social mobility. The drivers and headmen on individual plantations, and the slave elite in general, had a strong personal interest in the success of these strategies, for success meant an increase in their material benefits and a strengthening of their social positions.[54]

Indeed, labour-bargaining strategies signalled the increasing social investment of enslaved Africans and their descendants in plantation society and their emerging Creole sensibilities and commitment to the only home that they knew. It is this feature of plantation society which best explains how "a transitory and alienated nucleus of [white] workers, sharing no common economic ground with the ownership, was able to hold in subjection a massive body of restless slaves."[55]

This is not to argue that enslaved people in the Caribbean and their free descendants did not seek fundamental changes in slavery or plantation society. Their constant insistence on their humanity, which these labour bargaining strategies expressed, led them inexorably to pose a revolutionary alternative to the plantation and industrial disputes which began as peaceful attempts at labour bargaining were quickly transformed or went hand in hand with revolutionary challenges to the entire plantation system. This historical process is witnessed again and again in the late slave rebellions of the British Caribbean: in Barbados in 1816, Demerara in 1823 and in Jamaica in 1831–1832, as well as in the extensive labour rebellions in St Kitts in 1834 and 1896. There was no dichotomy between the role of peaceful and "trusted" negotiator taken on by drivers and other members of the plantation labour elite and that of rebel leader, and many individuals easily traversed both roles.

Ultimately, the labour-bargaining strategies of the slaves and their free descendants were impeded, at least initially, not so much by the inability of the plantations to satisfy the social and economic demands of their labouring population as by the ingrained racism of their White masters. The response of Edward Huggins Snr. to the industrial action of the slaves at Mountravers had as much, if not more, to do with the preservation of his racial honour as with the maintenance of plantation discipline. The racial fear of White enslavers and employers in St Kitts was well represented in the views of the island Treasurer, James Burns, who in a private letter to Sydney Olivier, expressed his fears of what would have happened but for the timely arrival of a British warship during the labour disturbances of 1896. Burns wrote:

> But for the chance arrival of the HMS Cordelia, the town would certainly have been burnt to the ground even if we had escaped with our lives. I have a full knowledge of the nigger and I know that full of rum and excited by plunder, the quasi-civilisation of the last fifty years fall from him and leaves him a greater savage than his African ancestors.[56]

The racial response of the White employer class to the bid for social equality which the labour-bargaining strategies of the enslaved people and their descendants implied was also an expression of their own Creole sensibilities. For, after centuries of creolisation and the heat of a Caribbean sun, whiteness remained their only personal distinguishing characteristic.

It was the enslaved worker and his/her free descendant who, both in trying to "make life" and to remake the world a new, expressed the strongest commitment to a new Creole existence which would embrace enslaved and enslaver, Black and White. This commitment to a new Creole order was fittingly expressed in the words and actions of an old estate worker who, at the end of the 1896 labour protest in St Kitts, is reported to have approached his estate manager and shook the manager's hand with the words, "Ole Massa, now everything is settled let us all be good friends."[57]

NOTES

1. "Driber tan mi' side" is a line from a traditional emancipation song unearthed by Michael Craton during his research on the Worthy Park estate in Jamaica for his book *Searching for the Invisible Man* (Cambridge and London: Harvard University Press, 1978).

2. See chapter two of Sidney Mintz and Richard Price, *The Birth of African-American Culture: An Anthropological Perspective* (Boston: Beacon Press, 1992). This work was originally published in 1976 as *An Anthropological Approach to the Afro-American Past: A Caribbean Perspective* by the Institute for the Study of Human Issues and

republished largely unrevised. W. Washabaugh and S. Greenfield, in keeping with the theoretical position of Mintz and Price, have noted that: ". . . Atlantic creole languages are developmentally and functionally related to the plantation as a social form. Consequently, we argue that Atlantic creole language first arose among the laborers on the earliest plantations in the Western World." See S. Washabaugh and S. Greenfield, "The Development of Atlantic Creole Language" in E.Woolford and W. Washabaugh, eds., *The Social Context of Creolization* (Ann Arbor, MI: Kanoma Publishers, 1983), p. 106.

3.   Michael Craton's invaluable and somewhat unique *Searching for the Invisible Man* (Cambridge and London: Harvard University Press, 1978) is perhaps the closest that we get to such a work in the field of Caribbean History. While employing the concept of creolisation, the author does not himself set out to explore the evolution of this historical process in the working world of his slave subjects. Ira Berlin and Philip Morgan, commenting on the prevailing approach to the study of slave culture which is regarded as "emanating from the quarter, household, and church rather than the field and workshop", observe that the "struggle over the slaves' labor informed all other conflicts between master and slave, and understanding that contest opens the way to a full comprehension of slave society." See Berlin and Morgan, eds., *Cultivation and Culture: Labor and the Shaping of Slave Life in the Americas* (Charlottesville and London: University Press of Virginia, 1993), Introduction, 2; Chapters 3 and 4 of Philip Morgan's, *Slave Counterpoint: Black Culture in the Eighteenth-Century Chesapeake and Lowcountry* (Chapel Hill and London: University of North Carolina Press, 1998) makes a significant contribution, in the context of North America, to the study of the creolisation process in the field of work but the discussion of creolisation tends to get lost in his systematic exploration of crop production techniques, fieldwork patterns, and occupational structures. Chapter 6, however, provides a very useful examination of the social interaction between slaves and masters in the economic sphere.

4.   Interview with Marjorie Nicholson by Glen Richards, St Albans, England, 14 April, 1987.

5.   Mary Turner, "Introduction" in M. Turner, ed., *From Chattel Slaves to Wage Slaves: The Dynamics of Labour Bargaining in the Americas* (Kingston, Bloomington and London: Ian Randle, Indiana University Press and James Currey, 1995), pp. 1–2.

6.   Mintz and Price, *The Birth of African-American Culture* (1992), p. 34. Nowhere is this argument more graphically represented that in Dale Tomich's recounting of Victor Schoelcher's account of his experience in Martinique of seeing large mango trees in the middle of cane fields stunting the growth of the cane plants in their shadows. The master was unable to cut them down because the mango trees, probably standing on land formerly used as slave provision grounds, had been

bequeathed to a slave who was not yet born. See D. Tomich, "The Other Face of Slave Labor: Provision Grounds and Internal Marketing in Martinique", in H.Beckles and V. Shepherd, eds., *Caribbean Slave Society and Economy: A Student Reader* (Kingston and London: Ian Randle and James Currey, 1991), p. 313.

7.   Mintz and Price, *The Birth of African-American Culture* (1992), p. 27.

8.   W. Green, "The Creolisation of Caribbean History: The Emancipation Era and a Critique of Dialectical Analysis", in H. Beckles and V. Shepherd, eds., *Caribbean Freedom: Economy and Society from Emancipation to the Present: A Student Reader* (Kingston and London: Ian Randle and James Currey, 1993), p. 29.

9.   See Mintz and Price, *The Birth of African-American Culture.*

10. One striking but most ironic example of this proprietorial attachment to plantation work was the action of the Mesopotamia slaves, led by their head driver, Samuel Williams, and a slave mason, Richard Gilpin, who during the Sam Sharpe rebellion started up the sugar works and began to take off the sugar crop on their own although all the White men on the estate had departed to help crush the rebellion. See Richard Dunn, "'Dreadful Idlers' in the Cane Fields: The Slave Labor Pattern on a Jamaican Sugar Estate, 1762–1831", in B. Solow and S. Engerman, eds., *British Capitalism and Caribbean Slavery: The Legacy of Eric Williams* (Cambridge: Cambridge University Press, 1987), pp. 163–90.

11. Mary Turner's *From Chattel Slaves to Wage Slaves* provides an extensive survey of labour bargaining techniques throughout the Americas. See particularly O. Nigel Bolland, "Proto-Proletarians? Slave Wages in the Americas: Between Slave Labour and Free Labour", pp. 123–46; Lucia Lamounier, "Between Slavery and Free Labour: Early Experiments with Free Labour and Patterns of Slave Emancipation in Brazil and Cuba", pp. 185–200.

12. O. Nigel Bolland writes: "Slaves who negotiated in this way engaged in a market transaction about the value of their own labour power, as a consequence of which they were able to improve their material standards of living and sometimes even to purchase their freedom, or the freedom of others, with the proceeds of their labour. Such slaves resemble a kind of 'proto-proletariat', engaged in subtly transforming their relations with their masters." See Bolland, "Proto-Proletarians? Slave Wages in the Americas", in Turner, ed., *From Chattel Slaves to Wage Slaves*, p. 136.

13. For a discussion of the seventeenth-century system of White indentureship and its operation in the Caribbean see D. Galenson, *White Servitude in Colonial America* (Cambridge: Cambridge University Press, 1981) and H. Beckles, *White Servitude and Black Slavery, 1627–1715* (Knoxville: University of Tennessee Press, 1989).

14. Beckles, *White Servitude and Black Slavery* (1989), pp. 111–12.

15. See D. Akenson, *If the Irish ran the World: Montserrat, 1630–1730* (Kingston and Montreal: UWI Press, and McGill University Press, 1997). Akenson notes that

"white indentured servitude was so different from Black slavery as to be from another galaxy of human experience." Ibid., p. 49.

16. Ibid., p. 114.

17. H. Beckles, "A 'Riotous and Unruly Lot': Irish Indentured Servants and Freemen in the English West Indies, 1644–1713", in *The William and Mary Quarterly*, 3rd ser. (47:1, 1990), p. 512; Beckles, *White Servitude and Black Slavery*, p. 127.

18. Beckles, *White Servitude and Black Slavery*, p. 99.

19. After the discovery of a slave conspiracy in 1686, 18 Irish indentured servants were arrested on suspicion of cooperating in the plot but had to be released for lack of evidence. In the 1692 slave conspiracy, "five or six" Irishmen were supposedly implicated in a plot to steal arms and ammunition from a military fort and supply them to rebellious slaves but the absence of any records pertaining to the trial or punishment of these Irishmen led Beckles to conclude that "there was no evidence and that English suspicion had reached paranoid levels". See Beckles, "A 'Riotous and Unruly Lot'", pp. 517–18.

20. Ibid., p. 514.

21. Governor Atkins, while not himself a plantation owner, was dependent upon the financial concessions he received from planters to supplement his official salary. Ibid., pp. 514–15.

22. *Mbakara* is an Efik word meaning "all-master" or "he who rules". See Richard Burton, *Afro-Creole: Power, Opposition and Play in the Caribbean* (Ithaca and London: Cornell University Press, 1997), p. 269; Michael Craton, *Testing the Chains: Resistance to Slavery in the British West Indies* (Ithaca, N.Y.: Cornell University Press 1982), p. 341. However, Sultana Afroz suggests that the term 'buckra' or 'baccra' is a corruption of the Arabic word baqarah or cow, which, when applied to persons, denotes the "fossilisation [or spritual death] of human beings". The open contempt and hatred which the term often conveys supports the interpretation advanced by Afroz. See Sultana Afroz "From Moors to Marronage: The Islamic Heritage of the Maroons in Jamaica", *Journal of Muslim Minority Affairs* (19:2 ,1999), p. 177.

23. See Paul Lovejoy, *Transformations in Slavery: A History of Slavery in Africa* (Cambridge: Cambridge University Press, 1983).

24. Lovejoy is not very specific in his definition of the term. He writes: "The cultivation of agricultural goods under plantation conditions sometimes reflected extensive market developments and sometimes not. Plantation output could be used to feed armies and palaces or it could be exported. The low level of technology meant that there was relatively little investment in capital or the improvement of land . . .". Paul Lovejoy, *Transformations in Slavery*, p. 270. James F. Searing questions Lovejoy's use of the term plantation to describe agricultural units which utilise slave labour in pre-colonial Africa, noting that it "can be

misleading if it suggests close parallels with the capitalist slave economies of the Americas". See J. Searing, *West African Slavery and Atlantic Commerce: The Senegal River Valley, 1700–1860* (Cambridge: Cambridge University Press, 1993), pp. 48–9.

25. See, for example, Paul Lovejoy, "Plantations in the Economy of the Sokoto Caliphate", in *Journal of African History* (19:3,1978), pp. 341–68; Lovejoy, "The Characteristics of Plantations in the Nineteenth Century Sokoto Caliphate (Islamic West Africa)", in *American Historical Review* (4, 1979), pp. 1267–92; Lovejoy, "Problems of Slave Control in the Sokoto Caliphate", in Paul Lovejoy, ed., *Africans in Bondage: Studies in Slavery and the Slave Trade* (Madison, WI: University of Wisconsin Press, 1986), pp. 235–72.

26. The sheer enormity of this task may, however, stand as a permanent discouragement for any such undertaking. For a fuller discussion of the extensive requirements of such a research project, see Mintz and Price, *Birth of African-American Culture* (1992).

27. In *Slave Counterpoint*, Philip Morgan notes that rice sowing techniques on the rice plantations of the South Carolina Lowcountry were an "amalgam of, perhaps even a conflict between, European and West African planting techniques" (p. 150). However, he notes that the African contribution to rice planting in the Lowcountry was severely limited because the majority of African slaves there were from coastal regions which were not rice-producing areas. Additionally, the irrigated rice culture of South Carolina differed sharply from the dry, upland, rice cultivation which most West Africans engaged in (pp. 182–83).

28. Mintz and Price, *Birth of African-American Culture*, p. 27.

29. Craton, *Searching for the Invisible Man*, p. 149. Richard Dunn observes that: "Among the black men, the drivers had the longest careers and died at the most advanced ages, which is not surprising, since they were elevated to this post in middle life, having been selected at least in part because of their proven durability." Dunn, "'Dreadful Idlers' in the Cane Fields", p. 178.

30. Dunn, "'Dreadful Idlers' in the Cane Fields", Table 47, 182–5. Barry Higman also points out that physical stature may have been another important criteria for the selection of drivers. In Berbice, Creole male drivers were consistently taller than all other sections of the slave population. See B.W. Higman, *Slave Populations of the British Caribbean, 1807–1834* (Baltimore and London: Johns Hopkins University Press, 1984), p. 288.

31. Craton, *Testing the Chains*. p. 54. Craton expresses the duality of the slave driver's position well when he writes: "Accordingly, the key figure on each plantation was the black slave driver, chosen by the planters as policeman and mediator but, being himself the quintessential slave, potentially and ultimately a rebel leader too." Ibid. Slave drivers, as with other elite plantation slaves, often combined other social leadership roles with their occupational role. Craton notes that on

William Wylly's estates in the Bahamas, the drivers were instructed to hold Sunday services. Ibid, p. 54. On Mountravers estate in Nevis, Wiltshire, the driver, was "specially skilled in compounding roots into remedies for venereal disease". See Richard Pares, *A West India Fortune* (London: Longmans, 1950), p. 128.

32.   Turner, "Introduction", in *From Chattel Slaves to Wage Slaves*, p. 8.

33.   Without making the explicit connection with the historical role of the slave driver and the slave elite, Richard Burton notes, in his commentary on political and spiritual leadership in modern Jamaica, that: ". . . the prophet-leader is he who has privileged access to the Big Massa in the Great House of heaven, who takes or is given some of Big Massa's power and transmits it to the suffering masses below, whence the almost irresistible appeal of Afro-Jamaican religion: Surrender yourself to 'Daddy' or 'Ruler' or 'Shepherd', and you in your turn – provided you *obey* his teaching and orders – will enter the Promised Land where, as in the Great House, you will be fed milk and honey (or if you prefer, jerked pork with rice and peas) for all eternity." See Burton, *Afro-Creole*, p. 141.

34.   The collective identity of slave drivers and slaves is fittingly illustrated in the traditional emancipation song collected by Michael Craton. The words of the song are as follows:

Driber tan me side, but let me talk to mi' busha

When 'busha gan, is mi an' yu deyah

Howdy 'busha, tenke Masa Craton, *Searching for the Invisible Man*, p. 367.

35.   Slave drivers have played key roles in most of the significant slave revolts and conspiracies in the British Caribbean from the seventeenth century to the end of slavery. Drivers who played leading roles in slave rebellions and conspiracies include Secundi and Jacko in the 1736 slave conspiracy unearthed in Antigua; Jackey in "Bussa's rebellion" of 1816 in Barbados named for its principal leader, Bussa, another elite slave; and Telemachus in the 1823 slave revolt in Demerara. For a full account of these instances of slave resistance, see Craton, *Testing the Chains*.

36.   Richard Sheridan, *Sugar and Slavery* (Rock Dundo Heights, Barbados: Caribbean Universities Press, 1974), p. 160.

37.   For a fuller account of the dispute see Pares, *A West India Fortune*.

38.   At 7.1 per cent African-born in 1817, the creolisation process was most advanced in the island of Barbados. See Barry Higman, *Slave Populations of the British Caribbean 1807–1834*, Table 5.7, Slave Sex Ratios and Percentages African and Colored by Colony, circa 1817 and circa 1832, p. 121.

39.   Richard Frucht, "From Slavery to Unfreedom in the Plantation Society of St Kitts, W.I.", in V. Rubin and A. Tuden, eds., *Comparative Perspectives on Slavery in New World Plantation Societies* (New York: New York Academy of Science, 1977), p. 386.

40. For a detailed account of the evolution of masters and servants legislation in England see Daphne Simon, "Master and Servant", in *Democracy and the Labour Movement*, ed., John Saville (London: Lawrence and Wisehart, 1954), pp. 160–200.

41. C.O. 240/20, Masters and Servants Act, no. 84 of 1849.

42. C.O. 152/203, Petition of Labourers, Boatmen, and Porters, 21 February, 1896, enc. Fleming to Chamberlain, 16 March, 1896. The names of the signatories are given but their respective occupations are given as "labourer", "porter" and "boatmen". These individuals, however, almost certainly held supervisory roles.

43. C.O. 152/279, Petition from James Clarke Taylor and Nevis Labourers, enc. Strickland to Chamberlain, 30 May, 1903.

44. *St Christopher Advertiser and Weekly Intelligencer*, 24 January, 1905; *St Christopher Gazette and Caribbean Courier*, 23 January 1905.

45. Karen Fog Olwig, *Global Culture, Island Identity: Continuity and Change in the Afro-Caribbean Community of Nevis* (Switzerland: Harwood Academic Publishers, 1993), p. 94.

46. *West India Royal Commission, 1897*, Evidence of the Hon. Francis Wigley, 236.

47. Craton, *Testing the Chains*, p. 300.

48. For a detailed account of the 1834 general strike in St Kitts see R. Frucht, "Emancipation and Revolt in the West Indies: St Kitts, 1834", in *Science and Society* 39 (1975), pp. 199–214.

49. See Glen Richards, "Masters and Servants: The Growth of the Labour Movement in St Christopher-Nevis, 1896–1956", Ph.D., Cambridge, 1989, pp. 145–68

50. C.O. 152/286, Bromley to Knollys, 1 March, 1905, enc. Knollys to Littleton, 8 March, 1905.

51. Bonham Richardson, *Caribbean Migrants: Environment and Human Survival in St Kitts and Nevis* (Knoxville: University of Tennesse Press, 1983), pp. 181.

52. See Glen Richards, "Masters and Servants", pp. 151–53. Largely anonymous in the archival records, even when names of these early working-class leaders do appear, as with John Bishop who was named by the *St Christopher Gazette and Caribbean Courier* of 30 May, 1896 as the organiser of the boatmen strike and urban demonstrations during the St Kitts labour protests of that year, there is no information on their occupational role. Although it is not possible to say with any certainty that the leaders of these workers' delegations or the working-class signatories of the petitions were headmen and drivers, the tradition of the leading role by elite members of the labour hierarchy witnessed during slavery, continued, in St Kitts and Nevis, to the eve of the legal formation of trade unions. The 1935 labour protests in St Kitts followed a meeting of the headmen on the various sugar estates held on 20 January to discuss wage demands for the coming sugar crop. C.O. 152/454/5, Nathan to head cutters and head cartmen on the various

estates, 2 January, 1935, enc. St Johnson to Cunliffe-Lister, 15 January, 1935; *Union Messenger*, 21 January, 1935, undated letter to the editor by Joseph Nathan.

53. C.O. 152/202, minutes of a meeting of planters held by invitation of the governor, 22 February, 1896, statement of F.A. Hall, enc. Fleming to Chamberlain, 28 February, 1896; *St Christopher Advertiser and Weekly Intelligencer,* 19 May, 1896, letter to the editor from James D. Adamson, undated.

54. Michael Craton and Jim Walvin write, "It was to the elites benefit not only to produce the finished goods but, following from this essential point, also to mould the slaves beneath them and to keep them as pliable and reliant a group as possible. In return for better facilities, the slave elite was the agent which impressed a work discipline on to the slave community." See M. Craton and J. Walvin, *A Jamaican Plantation: The History of Worthy Park, 1670–1970* (London and New York: W.H. Allen, 1970), p. 147.

55. Ibid.

56. C.O. 152/202, Burns to Olivier, 24 February, 1896, enc. Fleming to Chamberlain, 28 February, 1896.

57. *St Christopher Advertiser and Weekly Intelligencer*, 17 April, 1896.

Swithin Wilmot

Chapter 12

THE POLITICS OF
SAMUEL CLARKE

BLACK CREOLE POLITICIAN IN
FREE JAMAICA, 1851–1865*

Kamau Brathwaite's work on the development of Creole society has emphasised the active role of the ordinary men and women "who, from the centre of an oppressive system have been able to survive, adapt and recreate".[1] This struggle was maintained in the post-slavery period, where, despite the restrictions imposed by considerations of property and gender, Blacks in Jamaica were as determined as other Creole groups to have a say in how their society was governed. One such was Samuel Clarke, a Black carpenter and Vestryman from the parish of St David, which bordered St Thomas-in-the-East Although Clarke and George William Gordon were the only two of the political prisoners who were arrested outside the area of martial law and taken to Morant Bay where they were hurriedly tried and executed, only Gordon's fate is highlighted, thereby reflecting a bias to underscore the activities of the Creole Brown elite and to neglect the struggles of the Black Jamaicans who creatively attempted to utilise the institutions of governance to further the interest of the freed people.

Samuel Clarke's invisibility before 1865 reflects a broader failure in the historiography of post-slavery Jamaica to include Black Jamaicans' role in fashioning the politics of the island before the Brown and White elites surrendered the constitution after the rebellion in 1865. This article seeks to rescue Samuel Clarke from historical obscurity by tracing his public career which began a decade and a half before Paul Bogle and other Black men and women marched to Morant Bay in October 1865. Then perhaps one will be able to understand why Clarke was executed during martial law at Morant Bay, even though there was no evidence to implicate him.[2]

Samuel Clarke, a carpenter and small settler, bought 9.5 acres of land in Heartease in St David in 1850. As an influential member of the Black small settler community, Clarke came to public attention when he mobilised Black voters in the free Coloureds' aggressive campaign in 1851 to capture one of the two St David seats in the House of Assembly.[3] By the1850s in St David, this new class of Black small settlers, mostly ex-slaves, had become an important political force to be reckoned with and the planters' traditional control of the politics in the parish was certainly under serious threat.

Up until the abolition of slavery, sugar estates and pens dominated in the lower, dry areas of St David. At emancipation, the parish had 10 sugar estates, and by 1854, 70 per cent of them had been abandoned. Moreover, as the estates contracted their operations, the pen-keepers subdivided part of their holdings and sold lots to ex-slaves.[4] For instance, in 1839, 61.75 acres of Heartease Pen were surveyed and subdivided into nine lots of between five and ten acres and by 1841, freed people had already settled there. Similarly, Smithfield Pen, to the north of Albion sugar estate, was surveyed in 1842 and 14 lots totalling 44.5 acres were sold by 1843. In 1842 as well, of the total acreage of 65 acres at Mount Clare Pen, 21 were sold off in ten lots.

In the same period, sections of other pens near to the Yallahs area, such as Content, Cherry Garden, Colliers River, Highgate and Hopewell were purchased by freed people. Samuel Clarke joined an already established class of small settlers who grew provisions, raised livestock, planted sugar cane and cultivated minor exports such as honey, ginger and cotton. Some of the settlers, like Samuel Clarke, were skilled artisans, carpenters, masons and blacksmiths who serviced the nearby sugar properties at Albion, Norris, Mount Sinai and Windsor Forrest, and the pens, as well as the coffee properties higher up the Yallahs valley. As the number of this new class of small freeholders increased, it soon became apparent to the Kingston Coloured politicians that only 11 miles away to the east, in St David, a new electoral base was developing.

The related factors that linked Kingston and St David favoured their plans. Some ex-slaves in St David had previously been members of the Baptist community in Kingston and they and the free Blacks in St David formed the nucleus out of which Rev. Joshua Tinson, the Baptist minister in Kingston, established a church near Yallahs in 1830. As the new church flourished, with the chapel being built in 1835 and a school house opened on 1 August, 1838, links between the Kingston and St David Baptist communities were cemented. The 1844 Baptist electoral campaign against the Established Church (or Church of England) incorporated St David where the Vestry had remained the exclusive preserve of the Church of England and the Rector of the parish was notoriously lazy and indifferent to the educational needs of his parishioners.

Clearly, given the strong political tradition of the Baptist communities in the island, and the linkages between the Kingston and Yallahs congregations, the politicians had a good entree into the area.[5] Two of Kingston's leading Black political organisers, George William Cuthbert, a shoemaker, and Matthew Lutas, a tailor, who was also a trustee of the Native Baptist Church in Kingston, had purchased lands in St David, as did other Kingston Black electors such as Edward Duaney, a tailor, and Robert Wiltshire, whose father had been among the first Blacks to be elected to the Kingston Common Council in 1840.

These Kingstonians, well practised in electoral politics, linked with Samuel Clarke to mobilise the small freeholders in St David. In March 1849, Samuel Clarke chaired a meeting of upwards of 100 freeholders to prepare an address for the Stipendiary Magistrate Marah, who was leaving the island. This was the first of a series of meetings exclusively of the small freeholders, thereby providing them with a platform to articulate their views on issues that were of fundamental importance to them. Four months later, another such meeting was held. This time, the enforcement of the international treaties for the suppression of the slave trade was the theme that was used to bring together a large number of the small freeholders and the labouring population of the parish of St David. The St David political hopefuls, grasping the significance of such an issue for the ex-slaves, held such a gathering on Friday, 13 July, 1849, and the court house at Easington was surrounded by the horses, mules and asses of the labouring population of the parish. Significantly, wives and daughters were also present. At least three Blacks with Kingston connections addressed the gathering – Edward Duaney, Matthew Lutas and Robert Wiltshire.[6]

Any attempt to influence the formal politics of the parish required that a registration campaign be launched. This was forcefully underscored when just four days after the large meeting of the small freeholders at Easington, the 1849 election for two representatives of St David in the Assembly was held. This election was part of the general poll called by the governor to ascertain where the voters stood on the retrenchment disputes which had embittered the relations between the planters and Sir Charles Grey, the governor, whose main support in the Assembly was the Kings House Party, which was composed primarily of

Coloureds. The Coloureds put up Baron Maximilian Von Ketelholdt, a close friend of the governor, to oppose the two incumbents, Robert Carr and Alexander Finlay, Kingston merchants, who had commercial links with coffee and sugar properties in St David. Given future events, it was ironic that George William Gordon, a planter and magistrate in St David, nominated the Baron and was among the five men who voted for him.

In a small poll, Finlay and Carr easily won with 15 and 14 votes, respectively. Nonetheless, it is significant that this election was the first contested election in the parish for 31 years and a small crack had appeared in the hegemony of the planters in electoral matters.

Since the potential voters among the Black freeholders had not been canvassed and most had not registered their claim to vote, the mobilisation campaign now turned away from public meetings to the specific objective of registering those among the small freeholders entitled to the franchise. Within a month of the 1849 election, "The St David's Liberal, Recording, and Election Association" was formed. Robert Wiltshire, one of the Kingston Black politicians who owned a freehold at Poor Man's Corner in St David, was president, and Samuel Clarke was the vice president.[7] In addition to registering the small freeholders, the Association also monitored the developments in the island's politics which had important ramifications for Black Jamaicans.

Thus, when Charles Price, a Black builder from Kingston, won one of the two seats for the parish of St John in the Assembly in the 1849 general election, thereby becoming the second Black man to sit in the island's Assembly, the St David Election Association called a meeting and moved a special vote of thanks to the electors in St John "for the praiseworthy manner in which they have acted in returning a son of Africa as their representative in the Honourable House of Assembly".

Price had defeated John Aris, a Coloured sugar planter, and Francis Lynch, a White solicitor whose father-in-law, Dr Turner, was the senior magistrate for St Catherine and a member of the Legislative Council. This clearly underscored the electoral influence of the Black freeholders in St John and pointed the way to the Blacks in St David, once they registered. Furthermore, while Samuel Clarke busied himself in the drive to swell the St David electoral list, Edward Vickars, the other Black member of the House of Assembly, together with Robert Osborn and Robert Jordon, purchased 16 acres of land at the Eleven Miles District in St David in 1849. By becoming freeholders in the parish, they were positioning themselves to contest seats for the St David Vestry at the elections due in January 1850.

Robert Jordon who, along with Samuel Clarke, became the chief political organiser of the Black freeholders, requires some special comment. He was the brother of Edward Jordon and was the day-to-day editor of the *Morning Journal*. From 1847, he had used the columns of the newspaper to highlight the failure of the St David Vestry to promote education and the failure of the petty sessions courts to service the new small settler class. In particular, to the great inconvenience of and expense to the small freeholders, the court sittings were unreliable as the magistrates attended irregularly, and when they did show up, it was not uncommon for them to sit on cases that involved colleagues and small freeholders, thereby undermining the integrity of their decisions.

Moreover, the *Morning Journal* had also urged the relocation of the court sittings from Easington, which was over six miles from the Yallahs Bay area where many of the small freeholders had settled. In addition, Jordon provided coverage for the various meetings of Black small freeholders mentioned above. Thereafter, Robert Jordon's use of the *Morning Journal* to turn the spotlight on St David was part of the Kingston politician's strategy to alter the representation in the parish. Another important part of their plan was the political mobilisation of the freeholders and Samuel Clarke played a crucial role in this.

This partnership between the Kingston Blacks and Coloureds and the St David Blacks reaped its first success in the 1850 Vestry election when four Kingstonians, two Coloureds and two Blacks, George William Cuthbert, Robert Jordon, Robert Osborn and Edward Vickars won seats to the Vestry. More significantly, four other small freeholders who lived and worked in St David also won seats as Vestrymen. Three of these, George Barnett, a carpenter, Andrew Bogle, a blacksmith and Joseph Brown, a carpenter, were Black and the fourth, David Simpson, who was a blacksmith employed to Albion estate, was either Coloured or Black. Clearly, the class and colour composition of the St David Vestry had been irrevocably altered. That Samuel Clarke was not among the group of Black freeholders who won seats to the Vestry in 1850 is explained by the fact that he was not yet qualified as it was the same year that he purchased his nine acres freehold at Heartease. However, his efforts through the St David Liberal, Recording and Election Association had been crucial to this fundamental alteration in the configuration of the St David Vestry since the Blacks and Coloureds now controlled eight of the 10 seats for elected Vestrymen.[8]

Given their success in January 1850 at the level of local government, the Blacks and Coloureds now focused on the two St David Assembly seats. Within a year, Alexander Finlay, one of the two Kingston merchants who represented St David in the Assembly, died. Immediately, four individuals eyed the seat. First, there was James Porteous of the Kingston mercantile firm of Porteous, Carson and Company. Although he resided at Constant Spring in St Andrew, Porteous was the attorney for Albion sugar estate and Trustee for Sheldon coffee plantation, both in St David. Accordingly, the planters in the parish and elsewhere threw their support behind him as the "gentleman of talent and respectability" who was best suited to protect their interest.

Two Blacks from Kingston, George William Cuthbert, one of the Vestrymen elected in 1850 and who owned a freehold in St David at Four Mile Wood, as well as Nathaniel Tully, a butcher, also expressed interest in the seat. However, both withdrew and instead endorsed John Nunes, a Coloured proprietor of a livery stable in Kingston.[9] Nunes, who enjoyed the solid support of the Coloured leadership in the island, had a history of unsuccessful bids for seats in the Assembly, having failed to win electoral contests in Kingston in 1845, and in St George in 1844 and in 1849. James Porteous had also lost his two bids in 1849 to defeat Coloured candidates in the neighbouring parish of Port Royal. Thus, both candidates were eager to fulfil their political ambitions and St David, as it turned out, became the bloody battleground.

During the three-week period of canvassing, Samuel Clarke featured heavily in the organisational efforts to get Nunes elected. He, along with George William Cuthbert, held meetings at Poor Man's Corner, a settlement of small freeholders adjoining Albion estate on the main road linking St David with Kingston. Indeed, on the night before the poll, Clarke met there with Robert Jordon and John Nunes as they finalised election day strategy. Furthermore, Clarke pursued relentlessly Black freeholders who threatened to boycott the poll because the two Blacks had agreed to stand down in favour of the Coloured candidate.

Clarke particularly targeted Joseph Brown, a carpenter and one of the elected Black Vestrymen in 1850, who was disappointed that one of the "Sons of Ham" had been bypassed. Both Robert Jordon and John Nunes had met with Brown in Kingston and he still refused to support Nunes. Porteous' agent, Charles McLean, the Coloured overseer at Albion estate, also tried to woo Brown, but without success. Clarke made a final effort on the day before the election when, on Sunday, 26 January, 1851, he approached Brown in the Baptist Church yard at Yallahs and promised him that if he voted for Nunes, Brown would be among the St David Blacks whom the Kingston Coloureds would propose to the Governor to be appointed as Justices of the Peace. Since the two sides were almost evenly matched, Samuel Clarke's approach fitted into the general campaign which saw both sides bartering promises for votes.

Moreover, given that both sides anticipated a close poll, their respective agents, including Clarke, organised groups of non-voters, who were armed with sticks. Their task was to escort the respective voters to the poll and, if necessary, to intimidate their opponents from voting, a practice that had been used to great effect in the 1849 elections in the neighbouring parish of St Thomas-in-the-East, where two Coloured candidates from Kingston had defeated planters, capturing for the first time those two seats in the Assembly.

On Monday, January 27, 1851, the two candidates and their bands of supporters made their way to the court house at Easington. There, the Custos of St David, Honourable John Barclay, the proprietor of Woburn Lawn and Windsor coffee plantations, nominated James Porteous, while Edward Jordon, the senior member of the Coloured political grouping, who had travelled that morning from Kingston to St David, nominated John Nunes.

Initially, the poll proceeded in a very brisk but orderly fashion. Samuel Clarke distinguished himself by the zeal with which he ensured that Nunes' voters were brought forward, including Andrew Bogle, a Black Vestryman, who was brought on a stretcher from his sick bed to vote for Nunes. Indeed, William Girod, solicitor and editor of the planter newspaper *Colonial Standard and Jamaica Despatch*, who acted as one of Porteous' agents at the poll, was moved to compliment Clarke, whom he described as being "one of the most indefatigable advocates" that they had ever seen at elections.[10] Not only did Clarke ensure that Nunes' voters, hearty or sick, came to the poll, but he scrutinised the activities of the election officials, one of whom was David McLean, the Clerk of the Vestry, who had the responsibility of preparing the voters list for the election.

Since McLean's son, Charles, was Porteous' chief election agent, Clarke was particularly concerned to ensure that supporters of Porteous whose names were not on the agreed list, did not vote. When David McLean overruled Clarke and permitted William Wright, a Kingston merchant with coffee properties in St David, to vote for Porteous, even though Wright's name had been left off the electoral list, Clarke became abusive and threatened to assault the Clerk of the Vestry. The threats became more menacing when McLean, confronted by two individuals, each supporting the respective candidates, and claiming to vote in the same name, accepted the vote of the person who supported Porteous. By early afternoon, both candidates were tied with 35 votes each. Then Porteous' supporters, including the Custos, prevailed on Myer Benjamin, a parochial official, who had remained neutral, to come to the poll to vote.

Confronted by defeat, and convinced that David McLean had illegally permitted two votes for Porteous, Samuel Clarke mobilised his band of supporters, men and women, most of whom had no vote, to block the road between Benjamin's house and the court house, while he and others took possession of the poll. The Custos called up the police to clear the road and a riot ensued as the people, having put the grossly outnumbered police to flight, stoned the court house, chasing away the officials and the candidates and their respective gentlemen supporters. David McLean, the Clerk of the Vestry with whom Clarke had clashed, failed to

Table 12.1:   Acreage of Voters, St David, 1851

	Candidate – Nunes Voters' acreage Known (N = 22)		Candidate – Porteous Voters' acreage Known (N = 22)	
Acreage	Number	% of N	Number	% of N
1<5	14	63.6	2	8.7
5>20	7	31.8	5	21.7
20<100	–	–	2	8.7
>100	1	4.6	14	60.9
Not Known	13	–	13	–
Total	35	100	36	100

Sources: House of Assembly Poll Book, 1844–1865: Land Deeds; Jamaica Almanac, 1845; St David Vestry Minutes, 1850–1861.

make his escape. He was felled by a blow to the head from a stone, beaten with sticks, and later succumbed to his wounds.

When the poll reopened on the following day, Samuel Clarke clearly unrepentant for the previous day's confrontation, mobilised a crowd of over 60 people to intimidate Joseph Brown who, disgusted by the riot and the killing of McLean, made his way to the poll to cast his vote for Porteous, thereby breaking the tie and assuring a victory for the planters. They held the seat, but Jamaica had witnessed the first election fatality in the post-slavery period.[11]

Although Samuel Clarke's efforts had been defeated as he had been outmanoeuvred at the poll, the effectiveness of his organisational work among the Black small freeholders of St David was reflected in the voting patterns of the St David freeholders as depicted in table 12.1.

That 64 per cent of Nunes' voters in table 12.1 each owned less than the five acres is a statement of the extent of Samuel Clarke's success in mobilising the Black small settler votes. Thus, 14 or 88 per cent, of the voters identified as owning less than five acres supported Nunes. Significantly, of the 22 voters identified as Nunes' supporters, at least 13 were former slaves. Of the number, four were carpenters, four were masons, and one was a blacksmith. All 13 ex-slaves had purchased their respective freeholds between 1838 and 1843 in new settlements that mushroomed around the Yallahs area in lower St David, such as Cherry Garden Pen, Coco Walk, Content, Hamstead, Heartease, Mount Clare, Poor Man Corner and Smithfield.

The small freeholders' participation in the 1851 election underscored the extent to which rural Blacks had been integrated into the political culture of the island within a decade and a half of the granting of full freedom in 1838. It is a testament to the determination of Samuel Clarke and others to have a say in the affairs of free Jamaica that even though the small freeholders failed to carry the election in St David in 1851, their presence could no longer be disregarded in the politics of the parish. The political balance of the parish had been profoundly altered and the future "Black ascendancy" that Henry Taylor in the Colonial Office had predicted in 1839 seemed not far off, at least at the local level of politics in St David.

Meanwhile, once the dust settled after the violence in St David, Samuel Clarke was among the eight individuals who were indicted as accessories to the murder of David McLean. Through the skilful advocacy of Alexander Heslop, a Coloured barrister and one of the representatives for the neighbouring parish of St Thomas-in-the-East in the Assembly, Clarke and the other men were freed of the capital charge. However, Clarke, despite glowing character references from Edward Jordon and Edward Vickars, and 37 others were found guilty on the lesser charge of riot and assault, and sentenced to 18 months in prison. Clarke's influential political friends failed to get the governor to pardon Clarke after he served five months of his term. However, the governor eventually agreed to commute the sentences of all 38 individuals after they had served nine of the 18 months in April, 1852.

Despite paying the price for his over-exuberance and indiscretions during his mobilisation of the Black freehold voters for the 1851 election in St David, Samuel Clarke's appetite for politics remained unsatiated. At the earliest opportunity after his release from prison, Clarke, along with Robert Jordon, who had also served nine months for riot and assault, successfully contested in January, 1853, the two seats on the local vestry for elected church wardens, thereby replacing William Georges and William Mowatt, both sugar planters.

Furthermore, Clarke's victory was part of a clean sweep as the 10 elected posts of Vestrymen were won by Black freeholders, two of whom, David and Thomas Johnson, had also been convicted for riot and assault during the 1851 election. Significantly, six of the incumbents who were defeated, had voted for Porteous in the 1851 poll. Clearly, the small settler voters had pronounced their own verdict on the conduct of their Black political leaders as, within nine months of their release from prison, they had captured all the elected posts on the vestry. Not surprisingly, the Custos and the magistrates were alarmed and demonstrated their disgust by initially refusing to sit with the new team of vestrymen and church wardens. However, Samuel Clarke and his allies were acutely conscious that they had been elected by the people of the parish and as discomforted as the magistrates were, the parochial affairs had to be carried on. When the vestry eventually convened in February, 1853, the planters lodged a formal protest against Clarke's return as church warden, and then proceeded to do business.[12]

Once on the vestry, Samuel Clarke renewed his political battles with the planters and tried to block all patronage to their political supporters. First, he objected to Charles McLean, who had been proposed for the post of Clerk of the Vestry. McLean, who had been Porteous' campaign manager in 1851, had also given evidence against Clarke at the trial for the murder of his father. In this instance, Clarke failed to block his appointment because some of the other Black vestrymen were more interested in settling down to work, and endorsed McLean as a conciliatory gesture.

When Clarke moved a motion to change the vestry's solicitors, he received more support from the other Black vestrymen since Clarke's replacement, John Swaby Harrison, had assisted small freeholders in the St David Petty Sessions court in matters connected with tenancy and rent. Nevertheless, sufficient magistrates were present to thwart the vestrymen, and the incumbents held on to the post when the Custos gave his casting vote to them. Samuel Clarke next targeted the Rev. William Patterson, rector of the Parish, who had seconded James Porteous' nomination at the 1851 election.

Apparently, in June, 1852, Patterson had summarily dismissed a White domestic servant whom he had brought out from England eight months before. The young woman, who had no ties on the island, was taken in by a Black family in St David. When she requested assistance from the vestry to return to England, Samuel Clarke grasped the opportunity to embarrass the rector whom he accused of highhanded and immoral conduct. While he was full of praise for the Black small settlers who assisted the young woman, he demanded a vestry committee to look into the actions of the rector.

However, despite Clarke's efforts to publicly humiliate the rector, the issue was quietly resolved when other magistrates, clearly embarrassed at both the rector's conduct and the prospect of a White woman sheltering with Black families, arranged a subscription to send her home. Nevertheless, Samuel Clarke was still not finished with the rector as, despite being a church warden, he supported the efforts to reduce by 50 per cent the vestry's allowance to the rector in lieu of fees and grebe.

Clarke next turned his attention to William Georges, sugar planter and attorney, who had also supported Porteous and had given evidence against Clarke at his trial. In 1853, Georges was appointed to the post of Collecting Constable, which handled all the revenue collection for the parish as was his entitlement as a member of the vestry. Clarke, to Georges' disgust, incessantly scrutinised his accounts. No doubt, this further poisoned the relationship between the two men and fuelled the personal animosity that may have influenced Georges' testimony against Clarke at his trial in Morant Bay in 1865.[13]

It would be misleading however, to create the impression that Samuel Clarke's activities as a member of the St David Vestry up to 1865 were focused exclusively on settling personal scores and embarrassing political opponents. Along with the other Black freeholders, he took his responsibilities to conduct the parish affairs very seriously. From the outset and throughout the period, he was very involved with the various committees that looked after paupers, tax relief, the leasing of parish land, the maintenance of roads, the erection of a market at Yallahs and the local educational institutions. Indeed, Samuel Clarke was particularly passionate about the provision of education for the children of the small settlers and was very vigilant in monitoring the performance of the parish's educational institutions at Easington, Heartease, Wellington and Yallahs.

Clarke served on the committee that insisted on compulsory education and tightened the regulations governing the performance of the teachers, and whenever he thought it necessary, he pressed complaints against school masters for dereliction of duty. Significantly, his support for secular education was progressive for that period in Jamaica. When he addressed a meeting of small settlers called to discuss education and health facilities in the parish, he told them that "It mattered not in what form education was granted to the people, nor whether it was taught under the religion of Judaism, Romanism or Protestantism. Give the children a grammatical education and leave them to select their own religion afterwards."[14]

While Samuel Clarke and other Blacks monopolised the elected positions on the vestry, none of them had the requisite property qualifications to compete for seats in the Assembly. However, no candidate could win any of the two seats for St David without the endorsement of Samuel Clarke and the small freeholders. George William Gordon, who had also supported James Porteous in 1851, experienced this first hand in 1860 when he was defeated by John Nunes and Foster Henry March, two other Coloureds, who had Clarke's backing. Similarly, Aaron Salom, a Kingston retailer with a long record of support for the Blacks, had Clarke's endorsement when he defeated Samuel Constantine Burke in St David in 1862.

In the 1863 elections, with Clarke's support, Salom and Burke were elected together, blocking a challenge from William Jones, a Kingston merchant, who was the proprietor of the Ness Castle coffee plantation in upper St David. Clearly the Black peasant proprietors enjoyed the largest share of political power in St

David and Samuel Clarke was an important political broker for outsiders who courted this electorate.

Furthermore, outside the vestry, Samuel Clarke grasped every opportunity to extend the political education of the small freeholders. Between 1853 and 1865 he addressed a series of public meetings in St David which discussed pressing social issues. For example, when the St David Blacks assembled to prepare a farewell address to Sir Charles Grey in October, 1853, Clarke, whom Grey had pardoned the previous year, used the opportunity to launch a broadside against the Assembly's retrenchment policies.

He accused the legislators of favouring the planters and merchants at the price of betraying the interest of the "poor people". Furthermore, he emphasised that since "the masses were not considered" their food costs remained high because of the Assembly's fiscal policies of high duties on imported provisions. Utilising the refrain of "give the people cheap food", Clarke insisted that only when the duties were reduced would the freed people "consent to work for a low rate of wages".

He also denounced the political monopoly of the seats in the Assembly that the elite enjoyed, insisting that such restrictive qualifications were "totally unsuited to a nation of freemen". As for the notion that freedom had been granted too soon and that plantations were in decline, Clarke reminded the small settlers that such views were held by planters who believed that the "Black race" was "made purposely to do nothing but make sugar and rum for them." He criticised the planters and their allies in England who were particularly indignant that the Blacks "should presume to prefer owning and cultivating their own freeholds to working in the cane fields at inadequate wages for others."

Furthermore, Clarke reminded his Black audience that it was precisely because the Blacks asserted their freedom of the estates that "the planters thought to be even with the Blacks by importing coolies to cultivate their fields, and they had taxed the labouring population for the purpose of bringing out competitors among themselves." Clearly, Samuel Clarke was not one to mince his words and, if anything, his prison experience had only made him more defiant and doubly determined to champion the small settlers' interests.

Consequently, Clarke was among the Black vestrymen who were denounced by the planters as "agitators" who set out to "corrupt and deceive the Negro mind". Moreover, since the Vestries provided Clarke and other Blacks with their political base, by 1865 both Whites and conservative Coloureds urged that the institution be done away with since they had become "the training school for the demagogues".[15]

As social and economic pressures worsened in the 1860s, Samuel Clarke became a very vocal spokesman for the St David small settlers. When Governor

Eyre visited the parish as part of his island tour in August, 1864, it was Clarke who presented him with an address from the small settlers outlining the difficulties that affected them. Prominent among them were the costs of food and clothing, the lack of continuous employment on the failing estates, the destruction of small settlers' provisions by estate cattle and the deplorable conditions of the roads on which the small settlers had to transport their crops to market. Clarke was again in the forefront at another St David meeting held in November, 1864, where in addition to the points raised above, other issues having to do with the restrictive franchise, education and the proposed whipping bill were added.

Thus, months before the Underhill meetings were held all over Jamaica in 1865, Samuel Clarke in St David had already raised the burning social issues that were later highlighted at those meetings. Moreover, when Underhill's letter and the responses stirred up controversy in Jamaica, it seemed only natural that Samuel Clarke linked with others, like the "born again" George William Gordon, who, compared to Samuel Clarke, had somewhat belatedly in the early 1860s developed a radical critique of Jamaica's social and political ills. Clarke spoke at two of the Underhill meetings that Gordon chaired, one in Kingston in May, 1865, and the other at Morant Bay in August later that year. Between those meetings, Clarke organised the St David Underhill meeting which was held at the Easington Court House on 24 June, 1865.

Clarke's speech at the Kingston meeting provided us with a clear picture of his sentiments at the time. He denounced the ingrained prejudices that the Whites had against the Blacks whom "the white man looked down upon . . . as nothing better than a beast". Regarding the flogging bill to deal with the problem of praedial larceny, Clarke warned that "It was only intended for the black man not for the White or Coloured man . . . The Magistrate will act unjustly and send up a poor Negro for stealing a piece of cane to be flogged."

Moreover, he criticised the heavy taxes on the small settlers "donkey going to market", while "the proprietor's cows" were minimally taxed. He continued in his demagogic style. "The taxes were only made for the black man and not the white, there was one law for the black man and one for the white man." At both the Kingston and St David meetings he singled out William Georges, the Custos of St David, for particular abuse because he had planted cane in the slaves' burial grounds and had destroyed the tombs. Thus, the petition of the St David Underhill meeting that Clarke had organised described Georges as one of the "biggest enemies" of the Blacks.

Thus, by 1865 Samuel Clarke, like George William Gordon in the neighbouring parish of St Thomas-in-the-East, was at constant loggerheads with the authorities of the vestry and, in particular, the Custos and senior magistrate. Moreover, besides speaking at the Underhill meeting at Morant Bay in August, 1865, on at least two other occasions Clarke visited the parish in that year. In January he was active at the 1865 vestry elections in St Thomas-in-the-East where his brother George Clarke, who was Paul Bogle's son-in-law, was elected a vestryman. He was also at Morant Bay in September, 1865 when Samuel Ward, a Black independent Baptist minister, was hooted down by some of Gordon's supporters who objected to his presence since he had been recruited by planters to counteract the influence of Gordon.

Clarke also commented publicly on issues that poisoned the social relations in the troubled parish of St Thomas-in-the-East. One such example was in September, 1865, when the Custos and the magistrates prevailed upon Governor Eyre to remove Thomas Witter Jackson, the Coloured Stipendiary Magistrate, who had clashed with the local plantocracy. Clarke assured Jackson "in the most emphatic manner that people would not submit to it".[16]

Despite these associations with St Thomas-in-the-East and his link with George William Gordon at two of the Underhill meetings in 1865, there was not a shred of evidence which implicated Samuel Clarke with the events of 11 October, 1865 (the Morant Bay Rebellion). Yet, in the paranoid and vengeful panic that permeated Jamaica after the rebellion, Clarke was arrested in Kingston and along with other political prisoners sent to Morant Bay to face court martial. There on 3 November, 1865, after a hurried trial, he was executed. On the following day, the military authorities suggested, and Governor Eyre later agreed, that the remaining political prisoners should not be court-martialled. Instead they were to be held until civil proceedings were brought against them.

Thus, of all the political prisoners sent to Morant Bay, only Samuel Clarke and George William Gordon were tried by court martial and executed. While Governor Eyre selected Gordon for retribution, Samuel Clarke was confronted at his trial by his implacable political enemies, William Georges, the Custos of St David, and Charles McLean, the Clerk of the St David Vestry. Both Georges and McLean, as well as a newspaper reporter, recounted Clarke's public statements at Underhill meetings and at St David Vestry meetings which have been severely critical of the government. In addition, he had denounced the "Queen's Advice" as "lies, red lies", and denied that it had ever come from Her Majesty. Furthermore, months after Clarke's death, McLean, intent on justifying his execution, provided Eyre with a litany of his transgressions. First, in the months before the rebellion, Clarke had become more strident in his public attacks against the Custos, even to the point of threatening him with physical assault at a vestry meeting. Moreover, he was accused of launching a campaign against all the Coloured teachers in St David, hoping to replace them with Black men. Furthermore, Clarke on a visit to the school at Yallahs, had urged the Black children to be diligent in their studies since "shortly the island would be theirs, for nobody could keep it much longer from them".

Worse still, since the people looked to Clarke for "advice and instruction", Clarke "caused great mischief" because he always taught "the people to be insolent and rude to their employers".[17] Here indeed was Samuel Clarke's cardinal sin, his failure to know his station and to keep it. Clarke never had a chance to prove his innocence and even the *Morning Journal*, the Coloureds' newspaper which had been associated with Clarke's early political work in St David, allied itself with the general panic and hysteria and commented that Clarke had met his "just retribution" for having plotted "against peace and order, life and property".[18]

Thus, on 3 November, 1865, Samuel Clarke paid the ultimate price for his convictions and for his passion for politics. For him freedom was more than the absence of slavery. Rather, post-slavery society, to live up to its name, had to be one in which the Blacks received impartial justice and their interests were considered as important and legitimate, even when they conflicted with the demands of the plantations. In order to ensure this, Black men had to have access to the political institutions that governed the society in order to promote their own interests. Whenever property restrictions denied them this access, Clarke endorsed other politicians who could be relied on to oppose measures that were inimical to the interest of the Blacks.

During his 15 years in politics, as he enthusiastically pursued his aims, Samuel Clarke undoubtedly committed serious errors of judgement, as was best exemplified by his involvement in the St David election riot in 1851. Nonetheless, he was a fearless spokesman for the Black small settler class and the planters regarded him and other such Blacks as "loud mouthed demagogues".[19] At Morant Bay he was silenced forever.

NOTES

* This article was previously published in *The Jamaica Historical Review*, vol. xix (1996), pp. 17–29.

1.   Kamau Brathwaite, *Contradictory Omens: Cultural Diversity and Integration in the Caribbean* (Mona: Savacou Publications, 1974), p. 64.

2.   For a brief discussion of Clarke's imprisonment and execution, see Gad Heuman, *"The Killing Time": The Morant Bay Rebellion in Jamaica* (London: Macmillan, 1994), 154–55, pp. 169–70.

3.   Public Records Office, London (hereafter P.R.O.), C.O. 137/309, Charles Grey to Earl Grey, 7 February, 1851, folio. 17; *Morning Journal* 6 and 7 August, 1851; Land Deeds, Island Record Office (hereafter I.R.O.), Jamaica, Liber 900, folio 11. Probably Samuel Clarke was a free Black during slavery; he was at least 21 years of age in 1851.

4.   C.O. 137/330, Barkley to Labouchere, 6 March, 1856, no. 35 Enclosure: Report of Richard Hill, 25 January, 1856; Verene A. Shepherd, "Pens and Pen-keepers in a Plantation Society: Aspects of Jamaican Social and Economic History 1740–1845". Ph.D dissertation, University of Cambridge, 1988, pp. 341–42.

5.   *Morning Journal*, 8 July, 1847.

6.   *Morning Journal*, 16 July, 1849; 11 July, 1850.

7.   *Morning Journal*, 6 September, 1849; 7 August, 1851.

8.   I.R.O., Land Deeds, Liber 900, folio 11; *Morning Journal*, 31 December, 1849; 10 January, 1850.

9.   *Colonial Standard and Jamaica Despatch*, 1 and 12 February, 1851; *Falmouth Post*, 14 and 24 January, 1851.

10.   *Morning Journal*, 7 August, 1851.

11.   C.O. 1 37/309, Charles Grey to Earl Grey, 27 February, 1851, no. 17; *Colonial Standard and Jamaica Despatch*, 28 January, and 3 February, 1851; *Falmouth Post*, 4 February, 1853; *Morning Journal*, 7 August, 1851.

12.   Jamaica Archives 1B/11/9/6; St David Vestry Minutes, 1850–1862, 2 February, 1853; *Morning Journal*, 6 and 7 August, 1851.

13.   British Parliamentary Papers (hereafter P.P.), 1866, Jamaica Royal Commission (hereafter J.R.C.), Appendix, 1149; *Morning Journal*, 5 October, 1853.

14.   *Morning Journal*, 5 September, 1854.

15.   P.P., 1866, xxx (3682), Papers laid before the Royal Commission of Inquiry by Governor Eyre, p.123; P.P., 1866 xxxi J.R.C., Minutes of Evidence, p. 331. 17.

16.   P.P., 1866, xxxi, J.R.C., Minutes of Evidence, p. 362.

17.   P.P., 1866, xxx, Papers, p. 40; Gad Heuman, *"Killing the Time"*, pp. 146–51.

18.   *Morning Journal*, 7 November, 1865.

19.   P.P., 1866, xxx, Papers, p. 263.

PART FIVE

Creolisation and Caribbean Cultural Forms

Maureen Warner-Lewis

Chapter 13

CREOLISATION PROCESSES IN LINGUISTIC, ARTISTIC AND MATERIAL CULTURES

With the rise of "postcolonial" studies in the 1980s, hybridity has been endorsed as normative and "politically correct", so that new socio-political searchlights have been turned towards an examination of creolisation, much as the study of Creole languages has continued to move centrestage in the discipline of linguistics since the initial conference on these patently hybrid and therefore marginalised languages at the University College of the West Indies in 1959.[1] "Creole" is a term denoting various types of hybridity in the socio-historical evolution of Latin America, the Caribbean and francophone areas of the United States South, mirroring its socio-historical embeddedness among insular and coastal peoples of Portuguese West and West Central Africa, and in British colonial Sierra Leone. The abstract concept "creolisation" has been derived from the person- and culture-specific referent "Creole", a term first recorded in a 1570s Mexican text written by Juan Lopez de Velasco.[2] In 1602, Garcilaso, a hispanicised Inca, attributed the source of the word to Africans in Brazil for whom it designated their descendants born and socialised under slavery who were culturally alien from their parents.[3] On the basis of this observation as well as my etymological postulations,[4] the word signified "outsider", wherein lies the semantic ambivalence and contradictory applications which have characterised it over the centuries, since the identity of the outsider modulates according to the identity of the insider in any given context, carrying along with these perspectives overtones of positivity or negativity as personal, situational and temporal values dictate. This essay attempts to analyse various Caribbean cultural configurations of the creolisation process in order to demonstrate its multiple, dynamic and often paradoxical manifestations.

My point of entry into an examination of these processes is through African language texts from the island of Trinidad, recuperated during the 1960s and 1970s. The original speakers and singers of these texts had been captured into slavery but had, in the majority of cases, been freed by European anti-slave trade naval patrols. The African language residues articulated by their descendants indicate that African linguistic enclaves existed in the post-slavery (1838) era of British colonies as a continuation of the practice during slavery itself: contemporary social and religious commentators reported that slaves sang work, rebellion, and "pleasure" songs, used greetings, modes of address, and coded messages in African languages. Such linguistic practices were the result of several factors: enslaved persons wrenched from their native environments as teenagers and adults were already sufficiently socialised in their language cultures to find difficulty in adapting to new language demands; the more mature in age the enslaved, the more they would have tended to remember their family, associates and homeland with nostalgia and a sense of loss, emotions which militated in favour of language loyalty; ethnic clustering on estates and in maroon communities encouraged native language function.[5] But analyses of twentieth-century residual African languages in the Caribbean reveal them to be koines or amalgams of several regional dialects of a particular language, an indication of the variety of sources within the same language-group and geographical locale from which persons were wrested for the slave trade. Thus, based on Yoruba texts recovered in Trinidad, Yoruba was constituted by the phonology and syntax of the Oyo, Ekiti and Ijesha, in the main, but with input also from Egba and to a lesser extent Ijebu, all these areas and peoples belonging to the umbrella language-group called Yoruba. Apart from this inter-ethnic and inter-dialect contact and consolidation, the texts reveal contact between these Yoruba-speaking peoples and Hausa- and Fon-speaking peoples, both geographically proximate to the Yoruba and in mutual cultural contact as well as military friction.[6] The fact that all these peoples were drawn into the Atlantic slave trade meant a continuation of contact in the Caribbean. Comparable ethnic interaction is evident from the Akan, Temne, Limba, Koongo, Fula and Arabic words and phrases among Maroon communities in Jamaica.[7] Similar multiethnic sources of vocabulary are attested in the Maroon languages of Suriname, such as Saramaka and Ndjuka.[8] As such, Trinidad Yoruba and other Caribbean African-lexifier linguistic codes are themselves instances of trans-systemic languages formed out of contact situations among dialects of the same African language and involving other African languages and European ones into the bargain. However, until the 1980s African-lexified Caribbean languages were generally thought non-existent and thus had not been examined for their phonological, morphological, syntactic and lexical composition. But it is now apparent that such languages are microcosmic realisations of the more penetrative and structurally dissimilar syntheses that have engineered Creoles, which are indeed new languages. Instead, *the* Creoles, for the most part,[9] are understood as European-lexified contact languages. In this category fall Saramaka, Sranan, the other English-based Creoles, the French, Dutch, Portuguese and Spanish Creoles.[10] Indeed, it is the change in the lexical resource of their original speakers which has been one of the most overt features of Creoles, so that where, as in the case of Trinidad Yoruba, the lexical inventory has largely involved dialects of the same language, the resulting koine appears as an opaque instance of creolisation.

In attempting to identify the genetic relationship of Creoles to their adstrate constituents, other conceptual issues arise. One issue concerns the need for historical linguistics methodology to acknowledge more than one parent of a language, the orthodoxy being to privilege one genitor, even in the face of the biologically greater frequency of dual parentage over hermaphroditism. Languages emerge from dual or multiple heritages: the Romance languages, for example, are traced only to Latin, but what of the languages spoken by the Gauls and Iberians prior to Roman colonisation, languages which have wrought the differences in phonology and syntax which distinguish these languages one from the other? And given the massive borrowing of Latin words into the vocabulary of the Gauls and Iberians, in what way might that lexification process be considered different from the absorption of European words into the vocabulary resource of non-European peoples in the formation of Creoles? Rather, it is the historical recency of the formation of these new languages which allows for the clearer identification of the sources of their various components.

Another conceptual issue lies in the interrelation between earlier and later inputs into a new linguistic entity. Does it involve the dominance of the first input over later inputs, or the displacement of inputs by later elements? Clearly, both processes come into play. While a founder language is well placed to stamp its imprint on new language formation, the possibility of late arrival communities inputting idioms, calques and grammatical particles must be admitted. Indeed, the very lateness of the input may account for its salience and may even lead to the displacement of earlier lexical, grammatical and phonological characteristics.[11]

Complex and even multiple processes are at work in culture contact situations. Comparative data from disciplines other than linguistics allow one to arrive at the following deductions regarding the variety of processes at work in such encounters. These are discussed here with specific reference to the African contribution to Caribbean culture. Such research indicates, first of all, the need for sensitivity to factors of heterogeneity and chronological change within cultural experience.

Contact situations produce cultural artefacts and behaviours which exhibit syncretism, fragmentation, but also admit innovation. As far as cultural inheritance is concerned, African retentions in the Caribbean may be categorised as (i) the result of historically recent cultural inputs, which because of their recency have not been supplanted by other African, Creole, and/or European modalities, but are nevertheless affected by them, and (ii) constructs mapped on to a structural and/or conceptual framework established by another or an earlier group, whether Native American, African or European. Both these scenarios produce syncretic forms since they are structurally or functionally assimilations of elements within differing cultures. Syncretism may show in the crafting of an additional morphology – an element absent in the original structure – on to a pre-existing form. Furthermore, the donor group in one instance may also be the receptor in another. For example, non-adherents to the Yoruba-derived *orisha* religion of Trinidad may consult an *orisha* priest or priestess for healing or divination; on the other hand, the Christian iconography of the shepherd's crook and lighted candles may be incorporated in *orisha* ceremonial, just as it has been absorbed into the *mayal* African religion[12] of Jamaica to produce various types of Revivalism; Trinidad carnival is constructed out of the grafting together of the African "ole [old] mas" – ragged in appearance, satiric in emphasis, and using African religious colour symbolisms – and "pretty mas", utilising the decorative colour combinations of European masked ball and carnival costumery. Syncretism may also produce parallel morphologies, for example, the Catholic saint and Rada *vodun*[13] equivalences of Yoruba names for divinities in the *orisha* religion. As such, in Trinidad the Yoruba deity of thunder, Shango, is also called by the Fon name (O)sogbo, and is identified as the Christian St John of the Cross or St John the Divine. Another manifestation of syncretism lies in hybridised morphologies – for example, "bubulups" (Trinidad), meaning "fat", formed from Koongo *bubulu* "fat, ungainly", followed by the English word-ending "ps" suggesting, by analogy with terms like "oops", something out of control. Yet another form of syncretism occurs when, within a given typology, there is replacement of morphological elements, their re-distribution, and re-constitution into novel combinations. For example, steamed starchy flours – such as yam, cassava, corn/maize and breadfruit – are common as a carbohydrate meal base in West Africa. Also, boiled starches are pounded together to constitute a meal base. These two types of foods are retained to varying extents in the Caribbean. But extensions to the morphology and changes of methodology have taken place. In the Eastern Caribbean, cassava flour is mixed with grated coconut and optionally with grated pumpkin. To these spices, sugar and fat are added, and the pappy mixture is baked to make "pone". In Jamaica, grated sweet potato, grated coconut and wheat flour constitute the pap to which sugar and flavourings are added, and the mixture is baked. The identity of the carbohydrate base of such foods and their consistency are such that Africans can recognise a cognate food. However, in the Caribbean, "pones", being sweet, are eaten as cake or dessert. Such changes may be analysed as due to (a) use of high-profile agricultural products in the environment, such as sugar, coconut and pumpkin (a low prestige food in parts of West Africa), and (b) contact with non-African cultures, in this case European. Europe has contributed the concept of dessert and the salience of sweet foods.

The instance of *akara* betrays both the syncretistic substitution of morphological elements as well as a partial reassignment of function. Yoruba *akara* is composed of the flour of ground beans which is seasoned, made into a paste and fried. On the Caribbean islands of Trinidad, Tobago, Curaçao and Guadeloupe wheat flour is the base of *akra*, to which is added seasoning and pieces of cooked or salted fish. The paste is fried. And with regard to function, in both locales the food is primarily a breakfast meal, and can be publicly bought as a snack. However, in recent years it also serves as a cocktail hors d'oeuvre in the Caribbean.

Creolisation processes also involve loss or erasure. There may be loss of embellishment, as has occurred with the microtonality of some Yoruba sacred melodies which in Trinidad have been replaced by the wider pitch intervals of the seventeenth-century European "well-tempered" scale. In addition, the *bata*, the Oyo drum sacred to the deity Shango, so integrally a part of Cuban *regla de ocha* or *santeria*, in Trinidad has either been deleted from Yoruba religious ceremony over time or had never been incorporated into it. Similarly, unlike its vigour in Cuba, the Ifa divinatory system has not survived as an ancillary of the Yoruba *orisha* system in Trinidad and Brazil. Fragmentation of original unitary concepts and practices may therefore be part of the hybridisation process.

But fragmentation can also reproduce the transfer of multiple cultural options, as in the instance of the variety of labels for the same cultural item within a given geographical area. Here we may instance Jamaica, where *kumina* (discussed below) also goes by the name *kandungo*,[14] and marijuana – an Amerindian term – is more generally called by the Hindi word "ganja", although in communities with strong Koongo cultural influence it is also referred to as *dyamba*, *chianga* and *makoni.*[15] This latter example points to the fact that even in source environments a plurality of options may be available. These options may stem from regional differences within the overall cultural-linguistic area, or from status-influenced or context-defined variation. Indeed, as evidenced in the flexibility of dialect choice within the idiolects or individual utterances of Trinidad Yoruba speakers, and the variety of syntactic options available within continental Yoruba itself, more than one lexical token, more than one grammatical form, is available within a given African language. As such, judgment about what is or is not syntactically or lexically permissible in African languages cannot be pronounced on the basis of documented or present-day standard language forms only. In similar fashion, one of the factors for the variety of stickfighting forms in the West Atlantic – in Cuba, Martinique, Trinidad, Brazil – is the multiplicity of forms and purposes of this game in West Central and Southern Africa.[16] Another factor which precipitates an apparent inconsistency between form and meaning presents itself in instances where the same term exhibits polyvalency in differing geographical locations. The word *candomble* in Brazil applies to a religious ceremony and religion, whereas in Uruguay it applies to a musical type; *kandongo* in Puerto Rico pertains to a type of secular dance,[17] in Jamaica it is an alternative name for the *kumina* religious ceremony. This irregularity stems, however, from the omnibus nature of the terms themselves, since both are Angolan ethnonyms, the first referring to the Ndombe of the Benguela coast in the south, the latter to the Ndongo in the north.

Apart from syncretisms, fragmentations and erasure of form or function, contact situations also give rise to new cultural items and behaviours. These may be inspired by or patterned after features peculiar to artefacts, habits or concepts within one or more cultures in the environment. Trinidad steelband is a case in point. It was developed out of the percussive emphasis in African music and instrumentation, with the orchestra incorporating a cognate of the African gong-gong – the hand-held steel on steel – as metronome. In addition, the concept of an orchestra composed of the same instrument bearing differing pitch levels has many African precedents, whether the instruments are skin-headed drums or elephant horns. But the steel drum and the formation of an ensemble of such drums is neither African nor European. On the other hand, new cultural artefacts may be entirely new and outside the previous experience of the community. The motor car, satellite dish and cable television, computer, and all forms of the telephone are cases in point.

Amalgamation and bifurcation need also be looked at from the dimension of their occurrence in time. Are change and variety synchronic or contemporary occurrences or have they evolved diachronically? Jamaican *kumina*, and Trinidad *orisha,* calypso and *bele* will be considered in this light. *Kumina* is an ancestrally focused religious ceremony and belief system practiced, apparently since the latter part of the nineteenth century, by Central Africans and their descendants. It appears therefore to be a recent cultural input and utilises a Koongo cosmology, sung liturgy and drum rhythms. But its name – from Twi *akom*, "possession", and, *ana*, "ancestors" – and oral traditions of Maroon-Koongo fraternal relations in the nineteenth century,[18] suggest a previous association with Akan Maroon religious ritual. The latter is still practiced but carries the English-lexifer labels "business dance" or "play" or "Kramanti play" rather than a Twi-based term. Ancestral possession takes place in both Kumina and Kramanti play, but the dance movements and iconography differ.

For its part, the Eastern Caribbean dance form and social event called *bele,* at the turn of the twentieth century, became synonymous in certain contexts with the Hausa and Yoruba religious ancestral ceremony, *saraka.* On such occasions, it retained *saraka* religious elements, such as animal sacrifice and offerings of food to the ancestors, but it now became an African transnational event, known in Carriacou, Tobago and Trinidad as "nation dance" – "nation" referring to African ethnic groups, among them the Temne, Coromanti and Hausa. These various nations performed their dances and rituals at different times during one cere- mony, an amalgamation reminiscent of the clustering of devotionals to several Yoruba divinities within a one-week cycle of *orisha* ceremonials in Trinidad; such ceremonies take place at differing times and locations in Yorubaland itself. The nation dance religious ritual in some situations later gave way to a secular occasion featuring the *bele,* a further Creole mode with its distinctive and graceful dance vocabulary. However, all layers of form and function – *saraka,* sacred and secular *bele* – could co-exist simultaneously in any one geographical locale.

In the case of Trinidad's calypso – originally *kaiso,* a word of Efik (Calabari) provenance – it would appear that in the melodic line and rhythm of some early nineteenth-century performers, it manifested Senegambian influence, given that one of its earliest recalled exponents bore the ethnonym, Soso, the name of a Senegambian people (Soso or Susu). But later African adstrates have been the Koongo-Mbundu *kalenda* or stickfight, Yoruba *orisha* chants, and Efik-Ibibio-Igbo 2/2 staccato rhythms, not to mention the melodic intervals of Portuguese guitar chording, Latin American rhythms and tempo, African-American popular melody and Jamaican reggae rhythms. A calypsonian may use either of these adstrates as a dominant form or may elect to blend them. But can we any longer find evidence of its earliest layer? Was that earliest form itself monolithic? Or may it not have evinced different styles according to the ethnic provenance of its singers and in keeping with various song types even within the same ethnic culture? Has not the form itself changed radically and periodically, with certain news, satiric and entertainment functions remaining constant? All the same, if an earlier function such as lament now seems incongruous, functional change has certainly affected this artistic act as well.[19]

What we are dealing with is the dialectical relationship between dynamism and homeostasis, in nature, human society and culture. Dynamism suggests the capacity of an entity to generate new ideas, new institutions, new speech forms; on the other hand, homeostasis allows a community to absorb new features while retaining enough of its conventions to allow the community to recognise itself as the same as, or similar to, what it was before it admitted innovation. This is why innovation tends to carry the germ of some precedent. So the form/meaning/function correspondence between the old and the new cannot match exactly, and thus would be an inadmissible requirement for a genetic relationship to be acknowledged.

All these various paradigms of erasure, syncretism, adaptation, innovation and wholesale importation advanced here as characteristic and constitutive of creolisation emerge, in fact, as universal features of change. What has called attention to creolisation phenomena has first and foremost been the fact that the main body of Creoles has emerged out of the defining factor which created the modern historical era – European expansionism – and *these new constructs have destabilised European linguistic conventions*. The other startling feature has been the rapidity and qualitative intensity of the processes which have led to new language formations. Moreover, the fact that the circumstances of their occurrence have been fairly well documented, though not completely so, has allowed language formation and the dynamics of language use, choice and variability to be enriched by details regarding demographics, social status, functionality and power-relations between contesting groups.

The politics of identity and of centre/margin hostility and stratification have stamped their ideological and psychological mark on both the users and analysts of Creole languages over the centuries. In the slower-paced and more conservative contexts of earlier eras, the scale of economic and travel ventures which propelled Euro-African creolisation appeared to both European and African cultural insiders to have been abnormal. For ideological purposes of identity formation and maintenance, societies mythologise their own stability, establish their own markers of difference and set up their privileged cultural behaviours as normative. When these are abrogated or challenged, the new constructs – whether ethnic groups, art-forms or languages – are denounced as foreign and inferior. Unipolar and hierarchical models of society and culture are reinforced. It is therefore from this point of view that Creole linguistics – an offshoot of European scholarship –

has tended to emphasise the genetic relationship of a Creole to its European (the known) progenitors, even though elements of two or more donor languages are likely to be very closely interwoven at all linguistic levels of the new synthesis.

The intricate nature of such syntheses merits continuous investigation regarding the precise features of adstrate or donor languages within a Creole. Languages in contact would tend not to borrow entire systems, but would borrow selectively. In such a dynamic cross-cultural mix, and given important variables such as the force of individual personality, or the converse, collective impact, added to the advantageous catalyst of either early or late advent of linguistic groups to a location, or the favourable convergence of circumstances or of temporal confluences, any one language would not necessarily have dominated cultural domains across the board. Rather, it is evident that synchronically and also diachronically a linguistic group may put its stamp on religion, another on a musical form, yet another on masquerade, and so on. Analogically, then, may the influence of one ethno-linguistic group not be more significant in regard to certain domains of lexis, another in relation to certain features of syntax, another with respect to segmental phonology, and yet another in relation to suprasegmentals such as stress and intonation? The historical recency of creolisation processes in the Caribbean and the Americas allows us to analyse in microcosm the processes of evolution, systemic collapse and reconstitution which are endemic to the natural world and human societies, and which are re-enacted in the workings of conscious and unconscious human creativity.

NOTES

1. See David deCamp, "Introduction: The Study of Pidgin and Creole Languages", in Dell Hymes, ed., *Pidginisation and Creolization of Languages* (Cambridge: Cambridge University Press, 1971), pp. 13–39, and "The Development of Pidgin and Creole Studies", in *Pidgin and Creole Linguistics* (Bloomington: Indiana University Press, 1977), pp. 3–19.

2. See Antonio Benítez-Rojo, "Three Words toward Creolization", in Kathleen M. Balutansky and Marie-Agnès Sourieau, eds., *Caribbean Creolization: Reflections on the Cultural Dynamics of Language, Literature, and Identity* (Gainesville: University Press of Florida and Barbados: UWI Press, 1998), pp. 167–8, footnote 1.

3.   See Marius Valkhoff, *Studies in Portuguese and Creole, with special reference to South Africa* (Johannesburg: Witwatersrand University Press, 1966), p. 41; also quotation from Garcilaso in entry under *criollo* in *Diccionario crítico etimológico de la lengua castellana* (Berna: 1954).

4.   See Maureen Warner-Lewis, "Posited Kikoongo Origins of Some Portuguese and Spanish Words of the Slave Era", in *América Negra* 13, (1997), pp. 83–97. I suggest the Koongo source as *nkuulolo*, meaning "alien, outsider". In western Koongo word-initial pre-consonantal nasals tend to be dropped, a feature common in Koongo languages in Trinidad, Jamaica and Cuba. I propose further that *kuulolo* syncopated to *krolo* or *krulo*, alternation between *l* and *r*, even their indistinguishability, being common in many African languages including that of the Koongo.

5.   Of course, factors which encouraged native language-use were obviated by pressure to acquire new languages for work and social communication in new environments. But evidence of African ethnic-based clustering and solidarity is plentiful: see James Cruickshank, "Among the 'Aku' (Yoruba) in Canal no. 1, West Bank, Demerara River", in *Timehri* 3rd series, 4 (21), (1916), pp. 70–82; Lydia Cabrera, *El monte: igbo-finda, ewe orisha, vititi nfinda* (Miami: Collección de Chicherekú, 1986 [1954]); *Reglas de Congo, Mayombe, palo monte* (Miami: Ediciones Universal, 1986b [1979]); Monica Schuler, "Akan Slave Rebellions in the British Caribbean", in *Savacou* 1, (1970), pp. 8–31; Cleveland Eneas, *Bain Town* (Nassau: Cleveland and Muriel Eneas, 1976); Ulrich Fleichmann, "Los africanos del Nuevo Mundo", in *América Negra*, 6 (1993), pp. 11–34; Israel Moliner Castañeda, "Las sublevaciones de esclavos Congos reales: San Antonio de Trinidad", in *Islas*, 85 (1986), pp. 49–73; O. Nigel Bolland, "African Continuities and Creole Culture in Belize Town in the 19th Century", in Charles Carnegie, ed., *Afro-Caribbean Villages in Historical Perspective* (Kingston: African-Caribbean Institute of Jamaica, 1987), pp. 63–82.

6.   See Maureen Warner-Lewis, *Trinidad Yoruba: From Mother Tongue to Memory* (Tuscaloosa: University of Alabama Press, 1996); UWI Press (1997), pp. 168–9, 179–87, 199–203.

7.   See David Dalby, "Ashanti Survivals in the Language and Traditions of the Windward Maroons of Jamaica", in *African Language Studies*, 12 (1971), pp. 31–51; Kenneth Bilby, "How the 'Older Heads' Talk: a Jamaican Maroon Spirit Possession Language and its Relationship to the Creoles of Suriname and Sierra Leone", in *Nieuwe West-Indische Gids* 57 (1 and 2) (1983). Words such as *kinda* "a tree with ritual significance", *junga* "spear", *kandal* "clothes", *kimbombo* "vagina" are Koongo.

8.   See Jan Daeleman, "Kongo Elements in Saramacca Tongo", in *Journal of African Languages* 2 (1), (1972) pp. 1–44; Richard Price, "Kikoongo and Saramaccan: A

Reappraisal", in *Bÿdragen tot de Taal-Land-en Volkenkunde van Neerlandsch Indië*, 131 (1975), pp. 461–78; "George Huttar, Sources of Ndjuka African Vocabulary", in *New West Indies Guide*, 59 (1 and 2), (1985), pp. 45–71.

9. For example, the emergence of new languages evolving out of contact situations between/among African languages and also languages on the Indian sub-continent are also acknowledged as demonstrating linguistic processes characteristic of creolisation.

10. Initially, Spanish Creoles were cited only in respect of the Pacific. See Keith Whinnom, *Spanish Contact Vernaculars in the Philippine Islands* (London and Hong Kong: Hong Kong University Press, 1956). For later recognition of such Creoles in the Americas, see among others, Germán de Granda, "Sobre el estudio de las hablas criollas en el área hispánica", in *Thesarus* 23 (Bogotá), (1968), pp. 64–74; *Español de America, español de África y hablas criollas hispánicas: cambios, contactos y contextos* (Madrid: Editorial Gredos, 1994); Armin Schwegler, "Monogenesis Revisited: The Spanish Perspective", in John Rickford and Suzanne Romaine, eds., *Creole Genesis, Attitudes and Discourse* (Amsterdam/Philadelphia: John Benjamins, 1999), pp. 235–62.

11. As a corollary, one may instance the strength of Yoruba cultural influence in Cuba, Bahia and Trinidad, brought about in part by the relative lateness of sizeable Yoruba migration to these locations. Although Yoruba-speaking peoples began entering the slave trade in the late seventeenth century, their numbers radically increased as of the late eighteenth century and even more so during the nineteenth.

12. See Barry Chevannes, "The 1842 Myal Outbreak and Revival: Links of Continuity", paper presented to the Twenty-fifth Conference of the Association of Caribbean Historians, University of the West Indies, Jamaica (1993); Jean Besson and Barry Chevannes, "The Continuity-Creativity Debate: The Case of Revival", in *New West Indian Guide* 70:3 and 4 (1996), pp. 209–28.

3. Rada, an abbreviation of Allada, a kingdom south of Dahomey in West Africa. The *vodun* in concept are the equivalents of the Yoruba *orisha*, divinities epitomising natural and ancestral forces.

14. See Cheryl Ryman, "Kumina: Stability and Change", in *African-Caribbean Institute of Jamaica Research Review*, 1 (1984), pp. 81–128.

15. See Kenneth Bilby, "The Holy Herb: Notes on the Background of Cannabis in Jamaica", in *Caribbean Quarterly* monograph (1985), pp. 82–95.

16. Discussed in Maureen Warner-Lewis, *Koongo, Angola, and the Caribbean* (forthcoming).

17. See Hector Vega, "Some Musical Forms of African Descendants in Puerto Rico: *bomba, plena,* and *rosario francés*", in M.A. dissertation, Hunter College, City University of New York (1969), p. 29. Among names for various types of the *bomba* dance are *candungo* or *candungué*.

18.   See Beverley Hall-Alleyne, "Asante Kotoko: the Maroons of Jamaica", in *African-Caribbean Institute of Jamaica Newsletter* 7 (1982), pp. 12–13.

19.   The term "lament" is applied to certain types of nineteenth and turn-of-century calypso by Mitto Sampson in "Mitto Sampson on Calypso Legends of the Nineteenth Century", ed. Andrew Pearse in *Caribbean Quarterly* 4 (3 and 4), (1956), pp. 250–62, and by the veteran calypsonian Neville Marcano (The Growling Tiger) in the Trinidad and Tobago Government Broadcasting Unit's 1972 radio series on "The Story of the Calypso".

Lucie Pradel

Chapter 14

AFRICAN SACREDNESS AND CARIBBEAN CULTURAL FORMS

Is it possible for the Caribbean to affirm a cultural unity, in spite of its ethnic, linguistic and political heterogeneity? This region, a land of shelter and exile, became very early on the place of converging traditions. Four continents gave the Caribbean its specificity, while the population of these continents brought popular art forms, beliefs and religious practices. They gave to Caribbean religions a plural character. Caribbean spirituality is expressed as much through the dominant faiths as through Vaudou, Santeria and the worship of divinities such as Mariama, Mahibir or Kali. The list grows longer if we go back in time to the eighteenth-century "Stream of Power" in St Vincent, "The Awakening" movement in Jamaica or the "Shouters" of Trinidad and Tobago. This partial enumeration underlines the preponderant role played by religions in the genesis of Caribbean cultures. The forced conversion of the indigenes as well as the massive conversion of Africans to the Catholic faith also meant a close relation of the religious fact to resistance. Many were those who, following the rebellious Taino leader Hatuey, faced the stake to confirm their faith while others constantly found in their belief the liberating forces which proved victorious against oppression in the wars to combat slavery or during the struggles for independence.

If a relationship between religion and resistance is well established, there also exists a relationship between the sacred, popular and literary traditions of the Caribbean as illustrated by the experience of the Black population. Along with their beliefs, they brought all the traditional vehicles of their spiritual communication. The links between African sacredness and Caribbean culture are legitimised by the central role played by religion in the original societies of the slaves. Traditionally, in these societies there is no dissociation opposing sacred and secular, sacred and social, political or artistic domains. The absence of such a dissociation between art and sacred implies that religious faith is expressed in proverbs, myths, legends, as well as in the memory of millions of individuals deported from Africa to the Caribbean. These are the memories of divinities, sacred characters, rites of passage, rhythms, myths, dances, songs, prayers, ritual knowledge and craftsmanship: all the traditional vehicles of African sacred thought. The plasticity of this religious expression, the possibility of its resettlement, the faith of the followers, were factors favourable to the creolisation of African divinities and worships in the New World.

The major divinities: Ogun, Shango, Yemaya, Egungun, Fa, Oshossi, along with a plethora of secondary entities, followed the migration of their believers. They govern the Shango worship in Trinidad, Candomble in Brazil, the Vaudou pantheon in Haiti or Santeria in Cuba. The Anglophone oral tradition preserves the memory of these mythical beings in narratives with explicit titles such as, "Legend of the Singing Skull: Why Ogun Guards the Yoruba Gates" and "The Spell of Shango".[1] Not all the divinities transported to the Caribbean had the notoriety of Ogun or Shango, whose unifying designs bring the shores of the Atlantic closer and give a transnational dimension to their worship. However, many of them, in becoming secularised, found in the oral tradition of the Caribbean a place of survival. This tradition ensured the integration of deities within the Caribbean universe and their everlastingness in the local tradition. Similar to Anansi, a trickster god who was "humanised" in order to share the destiny of the common people, many such secularised divinities have contributed to the growth of the oral lore. The realm of water, Yemaya domain, offers water related creatures in the form of the fairymaid and mermaid. River Muma (Tanna), Manna Dlo or Fairmaid, all embody a generous creature, giving and possessing fertility and wealth. She appears during the night or at dawn from her sea or river habitat, in close proximity to a gold mine. Some think of her as the guardian of such a treasure and point out that the comb she uses to smooth out her long hair was cast from the precious metal. Promise of wealth is made to any individual who is able to return to her the comb when it is lost. Her male counterparts in "Les amours de Thezin et Zilia" (Georgel) or in "The Fish Lover: Timbo Limbo"

(Beckwith) have relationships with sincere and loving young women who do not hesitate to sacrifice their lives to love.[2]

The heroines in these initiation tales reach the watery realm during their journeys. Near a river, an orphan and her half-sister, mistreated and cherished respectively by their mother, encounter mature initiators. After travelling on an initiating path through which their moral and social qualities are tested, the initiates receive symbolic objects (eggs or jars). These contain rewards or punishments according to what was accomplished during the initiation process.

Other stories relating to passage rites encompass the character of the difficult girl who, contrary to the heroine of the initiation tale, does not demonstrate qualities, but stubbornly refuses every suitor presented to her by her family. Falling prey to her own stubbornness and to the tricks performed by her suitor, she is forced to follow her husband – sheep, grass-snake, python, bull, even the devil himself. The risk taken for such disobedient behaviour ranges from minor punishments to violent death. During her wedding night, her cries for help are denied through her husband's affirmation that these are only lover's games. In variations of the story, her saviour is her youngest brother who makes the authority of the biological family triumph over the family-in-law.

The African belief is an invisible world where the individual leads at the end of her/his earthly life a perennial life, contains multiple rites and narratives linked to death. After death, a precise ritual guides the funerary preparations. Precautions are taken to reduce contamination and the possible retaliation of the deceased. The funerary toilet, the construction of the coffin, the transport of the deceased to the graveyard, his/her burial are not left to novices. Relatives who do not respect the customary precautions expose themselves to the dead person's retaliations. The "duppie stories" state these facts. They also clearly state the difference between the malevolent, dangerous, violent and vindictive spirits who attack individuals in an attempt to kill them, and the spirits of a peaceful nature who come to earth to "make holidays".

Similar to the watery realm, sacred sanctuaries in the forest shelter secularised mythical beings who are integrated to the Caribbean oral tradition. Among them is Papa Bois who reveals his narrow connection with the creolised Ashanti god, Sasabonsam. He appears in "Papa Bois Saves a Deer" and in "The Night of Papa Bois", as a benevolent character, or defender of animals.[3]

The forest in Africa shelters divine beings as well as semi-divine beings such as the Abik-u, destined to death and multiple rebirths. In St Lucia, the child who dies prematurely is named Ti Bolom. The foetus has large eyes and bowed legs, and is usually born from a primiparous mother. The foetus drifts around naked and steals money for his master who gives him raw meat as a reward. In

Guadeloupe, the power and fortune owned by some people are attributed to the possession of a monster. Assigned to chores similar to Ti Bolom, he also must ensure his/her fortune and well-being. In Trinidad, the spirit of a child who dies before being baptised is named Douen. A being excluded from the human society, he is faceless and is identified by a straw hat. His physical appearance is comparable to the *mmotia*, fairies of the Ashanti forest, who have backward-pointed feet.

The domain of the forest is also a shelter of witches whose best known Caribbean line of descent are *Soukouyant* and *La Diablesse*. The first leaves her physical body hanging to a nail before flying. After she introduces herself in her victims' houses, she steals their blood. Contrary to *Soukouyant*, *La Diablesse* has the features of a young and elegant woman. Nevertheless, the search for her origin leads to the well-known myth about the evil origin of the supernatural fiancé.

The reprehensible character of the witches' actions is comparable to that of hideous supernatural beings who might well have appeared in the Caribbean, as their names point out their identity (Chinese Ghost, Coolie Ghost . . .). As dangerous as they are, Three-Foot-Horse blows unpredictably its malevolent and fatal breath. This creature may ride Whopping Boy who shouts human cries while dancing on tree branches. Some narratives describe Rolling Calf as a homeless goat: white, black or dotted, wearing a chain around the neck that hangs to the ground. Murders, butchers and sorcerers are incarnated in this being. All of them, including the Ghost With a Rope Around the Neck, perform aggressions whose consequences are deadly for humans.

The content of oral forms point out the fact that, although they are desacralised, divinities maintain their primary prerogatives of bestowing wealth, fertility, of encouraging resistance, combativeness and of conserving hope and faith. Important, as well, is the social function played by the repulsive and fearsome supernatural beings. While sending signals to the immigrant population, they ward off the many unpredictable dangers that could affect them in unknown countries. Thus, they facilitated their integration into the Caribbean world.

Parallel to social function, the didactic role given to Caribbean tales allows the diffusion of the Christian faith. In some texts, biblical messages create a syncretic dynamic between the dominant Christian religion and African beliefs. Supernatural belief and Catholic faith are juxtaposed in *Yo pitché on Soukouyant la epi bec mer la*. (They captured the Soukouyant with the jaw of a female swordfish). The story of the Soukouyant's capture, as it was under human disguise, and just as it was about to borrow salt on a Good Friday, is helpful to clarify a sign of religious nature. The Caribbean tale, similar to the African traditional function, helps in the dissemination of religion. The god mother is a privileged character who helps the spread of religious teachings: she holds a preponderant role in history as well as in fiction. She fulfills the function of a spiritual mother during slavery, a role confirmed in the tale. The godmother, in reality as in fiction, teaches her godson religious principles. Evidence in the oral tradition only shows that the conversion fails often because of the resistance in the candidate to conversion. The evangelist godmother watches in disbelief, stupefied in admiration. In another tale, conversion is equally mocked when the evangelist loses her credibility, because she is depicted as an ogress who abuses parents' trust and devours godchildren entrusted to her.

The creativity shown in the oral tradition points out the creolisation process that helped enslaved peoples to preserve ancestral beliefs from being eradicated. Such examples of cultural resistance are not isolated facts nor are they limited to oral expressions. If the oral tradition gathered the rites of passage and the achievements of mythical beings, both sacred and supernatural, these are also present in other art forms. African gods and rituals have pervaded the popular and artistic domains: desacralisation helped them to resist eradication and to follow the traditional path.

In carnival parades, characters and traditions from Europe and Asia can be seen side by side with Legba, the phallic-god; Egungun, the ancestor-visitor swiftly moving; the invincible spirit of Ogun; the shimmering colours of Shango, the mystical horns of the goddess Oya. The search for the origins between sacred ancestors and secular figures of carnival show that Vaval (king of Guadeloupe Carnival) was originally a phallic god, that the costume of Jack-in-the-Green made of vegetal matter is worn in Gambia by the Mandingo *fara-kankurang* during circumcision ceremonies, that Pitchy-Patchy wears a wildly coloured outfit, reminiscent of Egungun's costume. This carnival character also reproduces the dance steps and the swift turns of the ancestor-visitor. Oya and Shango, mystical parents, contributed to expand the array of carnival costumes with their attributes.

Desacralisation helped the growth of many artistic fields: dance, music, sculpture, painting, all rooted in the sacred. The example of Haiti is proof of this. Voudou, as many expert agree, has vitalised every art form on the island. Sacred rhythms inspired secular ones.

To different degrees, the secularisation process at work in the new worships, and the vitality which served as an impulse to foster popular artistic creativity, exist all over the Caribbean. In most islands, immigrated peoples from the African continent carried with them the same gods, put them on top of the local pantheons and expanded the oral tradition with their achievements. By using similar percussive instruments considered sacred in their original land, they transcribed musical messages to salute the arrival of the gods and ancestor-visitors during ceremonies. On the same sacred instruments, they play secular rhythms. Similar gestuality, honing phallic gods, is performed in traditional dances and is found again in carnival. In this transnational performance, carnival participants are speaking in harmony in diverse islands and seal the past and present, the living and the ancestors, the here and beyond and all celebrate life forces and rebirth. Oral art, popular forms, playful and carnival performances and artistic activities in the Caribbean show their relationship, their complementarity and in spite of political and linguistic differences reveal their identity. In acquiring part of this popular heritage, literature, as well as the oral tradition, binds the sacred and desacralised forms. In Jamaica, the first published literary works introduced a central character, at once a spiritual and rebellious leader: the obeah man/woman. This significant character becomes particularly interesting when recalling that, in the political and sacred fields in the Caribbean, religion played a central role as a cohesive space for the slaves and as a force in the rebellion. The struggle engaged between the Christian religion/dominant and the African religion/dominated is characterised in literature through the evolution of the character of the obeah man/woman. Described as a sorcerer in "Poems Chiefly on the Superstition of Obeah",[4] the leader is reinstated in his function of spiritual leader in "Hamel the Obeah Man".[5] History demonstrates that originally two distinct practices existed, Myal and Obeah (religious and magic). However, after the Myal man/woman performed in the political arena and gained victories against oppressive forces, she/he lost both her/his titles and her/his authentic function. The interest shown for both obeah and obeah/man/woman by many Caribbean writers in diverse languages is helpful to understand the evolution of the character and her/his practice, and write it as subtext to the bitter struggle between dominant and dominated religion. The obeah man/woman is constituted as a Caribbean literary archetype of undeniable importance.

Opting for the recognition of identity, Kamau Brathwaite writes in *The Arrivants* about an African pantheon with transnational boundaries.[6] Ogun, Shango: creolised gods survive in this writer's poetry. Other authors show the great similarities existing between the tricks played by characters in both oral and written forms. As an example: similar to "Ti Jean l'horizon"[7] a merciless righter of wrongs, responsible for death of a White god father's mother, vengeful slaves in *Wide-Sargasso Sea* by Jean Rhys, kill the White old masters' son.[8]

Oral forms give as much room to mythical heroes/heroines as to supernatural creatures, and the translation of the latter from oral to written form is made easily. Zombie, Soukouyant, Three-Foot-Horse are introduced in the writings of Herbert de Lisser and of Ismith Khan, *The White Witch of Rosehall* and *The Jumbie Bird* respectively.[9] Finding sources in local oral traditions, Jean Rhys is inspired by the belief in the zombie to frame the dramatic action and reinforce the theme of identity loss and alienation in *Wide Sargasso Sea*.[10]

The process of secularisation of the sacred as well as the process of resacralisation are convincingly illustrated in Earl Lovelace's prose. *The Wine of Astonishment*, on one hand, describes the struggles of the Bonasse community which claims the right to express its own spirituality.[11] While struggling against the imposition of a new religion and against the desacralisation and the suppression of their gods, they kept honouring them, giving them back their sacredness and operating a synthesis. On the other hand, *The Dragon Can't Dance* established an extremely fluid boundary between the sacred and secular realms.[12]

Although the majority of the above examples is taken from the Anglophone region, desacralisation, re-sacralisation and vitalisation processes are to be found in every linguistic region of the Caribbean. The Haitian example can be used here again as it perfectly illustrates the contribution of the sacred to the cultural field. Vaudou weaves the languages of literature, music, sculpture, painting. In the religious pantheon, as in oral art, Haitian divinities are characterised by their strength of character, their perennial quality, their resistance to annihilation. Haitian mythology is full of achievements which also appear in the Anglophone oral tradition where Shango/Ogun confirm their presence by pointing to the importance of the *loas nagos* family where they originate. Their divine counterparts are prestigious in Haiti as Atibon Legba, Damballah Huedo or Erzulie. The diversity of their fields of intervention characterises their prolixity.

The Cuban oral lore is similarly rich in mythical beings introduced by the Yoruba people. Their achievements found in the *babalochas* (narratives perpetuating the knowledge about divinities) can be compared to the achievements of the gods of the Francophone and Anglophone oral traditions. Haiti and Cuba get a preponderant position because of the exhaustive character of their mythologies. The prolixity of their respective myths helps to decode and to understand other stories from different parts of the Caribbean. Because of the depredations, adaptations or transformations that have occurred, the interpretation of some stories requires the clarity brought by more structured texts. After bringing together and comparing these texts, in spite of some variations, the presence of common characteristics between different characters confirm that they are mythical beings, designated through different names, described by story tellers with diverse idioms, who nevertheless show similar trends in the story of their achievements.

In conclusion, the secularisation of the sacred, the re-sacralisation process and the vitalisation of the cultural domain constitute a symbol of unity, valid throughout the Caribbean. This confirms that since the spiritual migration used collective memory as its privileged vehicle, then all the lands of slave migration potentially bear traces of the African sacred memory.

NOTES

1. "Legend of the Singing Skull: 'Why Ogun Guards the Yoruba Gates' ", in Jacob Elder, ed., *An Anthology of Rare and Strange Lands and Myths from Trinidad and Tobago* (Port of Spain: National Cultural Council of Trinidad and Tobago, 1972), pp. 23–27; "The Spell of Shango", in Michael Anthony, *Folk Tales and Fantasies* (Port of Spain: National Cultural Council of Trinidad and Tobago, 1976), pp. 53–58.

2. "Les Amours de Thezin et Zilia", in Thérèse Georgel, *Contes et Legendes des Antilles* (Paris: Fernand Nathan, 1963), pp. 173–77; M. Beckwith, *Jamaican Anansi Stories* (New York: G.E. Stechert, 1924)

3. M. Alladin, "Papa Bois Saves a Deer", in Michael Anthony, *Folk Stories and Legends of Trinidad* (Port of Spain, Trinidad: National Cultural Council, 1968), and "The Night of Papa Bois", in Michael Anthony, *Folk Tales and Fantasies* (Port of Spain: National Cultural Council of Trinidad and Tobago, 1976), pp. 41–6.

4. Anon, *Poems Chiefly on the Superstition of Obeah* (London: n.p., 1816).

5. Anon, *Hamel the Obeah Man* (London: 1827: New York: Schomburg, 1870)

6. Kamau Brathwaite, *The Arrivants: A New World Trilogy* (Oxford: Oxford University Press, 1988).

7. Thèrése Georgel, "Ti Jean l'horizon", in *Contes et Legendes des Antilles* (Paris: Fernand Nathan, 1963), pp. 208–77.

8. Jean Rhys, *Wide Sargasso Sea* (London: Andre Deutsch 1963 and Penguin Books, 1975)

9. Herbert de Lisser, *The White Witch of Rose Hall* (London: Ernest Benn Ltd., 1929 and Macmillan, 1982); Ismith Khan, *The Jumbie Bird* (London: New York, Trinidad: Longman, 1985).

10. Rhys, *Wide Saragossa Sea.*

11. Earl Lovelace, *The Wine of Astonishment* (London: André Deutsch, 1982).

12. Earl Lovelace, *The Dragon Can't Dance* (London: Longman, 1979).

Carolyn Cooper

Chapter 15

HIP-HOPPING ACROSS CULTURES

CROSSING OVER FROM REGGAE TO RAP AND BACK*

Nairobi's male elephants uncurl
their trumpets to heaven
Toot-Toot takes it up
in Havana
in Harlem

bridges of sound curve
through the pale rigging
of saxophone stops[1]
      [Kamau Brathwaite, "Jah"]

The African diasporic poet Kamau Brathwaite employs the reverberant metaphor "bridges of sound" to evoke the substrate cultural ties that reconnect Africans on the continent to those who have survived the dismembering middle passage. The paradoxical construct "bridges of sound" conjoins the ephemerality of aural sensation with the technological solidity of the built environment. This arresting metaphor affirms the cunning capacity of Africans in the diaspora to conjure knowledge systems out of nothing, as it were. Africans, taken away without tools, were able to rebuild material culture from the blue-print of knowledge carried in our collective heads. In long historical perspective, the middle passage thus functions like a musical bridge – the transitional passage connecting major sections of a musical composition. And that *magnum opus* is the survival song of generations of Africans who have endured the crossing.

The poem "Jah" acknowledges the immediate excremental details of the middle passage and, simultaneously, celebrates the therapeutic power of the imagination to transform the real into the surreal. In a clever metaphorical slide, the rigging of the slave ship becomes the stops of the saxophone: "bridges of sound curve/through the pale rigging/of saxophone stops". This dislocating shift from the literal to the metaphorical may be read as a sign of the delirium of enslaved shipboard Africans trapped in an hallucinogenic trip of anti-conquest. But the visionary turn from the rigging to the saxophone can also be conceptualised as a liberating trope of the processes of artistic creativity and aesthetic transforma-tion. Indeed, the poet as griot is moved to wonder if the drummer and the sound of the drum will continue to have potency after the debilitating sea-change of the middle passage. The answer is a resounding "yes"; for the capacity to make music anew does become, quite literally, the bridge of sound that rehumanises slaves who have been cannibalised by history:

the ship sails, slips on banana
peel water, eating the dark men.
Has the quick drummer nerves after the stink
Sabbath's unleavened cries in the hot hull?
From the top of the music, slack Bwana
Columbus rides out of the jungle's den.
With my blue note, my cracked note, full flat-
tened fifth, my ten bebop fingers, my black
bottom's strut
Panama
worksong, my cabin, my hut,
my new frigged-up soul and God's heaven
heaven, gonna walk all over God's heaven.[2]

Here Brathwaite names some of the musical forms that have emerged in the Americas – blues, jazz, work songs and spirituals. The reference to "Panama work song" alludes to the labour-intensive project of constructing the canal and the role of music in sustaining the spirit in adverse physical circumstances. The move-ment of Caribbean peoples to work in the zone made possible new processes of acculturation and reshaped old aesthetic forms. Indeed, the reference to Panama images the bridging of African diaspora cultures in the Americas. The canal, produced by the labour of so many remigrant African peoples, now separates continents and, simultaneously, joins the Atlantic to the Pacific Ocean, itself the locus of other African diasporas, both ancient and modern. There are so many diasporas within the diaspora. Metaphorical bridges of sound thus span not only the Atlantic, but also overarch the many bodies of water that dis/connect African peoples dispersed across the globe. The distinctive, neo-African musical forms that have emerged in the Caribbean, Latin America, North America and the Pacific, for example, are vibrant testimony to the longevity and durability of sound musical bridges.[3]

RHYTHMS OF RESISTANCE

Like jazz, the blues, work songs and spirituals, more recent music such as reggae, ragga and rap constitute sites of resistance to the ubiquitous brutalisation of African peoples. In the words of Bob Marley's "One Drop" from the *Survival* album:

So feel this drum beat
As it beats within, in
Playing a rhythm
Resisting against the system.

These new sounds of resistance are contemporary manifestations of a long tradition of African diasporic hybridity and bricolage. The evolution of reggae in Jamaica illustrates this cross-fertilising process. Garth White, research fellow in the International Reggae Studies Centre at the University of the West Indies, Mona, Jamaica, observes in an important 1982 monograph entitled "Traditional Musical Practice in Jamaica and its Influence on the Birth of Jamaican Popular Music" that mento, the indigenous folk music of Jamaica, absorbed influences from the Trinidad calypso and Cuban rumba. Indeed, White notes that:

... the calypso and the mento were often so similar that the terms were often used inter-changeably when referring to mento. At the same time, a number of differences can be observed between the two forms.

Mento could be either fast or slow tempo, but it was usually slower than calypso, encouraging more sinuous, horizontal, pelvic movement in, the dance.[4]

Later, African-American rhythm-and-blues influenced this already hybridised mento music, accelerating the process of transformation that resulted in ska. Ska decelerated into rock-steady, which, in turn, crescendoed into the dread beat of reggae. The current derivative of reggae is known as both dancehall and ragga.

The naming of Jamaican popular music reveals complex ideological meanings. The words "reggae" and "ragga" share a common ragged etymology, which denotes their identical origins in the concrete jungle of Kingston. The 1967 *Dictionary of Jamaican English* defines "reggae" as "a recently estab[lished] sp[elling] for *rege* (the basic sense of which is *ragged* – see *rege-rege* with possible ref[erence] to rag-time music (an early form of American jazz) but referring especially to the slum origins of this music in Kingston." "Rege-rege" is defined first as "rags, ragged clothing"; its secondary meaning is "a quarrel, a row". The dictionary entry invites readers to compare "rege-rege" with "raga-raga", which is defined in the nominative as "old ragged clothes"; as adjective, it means "in rags, ragged" and as verb, it means "to pull about, pull to pieces".[5]

In Jamaican Creole there are a number words formed from the consonants "r" and "g/k" which share essentially the same meaning of ragged and connote disorder and deviation from the habits of respectability.[6] Words such as "tegereg" (related to the English tag-and-rag, meaning "of or belonging to the rabble"); "Regjegs" (described in the *Dictionary of Jamaican English* as probably reduced from the English "rags and jags" – "jags" meaning "rags and tatters". A related word is "stregeh" meaning promiscuous woman.[7]

Stephen Davis, author of *Reggae Bloodlines*, acknowledges the singer Toots Hibbert as the first to use the word "reggay" in the title of a song – the 1967 "Do the Reggay". The spelling variation confirms the fluidity of the word in this early period of formation. Davis reports his conversation with the singer on the etymology of "reggae" thus:

> I once asked Toots Hibbert, lead singer of the Maytals and composer of "Do the Reggay," to tell me what the word meant, and his answer is as satisfactory a definition of reggae as you're likely to get: "Reggae means comin' from the people, y'know? Like a everyday thing. Like from the ghetto. From *majority*. Everyday thing that people use like food, we just put music to it and make a dance out of it. Reggae means *regular* people who are suffering, and don't have what they want.[8]

Hibbert's poetic reggae/regular word-play emphasises the everyday ordinariness of the basic survival strategies of "regular people who are suffering" and who use music and dance, like food, as essential nutrients for daily sustenance. In creolised Jamaican English "regular" is pronounced "regla", thus evoking the muted echo of "reggae". The reggae/regla semantic shift deftly underscores the regulatory, safety valve function of reggae music in Jamaican society. Without raga-raga music, the explosive class politics of stark deprivation versus vulgar privilege woud detonate even more resoundingly than it now does. To indigenise Karl Marx's classic dictum that religion is the opium of the masses, I propose that in Jamaica reggae is the ganja of the massive.

The word "ragga" is an abbreviation of "ragamuffin", which, in English, means "a ragged, dirty, disreputable man or boy"; also, "rough, beggarly, good-for-nothing, disorderly". In the contemporary Jamaican context, the semantic range of the word "ragamuffin" is widened to include the sense of glorified badmanism. There is thus enacted a process of subversion of the English meaning of the word whereby the outlaw condition of the ragamuffin is simultaneously transferred to and transformed in Jamaican usage. The Jamaican masses transgressively reclaim and celebrate the outlawry of ragamuffin-style dancehall music that now bears the same stigma that reggae endured in its 1960s period of formation. Conversely, the Jamaican elite marginalises both musics as outlaw sounds, though it must be conceded that, over time, the hard-hitting rebel music of Bob Marley has become respectable: classical "roots and culture" reggae.

In an article entitled "The Origins and Meanings of Dancehall and Ragamuffin", Mandingo observes that the term "ragamuffin" and its variant "ragamuffet", were first used in reggae in the 1978 tune "Ragamuffet", sung by Horace Andy and produced by Tappa Zukie for his "Star" recording label. Mandingo comments thus on the provenance of the term "ragamuffin":

> Shortened to 'Ragga' in England, it merely means those person[s] whom Jkans [Jamaicans] used to call Rudies, Rebels, Spengs, or Soldiers. The names simply describe rebellious youths who managed to survive and flourish . . . [9]

Mandingo emphasises the inventiveness of these ragamuffin youth who defy the Eurocentric conventions of middle-class respectability in Jamaica:

> These Ragamuffins have always clung to their grassroots culture and have created and continued to create new music, dance and styles that influence and inspire the rest of the world.
>
> There is positive and negative in everything and reggae dancehall Ragamuffin is no exception![10]

Ben Mapp, writing in the *New York Times* in June 1992 defines contemporary ragga/dancehall as "a cousin of both reggae and rap".[11] The metaphor of blood relation is apt. Mapp notes that dancehall music "relies on bouncy, heavy-hitting rhythms"; and distinguishes between reggae and dancehall instrumentation thus: "Dancehall draws on the basic structure of reggae, but its instrumentation is usually more sparse, with the rare horn section and guitar programmed by computer. The relentless drum and bass lines are often computer-generated." Mapp establishes the connection with rap: "The dancehall D.J. is the equivalent of hip-hop's M.C, or rapper, rhyming over the rhythms steeped in Jamaican patois."[12]

It is this bridging of reggae, ragga and rap that is the central preoccupation of this essay, which is very much work-in-progress. In the fervent hope of absolution, I must confess that I am a neophyte in the communion of rap. I am not at all versed in its polysyllabic catechism. Nevertheless, with the reckless presumption of the new convert, I dare to make a few generalisations about hip-hop culture and draw a few parallels with Jamaica's dancehall culture, parallels that seem worthy of further exploration. In this tentative, preliminary investigation I focus on two clearly inter-connected areas: language and ideology.

THE POLITICS OF NOISE

There are recurring themes in the various versions of the story of rap that I have reviewed. These I identify as (i) displacement (ii) cultural alienation (iii) technological inventiveness (iv) verbal virtuosity and (v) gender politics. In the 1960s and 70s, the South Bronx home of rap was the locus of radical social transformation precipitated by the construction of the Cross-Bronx Expressway, which was begun in 1959. In *Black Noise: Rap Music and Black Culture in Contemporary America,* Tricia Rose cites Marshall Berman's account of the devastating impact of construction work:

> Miles of streets alongside the road were choked with dust and fumes and deafening noise . . . Apartment houses that had been settled and stable for over twenty years emptied out, often virtually overnight; large and impoverished black and Hispanic families, fleeing even worse slums, were moved wholesale, often under the auspices of the Welfare Department, which even paid inflated rents, spreading panic and accelerating flight . . .
>
> Thus depopulated, economically depleted, emotionally shattered, the Bronx was ripe for all the dreaded spirals of urban blight.[13]

The dust, fumes and noise of the invasive expressway are sensational manifestations of class politics. The powerful are free to impose their deafening noise on the powerless. In the battle for the control of "public" space the poor usually lose. Displacement exacerbates the cultural alienation of the politically marginalised.

In *Noise: The Political Economy of Music,* Jacques Attali defines music as "the organisation of noise".[14] This brilliant aphorism alludes to the complex ways in which the power to organise noise is appropriated differently in different cultures. Black youth in the destabilised South Bronx used their skills in electronics to re-organise the dissonance in their environment. They learned to make music out of social noise. The metaphor of noise recurs in the discourse of rap. The *A 2 Z: The Book of Rap and Hip-Hop Slang* (1995) defines noise as "the sound or phenomenon of rap".[15] The citation selected to illustrate the entry on "noise" is a quote from Chuck D: "People try to come up with intellectual reasons for the noise, and it ain't nothing intellectual."[16] The reputed anti-intellectualism of the noise is, decidedly, an intellectual issue. Indeed, Chuck D himself elaborates a politics of noise in a television documentary, "Looking for the Perfect Beat": "What we saying can also be viewed as noise, irritating, oh no stop it, turn it off. And, ahm, we're gonna bring it regardless. So we're gonna be too black and too strong and just deal with whatever comes down the line."[17]

The politics of exclusion and inclusion reverberate in rap. Insiders understand the noise. They participate in a communicative field that gives meaning to the dissonant pain of everyday survival. Outsiders dismiss as mere "noise" the guttural sounds that affirm the African-American's right to speech in the public sphere. The recuperation of noise as a loud affirmation of the politics of inclusion is an excellent example of the way in which African-American speech subverts the lexicon of American English to articulate in-group identity. Geneva Smitherman locates hip-hop discourse within the broader context of subversive African-American speech practices:

> Today Hip-Hoppers call it *flippin the script* . . . This is a process much more profound than the creation of mere 'slang.' From its origin as a counter language, flippin the script has resulted in a coded Black Semantics, available only to Africans in America. This accounts for the fact that when a term crosses over and gains linguistic currency in the EAL [European American English] world AAL [African-American Language] speakers generate a new term to take its place.[18]

The hip-hop metaphor of "flippin the script" suggests the autonomy of authorship, the creative capacity of the artist to rewrite the submissive script of compliant silence that has been imposed on African-Americans. Chuck D's insistence on bringing the noise is remarkably similar to Bob Marley's obstreperousness expressed in his aggravatory line, "I want to disturb my neighbour", from the song "Bad Card" on the *Uprising* album. Music as "night noise" literally disturbs the peace. As metaphor, noise dislocates the lines of demarcation between those who have rights to "place" and those who do not:

You a go tired fi see mi face
Can't get mi out of the race
Oh man you said I'm in your place
And then you draw bad card
A make you draw bad card
I want to disturb my neighbour
Cause I'm feeling so right
I want to turn up my disco
Blow them to full watts tonight
Inna rub-a-dub style[19]

Put differently by Peter Tosh:

Everyone is crying out for peace, yes/
None is crying out for justice/
I don't want no peace/
I need equal rights and justice[20]

The cry for equal rights and justice is the universal noise of the ghetto. For example, The Fugees, Haitian-American (re)fugee rappers, appropriate Bob Marley's "No Woman, No Cry", transforming this song of consolation into "a dedication to all the refugees worldwide".[21] Forced to become refugees, the dislocated must endure "the pain of losing family".[22] In their rap re-contextualisation of Marley's lyrics, The Fugees reconfigure the boundaries of grief, thus widening the family of shared suffering and mutual consolation. Marley's "government yard in Trench Town" becomes The Fugees' "government yard in Brooklyn" and "project yard in Jersey". There, in Brooklyn, they observe the "crookedness as it mingle with the good people". Marley's "hypocrites [who] mingle with the good people" become The Fugees' generic "crookedness". This revision evokes the hip-hop signifying on Brooklyn as "Crooklyn". Bob Marley's poignant reference to Georgie lighting ghetto fires gets a new urban twist of "drive-by" violence in the Fugees' version: "Little Georgie would make the fire light/As stolen cars pass through the night". In an understandable gesture of inclusion, The Fugees draw even fugitive gunmen into the circle of uprooted refugees: "The gunman's in the house tonight/But everything's gonna be alright". Marley's culture-specific references assume new diasporic meanings as they cross borders.

TECHNOLOGICAL INVENTIVENESS

Rap, like reggae, is the noise of remembering. And technological inventiveness does amplify the noise – the verbal virtuosity – of the dispersed African community. David Toop, in *Rap Attack 2: African Rap to Global Hip-Hop*, traces the convoluted genealogy of rap right back across the Middle passage to West Africa:

> Rap's forebears stretch back through disco, street funk, radio DJs, Bo Diddley, the bebop singers, Cab Calloway, Pigmeat Markham, the tap dancers and comics, The Last Poets, Gil Scott-Heron, Muhammad Ali, acappelia and doo-wop groups, ring games, skip-rope rhymes, prison and army toasts, signifying and the dozens, all the way to the griots of Nigeria and the Gambia.[23]

Toop does acknowledge the immediate influence of Caribbean music in catalysing the processes of hybridisation that erupted as rap in late 1970s urban Black America. He underscores the role of Caribbean migration into New York and the resulting acculturation. For example, the parents of hip-hop DJ Grandmaster Flash migrated from Barbados, and his father was a connoisseur of both American and Caribbean music. He also notes the fundamental influence of Jamaican sound system technology on the evolution of rap. Reggae itself did not cross over widely into Black American culture in the 1970s. But its sound system mode of transmission did. The migrant Jamaican Clive Campbell, aka Kool DJ Herc, brought the noise to the Bronx. Toop observes that:

> . . . it was the 'monstruous' sound system of Kool DJ Herc which dominated hip hop in its formative days. Herc came from Kingston, Jamaica, in 1967, when the toasting or DJ style of his own country was fairly new. Giant speaker boxes were essential in the competitive world of Jamaican sound systems (sound system battles were and still are central to the reggae scene) and Herc murdered the Bronx opposition with his volume and shattering frequency range.[24]

In *Cut 'N' Mix*, Dick Hebdige documents Herc's inventiveness in responding to his audience's rejection of reggae. Herc " . . . began talking over the Latin-tinged funk that he knew *would* appeal. To start with he merely dropped in snatches of street slang, like the very first toaster djs who worked for Coxsone Dodd's system in the 1950s."[25] Herc isolated the particular organisation of noise that would capture the imagination of his predominantly African-American audience. This was the instrumental break. Hebdige notes that "[t]he lead guitar or bass riff sequence of drumming that he wanted might last only fifteen seconds. Rather than play the whole record straight through he would play this same part several times over, cutting from one record deck to the other as he talked through the microphone."[26]

Hebdige gives a classic example of the recycling of diasporic sound in his account of Herc's resuscitation of the record *Apache*, released in 1974 and performed by the Jamaican disco group, The Incredible Bongo Band. *Apache*, "written for the Shadows, Cliff Richard's backing group, in 1974 . . . had been 'covered' by an American group called The Ventures, who had a minor hit with it in the States."[27] The Jamaican group "used conga drums instead of the standard pop music drum kit. And they laid more stress on the percussion. Thanks to Kool Herc, *Apache* could be heard all over the Bronx in 1975."[28] But it was and was not *Apache*. Herc's inventiveness had transformed the instrumental break into a bridge of sound that made the Jamaican disco version of an American hit acceptable to African-American ears.

THE CREOLE CONTINUUM

Like African-American Language, Jamaican (Creole), the devalorised, hybrid language created by African peoples in Jamaica is the preferred medium for rewriting and voicing-over the flipped script of cultural autonomy. The reggae singers and ragga DJs of Jamaica and its diasporas in the Caribbean, Africa, North America and Europe, for example, draw on a tradition of resistance that is encoded in the language of Jamaican popular culture. Conservative, Eurocentric (mis)conceptions of Jamaican as "broken", "bad", "corrupt" English deconstruct the language as pathology, a degeneration of the idealised "Queen's English". Conversely, metaphors of freedom in the popular imagination – for example, "breaking out into patwa" – suggest the liberating discourse of emancipation from mental slavery, to cite Bob Marley's "Redemption Song".

Not surprisingly, in the crossing over of reggae, ragga and rap in the U.S. East Coast, some Jamaican words have made their way into the vocabulary of hip-hop. And a few hip-hop terms have migrated into Jamaican dancehall culture. Two examples of hip-hop crossovers are "chronic", a particularly strong strain of ganja and the honorific "G" for gangsta.[29] The *A 2 Z: The Book of Rap and Hip-Hop Slang* has 12 entries that are identified as being of Jamaican origin. These constitute a mere 0.6 per cent of the approximate 2,000 entries in the dictionary. Below is a list of these words with their assigned meanings, some of which are not accurate translations of the Jamaican:

chatting:	rapping
culture:	serious affirmative lyrics of an historical or social nature

dancehall:	contemporary reggae music or the club where it is played
dibi dibi:	i). n. a promiscuous female; ii) adj. vulnerable or weak
gal pikney [sic]:	an attractive female
level the vibes:	to calm down the atmosphere in a music club or elsewhere
natty or	
natty dread:	admirable
rewind:	i) vb. a DJ backspinning a record to the beginning
	ii) n. what an approving crowd shouts to the DJ
rude boy:	n. and adj. like ragamuffin. The West Indian equivalent of gangsta, gangsta rap music, gangsta-style clothes and street slang
selecta:	a DJ who favours reggae music slackness – lyrics that are sexually rather than socially significant
sound boy:	an MC, DJ or other fixture at a reggae club

There are nine additional entries, which, though not identified as of Jamaican origin, probably are: "dreads" is defined as "characteristic braided hair of Jamaican Rastafarians". Two entries point to the hybrid identities that are created in the movement between Jamaica and the U.S. "Jafakein" – "false Jamaican" – and "Jamericans" – "American-born people with Jamaican parents". There is also the word "Jamdown", meaning "Jamaica". Surprisingly, "ragamuffin", in its culture-specific Jamaican sense of glorified badness, is not identified as Jamaican although the definition in the dictionary clearly acknowledges its Jamaican roots: "rough-neck or gangsta-style West Indian reggae music, or the 'rude boy' Jamaican equivalent of gangstas, gangsta fashion and street slang." Similarly, "toastin" ("dissing or boasting in a story, rhyming verbal format preceding rap") is not identified as Jamaican, although the secondary meaning assigned it, "rhyming verbal format preceding rap", may be read as an allusion to the Jamaican art form imported by Kool DJ Herc. "Pum-pum", ("vagina") with the variant spelling "pom-pom" and "pum-pum shorts" are not identified as Jamaican. Neither is "poonani" ("vagina"), which does have African-American variants – "poontang" and "pootanany".[30]

Failure to assign Jamaican origin to these questionable entries may be simply an error on the part of the compilers. More profoundly, it may indicate the depth of penetration of Jamaican words into hip-hop culture. The Jamaican origin is effaced and words become naturalised like their Jamerican carriers. A classic example of this process is the emergence of the quintessential hip-hop word "B-boy". In *Black Talk: Words and Phrases from the Hood to the Amen Corner*, Geneva Smitherman defines "B-boy" as:

A male follower of Hip-Hop. Originally (in the Bronx and Harlem in the 1970s)
B-boys referred to Brothas who would regularly "break" out into a dance movement to the DJ's scratching of a record.

The term B-boy is believed to have been coined by the entertainer Kool DJ Herc.
"Break" dancing – a rhythmic, intense type of dancing with twirls, turns, and
intricate, fancy steps – is rooted in African and Caribbean dance movements.[31]

In the documentary, "Looking for the Perfect Beat", KRS One describes the
process of semantic widening of the term "B-boy" which now includes a specifically Jamaican "hardcore" meaning:

> Throughout the years a b-boy became a 'bad bwoy' [laughs] on another level
> because the term 'b-boy' began to go to everybody in the hip hop community
> that felt as though that in order to maintain strength in the community we had
> to show ourselves as hardcore.
>
> And a lot of us – the half that was trying to survive – got caught up in the 'bad
> bwoy' life.[32]

GENDERED NOISE

The cross-cultural reach of "poonani" confirms the magnetic pull of this female
body part in the predominantly homosocial world of both rap and ragga music
production. Clad – or, more accurately, barely clad – in pum-pum shorts, female
genitalia figure frontally in the discourse of both ragga and rap. Gyrating female
bodies are the standard visual vocabulary of both rap and dancehall videos. It is
this overexposure of the more often Brown than Black female body that accounts,
in part, for the characterisation of both rap and ragga as irredeemably misogynist.
I argue elsewhere that women's unrestrained participation in dancehall culture,
as fans, performers, producers and managers may signify not so much their
mindless complicity in subjugation to dominating male discourses, but their
self-conscious celebration of the power of female sexuality to command submissive male attention. I do concede that the line between celebration and exploitation of the Black female body is rather thin; as thin as some of fashionable
garments sported by women in the dancehall.[33]

There appears to be an unresolved contradiction between "slackness" and
"culture" in both African-American hip hop and Jamaican dancehall discourse.
These Jamaican words that have migrated into the vocabulary of rap denote two
ideological extremes. "Culture" signifies lyrics that have a social and political
"message". These lyrics decry the dehumanising conditions in which many
African diasporic communities eke out an existence. Racism, in particular, is the

focus of many "culture" lyrics. The names of rap groups such as Public Enemy articulate the oppositional stance that many rappers assume in relation to the dominant political order. In Jamaican dancehall culture, issues of race and class do surface in "conscious lyrics". Buju Banton's CD, *Til Shiloh*, exemplifies the new trend toward old-style message music of the "roots and culture" variety. Conversely, "slackness" is a gendered political space in which cocksure men assume absolute power in their sexual relations with women; and feisty women set them straight. This, too, is "message" music. Women are stereotyped as "bitches and (w)ho(re)s" and objectified in an overwhelmingly misogynist and verbally violent discourse. The gun-toting heroes and anti-heroes of countless Hollywood westerns and gangster flicks are alive and well in the macho world of Black popular music lyrics. Indeed, West Coast gangsta rap has decided affinities with Jamaican dancehall gun lyrics. But these very lyrics can be read subversively. In my analysis of Jamaican dancehall culture I argue that this aggressive verbalisation of male dominance may, in fact, be the impotent manifestation of a diminished masculinity seeking to exercise control in the only way it can. The recurring metaphor of the penis as gun in both rap and ragga lyrics is instructive.[34]

African-American psychiatrist Frances Cress Wesling argues in a provocative essay, "Guns as Symbols", that the gun as phallic icon bears the weight of White male sexual inadequacy in relation to Black males:

> The gun became not only the weapon, the developed technology to ensure white genetic survival, but it also became the symbolic white penis.
>
> Thus, it is no accident that white males often refer to one another as "son of a gun." ... This phrase deprecates the white male genital apparatus that "fathers" white people ... It says instead that the white male prefers the gun to be his phallus and the phallus of his father. The gun then becomes the desired all-powerful phallus of the white male, which he conceives of as being an equaliser to the phallus of Black and non-white males.[35]

This controversial reading of the gun as symbolic White phallus raises the problematic issue of Black male appropriation of the deadly authority of White males. In Black neighbourhoods – the hood – the Black man's literal gun is more often pointed at other Black males than at White males. Subversive hierarchies of impotence become established when Black men use the gun to assert authority over men and women of their own group.

In addition, Black women do not passively accept Black male violation of their person. Female rappers like Queen Latifah and female DJs like Lady Saw give as much as they get. They assume the power to give back chat. Flipping the script, they contest the negative roles assigned them. Cheryl Keyes concludes her illuminating article "'We're More than a Novelty, Boys': Strategies of Female Rappers in the Rap Music Tradition", with the following insight:

> There still exists among women of rap a conscious need to maintain a sense of womanliness and 'female respectability that is the ideal of feminine face' in this male-dominated tradition. Some have chosen to utilise the term ladies without having to justify their doing so, as in Queen Latifah's rap "Ladies First," while others like Yo-Yo, have started such organisations as the Intelligent Black Women's Coalition (I.B.W.C.) in response to the rap industry's ongoing sexism, including misogynist lyrics. In general, women express through the rap medium their personal feelings about female and male relationships, but more important, they speak for the empowerment of women.
>
> Although acceptance and recognition are crucial to contemporary women of rap, they want to be regarded as more than just a novelty.[36]

CONCLUSION

Reggae, rap and ragga originate in a complex ideological space in which identities are continually contested. Everyday issues of race, class and gender are voiced in the noisy discourse of African diasporic popular music: ragamuffin sounds. In the words of Chuck D, "Rap music makes up for its lack of melody with its sense of reminder."[37] And dancehall ragga, too often dismissed as noise, not music, tells its own story of cultural remembering. Similarly, the disturbing lyrics of "roots and culture" reggae tell an archetypal tale of displacement, cultural alienation and the search for home in the Diaspora. Chuck D's ominous sense of reminder is a bridge of sound that connects reggae, rap and ragga to their multi-vocal, middle-passage antecedents.

NOTES

*This paper was completed in 1996 while I was a Research Fellow at the UCLA Center for African-American Studies. I am indebted to the Centre – and to the University of the West Indies for unpaid leave which made it possible for me to accept the fellowship. I gratefully acknowledge the assistance of my faculty sponsor, Dr Marcyliena Morgan, of the Department of Anthology, who extended to me the hospitality of accommodation in her home in the first few weeks of my visit, and who also provided access to valuable research materials. I am especially indebted to Dr Cheryl Keyes of the Department of

Ethnomusicology for sharing her research findings with me. Thanks are also due to the administrative staff of the centre, Terri-Lynn Cross, Valerie Whittington and Rachel Gebler for their exceptional kindness.

1. Kamau Brathwaite, *The Arrivants: A New World Trilogy* (Oxford: Oxford University Press, rpt. 1978), p. 162.

2. Ibid., pp. 162–3.

3. For a brilliant reading of Brathwaite's use of musical allusion in "Jah", see Gordon Rohlehr, "Bridges of Sound: An Approach to Edward Brathwaite's 'Jah'", *Caribbean Quarterly*, 26, 1 and 2 (1980), pp. 13–31. For a classic account of the role of Harlem as a meeting place of dispersed African peoples, see, for example, Claude McKay's novel *Home to Harlem* (Chatham, New Jersey: The Chatham Bookseller, 1928 reprint)

4. Garth White, "Traditional Musical Practice in Jamaica and its Influence on the Birth of Modern Jamaican Popular Music", African-Caribbean Institute of Jamaica monograph, pp. 64–5, extracted from *ACIJ Newsletter*, 7 (March 1982).

5. F. Cassidy and R.B. LePage, *Dictionary of Jamaican English* (Cambridge: Cambridge University Press, 1967).

6. I am indebted to Prof. Hubert Devonish, Department of Language, Linguistics and Philosophy, University of the West Indies, for this insight.

7. Ibid.

8. Stephen Davis, *Reggae Bloodlines: In Search of the Music and Culture of Jamaica*. (London: Heinemann Educational Books, 1977, 1981 reprint), p. 17.

9. Mandingo, "The Origins and Meanings of Dancehall and Ragamuffin", in *Dance Hall* (February 1994), p. 114.

10. Ibid.

11. Ben Mapp, "First Reggae, Then Rap, Now its Dancehall", *The New York Times*, Sunday 21 June, 1992, p. 23.

12. Ibid.

13. Marshall Berman, *All That is Solid Melts into Air: The Experience of Modernity* (New York: Simon and Schuster, 1982), pp. 290–2, in *Black Noise: Rap Music and Black Culture in Contemporary America*, ed., Tricia Rose (Hanover, New Hampshire: Wesleyan University Press, 1994), p. 31.

14. Jacques Attali, *Noise: The Political Economy of Music* 1977; English Translation (Minneapolis: University of Wisconsin Press, 1985), p. 4.

15. Lois Stavsky, I.E. Mozeson and Dani Reyes Mozeson, *The A 2 Z: The Book of Rap and Hip-Hop Slang* (New York: Boulevard Books, 1995), p. 72.

16. Ibid

17. "Looking for the Perfect Beat", "The South Bank Show" (The British T.V. series broadcast in Los Angeles on the Bravo Cable Network, Sunday, 11 February 1996). Transcription by Carolyn Cooper.

18.   Geneva Smitherman, "'The Chain Remains the Same': Communication Practices in the Hip-Hop Nation". Revised version of an unpublished paper presented at the "English in Africa" conference, Grahamstown Foundation, Monument Conference Centre, Grahamstown, South Africa, 11–14 September 1995, pp. 18–19.

19.   Bob Marley, "Bad Card", *Uprising* (Island Records, 1980).

20.   Peter Tosh, "Equal Rights", *Equal Rights* (CBS Records, 1977).

21.   The Fugees, "No Woman, No Cry", *The Score* (Columbia Records, 1996).

22.   Ibid.

23.   David Toop, *Rap Attack 2: African Rap to Global Hip-Hop* (London: Serpent's Tale, 1991), p. 19.

24.   David Hebdige, *Cut 'N' Mix: Culture, Identity and Caribbean Music* (London: Routledge, 1987), p. 137.

25.   Ibid.

26.   Ibid., p. 138.

27.   Ibid.

28.   Ibid., p. 138.

29.   I am indebted to Dr Louis Chude-Sokei, assistant professor of English, Bowdoin College, for these examples.

30.   I am indebted to Terri-Lynn Cross, administrator, UCLA Center for African-American Studies, for informing me of the African-American terms which she speculates are of Portuguese origin.

31.   Geneva Smitherman, *Black Talk: Words and Phrases from the Hood to the Amen Corner* (New York: Houghton Mifflin, 1994), p. 51.

32.   Ibid.

33.   See "Slackness Hiding from Culture: Erotic Play in the Dancehall", in *Noises in the Blood: Orality, Gender and the 'Vulgar' Body of Jamaican Popular Culture*, ed., Carolyn Cooper (London: Macmillan, 1993; Durham, North Carolina: Duke University Press, 1995), pp. 136–73.

34.   See, for example, Carolyn Cooper, "'Lyrical Gun': Metaphor and Role Play in Jamaican Dance-hall Culture", *The Massachusetts Review* xxxv, 3 and 4 (1994), pp. 429–47.

35.   Frances Cress Wesling, *The Isis Papers: The Keys to the Colors* (Chicago: Third World Press, 1991), p. 110.

36.   Cheryl L. Keyes, "'We're More than a Novelty, Boys': Strategies of Female Rappers in the Rap Music Tradition", in Joan Newton Radner, ed., *Feminist Messages: Coding in Women's Folk Culture* (Urbana and Chicago: University of Illinois Press, 1993), p. 216. Keyes quotes Roger Abrahams, "Negotiating Respect: Patterns of Presentation among Black Women", in Claire R. Farrer, ed., *Women and Folklore: . . . Images and Genres* (Prospect Heights, Ill: Waveland Press, 1975), p. 67.

37.   Chuck D, "Looking for the Perfect Beat", video. Transcription by Carolyn Cooper.

PART SIX

Poetic Discourses

Lorna Goodison

Chapter 16

TWO POEMS

ANGEL OF DREAMERS

Angel, ever since I come back here trying to reopen this dream shop
I get so much cuss-cuss and fight down, these merchants don't want
me to prosper in this town.

Seraph mine you supervised and trained me, inspected my goods
declared it celestial first quality. But cherubim what a cherubam
since I land.

I set up my shop in this big sprawling bazaar, central, to draw them
from near and from far. Well the first thing that I notice all around
and about me

is other sellers living in fear and under necromancy. Every morning
they get up they squeezing lime to cut and clear and all I using
is the power of prayers.

Some consulting with D lawrence (darkness) writing down my name
on parchment. Some have taken to attacking my name in mal-
crafted, lopsided, imitations of my creations

all because of bad mind. Angel, if you see the spoilgoods they peddle
as dreamwares. Chuh, I leaving them to count the proceeds from
their bankruptcy sales.

For seraph, you should see how I fix up my shop, nobody around here
ever see a shop fix up like that. When I throw open the doors not
even the most bad minded

could come out with their usual naysaying, carping and fault finding.
For I have painted the walls in a deep evergreen, and all around the
cornices and along the ceiling

I have picked out the subtle patterns in the mouldings in the indigo
of discernment so that what was hidden has now become clear,
illuminate, and prominent.

Along the walls I have placed some long low cane seat couches,
the cushions all covered in the lavender of lignum vitae. It is there that
dreamers sit and drink rosemary tea.

On the floor I dropped a rug of lagoon blue with feathers floating free
on its surface, and if you look long and your eye is clear, you see
schools of goldfish swimming down there.

And my extraordinary dreamshop was opened with no fanfare,
not one high official, Pharisee or Tappanaris was there,
I just threw open the doors and sat there quietly

till some dreamseeker pass by and noticed me. Someone well-parched
from too much hard-heart life, they look up and see my sign a crescent
moon with a single star fixed

and dreamseller lettered in font Gazelle, lower case, sans serif.
And so they stumble in weary, having tried various health schemes
and bush medicines and ask me for a dream.

As soon as they ask me I go to work like Attar, the darwish chemist,
my ancestor. In a clean crucible I mix the fallout from stars and the
fragrant dyestuff of roses.

I add to this then, various elements for the restoration of lost shining.
Only one or two hearts that have lived too long in the dark
professed dissatisfaction with the dream they bought.

But most of the ones who acquire them always come back in to report
how acquiring their dream has alchemically changed and
altered their way of seeing and being.

They say to all visitors, "come see this dream I have received from the
seller in the bazaar, god child of Ghazali, student of Attar,
the love child of Rum! and Asi Itra.

One of the ancient keepers of dreams and songs,
great granddaughter of a psalmist and griot Guinea woman. They say if you deserve one
of these she will mix you one

to quicken your hopes and tune your heart to hear songs of bliss
All she takes for payment is sincerity and red roses". I have received
many referrals in this way.

The ones who acquire these dreams are inspired to light candles of
understanding which illuminate all they do thereafter with a clear
pervasive shining.

I am writing this to you seated at the shop door where the simurgh,
that cinnabar talisman of a bird, has just flown in and perched upon
one of the bunches of wine-fruit

which hang ripe from the ceiling. Sometimes ground doves fly in and
Barbary doves too. Let me attempt to describe the transcendent
Barbary dove song for you.

. . . .

The transcendent song as taught by a passing Tuareg woman

A Tuareg woman passing once taught me a song.
It was really a series of intricate notes
urgently sounded, like the fast forward call
of a rising flock of Barbary doves.

The song, if correctly and effectively done,
can lift me up to a cool place
above the burning chamber of the sun.
The woman said it is the transcendent song

known only to the ones like us.
I caught the song and held it.
I feel it is not wise to use it too frequently.
Just so, I have learned to save it for unbearable days.

First a series of fluttering notes
then a long low fluting coo.

Then a series of fast forward notes
till there occurs a wild breakthrough.

Then a joyful, joyful gurgling
like a full throttle rain replenished stream

and after that its just puresweet cooing.

The only way that I have been able to withstand
the undermining efforts of the job lot sellers
is to sound this transcendent song.

Until I see you face to face, I ask you to pray that God grant
me celestial insurance from the arsonist efforts
of the job lot sellers.

My Uncle

When my uncle died
he had daughters and sons
enough to bear his coffin
sufficient to lay him out.

One was a carpenter.
He built a fine casket
planed it from the trunk
of a fragrant cedar tree

that grew high as if heading
up to heaven ahead of uncle
lofty in his front yard
for the best part of a century.

One was a stone mason.
He constructed the vault.
While he was under ground
he smoothed out a second tomb

for the pious wife of my uncle
who to this day still lives
on the nourishment pressed
from thin bible leaves.

His daughters, fine seamstresses
lined his coffin with purple.
They washed and dressed him
in a serge suit of dark blue.

He'd cut and stitched it himself,
He was a tailor and farmer
with a gift in his hands
for good fit and perfect lucea yams.

His family fed all who came
to help them mourn
with the flesh of his goats
arid ground provisions of his land.

I dreamt I saw my uncle
enter the jubilee pavilion of Kings.
Osiris weighed his heart against a feather
and his heart was not found wanting.

Jean Small

Po'm For Kamau*

Sistren and Brethren
The lot has fallen to me
To sing the praises of the poet
Of the poet/historian
Kamao Bratliwaite
Who came out of the cold
To land on these warm shores
In the middle of the day
Yesterday

And he asked me to leave him alone
Alone, with his Gods, alone
For he needed to rest
After the long journey
Out of the cold
And he needed to be alone
As he made the markings on the page
Which will soon come to your ears
Specially created for this twenty-fourth day
Of the month of February
One day before the birthdate
Of Sir Philip, Founding Father
Of this place
Of this place
Of this place of learning.

The journeying has been long
For this son of the island
Of Barbados
This journey which started in 1949
When he emerged victorious
As the island scholar
And left those island shores
For Camhridge

To gain his honours in History
That was 1953
And having stayed one more year
To complete a certificate

In education
He forwarded to Ghana, Africa
To be an Education Officer.

This was the turning point in his life
This was the beginning
Of the opening of his eyes
To see
Africa
As the centre of Caribbean culture
And so, hearing
Many rhythms of music
Many sounds of language
Many tales of his ancestors
And so, learning
Of the sources of the black esse

Of the black spirit
Of the black tongue
Of jazz and bebop
And the sound of the drum
He began to write
He began to write
To the tap of his foot
To the stroke of his pen
To the beat of his heart

And so, many markings of words
Which started long ago in BIM
In his early days
From Ghana he travelled
To work in St Lucia
To work as Resident Tutor
And the year that followed
in 1963
He came to this University
In the Department of History

What can I tell you more
Than you already know
Of his seminal work
On the creole society in Jamaica
Of his collections of works
In which he told the history
Of his people, in poetry
I speak of that first trilogy
Masks, Rights of Passage and Islands
Now called the Arrivants
Which every one of you must read
And every one of your thrilldren
Must read to overstand
The rootless, restless psyche
Of the Caribbean
Wandering to Europe
Wandering to North America
Migrating and returning
Then there was the other trilogy
Not sure if it is he or you or me
Or all the people collectively
Of the Caribbean Sea

Many more are the poems
That speak of recovery
And affirmation, of imprisonment
And freedom from bonds
Especially that linguistic bond
That leaves the tongue tied
The head blank
And the heart sits in silence
And so, hurting for his people
He fathered and created

A nation language
That dubs out the Euro-
And dubs in the Afro-
Caribbean beat
To unify Black People

Some say that his greatness
Is to be found in this work
Some say that his greatness
is his nakedness seen
In the Zea Mexican Diary
Some say that his greatness
Is as a literary critic
And some say he is the greatest
Cultural historian

The breadth of his vision
The perfection of his poetic lines
The mission that he has taken unto himself
To restore a whole nation through
Himself, his life and the word
The Caribbeanised word
Is praised in every part of the world
For he has gained many Awards
and Honours
Both here and abroad
Like the Gramophone Award
In 1969
For a recorded version
Of Rights of Passage
And the Cholmondoley Award
The year after
The Yoruba Foundation
In his island home in 1972
Crowned him with the Bussa Award
Twice did he win
In 76 and 86
The Casa de las Americas
Prize
For Poetry
And Literary Criticism
Twice too did the Institute of Jamaica
Recognise his brilliance
By bestowing on him
The Centennial Award for Literature in 1980

And again the Musgrave Medal
For bibliography
In 1983

x/Self gained him
The Commonwealth Prize in Poetry
In 1987
And in that same year
He walked away
With the Bussa Award for Literature
And contribution to Bajan Culture
In that very same year
The year of 87
He was made Companion of Honour
Of Barbados, his island home
And a Special citation, to boot,
The Gabriela Mistral Inter-American
Prize for Culture

Now you know that not so long ago
Last year, in fact, he won
That famous famous Neustadt Award
For Literature
And was named
One of the golden dozen
At New York University
Where he teaches Comparative
Literature

It was that other poet
Kofi Awoonor of Ghana
Who said, Brathwaite
Is a poet of African consciousness
Is a poet possessing deep grasp of tones
Is a poet with reflexes of African Lingua
Encompassing the aboriginal sounds
Of West Africa
And the distinct echoes ever present
In the English-speaking Caribbean

Now we are in the poet-Neustadt phase
Works written
In the post modern
Video Sycorax style
Incorporating DREAM STORIES
BARABJAN POEMS
And TRENCH TOWN ROCK
All connected with past works
A summation
Of the psycho-ecological changes
In his whole life.

And so, Sistren and Brethren
We are gathered here today
Not only to celebrate
The nine score and three years
Of Sir Philip
Nor to commemorate the erection
Of this building
But we are gathered here
To celebrate greatness
The greatness of the sons of the Caribbean
The greatness that comes from persistence of effort
The greatness of Caribbean scholarship and creativity
The greatness of a commitment to a people

And so now will hold my tongue
For the time has come
For the poet
For the poet/historian
THE GRIOT OF THE CARIBBEAN
To tell the tale
Of the Gods
Of the Gods
Of the Gods of the Middle Passage.

(Introduction by Jean Small of Professor Kamau Brathwaite, Guest Lecturer, Annual Sir Philip Sherlock Lecture, PSCCA, UWI, Mona campus, February, 1995).

CONTRIBUTORS

Carolyn Allen lectures in the Department of Literatures in English at the University of the West Indies, Mona, Jamaica.

Hilary McD. Beckles is Professor of History and Pro Vice-Chancellor for Undergraduate Studies at the University of the West Indies, Mona, Jamaica.

O. Nigel Bolland, a former Research Fellow at the Institute of Social and Economic Research, University of the West Indies, Mona, is Professor of Sociology and Coordinator of Caribbean Studies at Colgate University, New York.

Carolyn Cooper is Senior Lecturer and Head of the Department of Literatures in English at the University of the West Indies, Mona, Jamaica.

Lorna Goodison is a well-known Jamaican poet who teaches part-time at the University of Michigan.

Veronica Gregg teaches at Hunter College, City University of New York.

Percy Hintzen is Chairperson of African American Studies at the University of California, Berkeley.

Paul Lovejoy is Professor of History at York University in Toronto, and Director of the York/UNESCO Nigerian Hinterland Project.

Pat Mohammed is Senior Lecturer and Head of the Centre for Gender and Development, University of the West Indies, Mona, Jamaica.

Mary Morgan, now retired, was for many years Senior Assistant Registrar at the University of the West Indies, Mona, Jamaica.

Rex Nettleford is Vice-Chancellor of the University of the West Indies and Editor of *Caribbean Quarterly.*

Lucie Pradel is a Lecturer in the Centre for Caribbean Studies and Research, Universite des Antilles et de la Guyane, Guadeloupe.

Rhoda Reddock is a Sociologist and Senior Lecturer in the Centre for Gender and Development at the University of the West Indies, St Augustine, Trinidad and Tobago.

Glen Richards is a Lecturer in the Department of History, University of the West Indies, Mona, Jamaica.

Verene A. Shepherd is Senior Lecturer in the Department of History, University of the West Indies, Mona, Jamaica and a 2000–2001 Network Professor of the York/UNESCO Nigerian Hinterland Project.

Jean Small is Tutor/Coordinator of the Philip Sherlock Centre for the Creative Arts, University of the West Indies, Mona, Jamaica.

David Trotman is Associate Professor of History at York University, Toronto, and Associate Director of the York/UNESCO Nigerian Hinterland Project.

Maureen Warner-Lewis of the Department of Literatures in English, is Professor in African Diaspora Studies at the University of the West Indies, Mona, Jamaica.

Swithin Wilmot is Senior Lecturer in the Department of History, University of the West Indies, Mona, Jamaica.

INDEX